Proceedings of the 15th World Sanskrit Conference

General Editor
Radhavallabh Tripathi

Vol. I
Veda Section

Vedic Studies: Language, Texts, Culture, and Philosophy

Vedic Studies

Language, Texts, Culture, and Philosophy

Edited by
Hans Henrich Hock

Rashtriya Sanskrit Sansthan
Deemed University
Under M/o Human Resource Development
Govt. of India, New Delhi

PRINTWORLD
Publishers of Indian Traditions

Cataloging in Publication Data — DK
[Courtesy: D.K. Agencies (P) Ltd. <docinfo@dkagencies.com>]

Vedic studies : language, texts, culture, and philosophy / edited by Hans Henrich Hock.
p. cm. — (Proceedings of the 15th World Sanskrit Conference ; v. 1, Veda section)
English and Sanskrit.
Includes bibliographical references.
ISBN 13: 9788124607275

1. Vedas. — Criticism, interpretation, etc. — Congresses. 2. Vedic literature — History and criticism — Congresses. 3. Vedic language — History — Congresses. 4. Hindu philosophy — Congresses. I. Hock, Hans Henrich, 1938- II. Rashtriya Sanskrit Sansthan. III. Series: Proceedings of the 15th World Sanskrit Conference ; v. 1, Veda section.

DDC 294.5921046 23

ISBN 13: 978-81-246-0727-5
First published in India in 2014

Published by:
RASHTRIYA SANSKRIT SANSTHAN
56-57, Institutional Area, Janakpuri, New Delhi - 110 058
Phones: (011) 2852 4993, 2852 1994, 2852 4995
e-mail: rsks@nda.vsnl.net.in
Website: www.sanskrit.nic.in

and

D.K. PRINTWORLD (P) LTD.
Regd. Office: *'Vedasri'*, F-395, Sudarshan Park
(Metro Station: Ramesh Nagar), New Delhi - 110 015-11
Phones: (011) 2545 3975; 2546 6019; Fax: (011) 2546 5926
e-mail: indology@dkprintworld.com
Website: www.dkprintworld.com

Printed by: D.K. Printworld (P) Ltd, New Delhi

Foreword

The 15th World Sanskrit Conference (WSC) was organized by Rashtriya Sanskrit Sansthan, New Delhi, in association with International Association of Sanskrit Studies (IASS) during 5 January – 10 January 2012. The Conference was conducted through twenty sections including Veda; Linguistics; Epics and Purāṇas; Tantra and Āgamas; Vyākaraṇa; Poetry, Drama and Aesthetics; Sanskrit and Asian Languages and Literatures; Sanskrit and Science; Buddhist Studies; Jain Studies; Philosophies; Religious Studies; Ritual Studies; Epigraphy; Sanskrit in Technological World; Modern Sanskrit Literature; Law and Society; and Manuscriptology along with the Paṇḍitapariṣad and Kavisamavāya. Apart from these sections, the event was marked with some special panels on the themes — Models and Theories in Sanskrit Grammar and Linguistics; Electronic Concordance of the Great Epics; Re-interpreting Pāṇini; Nāṭyaśāstra in Modern World; New Perspectives on Scientific Literature in Sanskrit; Boundaries of Yoga in Indian Philosophical Literature; Śaiva Philosophy; Innovations in Sanskrit Pedagogy; Sanskrit Inscriptions in South-East Asian Countries; Manuscripts and Their Intellectual Preservation; and Sanskrit in Global Perspectives.

Right from its inception, Vedic studies have been essentially in focus of the WSC. I am happy to note that during the 15th WSC, the deliberations under the Veda section were marked with versatile and profound discussions, covering a vast range of topics.

IASS has authorized Rashtriya Sanskrit Sansthan to bring out all the volumes of the proceedings of the 15th WSC. We are grateful to Prof. Hock for making a very judicious selection and for having edited the papers presented in the Veda section of the Conference.

Radhavallabh Tripathi

Contents

Introduction

Hans Henrich Hock

THE Veda Section was one of the most active of the 15th World Sanskrit Conference sections, with a total of thirty accepted contributions, of which twenty-five were presented. Presenters came from France, Germany, India, Japan, Rumania, the UK, and the US, with the largest contingent (sixteen) being from India.

The present volume contains selected papers, mainly by authors who presented their contributions at the Conference, but including two authors who were not able to attend the Conference for reasons beyond their control. Regretfully, several authors were not able to meet the final submission deadline and their papers had to be omitted. Even so, the resulting volume represents a broad cross-section of the issues and topics that were presented and discussed at the Conference.

The volume is organized in three major parts — Language and Linguistics; Textual Criticism and Text Edition; and Culture, Philosophy, Mythology. Language/linguistics papers range from syntax/semantics (Hock and Kümmel) to morphology (Tucker), onomastics (Pinault), and rhetorical structure (Klein). Remarkably, three of the papers devoted to textual criticism and edition deal with the tradition of the Atharvaveda (Bahulkar, Kulkarni, and Rotaru/Sumant); the remaining two address issues in the R̥gvedic tradition (Khare and Köhler). Two papers in the last part of the volume address matters of Vedic philosophy (Benedetti and Vedi), one is devoted to mythology and ritual (Gadgil), and one addresses ritual and material culture (Nishimura).

Along the different stages, from original abstract submission and evaluation, to feedback on individual papers at the Conference and the final editing process, several organizations and persons have been helpful. First and most important, Prof. Radhavallabh Tripathi and his team at the Rashtriya Sanskrit Sansthan in Delhi, as well as Prof. Bruno Dagens of the International Association of Sanskrit Studies, were instrumental in organizing the Conference, including the publication of abstracts. My convener colleagues, Profs. Gaya Charan Tripathi, Sannidhanam Sudarshana Sarma, and especially Shrikant S. Bahulkar lent their support in evaluating the submitted abstracts and/ or chairing sessions at the Conference and providing feedback on presented papers. I owe special gratitude to Prof. Shrikant Bahulkar for his support in the final editing process, ranging from extensive personal discussions with some of the authors to editing a paper submitted in a font that is not editable on my Macintosh computer.

Part I
Language and Linguistics

1

Predicate Order in Vedic Prose*

Hans Henrich Hock

1. Introduction

SINCE Delbrück's study of word order in the *Śatapatha Brāhmaṇa* (1878) scholars have generally agreed that in Vedic Prose predicates normally precede their subjects; see [1]. (Here as elsewhere, subjects are indicated in italics, predicates in small caps.)

[1] MUKHYAU vā *āvāṁ* yajñasya svo (*ŚB* 4.1.5.16)[1]
We two are the chiefs of the sacrifice.

This "predicate-initial" order is remarkable, both for its pervasive presence in Vedic Prose and for the fact that it conflicts both with the cross-linguistic preference for subjects to occur in initial position and with the generally assumed principle of discourse linguistics that the subject, which provides old information, should be placed at or near the beginning of the clause, and the predicate, the new information, should be ordered later.[2]

---

* This paper is a substantial revision of papers presented at the 1990 meeting of the American Oriental Society and the 2002 SALA meeting at Iowa City. (Part of the 1990 paper has appeared in Hock 2000.) I owe thanks to participants in the two meetings for feedback and comments, and to Stephanie Jamison for additional, written feedback on the 1990 version. I have also benefited from comments at the 15th World Sanskrit Conference, New Delhi. As usual, the responsibility for any errors and omissions is mine.

[1] I accept Cardona's (1993) argument for the validity of the bhāṣika accent system in the *Śatapatha Brāhmaṇa* and accordingly use underlining to transcribe the anudātta mark of the printed editions.

[2] This principle seems to have been first introduced into general linguistics by Mathesius (1928).

Delbrück (1878: 27) accounts for the phenomenon as in [2].

[2] Der Grund für diese Stellung liegt auf der Hand. Das Subject is nämlich bekannt, das Praedikatsnomen aber bringt etwas Neues hinzu, und tritt also nach dem allgemeinen Gesetz der occasionellen Wortstellung vor. (The reason for this position is obvious. The subject is known, but the predicate nominal adds something new and hence moves to the front according to the general law of occasional word order.)

While Delbrück thus considers PREDICATE-INITIAL order "occasional", he observes — correctly — that this ordering is virtually the norm in Vedic Prose and that SUBJECT-INITIAL structures of the type [3], with the subject preceding the predicate, generally are quite rare. Unfortunately, he fails to explain how this seeming contradiction can be resolved and why we should not consider predicate-initial structures of the type [1] unmarked, and subject-initial ones, as in [3], marked.

[3] *sa̱rve* ha vai̱ *devā̱* a̱gre SADR̥̱ŚĀ āsuḥ *sa̱rve* PU̱ṆYĀḤ (*ŚB* 4.5.4.2)
All the Gods were alike in the beginning, all (were) pure.

In fact, there are several difficulties with Delbrück's interpretation. One of these, of which Delbrück was fully aware, is that in many equational sentences of Vedic Prose it is difficult to tell subject and predicate apart. Delbrück (1878: 28) cites the example in [4] where both of the glosses, a. and b., are perfectly possible interpretations.

[4] ā́po váruṇasya pátnaya āsan (*TS* 5.5.4.1)
a. Varuṇa's wives were the waters.
b. The waters were Varuṇa's wives.

While ambiguities of this sort clearly are genuine, they nevertheless do not seem to be pervasive. The number of unambiguous examples is sufficiently large to establish that predicate-initial ordering does in fact predominate in Vedic Prose.

A further problem is that Delbrück's interpretation of predicate-initial structures conflicts with Speijer's claim for all of Sanskrit that "If the predicate be a noun [or adjective], it is put before the subject" (1886: 10).

In this paper, I argue that the unmarked order is subject-initial and that predicate-initial structures are marked. First, while predicate-initiality may predominate in Vedic Prose, subject-initiality is more common in both Mantra Vedic and Post-Vedic. Second, in the case of complex predicates, only part of the predicate is placed in initial position in Vedic Prose, with the rest of the predicate occurring later in the clause. Third, Vedic Prose predicate-initial structures dominate in a sub-genre of Vedic Prose, namely EQUATIONAL sentences, especially structures that equate instruments of the sacrifice (*yajñāyudhāni*) with more abstract or general phenomena or qualities (such as the Year or the Mind). Finally, in these structures, initial predicate placement can be attributed to an alternative, less commonly recognized principle of discourse linguistics — "FIRST (or more important) THINGS FIRST".

2. Mantra Vedic and Post-Vedic

As in Vedic Prose, predicate-initial structures seem to occur more frequently in the Mantra language and in Post-Vedic than they would in languages like English. In fact, however, they are not as frequent as subject-initial ones. Thus, in Book 3 of the *R̥gveda*, I counted twenty-four predicate-initial structures (plus three with part of the predicate preceding the subject, similar to [1] above) vs. 30 subject-initial constructions; see e.g. [5]. And in the Post-Vedic text of Nala (chapters 1-8) I found three predicate-initial structures (plus two with subject "extraposed" after the verb "to be") vs. 7 subject-initial ones; see e.g. [6].[3] These findings are consonant with those of Lahiri's 1933 dissertation on word order in Sanskrit prose.

---

[3] Because of Speijer's special rule for pronouns (see below), structures with pronouns were not counted, either in the *R̥gveda* or in Nala. I also excluded "possessive" structures of the type *ayaṁ loko 'kṣayas teṣām* (Nala 2.16) "this imperishable world is theirs" because in constructions of this type there can be some question as to which of the two elements, "possessor" and "possessee", functions as subject and which as predicate (Hock 1991b).

The references for the *R̥gveda* are as follows:

Predicate-initial: 3.2.2b, 3.3.4b, 3.5.4a, 3.11.5a/b, 3.11.6, 3.18.1c, 3.20.3a/b, 3.30.7c, 3.30.7d, 3.31.3c/d (3x), 3.31.4d, 3.31.14c, 3.53.17a (2x), 3.55.1d (repeated in all other verses of the hymn), 3.55.7a, 3.55.11b, 3.55.15b, 3.55.15c, 3.56.5b, 3.56.8a, 3.61.7b.

Part of predicate initial: 3.1.7c, 3.7.2a, 3.55.2c.

Subject before predicate: 3.2.8d, 3.6.5a, 3.7.9b, 3.11.1a, 3.20.4a/b, 3.26.7b, 3.27.5c, 3.28.2a, 3.30.13d, 3.31.2d, 3.31.7c, 3.32.8a (repeated at 3.34.6b), 3.32.12c, 3.39.8a, 3.45.2d, 3.46.1, 3.52.4c, 3.52.8c, 3.53.4a, 3.53.6b, 3.54.16a, →

[5] a. *agnír* HÓTĀ KAVÍKRATUḤ (*R̥V* 1.1.5a)
Agni is the Hotr̥ having a seer's power.

b. VIBHŪ́R vāṁ *yā́ma* . . . (*R̥V* 1.34.1b)
Wide is your course . . .

[6] a. *nalaś* ca NARAŚĀRDŪLO . . . abhavat . . . (*N* 1.14)
And Nala became a tiger of a man . . .

b. SAPHALAṀ te bhavej *janma* (*N* 1.27)
Your birth would be fruitful.

Notice further that Speijer restricts his claim that predicate-initial order is normal by stating that "Pronouns, it seems, may be put indiscriminately before or behind their noun-predicate" (1886: 10); and in his 1896 monograph, Speijer goes even farther by asserting, without further modification, that "Wenn jedoch das Subject ein Pronomen ist, erhält es die erste Stelle [If, however, the subject is a pronoun it takes the first position]."

In addition, predicate position can be subject to genre-specific conventions. Consider Pāṇini's grammar with its well-known pattern of placing terms to be defined at or near the end of the sūtra, as in [7]. Opinions may differ as to which is the subject and which the predicate in these structures. What is clear, however, is that this ordering implements a rhetorical strategy of "ascending prominence", placing the definiendum, the most significant part of the sūtra, into final position.

[7] a. adeṅ guṇaḥ (1.1.2)
a, e, o are (defined as) guṇa.
Or: Guṇa is (defined as) *a, e, o*.

b. halo 'nantarāḥ saṁyogaḥ (1.1.7)
Consonants in immediate succession are (defined as) saṁyoga.

→ 3.54.16b, 3.54.18a, 3.55.11c, 3.56.2d, 3.56.5c, 3.56.8c/d, 3.58.6a/b, 3.59.6 (2x).

The references in Nala are:

Predicate-initial: 3.4, 4.21, 8.22.

Subject extraposed, after "to be": 1.27, 2.2.

Subject before predicate: 1.14, 1.26, 1.29 (2x), 2.1, 2.14 (2x).

Or: Saṁyoga is (defined as) consonants in immediate succession.

3. Vedic Prose: General, Formal Concerns

Turning now to the evidence of Vedic Prose, it is possible to discern a number of problems with the claim that predicate-initial order is basic or unmarked.

First, in examples like [1] (repeated for convenience) it is not the entire predicate which is placed in initial position, but only a part (*mukhyau*); the remainder of the predicate (*yajñasya*) remains stranded in post-subject position. Other examples are not difficult to find. Consider for instance [8], where *āpaḥ* precedes, but *mahat salilam* follows the subject *idam*. Similarly, in [9a] the comparative *bhūyān* precedes, but the standard of comparison, *kṣatriyāt*, follows; and in [9b] the quasi-participle *ghātukaḥ* precedes, but its complement *paśūn* follows (the position of *asya* is due to its clitic nature).

[1] MUKHYAU vā *āvāṁ* YAJÑASYA svo (*ŚB* 4.1.5.16)
We two are the chiefs of the sacrifice.

[8] ĀPO vā *idam* agre MAHAT SALILAM āsīt (*JB* 1.238)
In the beginning, this (world) was water, a great ocean.

[9] a. BHŪYĀN vai *brāhmaṇaḥ* KṢATRIYĀD (*AB* 7.15.8)
A brahmin is better than a kṣatriya.

b. GHĀTUKO 'sya *rudraḥ* PAŚŪN bhavati (*KS* 8.6)
Rudra becomes liable to slay his cattle.

This evidence suggests that the order predicate before subject results from fronting the predicate, or in many cases just one part of the predicate — i.e. moving it to the front of the sentence, and that the predicate is not base-generated in pre-subject position.

Supporting evidence for this conclusion comes from structures like [10], where another constituent — neither subject nor predicate — has been fronted, and where placing the predicate before the subject appears to be blocked.

[10] agninā vai tejasā *rātris* TEJASVATY (*AB* 5.29.6)
By Agni, the brilliance, the night is brilliant.

Fronting of the predicate, or part of it, thus is no different from the fronting of any other constituent, as in [11]. In fact, in both cases fronting normally affects only one word and thus leads to the separation of elements in a complex constituent; see again the examples in [11].

[11] a. (a)sapatnāṁ vā etābhir devā vijitiṁ vyajayant(a) (*AB* 1.24.1)
By means of these the Gods won a victory that is without (successful) enemies.

b. vi̱śvebhyas tā̱ṁ deve̱bhya ālabhante (*ŚB* 5.5.2.10)
They seize her for all the Gods/the All-Gods.

Now, it is true that not all structures with predicate before subject can be easily accounted for through predicate fronting; see e.g. the examples in [12], where the predicate precedes the subject but is not in clause-initial position. In these structures, other material, an initial pronominal or particle precedes the predicate, which in turn precedes the subject.

[12] a. tasya BAHIṢPAVAMĀNAM eva *rathantaraṁ* (*JB* 1.129)
Of this (divine chariot), the chariot front is the bahiṣpavamāna

b. atha ha + INDRASYA TRIDIVE *soma* āsa (*JB* 1.287)
Now, Soma was in Indra's third heaven.

Structures of this type are complex and may involve multiple focus. The initial pronominals or particles establish discourse continuity and the topic follows [12a], or the subject may be placed in preverbal focus position [12b].[4]

In the following, I will not distinguish between structures with the predicate, or part of it, in initial position and structures of the type [12] and refer to both of them as PREDICATE-INITIAL (meaning, predicate before the subject).

Further evidence that predicate-initial structures are marked comes from "extended predicate" structures with a long series of equational constructions, such as [13] and [14]. As the examples illustrate, in many such passages, the order "predicate before subject" breaks down after a while, giving way to the order "subject before predicate" or beginning to fluctuate between the two. (Similar passages are found at *ŚB* 1.2.5.17, *ŚB* 3.1.2.18, *BAU* 3.2.13.)

---

[4] See Hock 1997 for the need to recognize a preverbal focus position for Sanskrit, and see the cross-linguistic evidence for such a position in Kim 1988.

[13] tasya BAHIṢPAVAMĀNAM eva *rathamukhaṁ*
BṚHADRATHANTARE *aśvāv*
ĀJYĀNI *yoktrāṇy*
abhīśū PAVAMĀNAU
pakṣasī AUŚANAKĀVE
āṇī NAUDHASAKĀLEYE
...
adhyāsthātā SA EṢA PURUṢA(Ḥ) (*JB* 1.129)

Of this (divine chariot), the chariot front is the bahiṣpavamāna, the two horses are the bṛhad and rathantara, the ropes are the ājya stotras, the two bridles are the two pavamānas, the two sides (= wheels) are auśana and kāva, the two axle pins are naudhasa and kāleya . . . , the controller (= charioteer) is this very human being.

[14] UṢĀ vā *aśvasya medhyasya śiraḥ*
SŪRYAŚ *cakṣur*
VĀTAḤ *prāṇo*
vyāttam AGNIR VAIŚVĀNARAḤ
SAṀVATSARA *ātmā*
ūvadhyaṁ SIKATĀḤ
SINDHAVO *gudāḥ*
yakṛc ca klomānaś ca PARVATĀḤ (*BAU* (*M*) 1.1.1)

The head of the sacrificial horse is the dawn; the eye, the sun; the breath, the wind; the open mouth, Agni Vaiśvānara; the body, the year . . . ; the food in the stomach, the sand; the blood vessels, the rivers; the liver and lungs, the mountains.

Most important is the fact that it is just one type of context in which predicate-initial order clearly dominates, namely EQUATIONAL structures as in [15]. In other constructions or discourse types predicate-initial ordering does not seem to predominate. Thus, in passages introducing the frequent mythological or quasi-mythological excursions, subject-initial order appears to be the norm; see [16]. Predicate-initial structures, such as [17], seem to be much less common in this context. Interestingly, subsequent, more didactically-oriented passages tend to exhibit predicate-initial order, as in the second line of [16bc]. Subject-initial order, as in [18], likewise predominates in causal structures with *tásmād*. Examples like [19], the *Maitrāyaṇī Saṁhitā* version of [18a], in which the predicate precedes (part of) the subject, are much less common. Finally, cited discourse — notorious for its stylistic independence from the surrounding didactic prose (see Jamison 1991)

— seems to exhibit structures with subject before the predicate, as in [20], more frequently than does "ordinary" Vedic Prose.

[15] a. TEJO vai BRAHMA *gāyatrī* (*KS* 25.5)
The Gāyatrī is brilliance, Brahman.

b. ṚTAVO vai SAṀVATSARO *yajñaḥ* (*ŚB* 4.4.1.2)
The sacrifice is the seasons, the year.

c. MANO vai *bṛhad* VĀG *rathantaram* . . . (*JB* 1.128)
The bṛhad is mind, the rathantaram is speech . . .

[16] a. *devā* vai *sarva* eva SADṚŚA āsan . . . (*KS* 29.7)
All the Gods were alike . . .

b. *prajāpatir* vāva + IDAM agra āsa
MANO ha vai *prajāpatir* devatā (*JB* 1.68)
In the beginning Prajāpati was here (alone). Prajāpati is mind as deity.

c. *oṣadhayas* TAD RŪPAM abhavann
OṢADHAYO vai *paśupatis* (*ŚB* 6.1.3.12)
The plants were/became that shape, for Paśupati is the plants

[17] TṚTĪYASYĀM diví sóma āsīt . . . (*KS* 30.10)
Soma was in the third heaven . . .

[18] a. tasmād *anyatarac cakṣuṣos* TEJASVITARAṀ (*KS* 27.8)
Therefore one of the two eyes is brighter.

b. tasmāt *prāṇā* antarato LOMAŚĀ UDANVANTO (*KS* 25.9)
Therefore the breaths are internally shaggy, watery.

[19] tásmād imé LOMAŚĀḤ *prāṇā(ḥ)* (*MS* 3.8.8)
Therefore these breaths are shaggy.

[20] ittham eva *sarve manuṣyā* AMṚTĀ bhaviṣyanty (*ŚB* 10.4.3.9)
In this way, all human beings will be(come) immortal.

Predicate-initial structures, thus, are most clearly dominant in just one context, namely equational structures. In other predicative constructions, the order of subject vs. predicate is less clearly fixed, or the order subject before predicate is more common.

4. Vedic Prose: Discourse and Genre

What, then, motivates predicate-initiality in equational structures?

In earlier versions of this paper, I attributed the phenomenon to a general Vedic Prose tendency toward FRONT HEAVINESS and motivated it along the following lines.

The major purpose of the bulk of the Vedic Prose texts is to provide oral instructions on how to properly employ or understand the ritual. Everything else is subordinate to this purpose, including the myths which, as is well known, are generally only alluded to, with just so much detail being provided as is absolutely necessary for ritual exegesis.

In this ritualistic instructional enterprise, predicate-initial order can be viewed as a rhetorical attention-getting device, an oral counterpart to a written headline, which immediately informs the student about the new subject matter that is being introduced. While this ordering violates the principle that the subject, providing old information, should be placed at or near the beginning of the clause, and the predicate, i.e. new information, should be ordered later (Mathesius 1928, Daneš 1974, Li 1976, Klein-Andreou 1983), it conforms to an alternative principle of discourse organization argued for by Gundel (1988), namely "FIRST THINGS FIRST".

In support of this view it is possible to point to the overwhelming tendency to place accented pronominals (*tád, etád, yád, kím*), discourse particles (such as *vaí, ha*), and clitic pronouns (*tvā, asya, enam*) into clause-initial strings. Such structures can be argued to provide a headline or signpost for the student, alerting him to what follows. In extreme cases, the initial strings, in fact, can be said to constitute a "mini-clause" in which all the major participants, objects, and circumstances of the action are briefly encapsulated, as a headline for the rest of the clause; see e.g. [21].

[21] **etām v evā + eṣā etasmai** viṣṇur yajño vicakrame (*ŚB* 1.1.2.13)
And **this** Viṣṇu, the sacrifice, stepped **this** stepping for **him** (the sacrificer).

Moreover, this pattern can be compared to the practice of the *Śatapatha Brāhmaṇa*, in one of its recitational variants, to separate the first "chunk" of a paragraph (the "pratīka") from the rest by means of applying avasāna sandhi (marked by a daṇḍa in the written version), as in [22].

[22] tasya vā etasya vāsasaḥ । agneḥ paryāso bhavati . . . (*ŚB* 3.1.2.18)
Of this very cloth, the woof is of Agni. . . .

I still feel that this account is at least part of the explanation for the dominance of predicate-initial structures in Vedic Prose. However, I now believe that it is not sufficient to explain why predicate-initiality is especially dominant in equational constructions.

To account for this fact, I believe it is necessary to realize that equational structures are widely used in a particular context, and for a particular purpose. This context is the equation of the "ordinary" instruments of the sacrifice (*yajñāyudhāni*) with more abstract or "supramundane" phenomena or qualities such as the Year (writ large) or the Mind (again, writ large), and the purpose seems to be to show that the significance of the sacrificial act extends beyond mere ritual action or recitation and that the sacrifice helps to establish and preserve the entire physical — and metaphysical — world. This "supramundane" significance of the sacrifice, thus, is what is most important in the equation, and for this reason this part of the equation is placed first by the principle "FIRST THINGS FIRST".

This perspective further helps explain the widespread use of the notorious "invariable *yad*" construction, as in [23]. Here, too, the part preceding the *yad*-construction focuses on the special SIGNIFICANCE of the ritual and its parts, while what follows refers to the "ordinary" components of the ritual.

[23] tad etad devamithunam yad gharmaḥ (*AB* 1.22.14)
That is a divine coupling, to wit the gharma. (= The gharma is a divine coupling)

The functional parallelism of this construction with simple predicate-initial equational structures is seen in passages such as [24a], where an initial *yad*-construction is continued by an equational one with predicate before subject. Further support for this interpretation comes from the fact that the parallel passage in [24b] only uses predicate-initial equational structures.

[24] a. ŚIRO vā etad yajñasya yad *ātithyam*
GRĪVĀ *upasado* (*KS* 24.8 = *AB* 1.25.1)
Now, the ātithya is the head of the sacrifice; the upasads, the neck.

b. ŚÍRO vā́ *ātithyám*
GRĪVĀ́ *upasádo* (*MS* 3.7.9)
The ātithya is the head; the upasads, the neck.

5. Conclusions and Outlook

If my arguments are on the right track, Delbrück was correct in his assessment of Vedic-Prose predicate-initiality as marked. The heavy dominance of this pattern in Vedic Prose can be attributed to the nature of its genre, just as the pattern of placing terms to be defined at or near the end of the sūtra is a genre feature of Pāṇini's grammar. More specifically, predicate-initiality is most dominant in equational structures, where it can be attributed to the special concerns of the tradition to establish a supramundane significance for the ritual and its components.

That issues of discourse and genre tend to play a strong role in determining which types of structure are favoured or disfavoured is, of course, not a novel insight. For the Vedic language, consider for example Gonda's remarks on "amplified sentences" and the principle of elaboration in Mantra Vedic (1959), and Jamison (1991) on the use of demonstratives in dialogue vs. didactic passages of Vedic Prose.

Moreover, as I show in Hock (1997), the difference between relatively loose verb-final order in Mantra Vedic and strict verb-finality in Vedic Prose can be attributed to genre differences — between hymnal poetry, liberally drawing on word order variations permitted by the grammar, and didactic texts, without any pretentions to poetic flourishes.

Interestingly, there is one area in which Vedic-Prose verb-finality is frequently overridden, namely the placement of purpose-dative phrases to the right of the verb, as in [25].[5]

[25] a. ta̲t paśū̲n evā̲smā eta̲t pa̲ri dadāti **gu̲ptyai** (*ŚB* 2.4.1.5)
Thereby he gives the cattle to him, for protection.

b. tāny āhur nānopetyāni । nāneva vā ime lokāḥ ।
eṣāṁ lokānāṁ vidhr̥tyā iti (*JB* 2.218)
They say these (sāmans?) are to be undertaken variously — these worlds are various, as it were — for keeping apart these worlds.

c. ta̲m indrāgnī̲ anusa̲matanutām । **prajā̲nām pra̲jātyai** (*ŚB* 4.3.1.2)
Indra and Agni preserved him (Soma); for the procreation of creatures.

[5] See Delbrück 1888: 149 for additional examples.

d. digvad bhavati **bhrātr̥vyasyāpanut[t]yai** (*PB* 12.4.10)
It contains the word "direction", for repelling the enemy.

Delbrück (1888: 25) considers such structures a Satzanhang (clause appendix), assuming that they are preceded by a slight pause, and Jamison (June 1991) even suggests that they are separate clauses. In terms of function within the larger structure, Delbrück and Jamison are no doubt on the right track, and Delbrück's proposal adumbrates Gonda's notion of sentence amplification. I am not convinced, however, that the structures are syntactically extra-clausal. I would prefer to consider them instances of simple syntactic extraposition, but with a special discourse/pragmatic effect.

In many instances, the extraposed dative phrase appears to simply elaborate on the preceding passage [25a]. In others, however, it refers to an "outside" benefit, beyond the ritual action, either a supramundane benefit [25c], or one that accrues to the sacrificer in the "real world" [25d]. Structures like [25cd] suggest that the reading of passages like [25a] as merely elaborating on what precedes may be missing the point, and that in all cases, the dative phrase indicates a benefit that extends beyond the simple sacrificial action. In that case, the contrast between the preceding structure and the extraposed dative phrase can be interpreted as an iconic reflex of the contrast between ritual-internal action and ritual-external benefit.

At any rate, I hope I have been able to show that there are strong reasons for paying closer attention to discourse and pragmatic factors governing syntactic choices, even in what since Delbrück's work on the *Śatapatha Brāhmaṇa* (1878) has appeared to be a "dry", didactic genre, representing the most basic, unmarked syntax of the language.

References

Cardona, George, 1993, "The bhāṣika accent system", *Studien zur Indologie und Iranistik,* **17:** 1-40.

Daneš, František, 1974 (ed.), *Papers on Functional Sentence Perspective,* The Hague: Mouton.

Delbrück, Bertold, 1878, *Die altindische Wortfolge aus dem Çatapathabrāhmaṇa dargestellt* (Syntaktische Forschungen, 3), Halle: Waisenhaus.

———, 1888, *Altindische Syntax* (Syntaktische Forschungen, 5), Halle: Waisenhaus, repr. 1968, Darmstadt: Wissenschaftliche Buchgesellschaft.

Gonda, Jan, 1959, *Four Studies in the Language of the Veda,* The Hague: Mouton.

Gundel, Jeanette K., 1988, "Universals of Topic-Comment Structure", in *Studies in Syntactic Typology*, ed. Michael Hammond et al., pp. 209-39, Amsterdam/Philadelphia: Benjamins.

Hock, Hans Henrich, 1991a (ed.), *Studies in Sanskrit Syntax*, Delhi: Motilal Banarsidass.

———, 1991b, "Possessive Agents in Sanskrit", in Hock 1991a: 55-69.

———, 1997, "Chronology or Genre? Problems in Vedic Syntax", in *Inside the Texts — Beyond the Texts: New Approaches to the Study of the Vedas*, ed. Michael Witzel, pp. 103-26 (Harvard Oriental Series, Opera Minora, 2), Cambridge, MA: Harvard University.

———, 2000, "Genre, Discourse, and Syntax in Sanskrit", in *Textual Parameters in Older Languages*, ed. S. Herring, P. van Reenen, and L. Schøsler, pp. 163-95, Amsterdam/Philadelphia: Benjamins.

Jamison, Stephanie W., 1991, "The Syntax of Direct Speech in Vedic", in *Sense and Syntax in Vedic*, ed. J.P. Brereton and S.W. Jamison (Panels of the VIIth World Sanskrit Conference, ed. J. Bronkhorst, vol. 1.), Leiden: Brill. — Also published in Hock 1991a: 95-112.

Kim, Alan Hyun-Oak, 1988, "Preverbal Focusing and Type XXIII Languages", in *Studies in Syntactic Typology*, ed. Michael Hammond et al., pp. 147-69, Amsterdam/Philadelphia: Benjamins.

Klein-Andreu, Flora, 1983 (ed.), *Discourse Perspectives on Syntax*, New York: Academic Press.

Lahiri, Prabodh Chandra, 1933, *Studies in the Word-Order of Sanskrit Prose*, University of London Ph.D. dissertation.

Li, Charles N., 1976 (ed.), *Subject and Topic*, New York: Academic Press.

Mathesius, Vilem, 1928, "On Linguistic Characterology with Illustrations from Modern English", in *Actes du 1er Congrès International de Linguistes à La Haye*, ed. C.C. Uhlenbeck, pp. 56-63, Leiden: Sijthoff.

Speijer, J.S., 1886, *Sanskrit Syntax*, Leiden: Brill, repr. 1973, Delhi: Motilal Banarsidass.

———, 1896, *Vedische und Sanskrit-Syntax* (Grundriß der indo-arischen Philologie und Altertumskunde, 1.6.) Straßburg: Trübner, repr. 1974, Graz (Austria): Akademische Druck- u. Verlagsanstalt.

2

Interstanzaic Repetition in the R̥gveda

Jared S. Klein

0. Introductory Remarks

ONE of the most surprising lacunae in R̥gvedic studies is the absence of a monographic treatment of the categories and functions of stylistic repetition from stanza to stanza within the individual hymns. There have of course been treatments of repetition in the Veda generally (Gonda 1959); and M. Bloomfield's monograph, *Rigveda Repetitions* (1916), deals with repetitions belonging to different hymns. In a series of twenty-one articles currently being reconfigured in book form (Klein, In preparation), I have closely studied repetition within the R̥gvedic stanza. But the issue of interstanzaic repetition within the hymn is significantly different in that it involves questions relating to the poetic or discourse structures of the hymns themselves. The material for this investigation, on which I am currently preparing a monograph, is of two types: repetitions that are primarily local, occurring for the most part in adjacent stanzas, and repetitions that are pervasive and have been elevated to a principle of hymnic composition. Material of the first type is closely related to intrastanzaic repetition in rhetorical terms. In this paper I will limit myself to non-local repetition, including repetition associated with entire sections of hymns, in order to demonstrate the role this plays in the overall structure of these compositions. In §§ 1-8 I will look at repetitions of various word classes, specifically nouns and adjectives, pronouns, simile words, and numerals. This will be followed in § 9 by a discussion of a select number of entire pādas repeated within individual hymns.

1. Repetition of Nouns and Adjectives: Names of Deities

Under this category we treat first instances in which a hymn to a given deity contains a reference to that deity in (nearly) every stanza. The most familiar instance of this is of course *Ṛgveda* I.1 to Agni, the relevant parts of which are presented below:

[1] ***agním*** *ī́ḷe puróhitam . . .* | | |

agníḥ *pū́rvebhir ŕ̥ṣibhir* | *ī́ḍyo nū́tanair utá* | *sá devā́ṁ éhá vakṣati* | | |

agnínā *rayím aśnavat . . .* | | |

ágne *yáṁ yajñám adhvaráṁ* | *viśvátaḥ paribhū́r ási* | *sá íd devéṣu gachati* | | |

agnír *hótā kavíkratuḥ . . .* | | |

yád aṅgá dāśúṣe tvám | ***ágne*** *bhadráṁ kariṣyási* | *távét tát satyám aṅgiraḥ* | | |

*úpa tv**āgne** divé-dive* | *. . . dhiyā́ vayám* | *námo bháranta émasi* | | |

rā́jantam adhvarā́ṇāṁ | *gopā́m ṛtásya dī́divim* | *várdhamānaṁ své dáme* | | |

sá naḥ pitéva sūnáve | ***ágne*** *sūpāyanó bhava* | *sácasvā naḥ svastáye* | | |

I call upon Agni, the purohita . . . /Agni (was to be called upon) by the previous ṛṣis and is to be called upon by the current ones. He will convey the heavenly ones hither./Through Agni one will attain wealth . . ./O Agni, which worship ceremony thou dost encompass on all sides, that alone goes to the heavenly ones./Agni is the hotar, the one having the intellectual power of a poet . . ./What auspicious thing thou wilt do for the worshipper, O Agni, that very thing of thine is real, O Angiras. Up to thee, O Agni, do we go day after day bearing reverence with our thought, the one ruling over the ceremonies, the gleaming protector of truth, increasing in his own home./So, O Agni, become of easy access to us, like a father to a son. Accompany us for well-being.

The name of this deity appears in eight of the hymn's nine stanzas. In the first five stanzas the name Agni appears fronted in pāda a in four different case forms: *agníḥ* (2 and 5), *agním* (1), *agnínā* (3), and *ágne* (4). In its remaining three occurrences the name is in the vocative, standing first in pāda b in stanzas 6 and 9. In both instances a topicalized structure has been fronted. Thus, in 6 *yád aṅgá dāśúṣe tvám* facilitates discourse cohesion via the correlative diptych *yá- . . . sá/tá-*

(6c *távét tát satyám aṅgiraḥ*). In 9 *sá*-figé in its second person deictic value is fronted as part of a discourse move seen repeatedly in the *R̥gveda*: the use of a final stanza to bring the hymn back from the abstract level of encomium to the here and now of the worship and those performing it. Following the opening matter of this stanza, which includes a simile (*sá naḥ pitéva sūnáve*) come the only two direct appeals to Agni in the hymn: *ágne sūpāyanó bhava* ı *sácasvā naḥ svastáye*). In stanza 7 the directional syntagm *úpa tvā* has been fronted in pāda c before the vocative. It is therefore only stanza 8, a collection of epithets describing Agni's station in advance of the final appeal (*rā́jantam adhvarā́ṇāṁ* ı *gopā́ṁ r̥tásya dī́divim* ı *várdhamānaṁ své dáme*) which lacks any reference to Agni.

2. Repetition of Nouns and Adjectives: Epithets and Other Keywords

A second important category involving nouns and adjectives encompasses instances in which the repeated items are not deities to whom the hymn is addressed but rather keywords such as epithets that occur in conjunction with the hymn's addressee. Prominent among these are the terms *vŕ̥ṣan-*/ *vr̥ṣabhá-* appearing frequently in hymns to Indra and often transferred to other things in his sphere. *Vŕ̥ṣan-* and *vr̥ṣabhá-* are of course themselves paronomastic variants. There are six hymns in the *R̥gveda* showing extensive interstanzaic repetition involving these terms in close juxtaposition to each other within a stretch of two or three stanzas. As representative of all of these we present II.16.4-6:

[2] *víśve hy àsmai yajatā́ya dhr̥ṣṇáve/krátum bháranti* ***vr̥ṣabhā́ya*** *sáścate//* ***vŕ̥ṣā*** *yajasva havíṣā vidúṣṭaraḥ/píbendra sómaṁ* ***vr̥ṣabhéṇa*** *bhānúnā///* ***vŕ̥ṣṇaḥ*** *kóśaḥ pavate mádhva ūrmír/****vr̥ṣabhā́nnāya vr̥ṣabhā́ya*** *pā́tave/* ***vŕ̥ṣṇādhvaryū́ vr̥ṣabhā́so*** *ádrayo/****vŕ̥ṣaṇaṁ*** *sómaṁ* ***vr̥ṣabhā́ya*** *suṣvati///* ***vŕ̥ṣā*** *te vájra utá te* ***vŕ̥ṣā*** *rátho/****vŕ̥ṣaṇā*** *hárī* ***vr̥ṣabhā́ṇy*** *ā́yudhā/****vŕ̥ṣṇo*** *mádasya* ***vr̥ṣabhá*** *tvám īśiṣa/índra sómasya* ***vr̥ṣabhásya*** *tr̥pṇuhi* (II.16.4-6)

For all bear resolve to him, the bold one worthy of worship, the bull who follows (that resolve). As a bull perform thy own worship, as the wiser one, with the oblation. Drink soma, O Indra, with its bull radiance./ The cup of the bull is purified, the wave of honey, for the bull whose food is a bull, to drink. The Adhvaryu's are bulls, the rocks (i.e. pressing stones) are bulls. They press the bull soma for the bull./A bull is thy cudgel and thy chariot is a bull. Thy two bay steeds are bulls, bulls thy weapons. As a bull, thou rulest over the bull exhilaration. O Indra, delight in the bull soma.

In this passage not just Indra alone but everything associated with him is described as a bull. The "bull-radiance" of 4d is no doubt the fire over which the soma is coured. Soma itself is then characterized as a bull in the phrase *vṛ́ṣṇaḥ kóśaḥ* "the cup of the bull" as well as in the bahuvrīhi *vṛṣabhā́nnāya* "for him whose food [i.e. soma] is a bull". There then follows in stanza 6 a series of copular equations of other things or individuals associated with the worship as bulls (Adhvaryu's, pressing-stones, soma explicitly, Indra's cudgel, his chariot, the bay steeds that lead it, and his weapons). From a formal point of view this sequence contains in stanza 4 an instance of polyptotic (*vṛṣabhā́ya . . . vṛṣabhéṇa*) and paronomastic (*vṛṣabhá-/vṛ́ṣan-*) repetition. Stanza 5 contains what I have called "4 x 4 + 3"[1] polyptotic and paronomastic anaphora: an occurrence of the repeated form in each pāda of a four-line stanza plus three additional occurrences, here in verses b, c, and d.

3. Pronominal Repetition

Pronominal sequences provide a rich repository of interstanzaic repetition in the *Ṛgveda*. Here we shall focus on only two of these, each of which is the most extensive instance of its genre. The first is I.61, a hymn to Indra in sixteen stanzas, the first fifteen of which begin with a form of *ayám* occurring in three different stanza-initial collocations: *asmā́ íd u* (1-6, 8, 12, 15), *asyéd u* (7, 11, 13, 14), and *asyéd evá* (9, 10):

[3] ***asmā́ íd u*** *prá . . ./. . . harmi stómam . . ./ / /*
asmā́ íd u *. . . prá yaṁsi/. . . āṅgūṣám . . ./ / /*
asmā́ íd u *. . ./bhárāmy āṅgūṣám . . ./ / /*
asmā́ íd u *stómaṁ sáṁ hinomi . . ./ / /*
asmā́ íd u *. . ./índrāyārkáṁ juhvā̀ sám añje . . ./ / /*
asmā́ íd u *tvā́ṣṭā takṣad vájram . . ./ / /*

---

[1] Read "four-by-four plus three". For this designation (also "4 x 4 +1", "4 x 4 + 2", etc.) cf. Klein 2007: 225.

asyéd u *mātúḥ sávaneṣu sadyó/maháḥ pitúm papivā́n . . .//*

asmā́ íd u *gnā́ś cid devápatnīr/índrāyārkám . . . ūvuḥ . . .///*

asyéd evá *prá ririce mahitvám/divás pr̥thivyā́ḥ páry antárikṣāt . . .///*

asyéd evá *śávasā . . ./ ví vr̥ścad vájreṇa vr̥trám índraḥ . . .///*

asyéd u *tveṣásā ranta síndhavaḥ . . .///*

asmā́ íd u *prá bharā . . ./ vr̥trā́ya vájram . . .///*

asyéd u *prá brūhi pūrvyā́ṇi/. . . kármāṇi . . .///*

asyéd u *bhiyā́ giráyaś ca dr̥ḷhā́/dyā́vā ca bhū́mā janúṣas tujete . . .///*

asmā́ íd u *tyád ánu dāyy eṣām/éko yád vavné . . .///*

evā́ te . . . suvr̥ktí/índra bráhmāṇi gótamāso akran . . . (I.61)

To him alone . . . I bring my praise . . ./To him alone I have extended my song of praise . . ./To him alone I bear my song of praise . . ./To him alone I impel my praise in its entirety . . ./For him alone, for Indra do I anoint my praise song entirely with my tongue . . ./For him alone did Tvaṣṭar fashion a cudgel . . ./At the pressings of the mother of him alone he straightway drank (lit. having straightway drunk) the drink of his great (father) . . ./For him alone, for Indra did the (heavenly) women whose spouses are the heavenly ones weave a praise song . . . / Indeed, of him alone is the greatness preeminent over heaven (and) earth, over the atmosphere . . ./Indeed, through the power of him alone did Indra hew apart Vr̥tra with his cudgel . . ./ Through the impetuosity of him alone did the rivers come to a standstill . . ./Upon him alone, upon Vr̥tra bear forth thy cudgel . . ./Of him alone speak forth the previous deeds . . ./Through fear of the birth of him alone the firm mountains and heaven and earth are in upheaval . . ./To him alone was that (soma drink: so Geldner with ref. to *somapéyam* at V.29.5b) conceded by them (sc. the heavenly ones), when he alone won (the right to it) . . ./Therefore, the Gotamas have made their formulations with a hymn for thee, O Indra . . ./

The structural principle of this hymn is clearly to declare the unique status of Indra as the recipient of the poet's praise based on his inimitable acts of heroic valour that have been acknowledged by the heavenly ones themselves. The force of *íd* is in all cases delimitative. The hymn moves from the delimitative force of *íd* to the lexical expression of the uniqueness of Indra, as signalled by *éka-* in stanza 15.[2] Once this has

2. Peculiar is stanza 12, where *asmā́ íd* refers to Vr̥tra (*asmā́ íd u . . ./vr̥trā́ya vájram* like *asmā́ íd u . . ./índrāyārkám* of 5 and 8). In the absence of the →

been established, the poet is free to end his hymn with the only stanza not beginning with one of the tours illustrated above. Here once again the final stanza possesses a cumulative and recapitulative value signalled by *evā́* "therefore", the function of which is very much like that of *sá*-figé in hymn I.1 discussed earlier.

4. Repetition of Correlative Diptychs

The next pronominal sequence we shall take up is the correlative diptych *yá- . . . sá/tá-*. This is a fundamental discourse strategy in the *Ṛgveda*. The best known extensive repeated structure of this sort in the *Ṛgveda* is seen in II.12, selected stanzas of which are presented in [4]:

[4] ***yáḥ*** *pṛthivī́ṁ vyáthamānām ádṛṁhad/****yáḥ*** *párvatān prákupitām̐ áramṇāt//* ***yó*** *antárikṣaṁ vimamé várīyo/****yó*** *dyā́m ástabhnāt* ***sá janāsa índraḥ****///* (2)

yásyā́śvāsaḥ *pradíśi* ***yásya*** *gā́vo/****yásya*** *grā́mā* ***yásya*** *víśve ráthāsaḥ//****yáḥ*** *sū́ryaṁ* ***yá*** *uṣásaṁ jajā́na/****yó*** *apā́ṁ netā́* ***sá janāsa índraḥ****///* (7)

yáṁ *krándasī saṁyatī́ vihváyete/páre (á)vara ubháyā amítrāḥ//samānáṁ cid rátham ātasthivā́ṁsā//nā́nā havete* ***sá janāsa índraḥ****///* (8)

yáḥ *śámbaram párvateṣu kṣiyántaṁ/catvāriṁśyā́ṁ śarády anvávindat// ojāyámānaṁ* ***yó*** *áhiṁ jaghā́na/dā́nuṁ śáyānaṁ* ***sá janāsa índraḥ****///* (11)

yáḥ *sunvántam ávati* ***yáḥ*** *pácantaṁ /* ***yáḥ*** *śáṁsantaṁ* ***yáḥ*** *śaśamānám ūtī́//* ***yásya*** *bráhma várdhanaṁ* ***yásya*** *sómo/****yásyedáṁ*** *rā́dhaḥ* ***sá janāsa índraḥ****///* (14)

Which one made firm the shaking earth, who brought to rest the quaking mountains, who measured out the atmosphere (so that it became) broader, who propped up heaven, that one, O peoples, is Indra./. . ./ Under whose direction are the horses, the cows, the communities of men, all the chariots; who begot the sun, who the dawn, who is the leader of the waters, that one, O peoples, is Indra./Whom the two battle lines coming together variously call, both (sides), the enemies near (and) far, the two mounting even the same chariot call (him) one on one side, one on the other, that one, O peoples, is Indra./. . ./Who found Śambara dwelling in the mountains in the fortieth year, who smote the serpent Dānu, showing off his power, lying (over the waters), that one, O peoples,

→ other stanzas this tour makes sense in that Vṛtra was, after all, Indra's greatest rival. But in the context of this hymn, was the poet trying to shock his audience to attention, lest they should have become lulled by the monotony of the structure?

> is Indra./. . ./Who aids the one pressing, who the one cooking, who the one praising, who the one toiling in worship with his aid, of whom the formulation is strengthening, of whom the soma, of whom this gift, that one, O peoples, is Indra.

All fifteen stanzas of this hymn to Indra are constructed in this fashion, all but the last showing the tour *yá-. . . sá janāsa índraḥ* "which one . . . that one, O peoples, is Indra". The actual number of occurrences of the relative pronoun in this hymn is 46, ranging from a low of one in stanzas 5, 8, and 15 to a high of seven in 7 and 14. On the other hand, *sá* occurs only once outside the core structure just noted (stanza 5). The diptych encompasses the stanza with the relative fronted in all instances but 13 and 15. In the former it is limited to the second distich and in the latter to the first. The correlatives are meant to identify Indra based on his deeds of cosmic significance as well as his accomplishments as a warrior, all of which are specified in the relative clauses. The absence of the correlative *sá janāsa índraḥ* in stanza 15 is yet another instance of the bards' tendency to differentiate the final stanza from the rest, and the hymn moves in its denouement back to the hic et nunc of the worship, speaking of Indra's aid to the one toiling in service to him and ending with the poet's expression of the wish that he and his cohort should "announce the distribution in possession of good heroes and as ever-dear ones to Indra" (15cd *vayáṁ ta indra viśváha priyā́saḥ/suvī́rāso vidátham ā́ vadema*), a variant of the refrain *bṛhád vadema vidáthe suvī́rāḥ* "May we speak loudly at the distribution in possession of good heroes" which ends twenty of the hymns in the second maṇḍala.

5. Repetition of Interrogative Pronouns

We turn next to interrogative pronoun sequences. In an earlier study of intrastanzaic repetition of interrogatives (Klein 2008) I noted that interrogativity in the *Ṛgveda* is associated with a type of discourse setting that tends to be self-contained and isolated from surrounding discourse stretches. That is to say, it is not common to find just a single interrogative but rather these tend to cluster both within the stanza and across stanza boundaries. One of the most extensive interrogative sequences in the *Ṛgveda* is IV.3.4-8:

[5] ***kadā́*** *ta ukthā́ sadhamā́dyāni/****kadā́*** *bhavanti sakhyā́ gṛhé te///* (4cd)
kathā́ *ha tád váruṇāya tvám agne/****kathā́*** *divé garhase* ***kán*** *na ā́gaḥ//*

kathā́ *mitrā́ya mīḷhúṣe pṛthivyaí/brávaḥ* ***kád*** *aryamṇé* ***kád*** *bhágāya///* (5)
kád *dhíṣṇyāsu vṛdhasānó agne/* ***kád*** *vā́tāya prátavase śubhaṁyé//párijmane nā́satyāya kṣé brávaḥ/* ***kád*** *agne rudrā́ya nṛghné///* (6)
kathā́ *mahé puṣṭimbharā́ya pūṣṇé/* ***kád*** *rudrā́ya súmakhāya havirdé//* ***kád*** *víṣṇava urugāyā́ya réto/brávaḥ* ***kád*** *agne śárave bṛhatyaí///* (7)
kathā́ *śárdhāya marútām ṛtā́ya/* ***kathā́*** *sūré bṛhaté pṛchyámānaḥ//práti bravo (á)ditaye turā́ya/sā́dhā divó jātavedaś cikitvā́n///* (8)

When will the hymns to thee be worthy of a common meal (with thee)? When do will friendships (with thee) in thy home arise?/How wilt thou, O Agni, complain about that to Varuṇa, how to heaven? What is our sin? How wilt thou speak to the reward-bringing Mitra, to earth? What (wilt thou say) to Aryaman, what to Bhaga?/What (wilt thou speak), O Agni, growing in the fireplaces? What to the very powerful Vāta (wind) driving for beauty? What wilt thou speak to Nāsatya wandering about, to the earth(?), what, O Agni, to man-slaying Rudra?/ How (wilt thou speak), to the great Pūṣaṇ, bearer of thrivance? What to the liberal Rudra, giver of the oblation? What seed wilt thou speak of to the broad-striding Viṣṇu, what (wilt thou condemn), O Agni, to the lofty arrow (of Rudra)?/How (wilt thou speak) to the troop of Maruts (driving) for truth? How, being asked, wilt thou speak to the lofty sun, to Aditi, to the powerful one? O Jātavedas, as a wise one set straight (the affairs) of heaven.

This is part of an Agni hymn in sixteen stanzas. What is remarkable about this passage is how the questions cascade one after another (seventeen in twenty pādas), and yet elsewhere in the hymn not a single interrogative pronoun is to be found. The hymn begins as an exhortation to the worshipper to praise Agni, an invitation to the god to sit down at the worship, and an appeal to him to take note of the ritual toil of the worshipper. But then suddenly the questions begin. Despite the many interrogatives here, it seems clear that this is merely a rhetorical tour and that there is only one question being asked, betraying a deep fear on the part of the singer that he has sinned and wants to know what he will be accused of in cosmic terms. The sense of *sā́dhā diváḥ* is probably that Agni should intercede for the singer and make things right with the heavenly ones. The singer then continues his song, praying that, among other things, he should not be held accountable for the sins of another and that Agni should become well inclined toward him on account of his song.

6. Repetition of Simile Markers

In three Ṛgvedic hymns a stylistic trope has been elevated to a compositional discourse principle. These are instances in which the entire hymn is composed of a series of similes. The first, X.78, is a hymn to the Maruts in eight stanzas, the first seven of which all constitute 4 x 4 repetitions involving *ná*. We have presented selected stanzas from this hymn in (6a). An even denser sequence of similes, this time involving *iva*, is seen in II.39 (6b, with selected stanzas), once again a hymn in eight stanzas, this time to the Aśvins:

(6) a. *víprāso **ná** mánmabhiḥ svādhyò / devāvyò **ná** yajñaíḥ svápnasaḥ // rā́jāno **ná** citrā́ḥ susaṁdṛśaḥ / kṣitīnā́ṁ **ná** máryā arepásaḥ ///* (1)

*vā́tāso **ná** yé dhúnayo jigatnávo / (a)gnīnā́ṁ **ná** jihvā́ virokíṇaḥ // vármaṇvanto **ná** yodhā́ḥ śímīvantaḥ / pitṝṇā́ṁ **ná** śáṁsāḥ surātáyaḥ ///* (3)

*áśvāso **ná** yé jyéṣṭhāsa āśávo / didhiṣávo **ná** rathyàḥ sudā́navaḥ // ā́po **ná** nimnaír udábhir jigatnávo / viśvárūpā áṅgiraso **ná** sā́mabhiḥ ///* (5)

*uṣásāṁ **ná** ketávo (a)dhvaraśríyaḥ / śubhaṁyávo **nā́ñjíbhir** vy àśvitan // síndhavo **ná** yayíyo bhrā́jadṛṣṭayaḥ / parāváto **ná** yójanāni mamire ///* (7)

(X.78.1, 3, 5, 7)

Having good thoughts like inspired poets with their hymns, of good wealth like those inviting the heavenly ones through their worship; of good appearance like resplendent kings, faultless like the young men of the (human) dwellings./. . ./Who are roaring, hastening like the winds, shining out like the tongues of fires; zealous like armoured warriors, granting good gifts like the proclamations of fathers./. . ./ Who are swift like the best horses, offering good gifts like charioteers eager to get (booty); hastening like waters along the watery depths, taking on all forms like the Angirases with their songs./. . ./Beautifying the ceremony like the beacons of the dawns, like those desirous of beauty they have glistened out with their ointments; hastening like rivers with their shining spears, they have measured the leagues like (men coming) from the distance.

b. *grā́vāṇ**eva** tád íd árthaṁ jarethe / gṛ́dhr**eva** vṛkṣáṁ nidhimántam ácha // brahmā́ṇ**eva** vidátha ukthaśā́sā / dūt**éva** hávyā jányā purutrā́ ///* (1)

*nāv**éva** naḥ parayataṁ yug**éva** / nábhy**eva** na upadh**ī́va** pradh**ī́va** // śvā́n**eva** na árisaṇyā tanū́nāṁ / khṛ́gal**eva** visrásaḥ pātam asmā́n ///* (4)

*vāt**evājuryā́** nady**èva** rītír / akṣī́ **iva** cákṣuṣā́ yātam arvā́k // hástāv **iva** tanvè śámbhaviṣṭhā / pā́d**eva** no nayataṁ vásyo ácha ///* (5)

óṣṭhāv ***iva*** *mádhv āsné vádantā/stánāv* ***iva*** *pipyataṁ jīváse naḥ//nās****eva*** *nas tanvò rakṣitā́rā । kárṇāv* ***iva*** *suśrútā bhūtam asmé///* (6)

(II.39.1, 4, 5, 6)

Like two pressing stones, you awake (to go) unto just that task; like two vultures to a tree, (you go) unto that possessing a store (of riches); like two formulators proclaiming hymns at the distribution ceremony, like two messengers you, belonging to the people, are to be called in many places./. . ./Like two ships, lead us across, like two yokes; like two naves (lead) us, like two wheel spokes, like two fellies; like two dogs not allowing injury to our bodies, like two suits of armour, protect us from breaking apart./. . ./Unaging, like two winds, like two streams (uniting) as a current, like two eyes with (a single) sight drive hither our way; like two hands bringing the most excellent benefit to the body, like two feet, lead us unto what is better./. . ./Like two lips speaking honey for the mouth, like two breasts, swell for us for living; like two noses serving as protectors of our body, like two ears become of sharp hearing for us.

In (b) again, as in virtually every case we have seen so far, the poet breaks off from his abstract reverie in the final stanza, referring to the purpose of the hymn in the here and now without any simile. Within the hymn as a whole one finds thirty-one occurrences of *iva*, and the distribution of the particle is not as regular as that of *ná* in X.78: stanzas 1-3 and 6 are 4 x 4, but 4 shows seven occurrences of *iva* 5 shows five, and 7 shows three. This eulogy of the Aśvins is therefore based totally on comparisons of their qualities to aspects of the world, nearly always presented in twos like the Aśvins themselves. These qualities are sometimes just stated as such but in many instances become material parts of a prayer on the part of the singer, whereby he and his entourage should benefit. In what we can now definitely state to be a discourse principle the final stanza is kept separate and free of similes as a summational, concluding statement of the poet's wish, ending in the signal final refrain pāda of Maṇḍala II quoted in our discussion of [4] above.

7. Repetition of Numerals

The longest instance of interstanzaic repetition involving numerals is seen in I.34, a hymn to the Aśvins in twelve stanzas, the first nine of which show thirty-four occurrences of *tráyaḥ/tríḥ*, presumably occasioned by the twin facts of their being invoked three times a day and their three-part chariot. This focus on the number "3" is the apparent raison d'être for the hymn. In [7] we present selected stanzas. The last three stanzas of this hymn for the most part abandon the play on *trí-*, stating the fact, rooted in the here and now, that the oblation has been poured and the Aśvins should come:

[7] ***tríś*** *cin no adyā́ bhavataṁ navedasā* . . . (1a)

tráyaḥ *paváyo madhuvā́hane ráthe/sómasya venā́m ánu víśva íd viduḥ//* ***tráya*** *skambhā́sa skabhitā́sa ārábhe/****trír*** *náktaṁ yāthás* ***trír*** *v aśvinā dívā///* (2)

trír *vartír yātaṁ* ***trír*** *ánuvrate jáne/****tríḥ*** *suprāvyè* ***tredhé****va śikṣatam//****trír*** *nāndyàṁ vahatam aśvinā yuváṁ/****tríḥ*** *pṛ́kṣo asmé akṣáreva pinvatam///* (4)

trír *no rayíṁ vahatam aśvinā yuváṁ/****trír*** *devátātā* ***trír*** *utā́vataṁ dhíyaḥ//* ***tríḥ*** *saubhagatváṁ* ***trír*** *utá śrávāṁsi nas/****triṣṭháṁ*** *vāṁ sū́re duhitā́ ruhad rátham///* (5)

trír *no aśvinā divyā́ni bheṣajā́/****tríḥ*** *pā́rthivāni* ***trír*** *u dattam adbhyáḥ// omā́naṁ śaṁyór mámakāya sūnáve/****tridhā́tu*** *śárma vahataṁ śubhas patī///* (6)

kvà ***trī́*** *cakrā́* ***trivṛ́to*** *ráthasya/kvà* ***tráyo*** *vandhúro yé sánīḷaḥ//*
(9ab) (I.34.1a, 2, 4, 5, 6, 9ab)

Thrice today become cognizant of us . . ./Three wheel-rims are on (your) honey-conveying chariot. All know of your longing for soma. Three supports are fixed for grabbing onto. Thrice do you drive by night and thrice, O Aśvins, by day./. . ./Thrice drive (your) path, thrice unto the man heeding your command. Thrice exert yourselves threefold, as it were, for the one serving (you) well. Do you thrice convey joy, O Aśvins; thrice swell the nourishment among us like an inexhaustible (cow swells with milk)./Do you thrice convey wealth to us, O Aśvins, thrice at the divine service, and thrice aid (our) thoughts. Thrice (convey) auspiciousness and thrice fame to us. The daughter of the sun has mounted your chariot having three standing positions./Thrice grant us, O Aśvins, (your) heavenly healings, thrice (your) earthly, and thrice (those) from the waters. Convey threefold protection as aid, the blessing of life to little me (as to) a son, O masters of beauty./. . ./Where are the three wheels of your three-part chariot, where are the three seats which offer equal sitting space?

8. Repetition of Entire Pādas

In this section I wish to investigate the repetition of entire pādas or groups of pādas within a single hymn. The best way to handle this material is to lemmatize it by hymn and pāda. The total number of repeated pādas are, depending on whether one follows Arnold (1905) or Oldenberg (1888), 213 or 214. I will focus on instances where the repetitions play a significant thematic role within their hymns, often employing in my commentary informal (telegraphic) style.

[8] *marúdbhir agna ā́ gahi* (I.19.1c-9c)

O Agni, come hither with the Maruts.

This line ends all nine stanzas of a Gāyatrī hymn to Agni and the Maruts. Stanzas 3-8 are introduced by relative pronouns signalling attributes or deeds of these deities; and *marúdbhir agne* are jointly anaphoric to these in each case. The petition to these deities to come to the worship is the point of the entire hymn.

(9) *ā́ tū́ na indra śaṁsaya/góṣv áśveṣu śubhríṣu/sahásreṣu tuvīmagha* (I.29.1c-e-7c-e)

Do thou, O Indra, give us hope for thousands of beautiful cows (and) horses, O thou of great liberality.

From a hymn to Indra in seven stanzas in Paṅkti metre. The repeated material therefore represents 60 per cent of the content of the hymn. The refrain fits best in stanza 1, where the singer and his cohort are said to be *anāśastā́ḥ* "bereft of hope", whence, in a paronomastic play, Indra is asked to give them hope (*ā́ . . . śaṁsaya*). In stanzas 3-7 Indra is asked to turn away various hostile forces or ill-omened beings.

[10] *dyumnaír abhí prá ṇonumaḥ* (I.78.1c-5c)

We (Gotamas) shout forth unto (thee) with heavenly splendour.

This is from a five-stanza Gāyatrī hymn to Agni. The refrain is integrated best syntactically in stanzas 1 and 4, where it provides the main clause verb. The object of *abhí prá ṇonumaḥ* is expressed in pāda 1a as *tvā*, in 2a-4a as *tám u tvā*. In stanzas 3 and 5 one finds *havāmahe* and *ávocāma*, respectively, as additional vocal gestures. These, and especially the iterative (intensive) act of shouting signalled by *abhí prá ṇonumaḥ*, constitute the fundamental statement made by the poet of this hymn.

[11] *yójā nv ìndra te hárī* (I.82.1e-5e)

Now I shall yoke thy two bays, O Indra.

This is a six-stanza hymn to Indra, 1-5 in Paṅkti and 6 in Jagatī metre. It deals with the harnessing of Indra's bay steeds following his partaking of the soma. In 1e-5e the singer states his intention to yoke the steeds (*yójā*: subjunctive) and then in 6a *yunájmi te bráhmaṇā keśínā hárī* "I yoke thy maned steeds with the formulation" he carries out his promise. The refrain can therefore be said to represent the basic theme of the hymn. Note how the variation in metre, another device frequently employed by the bards to separate the final stanza from those that precede, correlates both with the cessation of the refrain and the illocutionary change from intention to enactment.

[12] *marútvān no bhavatv índra ūtī́* (I.100.1d-15d)

Let Indra together with the Maruts be for aid for us.

From a Triṣṭubh hymn to Indra in nineteen stanzas. Stanzas 4-13 constitute a twenty-term *sá/tá* sequence detailing acts and attributes of Indra, 1-3 show relative clauses having the same purpose, and 14-15 show *yá- . . . sá/tá-* diptychs playing again the same role. In none of these stanzas is the name Indra mentioned outside the refrain pāda. Consequently, the purpose of the refrain is to overtly inform the listeners about the deity who is being praised and asked to come to their aid. Significantly, once the refrain has run its course, Indra's name does appear in 17 and 19. Note again the differentiation toward the end of the hymn.

[13] *marútvantaṁ sakhyā́ya havāmahe* (I.101.1d-7d)

We call the one accompanied by the Maruts for friendship.

From a hymn to Indra in eleven stanzas, 1-7 Jagatī, 8-11 Triṣṭubh. This hymn consists of two parts which follow the metrical variation: praise of Indra (1-7) and invitation to the worship. The refrain pāda is associated with a twenty-term relative sequence in stanzas 1-6 in which various attributes and deeds of Indra are rehearsed. Although Indra's name surfaces in 2c-7c, the refrain d-pāda provides the main verb, whose object is Indra each time it occurs. The acknowledgement of the poet's call to Indra is the theme of each stanza.

[14] *rátham ná durgā́d vasavaḥ sudānavo / víśvasmān no áṁhaso níṣ pipartana* (I.106.1cd-6cd)

Like a chariot from a difficult way, lead us out from every straitened circumstance, O Vasus, ye having good gifts.

Hymn to Viśvedevāḥ in seven stanzas. 1-6 are Jagatī, 7 Triṣṭubh. This hymn is a simple prayer for aid and therefore the refrain represents a general concluding prayer completely adapted to the theme. It is blocked from appearing in 7cd by the final refrain distich *tán no mitró váruṇo māmahantām / áditiḥ síndhuḥ pṛthivī́ utá dyaúḥ*, which appears 15 times in hymns I.94-115.

[15] *átaḥ pári vṛṣaṇāv ā́ hí yatám / áthā sómasya pibataṁ sutásya* (I.108.7cd-12cd)

Certainly drive around hither from there, O bulls, and drink of the pressed soma. (6d = 7d-12d)

A Triṣṭubh hymn to Indrāgni in thirteen stanzas. 7-12 all show the diptych *yád indrāgnī . . . átaḥ* "If, O Indra (and) Agni . . . from there". *Áthā . . . pibatam* is then always temporally dependent on this. 6d as well follows *ā́ hí yātám*, but the first part of 6c is different; and 5cd has *yā́ . . . tébhiḥ sómasya pibataṁ sutásya*. The basic theme of the hymn is therefore that wherever Indrāgni are, they should come to us from there and drink our pressed soma. The final stanza 13ab is as usual summational in nature: *evéndrāgnī papivā́ṁsā sutásya / víśvāsmábhyaṁ sáṁ jayataṁ dhánāni* "(And) so, O Indra (and) Agni, having drunk of the pressed (soma), completely win all the stakes for us." This is then followed by the refrain distich cited under I.106 [14].

[16] *tā́bhir ū ṣú ūtíbhir aśvinā́ gatam* (I.112.1d-23d)

With those aids, O Aśvins, come well hither.

Hymn to the Aśvins in twenty-five stanzas, the first twenty-three of which are Jagatī and made up entirely of correlative diptychs (*yā́bhiḥ . . . tā́bhir ū̥ ṣú . . .*) recalling other acts of aid the Aśvins have proffered and praying for them to render the same aids to the singer. As usual, 24 and 25, which are Triṣṭubh, abandon this tour, asking the Aśvins to reward the poet's words and grant strength in the battle for booty (24) and asking for protection day and night (25). The latter again ends in the refrain cited under I.106 [14].

[17] *dyā́vā rákṣatam pr̥thivī no ábhvāt* (I.185.2d-8d)

O heaven (and) earth, protect us from dissolution.

Triṣṭubh hymn to Heaven and Earth in eleven stanzas. As Geldner notes, this refrain is the point of the entire hymn. The idea is repeated in a different form in 10d *pitā́ mātā́ ca rakṣatam ávobhiḥ* The hymn-initial stanza begins with a barrage of questions about heaven and earth and stands thereby apart from 2-8. The hymn ends with the refrain pāda *vidyā́meṣáṁ vr̥jánaṁ jīrádānum*, which appears 21x as the concluding pāda of the group I.165-190.

[18] *sómasya tā́ máde índraś cakāra* (II.15.2d-9d)

In the exhilaration of soma did Indra do those things.

Triṣṭubh hymn to Indra in ten stanzas. 1-9 describe in each instance a heroic deed of Indra. The hymn begins much like I.32 with the poet's proclamation of his intention to recite these deeds; this time, however, focusing from the very beginning on the role of soma in his most important deed, the slaying of Vr̥tra:

prá ghā nv àsya maható mahā́ni/satyā́ satyásya káraṇāni vocam//

tríkadrukeṣv apibat sutásya/

asyá máde áhim índro jaghāna

Forth, indeed now shall I proclaim his deeds, the great deeds of the great one, the true deeds of the true one. He drank of the pressed soma in the *trikadruka* vessels. In the exhilaration of that did Indra slay the serpent.

Thus, the theme of soma-induced exhilaration as the source of Indra's heroic acts is stated at the outset and is prolonged throughout the hymn, representing its Leitmotif. Stanza 10 is merely a repetition of II.11.21 and is unrelated to the rest of the hymn.

[19] *saínaṁ saścad devó deváṁ/satyám índraṁ satyá índuḥ* (II.22.1gh.2fg.3fg)

That heavenly one will accompany him, the heavenly one: the real drop the real Indra.

Hymn to Indra in four unusual seven- and eight-line stanzas here again emphasizing the union of Indra and Soma. 1c states *tr̥pát sómam apibat* and 1e says *sá īm mamāda máhi kárma kártave* "He drank soma to satiety . . . that exhilarated him to perform a great deed." The first of these deeds is again his overcoming the "worm" (i.e. Vṛtra) in battle (2ab *abhí . . . krívim̐/yudhā́bhavat . . .*). The link between Indra and Soma is expressed on the levels of both content and form: on the former, both are *satyá-* "real"; on the latter, the antonomastic reference to soma as *índu-* "drop" is meant to create a phonetic figure (whether etymological, hence paronomastic or not must remain uncertain) with *índra-*.

[20] *yám̐-yam̐ yújam̐ kṛṇuté bráhmaṇas pátiḥ* (II.25.1d-5d)

Whomsoever Brahmaṇaspati makes his companion.

Jagatī hymn to Brahmaṇaspati in five stanzas. This hymn is a catalogue of all the good things that happen to the one whom Brahmaṇaspati makes his companion.

[21] *mahád devā́nām asuratvám ékam* (III.55.1d-22d)

Great is the unique Asura-power of the heavenly ones.

Triṣṭubh hymn to Viśvedevāḥ in twenty-two stanzas. In this hymn replete with riddles and the secrets of the powers of the heavenly ones, the one constant is this refrain, which must be interpreted as a kind of testimony of faith.

[22] *vā́yav ā́ candréṇa ráthena/yāhi sutásya pītáye* (IV.48.1cd-4cd)

O Vāyu, drive hither with thy golden chariot for the drinking of the pressed (soma).

Anuṣṭubh hymn to Vāyu in five stanzas. The hypermetrical quality of the c-pāda of this refrain is peculiar. But the idea is the fundamental one which pervades the hymn. The final stanza expresses essentially the same idea in different words:

vā́yo śatám̐ hárīṇām̐/yuvásva póṣyāṇām/utá vā te sahasríṇo/rátha ā́ yātu pā́jasā

O Vāyu, harness a hundred thriving bay steeds. Or let the chariot of thee having a thousand (bay steeds) drive hither with its firm structure.

Thus, the principle of separation of the final stanza from the rest is maintained on the level of expression if not of content.

[23] *íṣam̐ stotṛ́bhya ā́ bhara* (V.6.1e-10e)

Bear hither nourishment to the praisers.

Hymn to Agni in ten stanzas in Paṅkti metre. This final pāda of each stanza represents the basic point of the hymn.

[24] *mā́dhvī máma śrutaṁ hávam* (V.75.1e-9e)

O honey-lovers, hear my call.

Hymn to the Aśvins in nine stanzas in Paṅkti metre. In addition to a plea for the Aśvins to come to the worship, expressed in different words in stanzas 2, 3, 5, 6, and 7, this refrain represents the fundamental petition of the hymn.

[25] *ayáṁ sá sóma indra te sutáḥ píba* (VI.43.1c-4c)

This is that soma pressed for thee, O Indra. Drink!

Hymn to Indra in four stanzas in Uṣṇih metre. The double pronoun *ayáṁ sá* in this refrain represents a proximal deictic *ayám* plus an anaphor *sá*. In fact, each of the four stanzas of this hymn consists of a correlative diptych *yásya . . . mádam/máde/mandānáḥ/sá. . . .* Consequently, the refrain is a material part of the compositional structure of this hymn and of course its main point.

[26] *tā́ ā́po devī́r ihá mā́m avantu* (VII.49.1d-4d)

Let those heavenly waters aid me here.

Triṣṭubh hymn to the waters in four stanzas made up entirely of correlative diptychs in which nine relative pronouns appear in the a-c pādas of these four stanzas. The refrain is therefore intimately woven into the fabric of the hymn and its request is the raison d'être for the composition.

[27] *mā́ mā́m pádyena rápasā vidat tsáruḥ* (VII.50.1d-3d)

May a creeping thing not strike me with an injury to my foot.

Hymn to various deities in four stanzas. 1-3 are Jagatī, 4 Atijagatī. This hymn is an Atharvavedic-like charm against various substances noxious to the body. The only deities mentioned are Mitrāvaruṇā in stanza 1, Agni in 2, and Viśve Devāḥ in 3 (in stanza 4 the waters are asked to provide protection from various specified maladies). The refrain clearly states the point of the hymn.

[28] *mṛḷā́ sukṣatra mṛḷáya* (VII.89.1c-4c)

Be merciful, O thou of good dominion, show mercy!

Hymn to Varuṇa in five stanzas. 1-4 Gāyatrī, 5 Jagatī. This prayer for personal mercy on behalf of the singer, eloquent in its conciseness of expression, represents the point of the entire hymn. Stanza 5 is a much more expansive prayer for mercy expressed in the plural, thereby conforming to the usual differentiation of the final stanza from those preceding.

[29] *bhadrā́ índrasya rātáyaḥ* (VIII.62.1e-6e, 7d-9d, 10e-12e)

Auspicious are the gifts of Indra.

Hymn to Indra in twelve stanzas in Paṅkti metre with Bṛhatī variation in 7-9. A general praise of Indra in which the refrain expresses an important motif.

[30] *mádhvaḥ sómasya pītáye* (VIII.85.1c-9c)

for the drinking of the soma honey.

Gāyatrī hymn to the Aśvins in nine stanzas. This simple hymn consists of a prayer to the Aśvins to hear the singer's call and come to his home to drink soma. The refrain pāda therefore expresses the purpose of the Aśvins' journey.

[31] *tā́ vāṁ víśvako havate tanūkṛthé / mā́ no ví yauṣṭaṁ sakhyā́ mumócatam* (VIII.86.1cd-3cd) (1-3d = 4d.5d)

Viśvaka calls you two for (his) offspring. Do not separate us from (your) friendship. Release!

Jagatī hymn to the Aśvins in five stanzas. The Ṛṣi Viśvaka asks the Aśvins not to distance themselves from his friendship and that of his cohort, while at the same time asking them to free his son Viṣṇāpū, who has gone off to seek his fortune and not returned.

[32] *áthā no vásyasas kṛdhi* (IX.4.1c-10c)

And (then) make us better!

Gāyatrī hymn to Soma in ten stanzas. In eight of the stanzas Soma is asked to do various things in the imperative: 1-3 *sánā* "win!", 5 *ā́ bhaja* "give (us) a share", 7-8 *abhy àrṣa* "flow unto!", 10 *ā́ bhara* "bear hither!"; and the refrain asks for a special favour in addition to and subsequent to all these other things. It therefore expresses the constant prayer lying at the heart of the hymn.

[33] *mádeṣu sarvadhā́ asi* (IX.18.1c-7c)

In (thy) exhilarations thou art the granter of all.

Gāyatrī hymn to Soma in seven stanzas. The single all-pervasive thought in this hymn.

[34] *kásmai devā́ya havíṣā vidhema* (X.121.1d-9d)

To which heavenly one shall we worship with the oblation?

Triṣṭubh hymn to the unknown Urgott in ten stanzas. This important cosmogonic hymn consists of a string of twenty-two relative pronouns encompassing stanzas 2-6, 8 and 9 and serving for the most part as descriptors of the sort that would normally in R̥gvedic discourse be followed by the *sá/tá-* anaphor. But here, by a brilliant co-optation of this fundamental discourse strategy, what one finds in place of the anaphor, except in 7, where a quasi-temporal *yád . . . tátaḥ* diptych occurs, is its very antithesis: a completely non-referential *ká-* "who?" This non-identification of the Urgott is in fact the theme of the hymn. In stanza 1 the Urgott is designated as *hiraṇyagarbhá-* "golden embryo" but is still for all that unknown. In 10 it is identified with Prajāpati, but this is surely not part of the original hymn, as it completely undercuts the hymn's stunning power.[3] More specifically, the last five syllables of 10ab *prájāpate ná tvád etā́ny anyó/víśvā jatā́ni pári tā́ babhūva* "O Prajāpati, none other than thee has encompassed these things, all these creatures" is manifestly taken from the last five syllables of the Indra hymn I.32; and the final distich of this stanza, *yátkāmās te juhumás tán no astu/vayáṁ syāma pátayo rayīṇā́m* "With which desire we call to thee, let that come to pass for us. We would be masters of wealth" amounts to bathos in the face of the sturdy intellectual honesty which pervades the rest of the hymn.

9. Conclusion

Prior to this investigation, what study there has been of non-stanza-internal repetition in the *R̥gveda* has focused on repetition occurring from hymn to hymn throughout the collection in an effort to determine what this might be able to tell us about the internal compositional

3. I say this in full recognition of the fact that the later tradition understands *ká-* to refer to Prajāpati throughout this hymn.

history of the *Ṛgveda* (e.g. Bloomfield 1916[4]). Beyond this, one finds only very brief attention to pervasive repetition within a given hymn in the commentary to Geldner's translation and here and there in other anthologies or treatments of the *Ṛgveda* (e.g. Winternitz 1905-08). However, the study of such repetition within a single hymn is a critical undertaking for anybody interested in the internal structures of the hymns, their discourse development, and the motifs which characterize them. In this paper we have merely pointed out some of the most clear-cut instances of repetitions, including those that can hardly be overlooked by anybody with an interest in the collection as a whole. As for hymn-internal refrains, these convey the main ideas the ṛṣis wanted to articulate within their poems, taking the form of either a fundamental prayer, a catechismic-like confessional, or a statement of religious resolution on the part of the singer and his entourage.

References

Arnold, E. Vernon, 1905, *Vedic Metre in its Historical Development*, Cambridge: Cambridge University Press.

Bloomfield, Maurice, 1916, *Rigveda Repetitions* (Harvard Oriental Series, 20, 24), Cambridge, MA: Harvard University Press, repr. 1981, New Delhi: Meharchand Lachhmandas Publications.

Geldner, Karl F., 1951, *Der Rigveda . . . übersetzt*, 3 vols. (Harvard Oriental Series, 33-35), Cambridge, MA: Harvard University Press, cited as Geldner.

Gonda, Jan, 1959, *Stylistic Repetition in the Veda* (*Verhandelingen der Koninklijke Nederlandse Akademie van Wetenschappen, Afd. Letterkunde*, Nieuwe Reeks, Deel 65, No. 3), Amsterdam: N.V. Noord-Hollandsche Uitgevers Maatschappij.

Klein, Jared S., 2007, "Sequential Negation in the Rigveda", in *Verba Docenti: Studies in Historical and Indo-European Linguistics Presented to Jay H. Jasanoff by Students, Colleagues, and Friends*, ed. Alan J. Nussbaum, pp. 213-29, Ann Arbor/New York: Beech Stave Press.

———, 2008, "Interrogative Sequences in the Rigveda", in *Evidence and Counter-evidence, Essays in Honour of Frederik Kortlandt*, vol. 1: *Balto-Slavic and Indo-European Linguistics*, ed. Alexander Lubotsky, Jos Schaeken, and Jeroen Wiedenhof, pp. 297-308, Amsterdam/New York: Rodopi.

---

4. This work does include a listing of repeated pādas within individual hymns but does not discuss their roles within the thematic structures of their poems.

———, In preparation, *Stylistic Repetition in the Rigveda.*

Oldenberg, Hermann, 1888, *R̥gveda: Metrische und textgeschichtliche Prolegomena*, Berlin: Hertz, tr. V.G. Paranjape and M.A. Mehendale, 2005, New Delhi: Motilal Banarsidass.

Winternitz, Moritz, 1905-08, *Geschichte der indischen Litteratur*, Band 1, Teile 1-2, Leipzig: C. F. Amelang, tr. V. Srinavasa Sarma, 1981, New Delhi: Motilal Banarsidass.

3

Pāṇini 5.3.5 and the Function of Sanskrit *etád*[1]

Martin Joachim Kümmel

1. Introduction

WHEN we want to investigate a question of Sanskrit grammar, it is wise to consult our oldest authority on Sanskrit, namely Pāṇini. Even if we do not find explicit statements about the problem in Pāṇini's grammar, as in the case of the function of the different demonstratives, some statements often allow some indirect clues. One such case shall be discussed here, namely Sūtra 5.3.5:

> *etado 'n = etadaḥ an* (with var. lectio *etado 'ś = etadaḥ aś*)
>
> [before a vibhakti suffix] *án-* (or *a-*) is substituted for the pronoun *etad* [this yields in any case *á-tas, á-tra,* since *n* of *an* is lost according to 8.2.7]

To this we may also add Sūtra 2.4.33:

> *etadas tratasos tratasau cānudāttau*
>
> *a* is substituted for *etad* when suffixed with *-tra* and *-tas,* if unaccented (i.e., anaphoric).

Both of these statements imply that *átra, átas* belong to the demonstrative *etád* and are hence functionally and/or semantically equivalent to it. Before we shall investigate this by looking at the

---

[1] A similar talk was also given by me in March at Kyōto University. For valuable comments and discussion I wish to thank Hans Henrich Hock, Jared Klein, Georges-Jean Pinault, Olav Hackstein, Werner Knobl, and Aurelijus Vijūnas. This work was made possible by a Heisenberg grant of the DFG. Electronic versions of most texts, provided by the Frankfurt TITUS project (see http://titus.uni-frankfurt.de), have been very useful in doing my research.

actual usage of these adverbs and the demonstrative in Vedic Sanskrit, some terminological and typological preliminaries are in place.

1.1. PRELIMINARIES: THE TYPOLOGY OF DEMONSTRATIVE FUNCTIONS

Following typological investigations of demonstrative systems[2] we will use the following classification of usages and system types:

The prototypical usage of demonstratives is situational and exophoric (pointing to something outside the text), and normally implies spatial deixis seen from a centre (usually the speaker). Some systems seem to be based on relative distance from the centre, so that we find a proximal and a distal term, sometimes also a medial one. Others are person-oriented and distinguish the spheres of the speaker (1st person), the addressee (2nd person), or of none of the participants (3rd person). Beside this, demonstratives frequently show endophoric uses (pointing to something within the text), which are usually divided into anaphoric or tracking (pointing to something previously mentioned), discourse deictic (pointing to propositions), and recognitional (pointing to knowledge of the addressee); sometimes cataphoric usage (pointing to something to be mentioned later) is added as a fourth type.

2. The Usage of *átra, átas* in Vedic

2.1. TRADITIONAL INTERPRETATION

Traditionally, *átra* and *átas* have been glossed by "here/from here" as well as "there/from there".

Speyer (1886: 216) gives "अत्र (here), अतः (hence)", the PW "(von) hier; da, dort". Grassmann (1873) translated *átas* only three times by "von hier", otherwise "von da"; for *átra* he gives "here"/"there" (without distinction). Delbrück (1888: 197, 299) has *átas* "von da", *átra* "hier, dort, dorthin". Geldner (1951: passim) translates *átra* mostly by "da, dabei", rarely by "hier"; for *átas* he generally has "von da, von dort".

Thus the deictic function of these adverbs seems unclear.

2.2. SITUATIONAL DEIXIS

We will now investigate whether we can find evidence for concrete spatial deixis. First, we will discuss speaker deixis.

---

[2] Anderson & Keenan (1985); Himmelmann (1996, 1997, 2001: 833); Diessel (1999).

2.2.1. *Speaker deixis*

Collocations with 1st person pronouns may be an argument for speaker or proximal deixis. These are, however, rather rare in Early Vedic, and need not be interpreted in this way, since collocation does not necessarily mean a semantic connection. In the following verse, *átrā* seems to be anaphoric and is not connected to *nas*:

[1] *yád adó pito ájagan vivásva párvatānām* ।
átrā *cin no madho pitó 'raṁ bhakṣā́ya gamyāḥ* ।। (*R̥V* 1.187.7)

When, O Food, you have gone to the light of the mountains, even **in that case** may you, O sweet Food, come right to our enjoyment!

Other passages seem to show that the adverbs refer to the present situation. In the next passage, *átra* is better taken to be discourse deictic, referring to the whole preceding hymn:

[2] *ukthébhir* ***átra*** *matíbhiś ca vípró 'pīpayad gáyo divyā́ni jánma* ।।
(*R̥V* 10.64.16cd)

Thus the sage Gaya has strengthened **thereby** the celestial people with words and thoughts.

In other places, the adverb refers to the present situation, but not to the place of the speaker, but rather that of the addressee (however near to the speaker):

[3] *úd īrṣv**ā́taḥ*** *pátivatī hy* ***èṣā́*** (*R̥V* 10.85.21a)

Rise up **from hence**: **this** maiden hath a husband. (Griffith)

[4] *gókāmā me acchadayan yád ā́yam áp**ā́ta*** *ita paṇayo várīyaḥ* ।।
(*R̥V* 10.108.10cd)

They seemed to long for kine when I departed. **Hence**, into distance, be ye gone, O Panis. (Griffith)

All in all, there is no conclusive evidence for speaker deixis.

2.2.2. *Neutral deixis*

Amano (2009: 83-87) has investigated the usage of *átra, átas* in the prose of the *Maitrāyaṇī Saṁhitā*. She found that their use is mostly anaphoric, recognitional, and focusing/topicalizing, similar to *etád*. In two places, however, she assumes situational "neutral" deixis. In the first case, *átas* clearly contrasts with proximal *itás*, but certainly it refers to the present situation, probably accompanied by gestures (Amano 2009: 230 n. 520):

[5] *eṣó +'**taḥ** syā́d ayám **itáḥ*** (*MS* 1.6.6(2): 95.16)

That [fire] would be **there**, this one [the sacrificer] **here**.

In the second case, *átas* refers to the place of the addressee:

[6] *té vái svaryánto 'bruvann **áto** no yūyáṁ práyachata kénāyátanenā́**traivá** vetsyathéty abruvan* (*MS* 1.9.5: 135.6f.)

They (the gods) that went to the sunlight, said: "Give us something **from there** (where you are)." "On which basis?" "**There** you will find it.", they said.

As also the first case may be interpreted as hearer-deictic, we should now investigate whether we can find further evidence for this usage.

2.2.3. *Hearer deixis*

(a) Collocations with 2nd person pronouns and contrast to *ihá* connected to the 1st person is found in these two passages:

[7] ***átraivá tvám ihá vayáṁ** suvī́rā víśvā spŕ̥dho abhímātīr jayema* || (*R̥V* 10.18.9cd).

You (are) just **there**, we (are) **here** — may we with noble heroes overcome all rivals that go after us (cf. Oldenberg 1912: 219).

[8] *yé **'tra** pitáraḥ pitáro yé **'tra yūyáṁ** sthá **yuṣmā́ṁs** té 'nu **yūyáṁ** téṣāṁ śréṣṭhā +bhūyāsta*[3] || *yá **ihá** pitáro jīvā́ **ihá vayáṁ** smáḥ* | ***asmā́ṁs** té 'nu **vayáṁ** téṣāṁ śréṣṭhā bhūyāsma* || (*AV(Ś)* 18.4.86f.)

The Fathers who are **there**, the Fathers that **you** are **there** — [be] they after **you**; may **ye** be the best of them. The Fathers who are **here** alive, **here** are **we** — [be] they after **us**; may **we** be the best of them. (after Whitney-Lanman) — cf. *etád : idám* in [30] below.

(b) In quite a few passages we find actual reference to the addressee's location together with a 2nd person pronoun or verb, partly without a possible antecedent and thus difficult to interpret as anaphoric or discourse deictic:

---

[3] Thus in one MS, and the edition of Roth & Whitney for *bhūyāstha*, cf. Whitney-Lanman (1905) ad locum.

[9] ***átaś*** *cid indra ṇa úpā́ yāhi śatávājayā* । *iṣā́ sahásravājayā* ।। (*ṚV* 8.92.10)

From there (were you are), Indra, come to us with hundredfold, thousandfold gain.

[10] ***átaḥ*** *parijmann ā́ gahi divó vā rocanā́d ádhi* । (*ṚV* 1.6.9ab)

From there (where you now are), wanderer, come hither, or from the lighting of the sky.

[11] *yán nāsatyā parāváti yád vā sthó ádhi turváśe* । ***áto*** *ráthena suvṛ́tā na ā́ gatam* (*ṚV* 1.47.7abc)

Whether you, Nāsatya, are far away or with Turvaśa, **from there** come to us with the well-rolling chariot (referring to place of the addressees, whether medially distant or far).

[12] *ā́* ***vāṁ*** *ráthaṁ yuvatís tiṣṭhad* ***átra*** *juṣṭvī́ narā duhitā́ sū́ryasya* । (*ṚV* 1.118.5ab)

The girl steps/stepped on **your** chariot **there**, having found pleasure, O men, the daughter of the sun.

All this speaks for a rather clear connection to hearer deixis.

2.3. ENDOPHORIC USES

Of course, endophoric uses are much more common.

(a) For anaphoric function, cf. the following passages:

[13] *padáṁ yád asya paramé vyòmany* ***áto*** *víśvā abhí sáṁ yāti saṁyátaḥ* ।। (*ṚV* 9.86.15cd)

What his place in the highest heaven is, **from there** he gets towards all rows.

[14] *uttānáyoś camvòr yónir antár* ***átrā*** *pitā́ duhitúr gárbham ā́dhāt* ।। (*ṚV* 1.164.33cd)

Between the widespread world-halves is the birth-place: the Father laid the Daughter's germ **within it.** (Griffith)

Cf. also Amano (2009: 86) on *MS* 1.4.8(7): 57.1f. Often *átra* refers to the general situation mentioned before (translated as "dabei" by Geldner 1951, cf. Amano 2009: 85ff.):

[15] *dhī́rāś cit tát samínakṣanta āśat**ā́trā*** *kartám áva padāty áprabhuḥ* ।। (*ṚV* 9.73.9cd)

Only the wise that want to reach it have reached it; **in that situation** the unknowing will fall down in a pit.

(b) In some cases, the adverbs seem to be discourse deictic rather than anaphoric, e.g.

[16] *utá vā yáḥ sahasya pravidvā́n márto mártaṁ marcáyati dvayéna* ǀ ***átaḥ*** *pāhi stavamāna stuvántam ágne mā́kir no duritā́ya dhāyīḥ* ǀǀ (R̥V 1.147.5)

Or also if a knowing mortal harms a mortal with double play, **from that** save, O praised one, the praising one — Agni, do never expose us to trouble!

(c) In some other places they are used in a correlative construction which might be interpreted as cataphoric (or maybe also recognitional?):

[17] ***áto*** *devā́ avantu no* ***yáto*** *víṣṇur vicakramé* ǀ (R̥V 1.22.16ab)

Let the gods help us **from that (known) place from which** Viṣṇu has stepped out.

[18] ***átra*** *ná hā́rdi kravaṇásya rejate* ***yátrā*** *matír vidyáte pūtabándhanī* ǀǀ (R̥V 5.44.9cd)

There the heart of Kravaṇa does not shake, **where** a thought [= poem] bound to the purified [soma] is found. (Or rather temporal?)

2.4. CONCLUSION

átra and *átas* are mainly used endophorically (discourse-deictic, recognitional, anaphoric) in earlier Vedic. If they show exophoric usage, they seem to be associated with the addressee's space (hearer deixis).

3. The Usage of *etád*

Let us now compare this to the usage of the demonstrative *etád*.

3.1. PROXIMAL/SPEAKER DEIXIS

According to the tradition of Sanskrit grammar, *etád* is mainly a proximal demonstrative. Speyer (1886: 202) gives the following definitions: *eṣa* nearness : *asau* remoteness : *ayam* presence : *sa* absence, and cites the following *kārikā* in fn. 1 (with ref.):

idamaḥ pratyakṣarūpaṁ samīpataravarti vaitadorūpam adasas
tu viprakr̥ṣṭaṁ tad iti parokṣe vijānīyāt

Whitney (1879: 173) states that "the usual demonstrative of **nearer position** 'this here' . . . prefixes *e* to the simple root, — forming the nominatives *eṣás, eṣā́, etát*" (bolding supplied). Speyer (1896: 40) gives the following Greek and Latin equivalents "*eṣa* 'hic' οὗτος . . . *asau* 'ille' ἐκεῖνος . . . *ayam* 'hic' ὅδε " (but adds that *ayam* points to 1st person). According to Kielhorn (1912: 61) *etad* is closer to the speaker than *idam*. Also Klein (1998: 371) assumes a proximal deictic.

(a) Indeed, we find some collocations with a 1st person pronoun, but rather few (about ten in the *ṚV*), e.g.

[19] ***etā́*** *juṣata* ***me*** *gíraḥ* || (*ṚV* 1.25.18c)

Enjoy **these** songs **of mine.**

[20] ***etā́ no*** *agne sáubhagā didīhy ápi krátuṁ sucétasaṁ vatema* | (*ṚV* 7.3=4.10ab)

Shine **this** felicity **to us,** O Agni: may we attain to perfect understanding. (Griffith)

[21] ***eṣā́*** *syā́* ***no*** *duhitā́ divojā́ḥ kṣitī́r ucchántī mā́nuṣīr ajīgaḥ* | (*ṚV* 6.65.1ab)

That heaven-born daughter has now awakened the human settlements **for us** by shining.

(b) Also some other passages seem to indicate speaker-near reference:

[22] ***eṣá*** *syá kārúr jarate sūktáiḥ* (*ṚV* 7.68.9a)

With his fair hymns, **this** singer, too, extols you = speaker (from hearer's perspective?).

[23] *ástī**idám** adhimánthanam ásti prajánanaṁ kṛtám* |
etā́ṁ *viśpátnīm ā́ bharāgníṁ manthāma pūrváthā* || (*ṚV* 3.29.1)

There is **this** fire-rubbing **here,** there is the producing ready. Bring **that** clan mistress, let us rub fire in ancient fashion (cited by Kupfer 2002: 157 as the only example of proximal deixis).

This view is also supported by etymological arguments: *e-* (Indo-Iranian **ai-*) could be interpreted as a proximal deictic particle (Klein 1998: 371) from **a/i- = idám*. However, this is not convincing, as there is no good independent evidence for such a particle. It might be more promising to derive **ai-* from the old Nom. Sg. m. **ay* in **ay-ám* "this one". Many modern Indo-Aryan continuants of this pronoun have proximal function, viz. Bangla *e*, Hindi *yah/is*, Panjabi *e/is* "this" vs. distal *o, vah/us, o/us* "that". It may also be supported by possible proximal reference of Iranian **aita-*[4] and clear proximal function in Yaghnobi *iš/it* and Pashto *dā/de* "this". Cf. the following passages from Younger Avestan:

[24] ***aētahmi*** *aŋhuuō yaṯ astuuaiṇti* (passim)

in **this** bony existence (Skjærvø)

However, the function might as well be recognitional: "that well-known existence we are talking about", and this is also possible in the following case:

[25] *mā* ***mē aētaii å̄*** *zaoθraii* ***å̄*** *fraŋ*^{v}*harəṇtu* (Yt. 5.92)

let them not partake of **this** libation of mine (Skjærvø)

(c) However, there are some data that seem to contradict proximal and especially speaker-deictic function. Speyer (1886: 204) states that "अयम् – not एष – is the proper word, if the speaker wishes to denote something belonging to himself by a demonstrative". In addition, Pāṇ. 5.3.4 states that *etád* is substituted for *idám* in *etárhi* "now; then", which implies that the function of *etárhi* cannot entirely be derived from *etád* itself. Indeed it had a much wider scope than *idā́nīm* "now", as explicitly stated already in the Vedic texts.

[26] *yā́vanty etárhīṇi tā́vanti páñcadaśa kŕ̥tva idā́nīni* (*ŚB*(*M*) 12.3.2.5)

As many *etárhi* periods (there may be), they are fifteen times as much as the *idā́ni* periods.

In fact, in many of the passages cited above *etád* may be interpreted differently: [19] may be discourse-deictic; likewise [20] (in Geldner's interpretation). In [21], *uṣas* is certainly present and visible but not exactly near the speaker; maybe recognitional? In [23] the pronoun refers to something yet to be brought by the addressee (as noted by Kupfer herself). In the following passage, *eté* clearly is used contrastively with *vayám* "we" and thus excludes the speakers (cf. Kupfer 2002: 157f.):

[27] ***práité*** *vadantu prá* ***vayám̐*** *vadāma grā́vabhyo vā́cam̐ vadatā vádadbhyaḥ* । (*R̥V* 10.94.1ab)

Let **these** speak loudly forth, let us speak aloud: to the loud speaking Pressing-stones address the speech. (Griffith)

---

[4] See Schmitt (1989: 75); Skjærvø (2009: 82, 120).

3.2. NON-PROXIMAL DEIXIS

3.2.1. *Distal deixis*

Kupfer (2002: 157) cites just the following passage for possible distal deixis, as *eṣā́* surely refers to something outside the speaker's horizon:

[28] *yád agna* ***eṣā́*** *sámitir bhávāti devī́ devéṣu yajatā́ yajatra* ǀ (*ṚV* 10.11.8ab)

When, O Agni, **that** meeting will take place, the heavenly one among the heavenly gods, the venerable one, O venerable. . . .

However, the meeting of the gods is certainly not outside the addressee's horizon. This brings us to the third possibility, namely hearer deixis.

3.2.2. *Hearer deixis*

Already Speyer (1896: 40 n. 1) noticed the following: "Es wäre zu untersuchen, inwiefern *eṣa* zur 2. Pers., wie *ayam* zur 1. Pers. in Beziehung steht. Es giebt nämlich manche Stellen, wo *eṣa* wie lat. »iste« auf die zweite Person hinweist", then citing, e.g.

[29] *asmā́* ***etáṁ*** *pitáro lokám akran* ǀ (*ṚV* 10.14.9b)

ihm [dem Toten] haben die Väter diesen Raum [wo ihr eben standet] bereitet = For him [the dead] have the fathers prepared **this/that** space [where you just stood].

[30] *pítaro námo vaḥ. yá* ***etásmin*** *loké sthá* ***yuṣmā́ṁs*** *té 'nu yé* ***'smin*** *loké* ***mā́ṁ*** *té 'nu.* (*TS* 3.2.5.6 = *TB* 1.3.10.8)

O fathers, homage to you! Ye that are in **that** world, may they follow you; ye that are in this world, may they follow me. (Keith) — cf. *átra : ihá* in [8] above.

In fact, *etád* seems to be regularly used with 2nd person pronouns in Yajurvedic mantras, especially in the very frequent type ***eṣá te*** *yóniḥ/ lokáḥ/sómaḥ/bhāgáḥ* . . . "**this/that** is your . . ." (cf. Latin *iste tuus,* etc. Klein 1996b: 86ff. on Armenian *-d-*). And similar uses are also found in the *ṚV* (about fifty-five collocations), viz.

[31] *eṣá vāṁ stómo aśvinā̄v akāri* (*ṚV* 1.184.5a)

This song has just been made **for you**, Aśvins.

[32] *nákiṣ* ***ṭa etā́*** *vratā́ minanti* (*ṚV* 1.69.7a)

Nobody breaks **these** rules **of yours.**

[33] ***etā́ te*** *agne jánimā sánāni prá pūrvyā́ya nū́tanāni vocam* । (*ṚV* 3.1.20ab)

Those old births **of yours**, Agni, do I call forth, and the present ones for the ancient one.

[34] *kím* ***etā́*** *vācā́ kr̥ṇavā* ***távāhám*** (*ṚV* 10.95.2a)

What shall I do with **those** words of **yours**?

Even more clear are some passages where this is contrasted with *idám* + 1st person (cf. TS/TB above):

[35] *yā́* ***táva*** *tanū́r* ***iyáṁ*** *sā́* ***máyi*** *yó* ***máma*** *tanū́r* ***eṣā́*** *sā́* ***tváyi*** (*VS*(*M*) 5.6)

That form which is yours, may this be here on me, and that form which is mine, [may] **that** [be] on you

In direct speech (cf. Jamison 1991: 101), *etád* may be used with reference to the possession of a 2nd person subject:

[36] *ná máyi* ***tvám etám*** *asuryàṁ sómaṁ hoṣyasi* (*MS* 4.7.4)

You will not offer in me **that** Asuryan soma (that you have?).

Also in this case, some modern Indo-Aryan continuants show a similar function, cf. medial (= distal+visible/present-far) deixis in Dardic, e.g., Khowar *es/oró/et*, Kalasha *ása/ála/éli* (vs. proximal : invisible/absent from *idám : tád*[5]). This is supported by evidence for 2nd person deixis of Avestan *aēta-*[6]; in later Eastern Iranian this function is clearly established.[7] Cf. the following Younger Avestan passage:

(37) ***aēša*** *zaoθra paiti.jamiiāt̰* ***tauua*** *ahurāne ahurahe* (Y. 68.1)

May **this** libation (of yours) arrive, **yours**, O Lady of the Lord. (Skjærvø)

Original medial (2nd person) deixis has also been often assumed for the basis of this demonstrative, the PIE **só-/tó-* pronouns.[8] It may have been preserved in Armenian (cf. Klein 1996a) and Balto-Slavic. An important argument has also been the use of deictic "*sa* figé" in *sá*

---

[5] Cf. Morgenstierne (1975: 216ff.); Bashir (2003: 845, 852).

[6] Cf. Reichelt (1909: 285); Skjærvø (2009: 120).

[7] See Sims-Williams (1994); Wendtlandt (2011: 31-39, 305-19, 353ff.).

[8] Cf. Frei (1944: 125f.); Himmelmann (1997: 52 n. 33); Klein (1996b).

tvám "you there".[9] We can conclude that there are strong indications for the usage of *etád* as a 2nd person demonstrative rather than a proximal or distal one.

If it is so clearly represented in the data, why has this usage in Vedic then mostly been overlooked or neglected in the literature?[10] One reason may of course be the Sanskrit tradition which does not acknowledge this function. Another one may be inaccurate interpretation misguided by the influence of translation language with a two-term demonstrative system (like English and German): As presence in speech situation is implied, 2nd person deixis may also be translated as "here", which often wrongly suggests proximal reference.

3.3. NEUTRAL OR NON-DEICTIC FUNCTIONS

In any case, exophoric uses are clearly not the main function of *etád*. Delbrück (1888: 219ff.) described *etád* as a general "deictic", more emphatic than *tád*, often cataphoric and preceding relative clauses. Hock (1982: 14) described *etád* as "introducing new information, string-finally, pre-RC position" in contrast to *tád* "referring to earlier information, clause-initially, post-RC position". Hale (1991) has pointed to the 3rd position of *etád* as a (formerly) emphatic position. Kupfer (2002: 158, 164) states that there are no instances of situational 2nd person deixis (ignoring Speyer 1896 and the evidence above) and defines *etád* as "dér-deiktisch . . . häufig in relativer Nähe zum Sprecher". Amano (2009: 67-72) concluded that *etád* was mainly used "anamnestisch", i.e. recognitional (pseudo-cataphoric, euphemistic, rarely anaphoric) in Vedic prose (*MS*). A similar usage has been stated by Skjærvø (2009: 121) for Old Iranian *aēta-/aita-* in legal texts: "the X in question, this X we are discussing". It is also remarkable that Sanskrit *etad* is translated by Tocharian B *seṁ* which seems to be mainly recognitional and discourse-deictic, but pragmatically usable for 2nd person.[11]

---

9 See Jamison (1992); Klein (1996b, 1997: 261-69); Hock (1997, esp. 54-58) with references.

10 When I gave my talk in Kyōto, I learned that Werner Knobl had already argued for *etád* as a medial pronoun with so-called "da-deixis" some years before.

11 See Pinault 2009: 226-29; cognate Toch. A *saṁ* is a distal exophoric demonstrative with identical endophoric uses.

The main use of *etád* thus seems to be in recognitional function to introduce discourse — new information known to the hearer; this seems to be combined with an exophoric function of 2nd person deixis.

3.4. TYPOLOGICAL COMPARISON

When we try to look for cross-linguistic parallels, this combination is not infrequently found: Demonstratives with mainly endophoric functions seem to supply a second person or medial demonstrative in quite a few languages:

Lithuanian *tàs* "that" is described as primarily anaphoric and recognitional vs. deictic *šìs* "this": *anàs* "that", but it can also be used contrastively for medial deictic reference.[12] Similar uses are found for *to* "that" in Old Slavonic (vs. proximal *se* : distal *ono*) and modern Serbo-Croatian, cf. *òvō mèni, **tô tèbi**, ònō njèmu* "this is mine, **that** is **yours**, that is his/hers".[13]

In Hittite, *apāt* "that" is mainly emphatic-anaphoric (as elsewhere in Anatolian), but it is also a 2nd person deictic contrasting with proximal *kī* "this" and distal *ini* "that".[14]

Ancient Greek *toũto* may be defined as "this/that (best accessible to hearer)" vs. *tóde* "this (best accessible to speaker)" : *ekeĩno* "that, yon" (+ anaphoric *autó*).[15] Latin *istud* "that" is rather non-proximal and related to 2nd person[16] vs. proximal *hoc* "this" : distal *illud* "that, yon", anaphoric *id*. Vulgar Latin and Romance *ipse* > *isse* "that very, self" developed from an emphatic anaphoric to a medial demonstrative.[17]

Modern Turkish "medial" *şu* "this/that" points to something relatively near to the participants; it is described as a grammaticalized pointing

[12] Cf. Senn 1966: 195f.; Ambrazas 1997: 195: "neutral" but "contrasted to both" proximal and distal; Frei (1944: 120): "binaire + indifferent". I am grateful to Aurelijus Vijūnas for pointing out to me that the distinction is distance-based rather than person-based.

[13] Leskien 1919: 364; Vaillant 1958: 379ff.; cf. also Macedonian *-ot/-ta/-to* (Wendtland 2011: 31 with references).

[14] This was shown by Goedegebuure (2003a, b); cf. Hoffner & Melchert 2008: 142-46; Melchert 2009.

[15] Cf. Bakker 2010: 153-57.

[16] But secondary according to Hofmann & Szantyr (1965: 180, 183f.); only loosely connected according to Frei (1944: 113).

[17] Alkire & Rosen 2010: 301f.; Carlier & De Mulder 2010.

gesture and is often cataphoric, introducing new information vs. proximal *bu* "this (here)" : distal + anaphoric *o* "that (there)".[18]

Japanese *so-* "that" is described as anaphoric and 2nd person deictic (for something at least **identifiable** by the addressee) vs. 1st *ko-* "this" : 3rd *a-* "that" (Anderson and Keenan 1985: 284f.). Modern Mon *kɔ̀h* seems to combine medial, (most frequently) anaphoric, discourse deictic and recognitional uses (< Old Mon *goḥ* anaphoric, originally distal?), "marking identifiable information relevant to the ongoing discourse/topic marker" vs. proximal *nɔ̀?* : distal *tɤ̀?* (Jenny 2009).

This far from complete overview clearly shows that 2nd person deixis and frequent endophoric uses are very often combined in three-term systems, as seems to be in the case of Vedic *etád*.

3.5. SYNTHESIS: INTERRELATION OF HEARER DEIXIS AND "EMPHATIC" FUNCTIONS

What may be the reasons for that? 1. Recognitional and emphatic-anaphoric usage implies that the referent is (mentally or physically) present in the speech situation (especially to the addressee). In the case of physical presence, a demonstrative underspecified for person or distance might be blocked for 1st person by a contrasting pronoun which automatically leads to an interpretation as pointing to present but non-proximal referents, most typically near the addressee.

2. Starting from 2nd person deixis, what is related to the addressee typically belongs to the cognitive space of the hearer. Therefore a demonstrative with this function is especially apt to activate hearer's attention and to introduce discourse-new, hearer-old information, i.e. to be used in recognitional function.

4. Final Conclusion

The early Vedic usage of *átra, átas* confirms Pāṇini's assignment to *etád*. It also supports the interpretation of *etád* (and consequently, Proto-Indo-Iranian **aitá-*) as a "middle term" demonstrative pointing to the addressee's space and perspective and with a strong preference for endophoric functions, as often found in other languages.

How this is to be interpreted in diachronic terms, still remains an open question: Was Proto-Indo-Iranian **aišá-/aitá-*, clearly derived from

[18] Cf. Csató & Johanson 1998: 211; Göksel & Kerslake 2005: 180, 244f.

**sá-/tá-*, an originally endophoric demonstrative that came to be used for exophoric hearer deixis or vice versa?[19]

Primary Sources

Pāṇini's grammar = *Pāṇini's Grammatik*, Herausgegeben, übersetzt, erläutert und mit verschiedenen Indices versehen von Otto Böhtlingk, Leipzig: Haessel 1887.

Vedic Texts

AV(Ś) = *Atharvaveda (Śaunaka) with the Pada-pāṭha and Sāyaṇācārya's commentary*, vols. I, II, III, IV-1, IV-2, ed. Viśva Bandhu (Vishveshvaranand Indological Series, 13-17), Hoshiarpur: Vishveshvaranand Vedic Research Institute 1960-64.

= *Atharva Veda Saṁhitā* ed. Rudolph Roth, William Dwight Whitney Zweite verbesserte Auflage besorgt von Max Lindenau, Berlin: Dümmler 1924.

MS = *Mâitrâyaṇî-Saṁhitâ. Die Saṁhitâ der Mâitrâyaṇîya-Çâkhâ*, 4 vols., ed. Leopold von Schroeder, Leipzig: Brockhaus 1881-86 [= repr. Wiesbaden: Steiner 1970, 1971, 1972, 1972].

R̥V = *Rig-Veda-Samhitâ, The Sacred Hymns of the Brâhmans together with the commentary of Sâyanâkârya*, ed. F. Max Müller, 2nd edn., 4 vols., London: Allen 1890-1892 [= Chowkhamba Sanskrit Series 99, Varanasi 1966].

ŚB(M) = *The Çatapatha-Brâhmaṇa in the Mâdhyandina-Çâkhā with extracts from the commentaries of Sâyaṇa, Harisvâmin and Dvivedaganga*, ed. Albrecht Weber, Berlin/London: Dümmler 1855 [= Chowkhamba Sanskrit Series 96, Varanasi 1964].

TB = *The Taittirīya Brāhmaṇa with the commentary of Bhaṭṭa Bhāskara Miśra*, 4 vols., ed. A. Mahadeva Sastri et al. (Government Oriental Library Series, Bibliotheca Sanskrita 36, 57, 38, 42), Mysore: Government Branch Press 1908-21 [= Delhi: Motilal Banarsidass 1985].

TS = *The Taittirīya Saṁhitā of the Black Yajurveda with the Commentary of Bhaṭṭa Bhāskara Miśra*, 10 vols., ed. A. Mahadeva Sastri and K. Rangacharya (Government Oriental Library Series, Bibliotheca Sanskrita 4-18). Mysore: Government Branch Press 1894-98 [= Delhi: Motilal Banarsidass 1986].

VS(M) = *The Vâjasaneyi-Saṁhitâ in the Mâdhyandina and the Kâṇva-Çâkhâ with the Commentary of Mahîdhara*, ed. Albrecht Weber, Berlin/London: Dümmler 1852 [= Chowkhamba Sanskrit Series 103, Varanasi 1972].

Translations of Vedic Texts

AV(Ś) = *Atharva-Veda Saṁhitā*, tr. with a Critical and Exegetical Commentary by William Dwight Whitney. Revised and brought nearer to Completion

[19] For a similar problem in Anatolian, cf. Melchert 2009.

and edited by Charles Rockwell Lanman, 2 vols. (Harvard Oriental Series, 7-8), Cambridge (Mass.): Harvard University Press 1905.

R̥V = *Der Rig-Veda,* Aus dem Sanskrit ins Deutsche übersetzt und mit einem laufenden Kommentar versehen von Karl Friedrich Geldner, 4 vols. (Harvard Oriental Series, 33-36), Cambridge (Mass.): Harvard University Press 1951, 1957.

The Hymns of the Rigveda, tr. with a popular commentary by Ralph T.H. Griffith, 5th edn. (Chowkhamba Sanskrit Series, 35), Varanasi: Chowkhamba Sanskrit Series Office 1971.

TS = Arthur Berriedale Keith, *The Veda of the Black Yajus School entitled Taittiriya Sanhita*, 2 vols. (Harvard Oriental Series, 18-19), Cambridge (Mass.): Harvard University Press 1914.

Avestan Texts

Y. = Yasna, Yt.= Yašt

Avesta. The sacred books of the Parsis, ed. Karl F. Geldner, 3 vols., Stuttgart: Kohlhammer 1896, 1889, 1896.

References

Alkire, Ti, and Carol Rosen, 2010, *Romance Languages: A Historical Introduction*, Cambridge: Cambridge University Press.

Amano, Kyoko, 2009, *Maitrāyaṇī Saṁhitā I-II: Übersetzung der Prosapartien mit Kommentar zur Lexik und Syntax der älteren vedischen Prosa*, Bremen: Hempen.

Ambrazas, Vytautas (ed.), 1997, *Lithuanian Grammar*, Vilnius: Baltos Lankos.

Anderson, Stephen R. and Edward L. Keenan, 1985, "Deixis", in *Language Typology and Syntactic Description*, ed. T. Shopen, vol. 3, pp. 259-308, Cambridge: Cambridge University Press.

Bakker, Egbert J., 2010, "Pragmatics: Speech and Text", in *A Companion to the Ancient Greek Language*, ed. E.J. Bakker, pp. 151-68, Oxford: Wiley-Blackwell.

Bashir, Elena, 2003, "Dardic", in *The Indo-Aryan Languages*, ed. G. Cardona and Dh. Jain, pp. 818-94, London/New York: Routledge.

Carlier, Anne, and Walter De Mulder, 2010, "The Emergence of the Definite Article: *ille* in Competition with *ipse* in Late Latin", in *Subjectification, Intersubjectification and Grammaticalization*, ed. H. Cuykens, L. Van de Lanotte, and K. Davidse, Berlin/New York: Mouton de Gruyter.

Csató, Éva Á. and Lars Johanson, 1998, "Turkish", in *The Turkic Languages*, ed. L. Johanson and É.Á. Csató, pp. 203-35, London/New York: Routledge.

Delbrück, Berthold, 1888, *Altindische Syntax*, Halle: Verlag der Buchhandlung des Waisenhauses.

Diessel, Holger, 1999, *Demonstratives: Form, Function and Grammaticalization*, Amsterdam: Benjamins.

Frei, Henri, 1944, "Systèmes de déictiques", *Acta Linguistica* **4:** 111-29.

Goedegebuure, Petra, 2003a, *Reference, Deixis and Focus in Hittite: The Demonstratives* ka- *"this", apa- "that" and* asi *"yon"*, Academisch Proefschrift Leiden.

———, 2003b, "The Hittite 3rd person/distal Demonstrative *aši (uni, eni,* etc.)", *Die Sprache* **43: 1**.1-32.

Göksel, Aslı, and Celia Kerslake, 2005, *Turkish: A Comprehensive Grammar*, London/New York: Routledge.

Grassmann, Hermann, 1873, *Wörterbuch zum Rig-Veda*, Leipzig: Brockhaus [= 4th repr., Wiesbaden: Harrassowitz, 1964].

Griffith, Ralph T.H., 1896, *The Hymns of the Rigveda*, tr. R.T H. G., 2nd edn., Kotagiri (Nilgiri).

Hale, Mark, 1991, "Some Observations on Intersentential Pronominalization in the Language of the Taittiriya Saṁhitā", in *Sense and Syntax in Vedic*, ed. J.P. Brereton and S.W. Jamison, pp. 2-21 (Panels of the VIIth World Sanskrit Conference, ed. J. Bronkhorst, vol. 1), Leiden: Brill.

Himmelmann, Nikolaus P., 1996, "Demonstratives in Narrative Discourse: A Taxonomy of Universal Uses", in *Studies in Anaphora*, ed. B. Fox, pp. 205-54, Amsterdam: Benjamins.

———, 1997, *Deiktikon, Artikel, Nominalphrase*, Tübingen: Niemeyer.

———, 2001, "Articles", in *Language Typology and Language Universals*, ed. M. Haspelmath, E. König, and W. Oesterreicher, pp. 831-41, Berlin: Mouton de Gruyter.

Hock, Hans Henrich, 1982, "Clitic Verbs in PIE or Discourse-based Fronting?", in *Studies in the Linguistic Sciences* **12(2):** 1-38.

———, 1997, "Nexus and 'Extraclausality' in Vedic, or '*sa*-figé' all over again: A Historical (re)examination", in *Historical, Indo-European, and Lexicographical Studies: A Festschrift for Ladislav Zgusta on the occasion of his 70th Birthday*, ed. H.H. Hock, pp. 49-78, Berlin: Mouton de Gruyter.

Hoffner, Harry A., Jr. and H. Craig Melchert, 2008, *A Grammar of the Hittite Language*, Part 1: Reference Grammar, Part 2: Tutorial, Winona Lake (Ind.): Eisenbrauns.

Hofmann, J.B. and Anton Szantyr, 1965, *Lateinische Syntax und Stilistik*, München: C.H. Beck.

Jamison, Stephanie W., 1991, "The Syntax of Direct Speech in Vedic", in *Sense and Syntax in Vedic*, ed. J.P. Brereton and S.W. Jamison, pp. 40-57 (Panels of the VIIth World Sanskrit Conference, ed. J. Bronkhorst, vol. 1), Leiden: Brill. = *Studies in Sanskrit Syntax: A Volume in Honor of the Centennial of Speijer's Sanskrit Syntax (1886-1986)*, ed. H.H. Hock, pp. 95-112, Delhi: Motilal Banarsidass.

Jamison, Stephanie W., 1992, "Vedic '*sá figé*': An Inherited Sentence Connective?", *Historische Sprachforschung* **105:** 213-39.

Jenny, Mathias, 2009, "Deixis and Information Structure in Mon: The Multifuncional Particle kɔ̀h", *Journal of the Southeast Asian Linguistics Society* **2:** 53-72.

Keith, Arthur Berriedale, 1914, *The Veda of the Black Yajus School entitled Taittiriya Sanhita*, 2 vols. (Harvard Oriental Series, 18-19), Cambridge (Mass.): Harvard University Press.

Kielhorn, Franz, 1912, *A Grammar of the Sanskrit Language*, 5th edn., rev., Bombay: Nirnaya-Sagar Press.

Klein, Jared S., 1996a, *On Personal Deixis in Classical Armenian: A Study of the Syntax and Semantics of the* n-, s-, *and* d-*demonstratives in Manuscripts E and M of the Old Armenian Gospels*, Dettelbach: Röll.

———, 1996b, "'*Sá*-figé' and Indo-European Deixis", *Historische Sprachforschung* **109:** 21-39.

———, 1997, "The Contribution of Rigvedic Sanskrit to Indo-European Syntax", in *Berthold Delbrück y la sintaxis indoeuropea hoy: Actas del Coloquio de la indogermanische Gesellschaft Madrid, 21-24 septiembre de 1994*, ed. E. Crespo and J.L. García Ramón, pp. 253-81, Madrid/Wiesbaden: Reichert.

———, 1998, "Rigvedic *syá/tyá-*", in *MÍR CURAD: Studies in Honor of Calvert Watkins*, ed. J. Jasanoff, H.C. Melchert and L. Oliver, pp. 361-72, Innsbruck: Institut für Sprachwissenschaft.

Kupfer, Katharina, 2002, *Die Demonstrativpronomina im Rigveda*, Frankfurt am Main: Lang.

Leskien, August, 1914, *Grammatik der serbo-kroatischen Sprache: Lautlehre, Stammbildung, Formenlehre*, Heidelberg: Winter.

Melchert, H. Craig, 2009, "Deictic Pronouns in Anatolian", in *East and West: Papers in Indo-European Studies*, ed. K. Yoshida and B. Vine, pp. 151-61, Bremen: Hempen.

Morgenstierne, Georg, 1975, "Notes on Kalasha", *Norsk Tidskrift for Sprogvidenskab* **20:** 183-238.

Oldenberg, Hermann, 1909, 1912, *R̥gveda: Textkritische und exegetische Noten*, 2 vols., Berlin: Weidmann.

Pinault, Georges-Jean, 2009, "On the Formation of the Tocharian Demonstratives", in *Pragmatische Kategorien: Form, Funktion und Diachronie: Akten der Arbeitstagung der Indogermanischen Gesellschaft, Marburg, 24-26 September 2007*, ed. E. Rieken and P. Widmer, pp. 221-45, Wiesbaden: Reichert.

PW: Böhtlingk, Otto, and Rudolph Roth, *Sanskrit-Wörterbuch*, 7 vols. St. Petersburg: Kaiserliche Akademie der Wissenschaften 1855-75.

Reichelt, Hans, 1909, *Awestisches Elementarbuch*, Heidelberg: Winter.

Schmitt, Rüdiger, 1989, "Altpersisch", in *Compendium linguarum iranicarum*, ed. R. Schmitt, pp. 56-85, Wiesbaden: Reichert.

Senn, Alfred, 1966, *Handbuch der litauischen Sprache*, Bd. 1: Grammatik, Heidelberg: Winter.

Sims-Williams, Nicholas, 1994, "The Triple System of Deixis in Sogdian", *Transactions of the Philological Society* **92:** 41-53.

Skjærvø, Prods Oktor, 2009, "Old Iranian", in *The Iranian Languages*, ed. G. Windfuhr, pp. 43-195, London/New York: Routledge.

Speyer = Speijer, Jakob S., 1886, *Sanskrit Syntax*, Leiden: Brill.

Speyer, Jakob S., 1896, "Vedische und Sanskrit-Syntax", in *Grundriss der indo-arischen Philologie und Altertumskunde*, ed. G. Bühler, I. Band, 6. Heft, Strassburg: Trübner, pp. 1-101.

Vaillant, André, 1958, *Grammaire comparée des langues slaves*, Tome II, Morphologie: Flexion nominale, Flexion pronominale, Lyon/Paris: IAC.

Watkins, Calvert, 2000, "'sá figé' in Indo-Iranian and Anatolian", in *Anusantatyai: Festschrift für Johanna Narten*, ed. A. Hintze and E. Tichy, pp. 263-81, Dettelbach: Röll.

Wendtland, Antje, 2011, *Die Entwicklung von Demonstrativpronomina zu Artikeln im Soghdischen*, Wiesbaden: Harrassowitz.

Whitney, William Dwight, 1879, *A Sanskrit Grammar, including both the Classical Language, and the Older Dialects, of Veda and Brahmana*, Leipzig: Breitkopf & Härtel.

Whitney, William Dwight and Charles Rockwell Lanman, 1905, *Atharva-Veda Saṁhitā*, tr. with a critical and exegetical commentary by W.D. Whitney, rev. and brought nearer to completion and ed. by C.R. Lanman, 2 vols. (Harvard Oriental Series, 7-8), Cambridge (Mass.): Harvard University Press.

4

About the Names of Some Vedic Poets

Georges-Jean Pinault

1. Tracing the Authors of the Hymns

According to the Indian tradition of Vedic philology, each hymn (*sūkta*) of the *R̥k-Saṁhitā* (henceforth R̥S) has an "author", i.e. a *r̥ṣi*,[1] who is supposed to have uttered this poem for the first time. The names of individual authors, partly with their genealogy, have been compiled in an index (*anukramaṇī*) of *r̥ṣi*s, which has been integrated to the general catalogue (*Sarvānukramaṇī*)[2] of the R̥S, after the fixation of the whole text for ritual purposes. One can compare this invaluable material with the names of individual poets or of families that are given in the very text of the hymns. In addition, names of *r̥ṣi*s are known from various texts of the Brāhmaṇa and Sūtra periods. Some of these *r̥ṣi*s do appear in legends, recorded in the *Br̥haddevatā*, that have been transmitted for centuries. Names have been also adopted on the basis of the identification of the authors of melodies (*sāman*) with the poets themselves. The lists of ancestors (*pravara*) contain supplementary information about ancient *r̥ṣi*s that are the remote founders of families of brahmins.[3] One may assume that the majority

---

[1] I prefer to leave this term untranslated, although it is currently rendered as "seer", because the primeval poets are supposed to have first "seen" the poems (see the etymology recorded by *Nir.* 2.11) and afterwards they handed them down as memory heritage inside their family.

[2] See the edition of Sharma 1977. The book of Mayrhofer (2003: 106-50) has taken over this list of the poets of the R̥S, but it is devoid of a thorough critical sifting and classification of the material.

[3] Cf. Oldenberg 1888; Gonda 1975: 76-78; Jamison 2007: 20-21, 24-27.

of the record of the *anukramaṇī* reflects a genuine tradition from the time when the text of the R̥S had been fixed. In cases where the tradition was silent or defective, names have been extracted from the text according to the following principle: *yasya vākyaṁ sa r̥ṣiḥ* (*Sarvānukramaṇī* 2.4). As a consequence, each hymn, or even each part of a hymn, has now an author, even in the numerous cases where the author did not sign his poem by giving his name. A number of names are pure fiction: they have been gained on the basis of some words of the hymns.[4] In the case of dialogue hymns (*saṁvāda*), each speaking character, whose name is given in the text or has been deduced by the early commentaries, is taken as a *r̥ṣi*. Leaving aside these fictive names, the names of the *r̥ṣi*s of the R̥S are quite interesting from different angles: history of the composition of the hymns and of the books (*maṇḍala*), family traditions and mythology of poet's clans, relationships of the poets with their patrons, linguistic shape, and location of poet's clans in time and space. In the heart of the R̥S, the so-called "family books", the hymns of each *maṇḍala* are supposed to have been authored by the same *r̥ṣi* or by his descendants. While adding book VIII to this core, it is possible to draw some geographical conclusions about the location of the major poets' families, see the following chart (after Witzel 1995: 318):

Maṇḍala II:	Gr̥tsamada	W/NW, Panjab
Maṇḍala III:	Viśvāmitra	Panjab, Sarasvatī (the later Kurukṣetra)
Maṇḍala IV:	Vāmadeva	W/NW, Panjab
Maṇḍala V:	Atri	W/NW, Panjab → Yamunā
Maṇḍala VI:	Bharadvāja	W/NW, Panjab, Sarasvatī → Gaṅgā
Maṇḍala VII:	Vasiṣṭha	Sarasvatī (Sindhu/Panjab → Yamunā)
Maṇḍala VIII:	Kaṇva, Āṅgirasa	W/NW, Sindhu/Suvāstu, Panjab

2. Signatures Given Inside the Hymns

There are basically three devices through which the poets have signed their hymns.

1. Self-reference of the poets to their clan, i.e. to the name of their ancestor. Those names are found both in singular and in

[4] Examples are given by Oldenberg (1888: 227-29) and Mayrhofer (2002: 266-69).

plural, very rarely with patronymic derivative. One significant exception is *kāṇvá-* (7x, all in book VIII) "descendant of Kaṇva", attested beside *káṇva-* (singular 25x, plural 29x). Except in the passages where the legend of the *ṛṣi* is narrated or alluded to (Vasiṣṭha in VII.18 and VII.33, Atri in several passages, etc.), the singular refers to an individual member of the clan, parallel to the collective mention of the descendants of the *ṛṣi* in the plural. Therefore, *vásiṣṭha-* (singular 30x, plural 23x) is rarely the primeval Vasiṣṭha of the remote past. It means usually "one of the Vasiṣṭhas"; *átri-* (singular 38x, plural 8x) has in most occurrences the same meaning as the later derivative *ātreyá-* (*ŚB* +) "descendant of Atri". Actually, the plural refers collectively to the guild of poets of the same clan, although the author can speak his hymn in the first person, since each hymn has normally a single author.

2. The *ṛṣi*'s name as basis of an adverb in *-vát* that involves a link with the remote or mythical past: "as [did] N. in former times", cf. *manuṣ-vát, manu-vát, aṅgiras-vát*. See *atri-vát* 8x (7x in book V, cf. *átri-* 46x), *bharadvāja-vát* 6.65.6b (cf. *bharádvāja-* 19x), *vasiṣṭha-vát* VII.96.3d (cf. *vásiṣṭha-* 53x), *virūpa-vát* I.45.3b (cf. *vírūpa-* in plural, III.53.7a; X.62.5a and 6b, *vairūpá-* X.14.5b), *kaṇva-vát* VIII.6.11b, 52.8d (cf. *káṇva-* 54x), *vyaśva-vát* VIII.23.23b, 24.22a, 26.9b; IX.65.7a (cf. *vyàśva-* I.112.15c, VIII.9.10a, 23.16a, 24.28c, 24.29b), *vaiyaśvá-* VIII.23.24c, 24.23b, 26.11a), *sthūrayūpa-vát* VIII.23.24b.
3. The usage of a seal pāda, a kind of refrain (*udarka*), i.e. a pāda which is repeated identically at the end of several hymns of the same *maṇḍala*. This seal pāda helped to differentiate each poet's guild from others.

3. Self-Reference of Gṛtsamada

The name *gṛtsamadá-* occurs always in the plural (II.4.9a, 19.8a, 39.8b, 41.18c), e.g.

II.19.8 *evā́ te gṛtsamadā́ḥ śūra mánma, avasyávo ná vayúnāni takṣuḥ* ı
brahmaṇyánta indra te návīya, íṣam ū́rjaṁ sukṣitíṁ sumnám aśyuḥ ıı

(penultimate stanza) Just so the Gṛtsamadas, O hero, have built a poem for you, as people wanting a favour (make) enveloping plans.

May the makers of formulation obtain from you, O Indra, afresh invigoration, strength, good abode, benevolence.

II.39.8 *etā́ni vām aśvinā várdhanāni, bráhma stómaṁ gr̥tsamadā́so akran* ।
tā́ni narā jujuṣāṇópa yātam, br̥hád vadema vidáthe suvī́rāḥ ।। (last stanza)

The Gr̥tsamadas have made for you two, O Aśvin's, these reinforcements, the formulation (and) the praise. Enjoying these ones, O lords, come nearby. May we speak mightily at the distribution, provided with good men!

II.41.18 *imā́ bráhma sarasvati, juṣásva vājinīvati* ।
yā́ te mánma gr̥tsamadā́ r̥tāvari, priyā́ devéṣu júhvati ।।

O Sarasvatī, enjoy these formulations, O you provided with rewards, (enjoy) these poems, dear to the gods, which the Gr̥tsamadas have spent for you, O truthful one.

4. Self-Reference of Viśvāmitra

The name *viśvāmitra-* is mostly attested in the "family hymn" III.53: singular 7c, 9c, 12c for the hero of the legend; plural in the unique Gāyatrī stanza and elsewhere:

III.53.13 *viśvā́mitrā arāsata, bráhma índrāya vajríṇe* ।
kárad ín naḥ surā́dhasaḥ ।।

The Viśvāmitras have offered the formulation to Indra holding the club; he shall indeed make us provided with good presents!

Outside of the family books, it occurs in the hymns of Reṇu Vaiśvāmitra, in the penultimate stanza:

X.89.17 *evā́ te vayám indra bhuñjatīnā́ṁ, vidyā́ma sumatīnā́ṁ návānām* ।
vidyā́ma vástor ávasā gr̥ṇánto, viśvā́mitrā utá ta indra nūnám ।।

Just so may we partake of the renewed, enjoyable marks of the benevolence of yours, O Indra, and also may we now partake of the morning light, thanks to your favour, we the Viśvāmitras who are your adulators.

III.1.21 *jánmañ-janman níhito jātávedā, viśvā́mitrebhir idhyate ájasraḥ* ।
tásya váyaṁ sumataú yajñíyasya, ápi bhadré saumanasé syāma ।।

> The Jātavedas, being installed generation after generation, the indefatigable one, is kindled by the Viśvāmitras. May we dwell in the benevolence of him, who deserves worship, also in his blissful kindness. (Cf. Oldenberg 1897: 221-22)

III.18.4 *úc chocíṣā sahasas putra stutó, br̥hád váyaḥ śaśamānéṣu dhehi* ।
revád agne viśvā́mitreṣu śáṁ yór, marmr̥jmā́ te tanvàm bhū́ri kŕ̥tvaḥ ॥

> (Shining) forth with thy flame, O son of strength, praised (by us), bestow mighty vigor on those who toil for thee, wealth, O Agni, luck (and) welfare on the Viśvāmitras! We have polished thy body many times. (Cf. Oldenberg 1897: 277)

5. Self-Reference of Vāmadeva

Among the *r̥ṣis* of the family books, the name *vāmádeva-* is the least well attested, in the singular in one single instance, in the last part of a hymn:

IV.16.18 *bhúvo 'vitā́ vāmádevasya dhīnā́m, bhúvaḥ sákhā avr̥kó vā́jasātau* ।
tvā́m ánu prámatim ā́ jaganma, uruśáṁso jaritré viśvádha syāḥ ॥

> May you [Indra] become the helper of the thoughts of Vāmadeva, may you become an ally, opposed to the wolf, at the occasion of winning the victory prize. We have come to you for the sake of protection. Be at all times the one whose praise holds large for the adulator.

One finds however an indirect reference through word play in the last stanza of a hymn to Indra:

IV.30.24 *vāmáṁ-vāmaṁ ta ādure, devó dadātv aryamā́* ।
vāmám pūṣā́ vāmám bhágo, vāmáṁ deváḥ kárūḷatī ॥

> The God Aryaman shall give you, O Āduri, good in every instance, Pūṣan (shall give you) good, Bhaga (shall give you) good, the god with decayed teeth (shall give you) good.

The repetition of the word *vāmá-* and the sequence *vāmáṁ deváḥ* are certainly intentional, since *vāmá-* (*R̥S* 57x) is not a favorite word of the family; it occurs once more in IV.5.13a (last part of the hymn).

6. Self-Reference of Bharadvāja

The name *bharádvāja-* is found both in singular and in plural. In the singular, it refers to the mythical *ṛṣi*, in I.112.13c, I.116.8b, X.150.5a, X.181.2d, also in most instances of the book VI. See the dānastuti VI.63.9-10, where the verb is in the injunctive, so that it does not refer to a single poet, but to him as far as he is a member of the Bharadvāja clan:

VI.63.10 *sáṁ vāṁ śatā́ nāsatyā sahásrā, (á)śvānām purupánthā giré dāt* ।
bharádvājāya vīra nū́ giré dād, dhatā́ rákṣāṁsi purudaṁsasā syuḥ ॥

Together (with that) Purupanthan shall give hundreds, thousands of horses for the praise intended for you two, O Nāsatyas, he shall now give (them), O heroes, to Bharadvāja for his praise. May the demons be killed, O masters of many wonders.

Elsewhere the poet is associated to the patron as beneficiary of the hymn:

VI.17.14 *sá no vā́jāya śrávasa iṣé ca, rāyé dhehi dyumáta indra víprān* ।
bharádvāje nṛváta indra sūrī́n, diví ca smaidhi pā́rye na indra ॥

(penultimate stanza) Make thus, O Indra, our poets provided with brightness, for booty, for renown, for invigoration and wealth, make, O Indra, for Bharadvāja the patrons provided with heroes, and be definitely for us at the ultimate day, O Indra!

The plural is used in the family hymn VI.47 (25b) for referring to all members of the guild, including the present author of the hymn. In the dānastuti (22-25), one member of the family is mentioned, Pāyu, who is known as the author of VI.75, the last hymn of the book, cf. VI.47.24c. Besides, see the frequent locative plural: VI.10.6c, 23.10b, 35.4d and I.59.7b.

In one case, in the final stanza, the ancestor is made to speak, and he refers to this own descendants:

VI.50.15 *evā́ nápāto* ***máma*** *tásya dhībhír, bharádvājā abhy àrcanti arkaíḥ* ।
gnā́ hutā́so vásavo (á)dhṛṣṭā, víśve stutā́so bhūtā yajatrāḥ ॥

So the descendants of mine, the Bharadvājas, are praising with poems [and] with praises. The goddesses, the invincible Vasus, who receive oblations, O you worthy of worship, be all glorified! (following Geldner, *ṚV* II.153).

But the first pāda may contain a textual problem, and could be read differently (⁺*mamatásya*) "the descendants of Mamata", cf. VI.10.2, where the mother of Dīrghatamas, Mamatā, is mentioned.[5]

7. Name and Related Phraseology

The name *bharádvāja-* is based on Vedic phraseology that goes back to Indo-European poetic tradition, cf. the phrase *vā́jam bhar-* "to take along the victory prize", see also the compound *vā́jam-bhará-* "taking (away) the prize", epithet of running horses.[6] The poets can allude to the meaning of their name by mentioning the *vā́ja-* at the end of the hymns:

VI.10.6 *imáṁ yajñáṁ cáno dhā agna uśán, yáṁ ta āsānó juhuté havíṣmān* ।
bharádvājeṣu dadhiṣe suvr̥ktím, ávīr vā́jasya gádhyasya sātaú ॥

(penultimate stanza) Take pleasure, O Agni, gladly to this sacrifice, which the giver of oblation, being seated, spends for you. You have received a well-done praising on the side of the Bharadvājas. You shall help for the winning of the booty that is to be taken hold of.

VI.17.15 *ayā́ vā́jaṁ deváhitaṁ sanema, mádema śatáhimāḥ suvī́rāḥ* ॥

Through this (poem), may we gain the prize that has been put at stake by the gods, may we rejoice for hundred years (lit. winters), being provided with men of good value!

But this is not very significant, since *vā́ja-* is a quite frequent word in all books. One may however note that the presence of *vā́ja-* in the very last pāda reflects some intention:

VI.70.6cd *saṁrarāṇé ródasī viśváśambhuvā,*
saníṁ vā́jaṁ rayím asmé sám invatām ॥

Both Rodasī [heaven and earth], granting together, beneficial in every respect, shall bestow on us gain, booty, wealth.

VI.21.12cd *yé áśramāsa urávo váhiṣṭhās, tébhir na indra (a)bhí vakṣi vā́jam* ॥

Which are indefatigable, far-reaching, driving best, with those lead us towards the victory prize, O Indra!

---

[5] Oldenberg 1888: 212.

[6] Cf. Pinault 2006: 376-80.

The seal pāda of the family is the following: *mádema śatáhimāḥ suvī́rāḥ*, of limited extension: VI.4.8d, VI.10.7b, VI.12.6d, VI.13.6d (in the set of hymns to Agni, 1-16), VI.17.15b, 24.10d (in the initial set of hymns to Indra, 17-47). One may consider that the notions of possessing good men and of victory prize are related.

8. Hidden Reference to the Vasiṣṭhas in their Seal Pāda

The relationship between the poet's name and the phraseology apply to the seal pāda, which ought to be coined with much care and skill. The Vasiṣṭha family is certainly the most self-conscious of all guilds of poets. Their own name means "excellent, very best". They have a very frequent seal pāda, which is the most quoted of all such refrains in the *R̥S*:

> *yūyám pāta s(u)vastíbhiḥ sádā naḥ* (Triṣṭubh line)
>
> You, protect us always with supports for good return![7]

There are exceptions, in sum, in twenty-eight out of 104 hymns: VII.2 (āprī), VII.5, 6, 10, 15, 16, 17, 18 (first hymn to Indra), VII.32, 33, 38, 44, 49, 50, 52, 55, 59, 66, 74, 81, 82, 83, 89, 94, 96, and the appendix hymns VII.102, 103, 104. Since the addressee is in the plural, it should fit only for hymns to the Maruts, to the Viśvedevāḥ, or to the Ādityas, but it is used also if the addressee is in the singular or in the dual. One may wonder if it was composed initially for "all the gods". This pāda conceals in an astute way the name of the clan, which is based on the epithet *vásiṣṭha-*, superlative of *vásu-*. In the middle of the pāda, the keyword is *s(u)vastí-*, which ought to be read in three syllables in Ancient Vedic (prevalent in the *RS*). The prefix *su-* is the compound match of the adjective *vásu-*, cf. *su-mánas-* (32x) vis-à-vis of *vásu mánaḥ* = Av. *vohu- manah-*; *vásu-śravas-* (V.24.2a) as one variant of *su-śrávas-* (4x and *suśrávastama-* 6x). In addition the permutation of the two first syllables /su-vas/ gives /vas-su/≈ /vasu/, since the geminate *-ss-* is normally simplified.[8]

---

[7] I translate *s(u)vastí-* "fortune, luck, success" according to the etymological interpretation, cf. *EWAia* II: 796.

[8] *AiGr* I: 111, § 97a, α.

9. Interpretation of the Seal Pāda of the Gr̥tsamadas

Let us now examine more closely the seal pāda of the Gr̥tsamada clan, in book II (43 hymns):

br̥hád vadema vidáthe suvī́rāḥ

It is found in 1.16d, 2.13d (to Agni, 1-10), 11.21d (beginning of the set to Indra, 11-22), 12.15d (variant *suvī́rāso vidátham ā́ vadema* = I.117.25a, VIII.48.14d), 13.13d, 14.12d, 15.10d, 16.9d, 17.9d, 18.9d, 19.9d, 20.9d, 23.19d (beginning of the set to Br̥haspati, 23-26), 24.16d, 27.17d (beginning of the set to the Ādityas, 27-29), 28.11d, 29.7d, 33.15d (to Rudra), 35.15d (to Apāṁ Napāt), 39.8d (to the Aśvins), 40.6d (to Soma, Pūṣan, Aditi), 42.3d, 43.3d (to the oracle bird *śakúni-*); plus IX.86.48d (stanzas 46-48 ascribed to Gr̥tsamada). Translations of Geldner: "Wir möchten das groβe Wort führen als Meister in der weisen Rede" (*R̥V* I: 277, for II.1.16d); "Wir möchten das groβe Wort führen als Meister in der Weisheit" (*R̥V* I: 290 for II.11.21d); "Als Meister wollen wir (das Wort der) Weisheit reden" (*R̥V* I: 291 for II.12.15d, similarly II: 370 for VIII.48.14d). This pāda is very similar to the seal pāda of the Bharadvāja family (see above § 7); by contrast, its key word is certainly *vidátha-*, which refers actually to the appropriate distribution among the participants of the booty or of the prize gained in a competition. By extension, it may refer to the precise attribution of duties or tasks by a householder. This noun (< **vidhátha-*) is based on the verb *ví-dhā-* "to distribute, apportion, grant appropriately".[9] In the wedding hymn, the phrase *vidátham ā́ vad-* (X.85.26d, 27d) can be translated by "to tell the disposition(s) [in the household]". The two alternative phrases, while having in common the compound *suvī́rāḥ*, allow close renderings: *br̥hád vidáthe vad-* "Gute Mannen habend wollen wird Gewichtiges reden bei der Verteilung"; *vidátham ā́-vad-* "Gute Mannen habend wollen wir die Verteilung verkünden (die Anordnung ansagen)".[10] Along the same line, one may quote Renou's translations: "Puissions-nous parler puissamment dans la répartition-sacrificielle, (en sorte d'être récompensés par le don de) bons fils !" (*EVP* V: 69). "Puissions-nous parler haut dans la distribution-rituelle, (en sorte d'obtenir) des hommes-d'élite !" (*EVP* XII: 42). "Ayant des hommes valeureux (ou

---

[9] Cf. Thieme 1949: 35-49: "Verteilung", especially "anordnende Verteilung, Anordnung, Bestimmung" (42).

[10] Thieme 1949: 44.

mieux: en sorte d'obtenir des . . .), nous voulons annoncer la répartition (des biens)" (*EVP* XVI: 18). I would then propose the following translation of the first phrase: "May we speak high (with might) at the distribution (of goods), being provided with men of good value."

10. Gr̥tsamada, Vimada, and the Root Common to Both Names

The phraseology leads to put into question the meaning of the root *mad-* which is found apparently in the poet's names Gr̥tsamada and Vimada. The second member is taken routinely as related to the root *mad-* "to rejoice, be glad, be exhilarated, exult, delight, or revel in", and to the action noun *máda-* masc. (= OAv. *mada-*) "excitement, exhilaration", concretely "exciting drink" (*sóma-*).[11] This is reflected by the usual glosses: *gr̥tsa-madá-* (*R̥S* 4x) "sich auf erfahrene Weise berauschend", as per Mayrhofer (2003: 33, alternatively after R. Schmitt "den Gewandten (= Agni?) erfreuend/berauschend"). *vimadá-* (*RS* 11x, *ŚS* 4.29.4) "sich überaus berauschend, durch Rausch verwirrt" (Mayrhofer 2003: 83-84). In the first case, it corresponds to the internal or synchronic etymology, which contains however an additional etymology of *gŕ̥tsa-* as related to the root "to sing, praise": *Nir.* 9.5: *gr̥tsamado gr̥tsamadano gr̥tsa iti medhāvināma gr̥ṇāteḥ stutikarmaṇaḥ.* Nevertheless, a proper name meaning "exulting in a clever way" does not make much sense. It is true that the action noun *máda-* is very well attested in the *R̥S*, also in compounds: *mada-cyút-* (20x) "causing excitement" or "moved by excitement", *máda-cyuta-* (IX.98.3) "moved, delighted by excitement", *máda-vr̥ddha-* "invigorated by exciting drink" (I.52.3), *mada-pati-* "master of exciting drink" (VI.69.3, vocative dual, about Indra and Viṣṇu), *máde-raghu-* (VIII.101.3) "fleet under excitement", see "in Begeisterung flink" (*AiGr* II/1: 232), *ukthāmadá-* "hymn [and] exciting drink" (*ŚS* 5.26.3). Other names and epithets are built with derivatives from the root *mad-* or from the related new root *mand-* "to exhilarate, rejoice, delight", etc.: proper name **Sammada* presupposed by the patronymic derivative *Sāmmadá-* (*ŚB* +), used for Matsya, king of the aquatic animals, and also author of *R̥S* VIII.67 (Anukr.), cf. *sám-mad-* (*R̥V* +) "to rejoice together, rejoice with, delight in". See the adjectives *indra-mā́dana-* (VII.92.4a) "delighting Indra" (patrons), *deva-mā́dana-* (IX.84.1a, 107.3a, X.30.7d) "gladdening the

[11] Compare "Rausch, Rauschwirkung, Taumel; Rauschtrank" according to Kim 2010: 75.

gods" (*sóma-*), *mandád-vīra-* (VIII.69.1b) "gladdening men" (*sóma-*), *mandayát-sakha-* (I.4.7c) "gladdening friends" (idem). Concerning the name *vimáda-*, one faces a serious difficulty: the verb *mad-* is not found with preverb *ví* in the *R̥S*. When found with this preverb, it shows a very specific meaning, that does not fit the name of a poet: in *AV*, *ŚS* *ví-mad-* "to confound", *vi-mádan* XX.49.3, *ví . . . amīmadam* VII.74.3. It is found later mostly with negative connotation (*AitBr* +) "to become perplexed, discomposed, disturbed". See also *vi-matta-* "discomposed, perplexed", *vi-madita-* "discomposed, bewildered, confused". The adjective *vi-mada-* (ep. +) is based on *mada-* (*R̥V máda-*) with the privative meaning of *vi*: "free from intoxication, grown sober" (*R*), "free from pride or arrogance" (*MBh*), "joyless".

11. Self-Reference of Vimada Through Word Play

One notes some word play about the name of the poet Vimada, author of the hymns X.20-26, and protected by Indra.

X.23.6ab *stómaṁ ta indra vimadā́ ajījanann, ápūrvyam purutámaṁ sudā́nave* ।

> The Vimadas have created a poem of praise for thee, O Indra, which is unprecedented, most abundant, for you the quite munificent one.

X.23.7 *mā́kir na enā́ sakhyā́ ví yauṣus, táva ca indra vimadásya ca ŕ̥ṣeḥ* ।
vidmā́ hí te prámatiṁ deva jāmivád, asmé te santu sakhyā́ śivā́ni ।।

> Never shall our present relations of friendship break up with thee, O Indra, and with the R̥ṣi Vimada, because we know thy providence, O god, like the one of a blood relative. May thy gracious ties of friendship remain with us!

The legend of Vimada shows a major event: the Aśvins gave to him as wife a young woman named Kamadyū, daughter of Purumitra, cf. I.112.19a, I.116.1cd, I.117.20cd, X.39.7ab, X.65.12c (*kamadyū́-*), alternatively called *śundhyū́-* (X.39.7a). This name can be analysed as **ka-mad-yū́-* with hypocoristic prefix *ka-*, based on a derivative **mad-yú-*, agent noun, after the model of *manyú-*, *bhujyú-*, *śundhyú-*, *vipanyú-*, etc.[12] It would mean approximately, about a woman: "the dear rejoicing one", "what a rejoicing one!". Of course, this seems to be a fitting wife for a man called *vimadá*, whose name was related in synchrony

---

12 Remmer 2006: 44-52.

to the root *mad-*, but it does not entail that this connection holds historically, that is, as the original motivation of this name. Of course, the synchronic etymology is entertained in the refrain of X.25 (to Soma), in Āstārapaṅkti:

X.25.1c-f *ádhā te sakhyé ándhaso, ví vo máde, ráṇan gā́vo ná yávase, vívakṣase* ||

> 1d and 1f are repeated in the further 10 stanzas. Same device in X.21.1-8 (to Agni), X.24.1-3 (to Indra).
>
> Dann wollen wir uns in deines Trankes Gesellschaft ergötzen wie die Kühe auf der Weide — in der Begeisterung will ich es euch verkünden. — Geldner, *R̥V* I: 161
>
> Alors dans l'amitié de ton jus (nous allons nous réjouir) comme les vaches se réjouissent dans la prairie: dans l'ivresse je vais vous le révéler. — Renou, *EVP* IX : 71

The name of the poet is inscribed in his text, but in some obscured way. This has been much commented on, as an instance of anagrammatic or hypogrammatic display of the elements of a name.[13] It requires a minimum of attention to perceive this signature, which is given openly in other passages.

12. The Underlying Meaning of the Two Names

The seal pāda of the Gr̥tsamadas (see § 9 above) contains a hypogram of their name as well.[14] The major repeated phonemes are set in bold face in *br̥h**á**d **vad**ema **vid**áthe su**vī́**rāḥ*: alliteration in /d/, in /v/, consonance in /a/, /i/; furthermore, the permutation of syllables in ***vadema*** yields (*va*) ***made***, pointing to the second part of the poet's name: *gr̥tsa-**madá-***. One may even read under the line ***vi-made***, that would point to the name *vimadá-* ! But there is no legendary relationship between Vimada and Gr̥tsamada. I would guess that these word plays call to attention the lexeme *mad-* in both cases. Nevertheless, the two names had some meaning that precisely referred to a root *mad-* different from the usual root *mad-* of *máda-* "excitement". As a matter of fact, Old Iranian has as parallel combination *vī-mad-*, see Hintze 2000 — in *vīmāδas*, nom. pl. of a root noun *vī-mad-* "healing man, doctor", and in the verb *vīmāδaiia-* "to take measures in every

[13] Cf. Watkins 1995: 188-89.

[14] Watkins 1995: 114.

direction", in order to cure persons (*Vd.* 7.38, 40). The verb *mad-* "to grant with measure, appropriately" is attested also with preverb in *Y.* 54.1. See further the compound *vohumad-* (dat. sg. *+vohu-maiδe Y.* 12.1 and *Vd.* 19.11) "Gutes zumessend" = "allotting, granting good" (= Ved. **vasu-mád-*). Hintze (2000: 166) has proposed to compare the *R̥S* proper name *vimadá-*, while assuming with some reservation that its original meaning was "healer". An argument was the connection of Vimada with the Aśvins, as healing gods. But the legend of Vimada, as told in the *R̥S*, does not involve any special ability to cure other people. It is perfectly possible that the meaning of *YAv. vī-mad-* found in the Vidēvdāt results from a later specialization from the original meaning: "to take measures" or "to grant with measure" while distributing (*vi-*). In any case, this Av. root *mad-* goes back to the PIE root **med-* "to take appropriate measures", after Benveniste (1969, II: 123-32); hence, beside the notion of "measure", meanings such as "to heal, cure", "to think about, consider, meditate, plan", "to moderate, control", finally "to govern, rule", are attested in the different IE languages. The Indo-Iranian root **mad-* "to attribute, distribute in an appropriate way" has been replaced in Indo-Aryan by *ví-dhā-*, basis of *vidátha-* "appropriate distribution, ordering".[15] It survives only through the agent noun *-madá-* in the proper names *vi-madá-* and *gr̥tsa-madá-*. The former meant originally "granting appropriately". The latter would mean literally: "cleverly allotting, ordering".[16] Therefore, both names were connected with the notion of proper distribution, expressed otherwise by *vidátha-*. Their names claimed that these poets are able to get the best share at the distribution of goods following the conquest of the victory prize (*vā́ja-*) by the patrons, of course with the help of the gods.

13. Concealed Formation of the Name of Dīrghatamas

The Indo-Iranian phraseology, as displayed in compound names of the aristocracy, may be used to name a poet with some kind of pun: the case in point is Dīrghatamas, son of Mamatā. By itself, this noun

[15] The occurrence of this noun in the seal pāda of the Gr̥tsamadas is then fully justified from the historical point of view.

[16] The first member is the adjective *gr̥tsa-* (*R̥S* 9x) "clever, dexterous, judicious, wise" (MW: 361b), compare Fr. "adroit, agile-en-pensée, habile, vif d'esprit" (Renou, *EVP*, ad loc.).

does not make sense: "characterized by having long darkness" (?). The legend has him as a blind man, probably from birth.

I.158.6 *dīrghátamā māmateyó, jujurvā́n daśamé yugé* | *apā́m ártham yatī́nām, brahmā́ bhavati sā́rathiḥ* || (final stanza)

Dīrghatamas, son of Mamatā, having become decrepit in the tenth age, becomes the master of formulation, the driver of the running waters going to their goal.[17]

VIII.9.10 *yád vāṁ kakṣī́vām̐ utá yád vyàśva, ṛ́ṣir yád vāṁ dīrghátamā juhā́va* | *pṛ́thī yád vāṁ vainyáḥ sā́daneṣu, evéd áto aśvinā cetayethām* ||

(in the middle of a hymn by Śaśakarṇa Kāṇva, twenty-one stanzas) When Kakṣīvat, and when Vyaśva, when the Ṛṣi Dīrghatamas has called you two, [and] when Pṛthī Vainya (has called) you two at the seats (of the worship), thence straightaway take note, O Aśvins.

As Dīrghatamas Aucathya (cf. the Ṛṣi Ucathya, name based on the epithet *ucath(í)ya-*, Ucathya Āṅgirasa as author of IX.50-52), he is known as the author of the hymns I.140-164. The *Bṛhaddevatā* (4.11-23) takes over the legend of Dīrghatamas as a blind boy, who lost his sight and then recovered it by the favour of the gods. The *JB* (3.239) tells that Dīrghatamas, son of Mamatā, spoke in the womb: this can be a story based on his blindness, since "in the womb" would mean "still in the dark, not seeing the light". Nevertheless, the *ṚS* mentions him as a blind man.[18] I would suggest that his poet's name was invented so as to explain and justify his blindness. According to *ṚS* I.152.6, he received the favour of the rains as he was still an embryo.

I.147.3 *yé pāyávo māmateyáṁ te agne, páśyanto andháṁ duritā́d árakṣan* | *rarákṣa tā́n sukṛ́to viśvávedā, dípsanta íd ripávo nā́ha debhuḥ* ||

Thy guardians, O Agni, while watching over (him), saved the blind son of Mamatā from distress — (with them) the one who has knowledge of everything has saved them who have done good deeds. The impostors, trying to deceive, have not deceived indeed. (Somewhat different from Oldenberg 1897: 170, see Geldner, *ṚV* I: 206.)

---

17 The two preceding stanzas tell some episodes of his life, which remain difficult to interpret, however.

18 Cf. Tokunaga 1997: 209-10.

I.152.6 *ā́ dhenávo māmateyám ávantīr, brahmapríyam pīpayan sásmin ū́dhan* ।
pitvó bhikṣeta vayúnāni vidvā́n, āsā́vívāsann áditim uruṣyet ॥

The milch cows, favouring the son of Mamatā, have swollen in the same udder the one who cherishes the formulation. He [Agni] who understands our enveloping plans should partake of the food with his mouth. By trying to win innocence (for us), he would grant (us) freedom. (Cf. Brereton 1981: 200)

The first part of his name puts him at the same level as epithets belonging to old Indo-Iranian phraseology, connected with glory and fame[19] or with long life: *dīrghá-yaśas-* (epithet of *vípra-* in V.61.9d) "having long standing glory", *dīrghá-śravas-* "having long standing fame", *dīrgha-śrút-* (epithet of *vípra-* in VII.61.2b) "widely heard of, famous", superlative *dīrgha-śrút-tama-, dīrghā́yu-, dīrghā́yuṣ-* "provided with long-standing vital force".[20] The second part is based on *andhá-* "blind, opaque, obscure" as epithet of *támas-* "darkness", and on the synonymy between *ándhas-* (3x) and *támas-*. See *andhéna . . . támasā* X.89.15c (=X.103.12d), *andhé cit támasi* I.100.8c, *andhā́ támāṁsi* IV.16.4c. Actually, the phrase *dīrgháṁ támas* "long darkness" is known only in heroic context, as something negative, connected with death:

I.32.10cd *vr̥trásya niṇyáṁ ví caranty ā́po, dīrgháṁ táma ā́śayad índraśatruḥ* ॥

The waters flow widely over Vr̥tra's secret place, the one having Indra as adversary sank into long darkness.

X.124.1cd *áso havyavā́ḷ utá naḥ purogā́, jyóg evá dīrgháṁ táma ā́śayiṣṭhāḥ* ॥

(Indra to Agni) You shall be conveyor of the oblation and the one going before us. For a long time already you lay in long darkness.

II.27.14cd *urv àśyām ábhayaṁ jyótir indra, mā́ no dīrghā́ abhí naśan támisrāḥ* ॥

May I reach the wide light that protects from danger, O Indra, may the long veils of darkness not reach us.

[19] This notion is commonplace in Vedic names of princes: *Pr̥thuśrávas-, Suśrávas-* (also epithet), *Satyáśravas-, Upamáśravas-* (also epithet, cf. the superlative *upamáśravas-tama-*), etc.

[20] Cf. *EWAia* I: 172 and 729.

This phrase "long darkness" goes back to Indo-Iranian, cf. Yasna 31.20 *darəgə̄m āiiū təmaŋhō* "a long life of darkness" as fate of the enemy of the truthful one.

Therefore, the negative connotation of the "long darkness" seems to have been reversed as positive in the noun of Dīrghatamas.

14. The Problematic Origin of Kurusuti

Besides names of Indo-Aryan, or even Indo-Iranian pedigree, we do find in the *Sarvānukramaṇī* names that cannot be readily explained.[21] A poet called Kurusuti Kāṇva is recorded as the author of R̥S VIII.76-78 (to Indra).[22] According to Kuiper, some of the *r̥ṣis* outside of the family books were of Munda descent: prefix **kĕr-* pronounced as *kar-*, *kara-*, *kuru-* (1991: 40-42; 2000: 158). But the name *káṇva-* itself can be interpreted from Indo-Aryan, Prakritic < **kr̥ṇva-* (cf. Hoffmann 1975: 21-25). Otherwise, *kurusuti-* contains the name of a people and of a country *kúru-* (*MS* +). R̥S has it only in the name of a king, *Kuru-śrávaṇa-* (X.32.9, 33.4), descendant of the famous king Trasadasyu. One should leave aside *Kuruṅgá-*, name of a king (VIII.4.19), probably variant with /r/ of *kuluṅgá-* (*VS*, *TS*), *kulaṅgá-* (*MS*) "antelope".

X.33.4 *kuruśrávaṇam āvr̥ṇi, rā́jānaṁ trā́sadasyavam* ǀ
máṁhiṣṭhaṁ vāghátām r̥̄́ṣiḥ ǀǀ

> I chose for myself the King Kuruśravaṇa, progeny of Trasadasyu, the most generous one, I the best sage among the ones who proclaim prayer.

This name can be interpreted as "the glory of Kuru" or "bringing glory to the Kurus", as fitting name for a king — a rare occurrence of the action noun *śrávaṇa-*, otherwise unknown in the R̥S, except in the compound *pitr̥-śrávaṇa-* (I.91.20d), epithet of *vīrá-* "Sohn . . . , der dem Vater Ruhm bringt" (Geldner). The usual word for glory is *śrávas-* or *yáśas-*. Later, *śrávaṇa-* nt. (*ŚB* +) is known as meaning "hearing", also concretely "that which his heard" (= *śrúti-*), hence "sacred knowledge", etc. but rarely as meaning "fame, renown". The hymn I.91 is somewhat

[21] I shall leave aside in the present context the important issue of the various origins of "foreign" names, as well as the usage of "foreign" vocabulary by some poets, cf. Witzel 1999. One may suspect that some poets had the mastery of different languages, see in this vein Kuiper 2000.

[22] Belonging to the "Strophic" period according to Arnold 1905: 283.

older (less recent) than X.33, according to Arnold (1905: 271, 206).

The form *kurusuti-* looks phonetically odd: for **kuru-ṣuti-* "offspring of Kuru"? Alternatively **kuru-śruti-* (*kuruśrutiḥ kāṇvaḥ* as per Sharma 1977: 69b), meaning approximately the same as *kuru-śrávaṇa-*. Objections are:

1. *R̥S* **suti-* as derived from *su-* "to give birth" is only attested in the compound *súṣuti-* "easy birth" (X.39.7); otherwise, *suti-* belongs to the root *su-* "to press", or to the root *su* "to impel", cf. *āsutí-* "invigorating drink, cordial" (I.104.7, II.1.14, VII.97.7, VIII.1.26), also in *ghr̥tā́suti-* (4x), *bhū́ry-āsuti-* (1x), *sarpír-āsuti-* (6x).
2. *Śrúti-* is not attested in the meaning "fame, reputation", and is absent from the *R̥S*. The form *śrút(i)yai* is infinitive II.2.7b, VIII.96.3d, X.111.3a "in order to be heard". The characterization of this name as "popular" because of its shape ("volkssprachlich", as per Mayrhofer 2002: 269) remains vague.

15. Naming as Token of Cultural and Political Integration

As a new proposal, the underlying form would be **kuru-sruti-* with correct sandhi[23] and dissimilation of the liquid /r/ > *kurusuti-*. The second member is *srutí-*, known in the *R̥S* (8x, partly ancient) action noun of *sru-* "to flow": literally, "flowing", "running", hence in the *R̥S* "course, path" in most passages. This noun applies to running animals by way of comparison or metaphor:

VI.24.4ab *śácīvatas te puruśāka śā́kā, gávām iva srutáyaḥ saṁcáraṇīḥ* | (to Indra)

> Thy forces, O provided with many forces, accompanied by forces, (are) like the movable flows of bovines.

IX.78.2cd *pūrvī́r hí te srutáyaḥ sánti yā́tave, sahásram áśvā hárayaś camūṣádaḥ* ||

> (to Soma) because you have many courses to run, thousand bay horses, when you sit in the vessels.

The warriors[24] or the competing horses run like torrents flowing from the mountain:

---

[23] *AiGr* I: 232.

[24] About the Maruts, see V.60.3, VIII.94.7, X.77.4, 78.5, 78.7.

VII.18.15ab *índreṇaité tŕ̥tsavo véviṣāṇā, ā́po ná sr̥ṣṭā́ adhavanta nī́cīḥ* ।

> These Tr̥tsus,[25] having been impelled by Indra, ran downwards like liberated waters.

The priests and poets are compared both to flows and to horses, VI.24.6. The Kaṇvas compare themselves or their praises (VIII.32.23) to running waters. This can be expressed without the root *sru-* or with synonymous verbs; the notion of running or flowing can be inferred from similes, as in the next two passages:

VIII.33.1ab *vayáṁ gha tvā sutā́vanta, ā́po ná vr̥ktábarhiṣaḥ* । . . . *pári stotā́ra āsate* ।।

> We for sure, provided with pressed somas, having spread the bed of grass, we (resound) like flowing waters. The praising ones are seated around.

VIII.6.4 *sám asya manyáve víśo, víśvā namanta kr̥ṣṭáyaḥ* ।
samudrā́yeva síndhavaḥ ।।

> The clans bow together before his wrath, all the peoples, like the rivers running towards the ocean.

In the beginning of the latter stanza, a form of the verb *svar-* "to sound, resound" (here "to utter a praise") has to be transferred from the beginning of the next stanza, VIII.33.2a *sváranti tvā suté náraḥ* "the men sound (praises) towards thee (Indra), at the pressed soma".

Hence **kuru-sruti-* meant "the running force [of the youth] of Kuru". It is possible that this name was blurred with **kuru-śruti-*, according to the otherwise known appearance of the root *sru-* "to flow" as *śru-*.[26] This could be replaced (or explained) by the equivalent *kuru-śrávaṇa-*, from the root *śru-* "to hear", giving an acceptable and straightforward meaning. The poets of the Kuru clans did not know or use the compound epithets with *śrávas-* as second member, and their princes did not have such names. Otherwise, one may surmise that a proper name **kuru-śrávas-* would have been kept in the *R̥S*, since it would fit the noble naming model. Both *kuru-śrávaṇa-* and **kuru-sruti-* betray the (partly clumsy and snob) efforts of latecomers

[25] Vasiṣṭha, who tells the battle hymn VII.18, was the leader of the priestly clan named Tr̥tsu, cf. Witzel 1995: 334.

[26] Bloomfield-Edgerton 1932: 144, § 27.

to adopt the phraseology of the old Ārya clans of poets. This would be consistent with the late integration of the poems of the Kaṇvas to the *R̥S*: book VIII, and parts of book I and X. As noted by Witzel (1997: 265 n. 30) Kurusuti, by a typical archaizing trend, stresses his telling of an "old poem" (VIII.76.6a *pratnéna mánmanā*), but his poems are otherwise of late date, since he knows of the boar Emuṣa (VIII.77.10d) and of meals prepared with rice (*pakvám odanám* VIII.77.6b, *kṣīrapākám odanám* VIII.77.10c, *puroḷā́śam* VIII.78.1a). According to the historical scenario of Witzel (1997: 262-66), the stylistically divergent Kāṇva collections may have been initially excluded from the original Bharata collection; then follows the building of a "national Bharata-Puru collection", and addition of the strophic hymns of the (originally pro-Puru) Kāṇva poets. Finally, the Kuru realm emerges, somewhat at the level of book X; the new dynasty living in Kurukṣetra unified most of the R̥gvedic tribes.

16. Vedic Onomastics and Poetics

To sum up, most names of the poets, especially those of the ancient core of the *R̥S* (books II to VII), are interchangeable, since they express values and notions that are common to the ancient Vedic, and Indo-Iranian, phraseology; they are compounds of the same type as the names of princes, and have a laudatory meaning. Being names of poets, they are also poetic by themselves. In general, these names do not show any connection with the legends or historical facts that have become mythological, surrounding these *r̥ṣis*. Due to constraints of time and place, it is safer to postpone until further study the case of Atri, whose name is the only one which is not laudatory and based on ancient phraseology. The name *átri-*, obviously not a compound, has been traditionally connected with the root *ad-* "to eat" (*ŚB* 14.5.2.6), and related at face value with the names *atrá-* and *atrín-*, that are given to demons, the "devouring" ones. This may hold in synchrony,[27] but it remains to be evaluated in the context of some traditional features that are common to all *r̥ṣis*.

---

[27] Cf. Jamison 1991: 282.

References

AiGr = Wackernagel, Jacob, and Albert Debrunner, 1896-1957, *Altindische Grammatik*, I-III, Göttingen: Vandenhoeck & Ruprecht.

Arnold, E. Vernon, 1905, *Vedic Metre in its Historical Development*, Cambridge: Cambridge University Press.

Benveniste, Émile, 1969, *Le vocabulaire des institutions indo-européennes*, 2 vols. — 1. *Économie, parenté, société.* — 2. *Pouvoir, droit, religion*, Paris: Minuit.

Bloomfield, Maurice, and Franklin Edgerton, 1932, *Vedic Variants*, vol. II: *Phonetics*, Philadelphia: Linguistic Society of America.

Brereton, Joel P., 1981, *The R̥gvedic Ādityas*, New Haven (Conn.): American Oriental Society (American Oriental Series, vol. 63).

EVP = Renou, Louis, 1955-69, *Études védiques et pāṇinéennes*, I-XVII, Paris: Institut de Civilisation Indienne.

EWAia = Mayrhofer, Manfred, 1986-96, *Etymologisches Wörterbuch des Altindoarischen*, I-II (Ältere Sprache), Heidelberg: Carl Winter.

Geldner, Karl Friedrich, 1951, *Der Rig-veda aus dem Sanskrit ins Deutsche übersetzt und mit einem laufenden Kommentar versehen*, I-III, Cambridge (Mass.): Harvard University Press (Harvard Oriental Series, vols. 33, 34, 35).

Gonda, Jan, 1975, *Vedic Literature (Saṁhitās and Brāhmaṇas)*, Wiesbaden: Harrassowitz (A History of Indian Literature, vol. I, fasc. 1).

Hintze, Almut, 2000, "Die avestische Wurzel *mad* 'zumessen'", in *Indoiranisch, Iranisch und die Indogermanistik: Arbeitstagung der Idg. Gesellschaft vom 1. bis 5. Oktober 1997 in Erlangen*, ed. Bernhard Forssman and Robert Plath, pp. 163-75, Wiesbaden: Reichert.

Hoffmann, Karl, 1975, *Aufsätze zur Indoiranistik*, ed. Johanna Narten, Bd. I, Wiesbaden: Reichert.

Jamison, Stephanie W., 1991, *The Ravenous Hyenas and the Wounded Sun: Myth and Ritual in Ancient India*, Ithaca/London: Cornell University Press.

———, 2007, *The Rig Veda between Two Worlds*, Paris: De Boccard (Publications de l'Institut de Civilisation Indienne, fascicule 74).

Kim, Jeong-Soo, 2010, *Untersuchungen zu altindischen Abstrakta und Adjektiven im Rigveda und Atharvaveda*, Bremen: Hempen Verlag.

Kuiper, F.B.J., 1991, *Aryans in the Rigveda*, Amsterdam/Atlanta: Rodopi.

———, 2000, "A Bilingual *r̥ṣi* (RV X.106)", in *Anusantatyai: Festschrift für Johanna Narten*, ed. Almut Hintze and Eva Tichy, pp. 157-60, Dettelbach: J.H. Röll.

Macdonell, Arthur A., 1904, *The Br̥haddevatā attributed to Śaunaka: A Summary of the Deities and Myths of the R̥gveda*, 2 vols. — Part I: Introduction and text and appendices; Part II: Translation and Notes, Cambridge (Mass.): Harvard University Press (Harvard Oriental Series, vols. 5, 6).

Mayrhofer, Manfred, 2002, "Zu den Namen der Dichter rigvedischer Hymnen in der Anukramaṇī", *Historische Sprachforschung*, **115:** 265-73.

———, 2003, *Die Personennamen in der R̥gveda-Saṁhitā: Sicheres und Zweifelhaftes*, München: Bayerische Akademie der Wissenschaften.

MW = Monier-Williams, M., 1899, *A Sanskrit-English Dictionary*, Oxford: Clarendon Press.

Oldenberg, Hermann, 1888, "Ueber die Liedverfasser des Rigveda, Nebst Bemerkungen über die vedische Chronologie und über die Geschichte des Rituals", *Zeitschrift der Deutschen Morgenländischen Gesellschaft*, **42:** 199-247 (= 1967. *Kleine Schriften*, ed. Klaus L. Janert, 2 vols, pp. 568-616, Wiesbaden: Franz Steiner Verlag).

———, 1897, *Vedic Hymns*, Part II: *Hymns to Agni (Maṇḍalas I-V)*, London: Oxford University Press (Sacred Books of the East, vol. 46).

Pinault, Georges-Jean, 2006, "Compétition poétique et poétique de la compétition", in *La langue poétique indo-européenne: Actes du Colloque de travail de la Société des Études Indo-européennes (Paris, 22-24 octobre 2003)*, ed. G.-J. Pinault and Daniel Petit, pp. 367-411, Leuven/Paris: Peeters.

Remmer, Ulla, 2006, *Frauennamen im Rigveda und im Avesta: Studien zur Onomastik des ältesten Indischen und Iranischen*. Wien: Österreichische Akademie der Wissenschaften.

Sharma, Umesh Chandra, 1977, *R̥gveda-Sarvānukramaṇī of Kātyāyana and Anuvākānukramaṇī of Śaunaka*, Aligarh: Viveka Publications.

Thieme, Paul, 1949, *Untersuchungen zur Wortkunde und Auslegung des Rigveda*, Halle a. d. Saale: Max Niemeyer Verlag.

Tokunaga, Muneo, 1997, *The Br̥haddevatā: Text Reconstructed from the Manuscripts of the Shorter Recension with Introduction, Explanatory Notes and Indices*, Kyoto: Rinsen Book Co.

Watkins, Calvert, 1995, *How to Kill a Dragon: Aspects of Indo-European Poetics*, New York/Oxford: Oxford University Press.

Witzel, Michael, 1995, "R̥gvedic History: Poets, Chieftains and Politics", in *The Indo-Aryans of Ancient South Asia: Language, Material Culture and Ethnicity*, ed. George Erdosy, pp. 307-52, Berlin/New York: Walter de Gruyter.

———, 1997, "The Development of the Vedic Canon and its Schools: The Social and Political Milieu", in *Inside the Texts, Beyond the Texts*, ed. M. Witzel, pp. 257-345, Cambridge (Mass.): Harvard University Press.

———, 1999, "Aryan and non-Aryan names in Vedic India", in *Aryan and non-Aryan in South Asia*, ed. Johannes Bronkhorst and Madhav M. Deshpande, pp. 337-404, Cambridge (Mass.): Harvard University Press.

5

Compounds of the type *vājaṁbhará-* and *brahmakārá-* in the R̥gveda and Atharvaveda

Elizabeth Tucker

1. Introduction

R̥gvedic compounds of the type *vājaṁbhará-* "bringing booty", *brahmakārá-* "making a sacred formula" have frequently been discussed in historical linguistic studies because of the problems they raise for the conditions under which the sound change known as Brugmann's Law operated.[1] According to Brugmann's own formulation of the sound change (Brugman(n) 1876) Indo-European apophonic **o* developed to Indo-Iranian *ā* in medial open syllables. The thematic verbal nouns such as *-bhará* from *bhr̥-*, which form the second elements of the *R̥V* compounds, are traditionally compared to verbal nouns in other Indo-European (IE) languages such as Greek -φόρος <*-φορός.[2] These comparisons point to an IE reconstruction of the type **-bhoró-*, but, according to the operation of Brugmann's Law, the expected reflex in Indo-Iranian (IIr.) should regularly be **-bhārá-*. In the early *R̥V* thematic verbal nouns with both short *a* (*vājaṁbhará-*) and long *ā* (*brahmakārá-*) occur, and sometimes both forms are attested for the

[1] This paper discusses one part of a larger study concerned with all the categories of thematic verbal nouns in early Vedic that are relevant for the sound change in question. A report on this full investigation has been published in *Laws and Rules in Indo-European*, ed. by P. Probert and A. Willi, Oxford: Oxford University Press, 2012, pp. 229-59.

[2] Here the accent has shifted to the penultimate syllable according to Wheeler's Law in Greek (see Probert 2006: 93-94), cf. uncompounded verbal nouns of the type *τομός* "cutter".

same root (*yataṁkará-* and *brahmakārá-* with *-kará-*/*-kārá-* from *kr̥-*).

The most generally accepted modification to Brugmann's Law is that proposed by Kuryłowicz (1927), according to which apophonic **o* in a syllable closed by an inherited laryngeal did not develop to IIr. *ā*. However, this does not resolve all the problems presented by the Vedic verbal nouns under consideration here, and it highlights some further difficulties: for example, why does the verbal noun *-grābhá-* (*R̥V udagrābhá-* "holding water", *grāvagrābhá-* "holding the pressing stones") from *gr̥bh-* have long *ā* when this is a *seṭ* root which is reconstructed with a prehistoric final laryngeal (cf. present *gr̥bhṇā́ti*, root aorist *ágrabhīt*)? Kuryłowicz (1956: 325-35) later denied the validity of Brugmann's Law as a phonological rule, just as Brugmann himself had done later in his life. However, the exact conditions for a sound change IE **o* > IIr. *ā* have continued to be debated (cf. Burrow 1975, Collinge 1985: 13-21, Volkart 1994, Holst 2004). In addition some detailed philological studies devoted to categories of the Vedic verb, such as Jamison (1983) and Kümmel (2000), have indicated that Brugmann's Law is basically valid and that the anomalies result from inner IIr. morphological developments.

The evidence for the thematic verbal nouns (both in compounds and uncompounded) has been discussed in some detail by Lubotsky (1988) and Hajnal (1994) but their perspective is diachronic and focused on the IE problems. This paper will be concerned with the philological details of the *R̥V* and *AV* synchronic situations on the one hand, and on the other hand with the developments that can be traced within a limited IIr. chronological time-span. It will take into account evidence from three sources: first, the hieratic language of the early *R̥V* (Maṇḍalas I-IX), second, the "popular" *R̥V* (Maṇḍala X) + *AV*, and third, comparative evidence from Old Iranian (Old Persian and Avestan). The aim is to show which types of form were productive, which are moribund and thus likely to represent archaisms, and which are likely to represent artificial/nonce creations of the Vedic poets. It will also place emphasis on the function of the forms in the texts because this is not always immediately apparent from formal shape and accentuation. In addition, reference will be made to other categories of verbal nouns with which there was interplay, since compounded forms such as those seen in *vājaṁbhará-* and *brahmakārá-* did not exist in isolation at any period.

2. The Wider Synchronic Situation

It is possible to distinguish the following morphological and semantic categories of thematic verbal noun in the early *ṚV* where the effects of Brugmann's Law might be expected:

1. Simple (uncompounded) action nouns with accent on the root (*bhára-* m. "act of carrying away (booty), battle", *váśa-* m. "wish, will", *máda-* m. "exhilaration").
2. Nouns prefixed by *su-* or *duṣ-* with accent on the root (*subhára-* "easy to bear").
3. Simple nouns, whose meaning frequently shows a passive value of the root, with accent on the thematic vowel (*bhārá-* m. "burden, load", *grābhá-* m. "handful, grasp").
4. Prefixed action nouns based on compound verbs with accent on the thematic vowel (*saṁgamá-* "meeting", *saṁvādá-* "conversation", *prasavá-* m. "impulse).
5. Action nouns as the second element of nominal compounds with accent on the thematic vowel (*namovāká-* m. "speech of homage", *indrahavá-* m. "invocation of Indra").
6. Agent nouns as the second element of nominal compounds with accent on the thematic vowel (*vājaṁbhará-* "bringing booty", *dhārāvará-* "loving streams", *brahmakārá-* "making a sacred formula", *udagrābhá-* "holding water").
7. Simple agent nouns or adjectives with accent on the thematic vowel (*ghaná-* m. "murderer", *vará-* m. "suitor", *dravá-* "running", *vāhá-* m. "conveyor, draught animal").
8. Prefixed agent nouns based on compound verbs with accent on the thematic vowel (*para śará-* m. "smasher", *ātapá-* "burning", *vibādhá-* m. "oppressor").

Categories 6, 7 and 8 arguably form one large class where in all cases the thematic verbal noun has agent-noun or adjectival value, even though in Old Indo-Aryan (OIA) it is not a distinct formal class because the prefixed action nouns are also accented on the thematic vowel, as are the simple nouns of the *bhārá*-type (categories 3-4). Categories 7 and 8, although closely linked with 6, involve some more extensive problems which cannot be treated in this paper. Hence the paper will only discuss the data for the well-defined category of thematic verbal nouns which function as an agent noun or adjective and which stand in a compound whose first element is a noun or an adverb (e.g. *punaḥsará-* "running back", *evāvadá-* "speaking so, speaking the truth").

3. The Data from R̥V Maṇḍalas I-IX

In the tables below, the evidence from *R̥V* Maṇḍalas I-IX for these thematic verbal nouns as second elements of compounds is divided into two formal sub-categories, first, the cases where the verbal noun shows short *a* vocalism (Table 1) and second, the less numerous cases where it shows long *ā* (Table 2).

Table 1: Second Elements of Compounds with short -*a*- Vocalism in R̥V I-IX

khajaṁkará- "making a battle-din" (I.102.6), *yataṁkará-* "making constraint" (V.34.4), *satrākará-* "always performing" (I.178.4)	*kar-* "do, make", *kr̥ṇóti*
araṁgamá- "coming fittingly" (VI.42.1, VIII.46.17), *makṣuṁgamá-* "coming quickly" (VIII.22.16)	*gam-* "come", *gácchati*
vr̥taṁcayá- "punishing the enemy" (II.21.3)	*cay-* "punish", *cáyate*
kucará- "going about anywhere" (I.154.2), *dhanvacará-* "going about on the plain" (V.36.1)	*car-* "go about", *cárati*
dhanaṁjayá- "winning wealth" (III.42.6 = VIII.45.13, VI.16.15, IX.46.5, IX.84.5)	*jay-* "win", *jáyati*
rathaṁtará- "overcoming chariots" (I.164.25) (x1 *R̥V* X), *druhaṁtará-* "overcoming falsehood" (I.127.3 [x2])	*tari-* "overcome", *tárati*
puraṁdará- "attacking fortresses" (x11)	*dar-* "attack", *daráyati*
puṣṭiṁbhará- "bringing prosperity" (IV.3.7), *vājaṁbhará-* "bringing booty" (I.60.5, IV.11.4) (x1 *R̥V* X), *sahasraṁbhará-* "bringing a thousand(fold)" (II.9.1), *sutaṁbhará-* "bringing the pressed drink" (V.44.13)	*bhar-* "bear", *bhárati*
evāvadá- "speaking so, speaking the truth" (V.44.10)	*vad-* "speak", *vádati*
dhārāvará- "loving streams" (II.34.1)	*var*[i]*-* "choose", *vr̥ṇīté*
tadvaśá- "wanting that" (II.14.2, II.37.1)	*vaś-* "wish", *váṣṭi*
cakramāsajá- "dragging its wheel" (V.34.6)	*sañj-* "hang", *sájati*
janaṁsahá- "conquering people" (II.21.3)	*sah-* "conquer", *sáhate*
aśvahayá- "driving horses" (IX.96.2) (x1 *R̥V* X)	*hay-* "incite, drive", *hinóti*, ptcple *háyantā* (*R̥V* I.11.18)

Table 2: Second Elements of Compounds with long -*ā*- Vocalism in ṚV I-IX

brahmakārá- "making a sacred formula" (VI.29.4)	*kar-* "do, make", *kr̥ṇóti*
vr̥trakhādá- "injuring Vr̥tra" (III.45.2, III.51.9) (x1 *ṚV* X)	*khād-* "tear at, consume", *khā́dhati*
udagrābhá- "holding water" (IX.97.15), *grāvagrābhá-* "holding the pressing stones" (I.162.5), *tuvigrābhá-* "seizing strongly" (VI.22.5)	*grabhⁱ-* "seize", *gr̥bhāyáti, gr̥bhṇā́ti*
nakṣaddābhá- "harming the one who approaches" (VI.22.2)	*dabh-* "deceive", *dabhnóti*
kṣīrapāká- "cooked in milk" (VIII.77.10)	*pac-* "cook", *pácati*
hiraṇyapāvá- "purifying gold" (IX.86.43)	*pavⁱ-* "purify", *pūnā́ti, pávate*
tuvibādhá- "oppressing strongly" (I.36.6)	*bādh-* "oppress", *bā́dhate*
udavāhá- "conveying water" (I.38.9, V.58.3), *yūpavāhá-* "conveying the sacrificial post" (I.162.6)	*vah-* "convey", *váhati*
sarvaśāsá- "ruling all" (V.44.4)	*śās-* "instruct", *śā́sti*
vrātasāhá- "conquering troops" (VI.75.9) *satrāsāhá-* "conquering completely" (II.21.3)	*sah-* "conquer", *sáhate*

4. Additional Data from ṚV Maṇḍala X and the AV

The data for new compounds that are first attested in the late *ṚV* and *AV*[3] is likewise divided into two formal sub-categories according to vocalism. It is immediately apparent that some new forms are similar to those found in the earlier *ṚV*, but others differ and, above all, new forms with *ā* vocalism are more numerous than those with *a*.

[3] The *Atharvaveda* evidence is gathered primarily from Whitney (1881) for the Śaunaka recension (*ŚS*), and from the books of the Paippalāda recension (*PS*) that have been recently edited on the basis of both the Orissa and Kashmiri manuscripts (Zehnder 1999, Lubotsky 2002, Griffiths 2009). Forms attested in other parts of *PS* have been identified by searching the text of *PS* 1-15 published by Dipak Bhattacharya (1997), and from my own editorial work on *PS* 11. Hence, the *PS* evidence should not yet be regarded as 100 per cent complete, but the outlines of the *AV* picture are clear.

Table 3: Second Elements of Compounds with short *a* Vocalism in R̥V X and AV

abhayaṁkará- "making freedom from fear" (*R̥V* X.152.2, *PS* II.88.4), *kācitkará-* "performing everything" (*R̥V* X.86.13), *divākará-* "day-maker, the sun" (*ŚS* IV.10.5, XIII.2.34), *kiṁkará-* "attendant" (*ŚS* VIII.8.22)	*kar-* "do, make"
yudhiṁgamá- "going to battle" (*ŚS* XX.128.11)	*gam-* "come"
ajagará- "python" ("goat-swallower") (*ŚS* IV.15.7, IV.15.9, XI.2.25, *PS* V.7.6)	*gar*[i]*-* "swallow"
araṁgará- ?"singing fitly" (*ŚS* XX.135.13)	*gar*[i]*-* "praise, sing"
bhuvanacyavá- "setting the world in motion" (*R̥V* X.103.9)	*cyav-* "move"
vr̥ṣabhará- "bearing men" (*R̥V* X.63.3), *hariṁbhará-* "bearing the golden one" (*R̥V* X.96.4), *viśvaṁbhará-* "bearing everything" (*ŚS* II.16.5, XII.1.6), *śakaṁbhará-* ?"dung-carrier" (*ŚS* V.22.4)	*bhar-* "bear, carry"

Table 4: Second Elements of Compounds with long *ā* Vocalism in R̥V X and AV

medhākārá- "making wisdom" (*R̥V* X.91.8), *yutkārá-* "making battle" (*R̥V* X.103.2), *rathakārá-* "chariot-maker" (*ŚS* III.5.6), *jyotiṣkāra-* "making light" (*PS* I.86.1), *sphātikāra-* "making prosperity", *bahukāra-* "making plenty" (*PS* VIII.18.9)	*kar-* "do, make"
amitrakhādá- "injuring enemies" (*R̥V* X.152.1)	*khād-* "tear at, consume"
hastagrābhá- "taking the hand" (*R̥V* X.18.8, *ŚS* XVIII.3.12), *urugrābhá-* "broad-gripping" (*ŚS* XI.9.12), *śūrpagrāhī́-* "holding the winnowing-fan" (*ŚS* XI.3.4), *kūṭagrāha-* "holding the plough-end" (*PS* XI.15.1), *hanugrābha-* "seizing the jaw" (*PS* XI.2.9)	*gra(b)h*[i]*-* "seize"
odanapāka- "cooking rice, cooker of rice" (*PS* V.13.3)	*pac-* "cook"
ripravāhá- "carrying (away) impurity" (*R̥V* X.16.9), *vipathavāhá-* "drawer of a wagon" (*ŚS* XV.2.1-4), *śatavāhī́-* "conveying a hundred" (*ŚS* V.17.12), *havyavāhá-* "conveying the oblation" (*ŚS* XVIII.4.1)	*vah-* "convey"
abhimātiṣāhá- "conquering opponents" (*R̥V* X.83.4, *ŚS* XX.2.1), *amitrasāhá-* "conquering enemies" (*ŚS* I.20.4)	*sah-* "conquer"
balihārá- "carrying tribute" (*ŚS* XI.1.20), *aghahārá-* "evil carrier" (*ŚS* VI.66.1), *rasahārī-* "taking (away) sap", *sphātihārī-* "taking (away) prosperity" (*PS* II.91.4)	*har-* "take, carry"

5. Rhythmical Variants?

In the formal sub-category with short *a* (type *vājaṁbhará-*) one of the most salient features is the frequent accusative inflection on the first element of the compound. These inflected first elements are not a sign of archaism as they are totally absent from the corresponding class in Old Iranian and in other branches of IE.[4] Such inflections clearly serve a metrical purpose as they create a heavy syllable which can make a long compound of this sort fit the scheme of a Jagatī cadence (*khajaṁkará-*, *yataṁkará-*, *janaṁsahá-* appear in such a position) or make it usable as first word of any verse-line, where without the accusative inflection there would be a succession of four light syllables (e.g. first word in a Triṣṭubh line: *vr̥taṁcayá-*, *dhanaṁjayá-*, *sutaṁbhará-*). Hajnal (1994: 208-10) builds on such observations and suggests that this whole category of compounds conform to a set of rhythmical patterns, and that the appearance of a long or short vowel in the root syllable of the verbal noun depends on the quantities in the rest of the compound. According to Hajnal's account, in cases where an accusative inflection in *-m* is not possible for the first element, verbal nouns with a long radical vowel supply the necessary heavy syllable, e.g. *udagrābhá-* "holding water" (*udán-* n.). However, it is not possible that either metrical licence or rhythmical laws governing quantities — for which there is no other evidence in OIA — can explain all the variations. Hajnal is obliged to postulate a large number of rhythmical patterns, and even then there are exceptions. For instance, why are *aśvahayá-* "driving horses" and *dhanvacará-* "going about the plain" possible if *brahmakārá-* "making a sacred formula" demands vowel lengthening in the second element? Furthermore a number of *R̥V* X and *AV* examples show no alternations of quantity at all, e.g. *vr̥ṣabhará-* "bearing men", *ajagará-* "goat-swallower", *medhākārá-* "making wisdom", *jyotiṣkāra-* "making light". While it is clear that the *R̥V* poets' choice of compound was influenced by metre, there is also no doubt that verbal nouns such as *-kará-* and *-kārá-* had a linguistic reality beyond R̥gvedic verse as they were productively extended to form new compounds in the *AV* and also both variants occur in non-metrical Vedic texts

[4] Wackernagel *AiGr* II.1: 45-46 suggested that OIA extended the possibility of clarifying the syntactic relations between the elements of compounds by means of a case inflection on the first member to a greater extent than other branches of IE.

(e.g. *mayaskará- VS* 16.41, *karmakāra- TB* 3.11.10.3, *mahādyutikāra- TA* 10.1.7b, *garbhakāra- VaitS* 48.17, *kumbhakāra- VaikhGS* 41.12, and, less frequently, *karmakara- VaikhGS* 42.14, *karaskara- BaudhGS* 15.30).

6. Discussion of Forms with Short *a* (type *vājaṁbhará-*)

The two elements of some very frequent compounds of the *vājaṁbhará*-type are reflected elsewhere in the *R̥V* by collocations of finite verb + object:

vājaṁbhará- : *vā́jam bharati* "brings booty" (IV.16.16, IV.17.9)
sahasraṁbhará- : *indra sahásram ā́ bhara* "O Indra, bring a thousand" (VIII.78.1)
dhanaṁjayá- : *jayati sáṁ dhánāni* "he wins riches" (IV.50.9)

In addition a high proportion of the second elements correspond in vocalism to the verb's present stem, most often a Class I present (*vājaṁbhará-*: *bhára-*, *dhanaṁjayá-*: *jáya-*, *dhanvacará-* : *cára-*, *evāvadá-*: *váda-*, etc.). Hence from a synchronic perspective most possess a deverbative character which is no different from that of *R̥V* compounds such as *valaṁrujá-* "breaking the cave" (*ruj-*, *rujáti*), *agnimindhá-* "kindling the sacred fire" (*idh-*, *indháte*), *viśvaminvá-* "moving everything" (*inv-*, *ínvati*), *dhiyaṁjinvá-* "enlivening thought" (*jinv-*, *jínvati*). In the latter cases the verbal noun's recent origin is clear because it is based on a present stem that originated via a process of thematicization that took place within historical OIA (cf. *inóti*, *inváti*). As many of the compounds of the *vājaṁbhará-* type are hapax legomena in the *R̥V* and never occur again in Vedic, it appears likely that some were created recently on the basis of the verb's present stem in exactly the same way that *viśvaminvá-* must have been created. Additional confirmation that a synchronic process of deverbative derivation existed in the early *R̥V* language is provided by *atipārayá-* "making cross beyond" (*R̥V* VI.47.7) which can only be based on the present *pāráyati* "makes cross".

Such considerations indicate that even the compounds with archaic-looking verbal nouns as their second element need to be examined critically before they can be used for the purposes of historical linguistic reconstruction. The category has often been treated as if every *R̥V* form must represent the reflex of an IE proto-form, but some probably do not much predate the *R̥V*, let alone descend from forms of the type **-bhoró-* in PIE. For instance, the verbal noun of *vr̥taṁcayá-* is from an IE root (**ku̯ei̯* "punish") but its initial *c-* points to recent derivation from the present *cáyate*, not a form continuing

PIE*$k^{u̯}$*oi̯o-*. It and other hapax legomena (such as *janaṁsahá-* which shows a second element *-sahá-* rather than more frequent *-sāhá-* and occurs in the same verse as a compound in *-sāhá-*) could even represent new creations by the *R̥V* poets who were able to derive new compounds after the analogy of older models (*dhanvacará-*, *vājaṁbhará-*) from the verb's present stem. On the basis of the OIA evidence alone it is possible to conclude that this formal sub-category contains various layers of forms belonging to different chronological periods, and this impression is supported by the details of the comparative evidence from Old Iranian.

7. The Comparative Evidence of Avestan and Old Persian

The Old Iranian comparative evidence indicates that a sub-category with the same formal shape, except for the lack of first elements with accusative inflection, must have existed at least during the common IIr. period. Just as in the *R̥V*, the verbal nouns with short *a* vocalism represent the most frequent type in Old Iranian, and some exact word equations can be observed.

Table 5: Second Elements of Compounds with short *-a-* in Old Iranian

frašō.kara- "making wonderful", *maēγō.kara-* "making clouds", *raθakara-* "forming a chariot", *raēθβiš.kara-* m. "mixture-maker", etc. (YAv.); *dāraniyakara-* m. "gold worker", *hamaranakara-* m. "battle-maker", *zurakara-* m. "evil-doer" (OP)	*kar-* "make"
t̰baēšō.tara- "overcoming enmity" (YAv.)	*tar*^{i}- "overcome, go over"
zaoθrō.bara- "libation-bearer", *nəmō.bara-* "bearing homage", *gaδauuara-* (*-uuara- < -βara-) "club-bearing", *gaošāuuara-* "wearing earrings", *sruuara-* (< *srūβara-*) "horn-bearing" (YAv.); *arštibara-* "spear-bearer", *vaçabara-* "mace-bearer", *takabara-* "wearing the petasos" (OP)	*bar-* "bring"
drujim.vana- "conquering the Lie" (YAv.)	*van-* "conquer"
mašiiō.vaŋha- "clothing men" (YAv.)	*vah-* "wear"
mazdā.vara- "choosing Mazda" (OAv.)	*var*^{i}- "choose"

Table 6: Second Elements of Compounds with long -*ā*- in Old Iranian

nauuāza- "boatman", *gauuāza*- "cow-goad" (YAv.)[5]	*az*- "drive"
ašanāsa- "attaining truth", *ahu.nāsa*- "attaining life", *vahišta.nāsa*- "attaining the best" (YAv.)[6]	*nas*- "attain"
nasupāka- "cooking dead matter"[7], *uruzdipāka*- "cooking entrails" (YAv.)	*pac*- "cook"
asabāra- "horse-borne, horse-rider" (OP)	*bar*- "bear"

Word-equations with some of the *R̥V* verbal nouns make it possible to reconstruct IIr.**-kará-,*-cará-, *-tarHá-, *-bhará-, *-varHá-*. Among this group **-kará* and **-varHá-* do not correspond to thematic present stems but rather to nasal presents (Vedic *kr̥ṇóti*, Younger Avestan *kərənaoiti*, OP *kunautiy*; Vedic *vr̥ṇīté*, Old Avestan *vərəṇtē*). Hence the whole subcategory with short *a* vocalism cannot have been derived from present stems of the verb during the common IIr. period. On the other hand, the agreement in vocalism between some of the IIr. verbal nouns such as **-cará-* and **-bhará-* and the corresponding IIr. thematic presents (**cárati, *bhárati*) may have provided the starting point for an expansion of this class based on present stems of the verb, which resulted in a deverbative character by the early OIA stage. There is no recoverable explanation for why short *a* vocalism was regular for this class of thematic verbal nouns already in IIr., but it must be stressed that, if they descend ultimately from IE forms with **o* vocalism, the problem belongs to the remoter prehistoric period between the IE parent language and the intermediate ancestor IIr., and is not one that can be solved either within OIA or Iranian.[8] Short *a* vocalism is also regular

---

[5] -*āza*- could show lengthening of its vowel at the compound boundary (Wackernagel's Dehnungsgesetz).

[6] The vowel quantity shown by -*nāsa*- may not be original because long vocalism has spread throughout forms of the corresponding verb, cf. de Vaan (2003: 100, 181).

[7] Once attested ablative singular *nasupakāt̰* shows secondary shortening according to de Vaan (2003: 137, 159).

[8] All the individual forms that may be reconstructed for common IIr. have the phonological shape **-Cará-* or **-CarHá-* and this fact appears at first sight to support the hypothesis first proposed by Kuryłowicz (1956: 330) and repeated by Hajnal (1994: 208, 218-19) according to which **-Cārá-* < PIE **-Coró-* was remodelled to **-Cará-* on the analogy of **-Cará-* < **-CarHá-* < PIE **-CorHó-*, after the post-consonantal laryngeal was lost. However, →

for the simple uncompounded action nouns with accent on the root, e.g. *bhára-* m. "act of carrying away (booty), battle", *dábha-* m. "harm", *váśa-* m. "wish, will". For this category too the Old Iranian evidence indicates that the short vocalism must date at least from the IIr. period.[9] If it is correct that both the IIr. action nouns and agent nouns ultimately reflect associated IE forms of the type **bhóro-* and **-bhoró-* (cf. Greek -φόρος and -φόρος < *-φόρος), possibly the short *a* vocalism that is regular for both classes (simple action noun **bhára-*/compounded agent noun **-bhará-*) has one and the same prehistoric explanation.[10]

8. Discussion of Forms with Long *ā* (Type *brahmakārá-*)

The employment of forms of the *brahmakārá-* type in *ṚV* I-IX is quite limited, especially if the forms with second element *-khādá-*, *-bādhá-*, *-śāsá-* are excluded because they may be recent deverbative forms and owe their vocalism to the invariable long vocalism of the corresponding verb. For the rest of this sub-category two distributional facts are to be noted:

→ would it have been possible to generalise **-Cará*-type forms with short *a* vocalism already in common IIr.? Such a chronological assumption is necessary to account for e.g. *-kará-* and *-b(h)ará-* which are shared by both branches, but would not the inherited laryngeal in e.g. **-tarHá-* have still been present throughout the common IIr. period? Views may differ on this point of historical phonology, but a further difficulty is why *aniṭ* roots would have followed the analogy of *seṭ* roots rather than vice versa. The much greater frequency of the verbal nouns from **kṛ-* and **bhṛ-* in particular casts some doubt on such an analogical explanation as it might be expected that this pair would have served as the model for the roots which once ended in a laryngeal rather than vice versa.

9 Word equations such as *ṚV máda-* "intoxication" : Old Avestan *mada-*; *ṚV bhága-* "action of allotting" (also personified as god Bhága) : OP and Younger Avestan *baga-* "god", and also Avestan forms such as *taka-* m. "act of running" indicate that for the action nouns short *a* vocalism was already established in the common IIr. period. *ṚV* forms with long *ā*, e.g. *jā́na-* n. "birth", are mostly innovations.

10 Alternatively the IE reconstruction may not be correct or at least not applicable to IIr. For instance, it is suggested by Lubotsky (1988: 70) that the **bhóro-/*-bhoró-* distribution was not a law of PIE but merely a tendency that was developed in some branches but not others.

1. There is a preponderance of compounds whose meaning is associated with ritual.
2. The rest are concentrated in *R̥V* Maṇḍala VI Triṣṭubh hymns to Indra from the Bharadvājas.

At first sight it looks as if we may be dealing with forms that belong to particular registers or dialects of the earliest stage of OIA, and we need to ask whether they are archaisms or innovations. *R̥V* X and the *AV* show that some verbal nouns with long *ā* vocalism were extremely productive in agent noun function, and formed many new compounds which in meaning belong to more popular spheres of culture such as agriculture, e.g. *sphātikāra-* "making prosperity", *bahukāra-* "making plenty", *śūrpagrāhī́-* "holding the winnowing-fan", *kūṭagrāha-* "holding the plough-end", *vipathavāhá-* "drawer of a wagon". Apart from *-hārá-* from the root *hr̥-*, which does not occur anywhere in the early *R̥V*, it is precisely the same verbal nouns which provide the second element for several agent noun compounds in the early *R̥V* (*-kāra-*, *-grā(b)ha-*, *-vāhá-*, *sāhá-*) that go on forming new compounds in the late *R̥V* and *AV*. Thus two possibilities need to be considered: either these second elements are old in the early *R̥V* and take on a new lease of life or they are innovations which start to appear in the early *R̥V* and then gain ground. In order to decide between these alternatives the individual history of each form must be examined.

-vāhá- and *-sāhá-* have often been traced back to IE **-u̯oǵhó-*, **-soǵhó-* and compared to Greek *-ϝοχός and *-οχός.[11] The explanation of *-vāhá-* as a relic finds chronological support from within OIA since *udavāhá-* "conveying water" (I.38.9, V.58.3), *yūpavāhá-* "conveying the sacrificial post" (I.162.6) are found in *R̥V*, whereas *udvahá-* "one who conveys upward", which could be based on present *váhati*, is first attested in the *AV*. *R̥V vrātasāhá-* (VI.75.9), *satrāsāhá-* (II.21.3) could be older than *janaṁsahá-* (also II.21.3, cf. *sáhate*), although all three are found in the *R̥V* Family Books. On the other hand, there is also evidence that the

[11] But the Avestan compound *xšuuiβi.vāza-* which is normally translated "flying swiftly" is more likely to be a bahuvrīhi "whose flight ('conveyance') is swift" in view of the fact that *xšuuiβi-* is a Caland *i*-stem corresponding to simple adjective *xšuuiβra-* "swift": cf. *xšuuiβi.išu-* "whose arrow is swift".

apparent productivity of *-vāhá-* and *-sāhá-* in fact results from the thematicization of the root nouns *-vāh* and *-sāh* which appear as the second element of numerous compounds in the R̥V. On the distribution of the root nouns see Scarlata 1999: 473-80, 599-613. The early R̥V only has *havyavā́h-* "conveying the oblation" (very frequent) and *abhimātiṣā́h-* "conquering opponents", but *AV* has *havyavāhá-* and R̥V X *abhimātiṣāhá-*. Once occurring R̥V *satrāsāhá-* (II.21.3) stands beside more frequent *satrāsā́h-* (Scarlata 1999: 611-12). *-vāhá-* and *-sāhá-* illustrate the dangers of invoking an IE reconstruction for every individual Vedic form where it might seem plausible from a phonological point of view without examining its synchronic situation. Although R̥V *udavāhá-, yūpavāhá-* (both ritual terms) may contain inherited thematic verbal nouns, the later forms result from a morphological innovation rather than an extension of such relics.

A more certain inheritance is *-pāká-* "cooking, one who cooks", which only occurs in compounds to do with ritual cooking, R̥V *kṣīrapāká-* "cooked in milk", *PS odanapāka-* "cooking rice". This second element -*pāká-* can be reconstructed for IIr. by comparing Younger Avestan *nasupāka-, uruzdipāka-* "cooking solid dead-matter", "cooking liquid dead-matter" (with reference to a fire used for evil ritual purposes). Furthermore, *-pāká-* can be identified without problem as the reflex of IE **-pok^{u}ó-* which is also continued in compounds in other branches of IE, cf. Mycenaean *a-to-po-qo* "baker", Greek (metathesized) ἀρτοκόπος "baker". The alternation between active and passive value for the verbal noun that is seen in the two early Vedic compounds is characteristic of such IE verbal nouns, cf. Greek ἱπποτρόφος "horse-rearing" and ὀρειτρόφος "reared in the mountain". This example provides the best evidence we have that at least some of the IIr. thematic verbal nouns considered here may continue IE **o*-grade forms where Brugmann's Law operated as expected.

In the case of *-kārá-* there is the difficulty that *-kará-* with short *a* vocalism builds more compounds in the early R̥V (*khajaṁkará-* "making a battle-din", *yataṁkará-* "making constraint", *satrākará-* "altogether active") and it is the latter form which corresponds to the frequent second element *-kara-* in Old Iranian. If *-kārá-* represents a relic form (<IE **-k^{u}oró-*), it must have coexisted alongside "regular" **-kará-* in IIr. just as in Vedic. However, since Old Iranian does not possess any

compounds in *-kāra-* this hypothesis is doubtful.[12] On the other hand, *-kārá-* can be explained as an OIA innovation, but in order to demonstrate this it is necessary first to consider *-grābhá-* whose case is clearer since there is only one form of this agent noun in early Vedic. Moreover, it has no Iranian cognate.

The verbal noun *-grā(b)há-* occurs in a range of functions in OIA. These may be illustrated by:

> *grābhá-* m. "handful, grasp" (*R̥V* VIII.81.1, IX.106.3)
> *udagrābhá-* "holding water" (*R̥V* IX.97.15), *grāvagrābhá-* "holding the pressing stones" (*R̥V* I.162.5), *tuvigrābhá-* "seizing strongly" (*R̥V* VI.22.5)
> *nāmagrā(b)há-* m. "action of seizing the name" (*ŚS* X.1.12, *PS* VII.8.6, XVI.36.2)
> *grā(b)há-* "one who seizes" (*ŚS* XIV.1.38, *PS* IX.10.9, XVII.37.8, XVIII.4.7)
> *udgrābhá-* m. (*Vājasaneyī Saṁhitā*, *Taittirīya Saṁhitā*) "action of holding upwards"

Both *-kārá-* and *-grā(b)há-* possesses a dual function in compounds of two nouns as they can have the value of an action noun (*namaskārá-* m. "action of making obeisance", *nāmagrā(b)há-* m. "action of seizing the name") in addition to that of an agent noun/adjective (*brahmakārá-* "who makes a sacred formula", *udagrābhá-* "who holds water"). The function as an agent noun/adjective accords with an inherited IE distributional pattern, but the function as an action noun represents an OIA innovation. A new class of such OIA action noun compounds first appears in the early *R̥V*, but it has no equivalent in Old Iranian (Table 7).

Table 7: An Innovation of OIA: Action Noun Compounds in R̥V I-IX

indrahavá- m. "invocation of Indra" (IX.96.1)	*havi-* "call"
jīvayājá- m. "offering of living (animal)" (I.31.15)	*yaj-* "offer"
r̥tavāká- m. "act of speaking the truth" (IX.113.2), *joṣavāká-* m. "act of speaking what is pleasing" (VI.59.4), *namovāká-* m. "speech of homage" (VIII.35.23)[13]	*vac-* "speak"
sahasrasāvá- m. "pressing of a thousand, thousand(fold) Soma-pressing" (III.53.7 = VII.103.10), *prātaḥsāvá-* m. "morning Soma-pressing" (III.28.1, III.52.4) (x1 *R̥V* X)	*sav-* "press"

[12] Middle Iranian *-kār-/-gār-* might possibly provide some support. However, its extension as a suffix makes it difficult to tell precisely what Old Iranian word is involved.

[13] *dhāravāká-* 5.44.5, although its accent is similar, appears to be an adjective with bahuvrīhi meaning "having the speech of streams".

By the late *R̥V* and *AV* many new formations of this type are attested and it is notable how it develops via particular semantic fields:

Table 8: An Innovation of OIA: Action Noun Compounds in R̥V X and AV

namaskārá- m. "performance of obeisance" (*ŚS* IV.39.9), *vaṣaṭkārá-* m. "performance (of the ritual) call *vaṣaṭ*" (*ŚS* XI.7.9, XIII.1.15, XIII.4.26), *svadhākārá-* "performance of (the ritual call) *svadhā*" (*ŚS* XII.4.32, XV.14.7), *svāhākārá-* "performance of *svāhā*" (*ŚS* XV.14.8), *srukkārá-* "making of a swallowing noise" (*ŚS* IX.6.22), *hiṁkārá-* "making of the sound *hin*" (*ŚS* XI.7.5), *ailabakārá-* m. "making of *ailaba-* (Rudra's howling)" (*ŚS* XI.2.30),	*kar-* "do, make"
nāmagrāhá- m. "seizing of the name" (*ŚS* X.1.12, *PS* VII.8.6, XVI.36.2)	*gra(b)hⁱ-* "seize"
sūktavāká- m. "recitation of a hymn" (*R̥V* X.88.7, X.88.8)	*vac-* "speak"
pāpavādá- m. "evil speech" (*ŚS* X.3.6)	*vad-* "say"
kṣudhāmārá- m. "death by hunger", *tr̥ṣṇāmārá-* m. "death by thirst" (*ŚS* IV.17.6, IV.17.7)	*mar-* "die"

The verbal nouns that form the second elements of such compounds show long *-ā*-vocalism (with one early exception, *indrahavá-*). If *-kārá-* and *-grābhá-* originated in such formations, their long *ā* vocalism could be attributed to the morphology of this new type of OIA compound.

Expressions such as *R̥V* I.23.12 *haskārā́d vidyútas pari* which may mean "from the has-noise-making of the lightning" (action noun) or "from the has-noise-making lightning" (agent noun, used as adjective) illustrate how the same form could easily switch between the two functions. However, it would be necessary to assume that compounds with *-kārá-* and *-grābhá-* as their second element were already used as action nouns by the time of the early *R̥V*, and this is not certain from the chronology of the attestations (the ambiguous *haskārá-* occurs in a hymn from the family collection of Medhātithi Kāṇva in *R̥V* Maṇḍala I, and this is the only piece of evidence in *R̥V* Maṇḍalas I-IX). On the other hand, there can be no doubt that the extension of *-kārá-* and *-grābhá-* in agent noun function went hand in hand with their productivity in creating action-noun compounds of the type *namaskārá-* m. "performance of obeisance", *vaṣaṭkārá-* m. "performance (of the ritual) call *vaṣaṭ*".

If, however, the second elements *-kārá-* and *-grābhá-* originated first of all in compounds with agent noun value, it is still possible that they represent OIA innovations. An alternative possibility is that *-kārá-* and *-grābhá-* in composition should be traced to the simple nouns *kārá-* m. "battle, decisive action" (*R̥V* III.49.3, IV.1.14, V.29.8, etc.) and *grābhá-* m. "handful, grasp" (*R̥V* VIII.81.1, IX.106.3).[14] That the latter form could be at the origin of the long vocalism seen in *udagrābhá-* "holding water", *grāvagrābhá-* "holding the pressing stones" is suggested by a third compound that occurs in the *R̥V*, *tuvigrābhá-* "seizing strongly" (*R̥V* VI.22.5). *R̥V tuvigrābhá-* and *AV urugrābhá-* could represent old bahuvrīhis containing the simple noun *grābhá-* "grasp". In the early *R̥V* when the first element of a bahuvrīhi is a disyllabic nominal stem in *-i* or *-u* the second element is frequently accented, cf. *R̥V tuvidyumná-* "whose splendour is strong". But in the later Saṁhitās this accentuation is replaced by the normal bahuvrīhi-type accentuation on the first element (Wackernagel *AiGr* II.1: 296). Because of its accent an original bahuvrīhi such as *tuvigrābhá-* "whose grasp is strong" could have been reinterpreted as a determinative compound "grasping strongly". Such reinterpretations would have been particularly favoured as accentual patterns for bahuvrīhis with first element *tuvi-*, *uru-*, *puru-*, etc., changed. This change is already under way in the *R̥V*, cf. *tuvimaghá-* (*R̥V* V.33.6) but *tuvī́magha-* (*R̥V* VIII.61.18, VIII.81.2). The reinterpretation of the forms showing the old accentual pattern as agent nouns could have provided the starting point for the extension of a second element *-grābhá-* in agent noun or adjectival function. At a later stage the numerous new agent noun compounds in *-grā(b)há-*, e.g. *AV hanugrābha-* "seizing the jaw" (of an illness like tetanus) led to the backformation of a new simple noun with agent noun function, *grā(b)há-* m. "seizer" (a demon of illness in the *AV*).

[14] The long *ā* vocalism seen in these two nouns is exceptionless for this class of simple verbal nouns with accent on the thematic vowel which show a passive or intransitive value of the root and often develop a concrete sense, cf., e.g. *bhārá-* m. "burden, load", *bhāgá-* m. "what is allotted, share" (Avestan *bāga-*). This IIr. class may tentatively be compared with the Greek type exemplified by adjective *λοιπός* "left over, remaining", or noun *ὁλκός* "furrow, what is drawn". In other words, some forms may represent a remnant of the IE uncompounded *bhoró-type, but the class has expanded particularly within OIA. This category is discussed further in my paper mentioned in footnote 1.

A parallel historical development would also be conceivable in the case of *-kārá-*. A simple noun *kārá-* m. "decisive act, battle" is relatively frequent in the early *R̥V*, and in origin it probably represents a verbal noun "thing done, deed, action" from *kr̥-* "do, make" but it has developed in meaning.[15] If the earlier meaning "thing done, action" was preserved in old bahuvrīhis such as **purukārá-* "whose deeds are many", this could have been reinterpreted as "doing much", a possible starting point for the spread of second element *-kārá-* with agent noun value.

hārá- might conceivably represent a replacement for earlier **-bhārá-*, given the contamination between forms of the verbs *hr̥-* and *bhr̥-* that develops in post-*R̥V* OIA. However, although Old Persian *asabāra-* "horse-borne" probably preserves IE **-bhoró-* in agent noun function with a passive sense, a second-element agent noun **-bhārá-* does not occur in the *R̥V*. It must be stressed in this connection that Vedic *-bhārá-* "bearer, who bears", which is quoted in some handbooks of IE, is a ghost-form. An uncompounded verbal noun *bhārá-* m. "burden, load" occurs at *R̥V* III.56.2, IV.5.6, VII.37.7, I.31.3, I.152.3, and the *R̥V* compounds in *-bhāra-* are both bahuvrīhis, as their accentuation shows: *bhū́ribhāra-* means "having a large load, much burdened" (*R̥V* I.164.13, cf. *R̥V* *bhū́rivāra-* "having much treasure") and *muṣkábhāra-* (*R̥V* X.102.4) means "having a load of testicles" (description of Indra).

Therefore it seems more likely that *-hārá-/-hārī́-* is indeed a late formation, as its distribution suggests, and that it should be explained via developments within OIA of the sort already discussed in connection with the nouns *-kārá-* and *-grābhá-*. A prefixed action noun *pratīhārá-* "response" (action of taking back) is attested in the *AV* (*ŚS* XI.7.12), and there is a pattern according to which such prefixed action nouns[16] stand beside compounds of two nouns also with action-noun

---

15 Mayrhofer (1986-2001: 1.340), cf. Renou's discussion (1964: 103-04) of this difficult word. *R̥V* 1.112.1 *kārá-* may represent the cognate of OP *kāra-* m. "army, people".

16 Prefixed action noun forms with long *ā* vocalism increase in *R̥V* X and the *AV*. Originally the distribution of quantities in this category may have resulted from the operation of Brugmann's Law, cf. *āhavá-* "challenge" from *hav^{i}-/hū-* "call" versus *āhāvá-* "bucket" from *hav-/hu* "pour", and *prasavá-* "impulse" versus *sāvá-* "pressing", examples first cited by Kuryłowicz (1927).

value. The latter class probably developed from the former, cf. *R̥V upavākā́-*, Avestan *frauuāka-*, but the type *namovākā́-*, with a noun as first element, is peculiar to OIA:

Table 9: OIA Prefixed Action Nouns beside Action Nouns Composed of Two Nominal Stems

R̥V āhavá-, vihavá-	*R̥V indrahavá-* "invocation of Indra"
R̥V adhivākā́-, upavākā́-	*R̥V r̥tavākā́-* "speech of truth", *joṣavākā́-* "speech of pleasure", *namovākā́-* "speech of homage"
R̥V atiyājá- (?), *anuyājá-, prayājá-*	*R̥V jīvayājá-* m. "offering of a living (animal)"
R̥V saṁvādá-	*AV pāpavādá-* "evil speech"
AV pramārá-	*AV kṣudhāmārá-* "death by hunger", *tr̥ṣṇāmārá-* "death by thirst"

Thus a compound of two nominal stems *balihārá-* could have been created beside a prefixed action noun such as *pratīhārá-* "response", and *balihārá-* might be expected in the *AV* language to have possessed both the action-noun value "action of bringing tribute" and the agent-noun value "who brings tribute" (the sense attested at *ŚS* XI.1.20).

This discussion has so far passed over the early *R̥V* hapax legomena *hiraṇyapāvá-* "purifying gold" (*R̥V* IX.86.43) and *nakṣaddābhá-* "harming the one who approaches" (*R̥V* VI.22.2). Both are likely to represent nonce creations for the sake of the particular hymn where they occur. In the case of *hiraṇyapāvá-* "purifying gold", it may be noted that all *R̥V* nominal compounds with first element *hiraṇya-* have a second element that begins with a heavy syllable and **hiraṇyapavá-* would present metrical difficulties. It is also in a ritual context (*R̥V* Maṇḍala IX) since the gold is Soma and the agent noun compound describes the priests who purify him. *nakṣaddābhá-* with its unique present-participle first element may provide a rhyming counterpart to *tuvigrābhá-* in a Bharadvāja hymn to Indra which abounds in unusual epithets (*tuvikūrmí-, rabhodā́-*, etc.), and explicitly instructs "shake him all round by means of your very new poem" (*táṁ vo dhiyā́ návyasyā . . . paritaṁsayádhyai R̥V* VI.22.7ab).

The results reached in this section suggest that the formal sub-category with long *ā* vocalism like the sub-category with short *a* is composed of a mixture of forms, one or two of which may be of great antiquity (*-pākā́-, -vāhá-*), but the rest of which are likely to represent new creations of OIA that were consequential to developments in other categories involving thematic verbal nouns (especially the development of compounds with action noun value of the type *namaskārá-*, *namovākā́-*). The relic forms are linked to the vocabulary of ritual, a part of the lexicon which might be expected to be conservative and archaic. Verbal nouns such as *-pākā́-* in ritual terms must have escaped the innovation in agent noun compounds that occurred at a stage prior to IIr. and which resulted (for unknown reasons) in short *a* quantity being established as regular for most second element agent nouns.

9. Conclusion

This paper has attempted to reconstruct the development of individual cases by considering the philological details of attestations, etc. instead of relying exclusively on considerations of historical phonology. Hitherto little attention has been paid to the fact that there is a multi-layered category of formations even within the earliest texts, and that some productive processes can be observed that led to changes in the category even between the time of the *R̥V* Family Books and the late *R̥V* and *AV*. It has been suggested here that, despite their archaic appearances, the *vājaṁbharā́-* and *brahmakārá-*type compounds belong to some larger dynamic systems within IIr. and they by no means represent a static class of relic forms. An advantage of this approach is that it turns out to be possible to explain as OIA innovations not only some forms with *ā* vocalism which at first sight look as if they show the effect of Brugmann's Law and continue IE **o*-grade forms (e.g. *-kārá-* "maker", *-hārá-* "taker"), but also others which would contradict Brugmann's Law if interpreted as inheritances (*-grābhá-* "seizer, holder"). Apart from the troublesome question of the uniform short quantity that must be reconstructed for some verbal nouns at an IIr. stage (**-kará-*, **-bhará-* besides *-varHá-*, *-tarHá-* where short quantity would be expected according to Kuryłowicz's version of Brugmann's Law), this early OIA class does not include any forms that indicate that a revision of our understanding of Brugmann's Law is necessary. On the other hand, the prehistoric problem just mentioned may suggest that it is necessary to accept that there are only a very few remnants of the IE type **-bhoró-*, and that the IE starting point should be reconsidered at least as far as IIr. is concerned.

Abbreviations

AV	*Atharvaveda*
BaudhGS	*Baudhāyana Gr̥hyasūtras*
IE	Indo-European
IIr.	Indo-Iranian
OIA	Old Indo-Aryan
OP	Old Persian
PS	*Paippalāda Saṁhitā*
R̥V	*R̥gveda Saṁhitā*
ŚS	*Śaunaka Saṁhitā*
TĀ	*Taittirīya Āraṇyaka*
TB	*Taittirīya Brāhmaṇa*
VaikhGS	*Vaikhānasa Gr̥hyasūtra*
VaitS	*Vaitāna Sūtra*
VS	*Vājasaneyi Saṁhitā*
YAv.	Younger Avestan

References

Bartholomae, Christian, 1904, *Altiranisches Wörterbuch*, Straßburg: Trübner.

Bhattacharya, Dipak, 1997, *The Paippalāda-Saṁhitā of the Atharvaveda*, vol. 1, consisting of the first fifteen Kāṇḍas, Calcutta: Asiatic Society.

Brugman(n), Karl, 1876, "Zur Geschichte der stammabstufenden Declinationen. Erste Abhandlung: Die Nomina auf *-ar-* und *-tar-*." (*Curtius'*) *Studien zur griechischen und lateinischen Grammatik*, **9:** 361-406.

Burrow, Thomas, 1975, "A New Look at Brugmann's Law", *Bulletin of the School of Oriental and African Studies*, **38:** 55-80.

Collinge, Neville, 1985, *The Laws of Indo-European*, Amsterdam/Philadelphia: Benjamins.

de Vaan, Michiel Arnoud Cor, 2003, *The Avestan Vowels*, Amsterdam/New York: Rodopi.

Geldner, Karl Friedrich, 1951, *Der Rig-Veda*, 3 vols., Cambridge, Mass.: Harvard University Press.

Griffiths, Arlo, 2009, *The Paippalāda Saṁhitā of the Atharvaveda*, Kāṇḍas 6 & 7, Groningen: Forsten.

Hajnal, Ivo, 1994, "Das Brugmannsche Gesetz in diachroner Sicht und seine Gültigkeit innerhalb der arischen *a*-Stämme", *Historische Sprachforschung*, **107:** 194-221.

Holst, Jan Henrik, 2004, "Das Brugmannsche Gesetz und sein Bezug zum Winterschen Gesetz", *Historische Sprachforschung*, **117:** 159-78.

Jamison, Stephanie W., 1983, *Function and Form in the -áya-Formations of the Rig-Veda and Atharvaveda*, Göttingen: Vandenhoeck & Ruprecht.

Kümmel, Martin, 2000, *Das Perfekt im Indoiranischen*, Wiesbaden: Reichert.

Kuryłowicz, Jerzy, 1927, "Les effets du ə en indo-iranien", *Prace Filologiczne*, **11:** 201-43.

———, 1956, *L'apophonie en indo-européen*, Wrocław: Polska Akademia Nauk.

Lubotsky, Alexander, 1988, *The System of Nominal Accentuation in Sanskrit and Proto-Indo-European*, Leiden: Brill.

———, 2002, *Atharvaveda-Paippalāda*, Kāṇḍa Five, Cambridge, Mass.: Department of Sanskrit and Indian Studies, Harvard University.

Macdonell, A.A., 1916, *A Vedic Grammar for Students*, Oxford: Oxford University Press.

Mayrhofer, Manfred, 1986-2001, *Etymologisches Wörterbuch des Altindoarischen*, 3 vols., Heidelberg: Winter.

Probert, Philomen, 2006, *Ancient Greek Accentuation: Synchronic Patterns, Frequency Effects, and Prehistory*, Oxford: Oxford University Press.

Renou, Louis, 1964, *Études védiques et pāṇinéennes*, vol. XII, Paris: de Boccard.

Scarlata, Salvatore, 1999, *Die Wurzelkomposita im R̥g-Veda*, Wiesbaden: Reichert.

Volkart, Marianne, 1994, *Zu Brugmanns Gesetz im Altindischen*, Bern: Universität Bern (Institut für Sprachwissenschaft, Arbeitspapier 33).

Wackernagel *AiGr* = Wackernagel, Jacob, and Albert Debrunner, 1896-1957, *Altindische Grammatik*, I: *Lautlehre*, II.1: *Nominalkomposition*, II.2: *Die Nominalsuffixe*, Göttingen: Vandenhoeck & Ruprecht.

Whitney, William Dwight, 1881, *Index Verborum to the Published Text of the Atharva-Veda*, New Haven: American Oriental Society.

Zehnder, Thomas, 1999, *Atharvaveda-Paippalāda*, Buch 2: *Text, Übersetzung, Kommentar*, Idstein: Schulz-Kirschner.

Part 2
Textual Criticism and Text Edition

6

Medhājanana in the Atharvaveda Tradition*

S.S. Bahulkar

ONE who is familiar with the Hindu saṁskāras described in the Gṛhya-Sūtras, which are further elaborated in the commentaries, the Prayoga literature pertaining to those texts, and the medieval religious digests (*nibandha*), knows that the *medhājanana* is a rite to be performed at the birth of a child in order to generate intelligence (*medha*) in that child. It is sometimes combined with another rite called *jātakarman* (ceremony at the time of birth of a child) and sometimes both rites are performed together under the designation *jātakarman*, where the former is a part of the latter.[1] In this ceremony, the father of the newborn child, with his fourth finger and a golden instrument, gives the boy/girl[2] honey and ghee, or simply ghee. Substances such as honey, gold, and ghee are used as they are thought to be conducive to mental health. Some Gṛhya-Sūtras also prescribe sour milk, rice, barley, and whitish black or red hairs of a black bull (Pandey 1949: 74).

---

* I am thankful to my friend, Dr. Andrew Rotman of Smith College, MA, U.S.A. for going through my paper, correcting my English and making useful suggestions.

[1] See *ĀGS* I.15.2; *ŚGS* 1.24.9; *PGS* I.16.3; *HGS* II.3.9; *GGS* II.7.20; *KhGS* II.2.34. The references to these texts are according to Oldenberg 1892: 302.

[2] "Although the grammatically masculine words in the descriptions do not exclude the performance of the ceremonies for a newborn girl, the explicit reference to a boy . . . shows that they . . . were primarily intended for sons" (Gonda 1980: 371). Haradatta, in his commentary on the *Āpastamba-Gṛhya-Sūtra* (*ĀpGS*) 15.1, says that since by the (declined form) *jātam* the masculine is expressly meant, the ceremony called *jātakarman* is meant solely for a male (child), not for a female (*jātam iti puṁliṅgasya vivakṣitatvāt puṁsa evāyaṁ jātakarmākhyaḥ saṁskāraḥ* I *na striyaḥ*).

In the tradition of the *Atharvaveda* (*AV*), domestic rites are described in the *Kauśika-Sūtra* (*KauS*), a major Sūtra text traditionally regarded to be the Gṛhya-Sūtra belonging to the Śaunakīya recension (*śākhā*) of that Veda (*AVŚ*). It is, however, not a Gṛhya-Sūtra in the ordinary sense of the term, as it describes a number of rites such as medical ritual (*bhaiṣajya*), divination (*vijñāna*), Savayajñas, omens and portents (*adbhuta*), and so on that are peculiarly of Ātharvaṇic character.[3]

In the *Kauśika-Sūtra*, the rite of *medhājanana* is mentioned as the first in the series of domestic rites (*KauS* II.1[10].1-15).[4] There are certain rites such as *puṁsavana*, *garbhādhāna*, and *sīmantakarman* that are performed before the birth of a child. These rites have been described in the *KauS* as a part of women's rites (*KauS* 35.1-28). The Gṛhya-Sūtras generally describe the rites in two ways: the transition from studentship to that of marriage or from marriage to that of studentship (Oldenberg 1892: xxv-xxvi).[5] The order of the domestic rites in the *KauS* is different from that found in other Gṛhya-Sūtras. It divides the rites into roughly 21 sections covered in the first 11 adhyāyas — out of a total of 14 — some of which are devoted to specific domestic rites, such as the initiation of a student (adh. 7), marriage (adh. 10), and ancestral rites (adh. 11).[6] It follows a special method of describing

[3] On the basis of stylistic peculiarities and the contents, Bloomfield argues that the *KauS* was composed by more than one author and that it can broadly be divided into two parts, the Atharva-Sūtras and the Gṛhya-Sūtras (Bloomfield 1890: xxi ff.).

[4] In his editio princeps, Bloomfiled divides the text of the *KauS* into kaṇḍikās and sūtras. However, the traditional division is a threefold one: adhyāya, kaṇḍikā, and sūtras. Lanman (1905: 1012) suggests a way to harmonize the two methods that includes the number of adhyāya, the number of kaṇḍikā in that adhyāya, and the number of kaṇḍikā from the beginning. It is, however, better to put the consecutive number of kaṇḍikā given by Bloomfiled into a square bracket, followed by the number of sūtra. The same is adopted here. Cf. Griffiths 2009.

[5] For instance, the *HGS* follows the first order while the other text follows the second. Cf. Müller 1926: 106ff.

[6] *vidhisambandhe 'nena tu kauśikena sājātyena caikaviṁśatividhimantragaṇaṁ pravibhajya vidhiḥ kathitaḥ* (*DB*, p. 4). He then enumerates the 21 topics, beginning with the *śantyudakasaṁhitā* (*KauS* I.9.1) to the *pitṛmedha* (adh. 11). The editors, without warrant, insert one more topic: namely, the *manthāntāni* (*KauS* II.3[12].4) between the *sarvasāmpadāni* (*KauS* II.2[11].11ff.) and the *sāṁmanasyāni* (*KauS* II.3[12].5ff.), and they change the number to 22.

the rites in connection with the hymns that they employ. In the tradition of the *AV*, this Sūtra is therefore called *saṁhitāvidhi* — "(a text describing the employment of) the Saṁhitā in the (respective) rites".

The hymn that is employed in the *medhājanana* is the first one in the Saṁhitā and, therefore, the *medhājanana* is placed first in the order of the rites described in that Sūtra.[7] Then follows the rite of *jātakarman*, where the next hymn, appropriate for the rite, is employed. It occurs as the 30th hymn of the fourth kāṇḍa of the Saṁhitā. While it is not possible here to elaborate upon the methodology adopted by the *KauS* for the employment of the *Śaunaka Saṁhitā* of the *AV* (*AVŚ*), it may be pointed out that the hymn *AVŚ* I.1 has been employed in a variety of rites that do not apparently have a direct relation with the meaning of the hymn. In the introduction to his commentary on the *AVŚ* I.1, Sāyaṇa points out that Kauśika, the author of the *KauS*, has done this in order to show the immeasurable potency (*aparimitavīryatvapradarśanārtham*) of the Atharvavedic mantras.[8] It may, however, be pointed out that among all the rites in which the first hymn is employed, the *medhājanana* is the most relevant to the meaning of the hymn and may be regarded as the primary employment (*viniyoga*) of the hymn concerned.[9]

The substances such as gold and honey that are prescribed by the Gr̥hya-Sūtras have also been mentioned in the *KauS* with respect to the performance of the *jātakarman* (*KauS* 10.16-19). The rite of *medhājanana* described in the *KauS* is, however, peculiar to the Atharvavedic tradition. Accordingly, the rite is to be performed on two occasions: first, at the time of the birth of a child; and second, as a part of the rites to be performed by a student and for the student

---

7 The method adopted by the author of the *KauS* is a combination of what Dārila, the author of the *Bhāṣya* on the *KauS* (*DB*), calls *mantrādhikāra* "(arrangement of sections according to) the order of mantras (in the Saṁhitā)" and *phalādhikāra* "(arrangement of sections according to) the order of topics" (*DB*, pp. 1, 4). For a detailed explanation, see Bahulkar 1994: 27ff.

8 *tad evam ātharvaṇamantrāṇām aparimitavīryatvapradarśanārtham ādimasūktasya vistarataḥ sarveṣu karmasu upalakṣaṇatvena sūtrakr̥tā viniyogo 'bhyadhāyi* | Sāyaṇa's commentary on *AV* I.1; Vishva Bandhu et al. 1960: 32-33.

9 The hymn is also found in the *Paippalāda Saṁhitā* of the *AV* (*AVP* I.6) and the *Maitrāyaṇī Saṁhitā* (*MS* IV.12).

who has approached his teacher to pursue Vedic study. It is quite logical that the rite of *medhājanana* should also be performed in order to develop the intelligence of a student of the Veda, for he is supposed to memorize the Saṁhitā and other texts under the instructions of his teacher. This is the standard way of learning the Vedas, for one is enjoined not to make use of a written text.[10]

The student who has been initiated and introduced to the study of the Veda, with the performance of the *upanayana*, is supposed to have been "reborn" after the teacher has conceived and delivered him and, hence, he gets the status of a twice-born (*dvija*).[11] The student, the de facto newborn child, is therefore required to undergo the rite of *medhājanana* and is also given a new name through the *nāmakaraṇa*, performed as a part of the *upanayana* ceremony.

The mantras of this hymn (*AVŚ* I.1), like many others, possess some indication of the rite that the hymn is to accompany. There are four verses in this hymn, and though the word *medha* does not appear in them, there are some words and expressions that show that the person who recites the verses (*AVŚ* I.1.2-4) is praying to Vācaspati, the "Lord of Speech", so that the latter's knowledge may come to abide in him (Gonda 1980: 159). The prayer is obviously intended to be made by a Vedic student, not a newborn child, and the *medhājanana* rite is to be performed for the sake of that student. Kauśika, however, employs the hymn in the *medhājanana* for the newborn child and the student.[12] This is one of the unique features of the *medhājanana* in the *Atharvaveda* tradition.

---

[10] According to the *Pāṇinīya Śikṣā* (verse 32), one who recites the Veda with the help of a written text is one of the six wretched reciters (*pāṭhakādhama*). Kumārila argues that the efficacy of the Veda would be destroyed if the text were learned with the help of a written text (. . . *anyāyavijñātād vedāl lekhyādipūrvakāt*) and lays great stress on the method of recitation by repeating what is pronounced by the guru (*gurumukhoccāraṇānūccāraṇa*) (*Tantravārttika* on *Pūrva-Mīmāṁasā-Sūtra* 1.3.7).

[11] The notion of the conception of the teacher giving birth to the student occurs in *AVŚ* XI.5.3 and further in *ĀpDhS* I.1.15-17; *GDhS* I.10; *ManuSm* II.146-48; *VasiṣṭhaSm* II.3-5; and *ViṣṇuSm* 30.44-46. See also Bloomfield 1897: 626.

[12] *KauS* VII.8[57].31: *medhājanana āyuṣyair juhuyāt* I "In the (ceremony of) *medhājanana*, one should make oblations (of clarified butter into the fire) →

Another unique feature of the *medhājanana* in the *Atharvaveda* tradition involves the acts to be performed and the substances to be used in the rite. It is valuable, therefore, to see how the *KauS* describes the *medhājanana* (*KauS* II.1[10].1-15):

1. With (the hymn designated as) *pūrva* are associated the acts that generate intelligence.
2. (The priest) hangs (an amulet made of) the tongues of a parrot, (birds called) *sāri* and *kṛśa* (around the neck of the person for whom the *medhājanana* is to be performed).[13]
3. (He) makes (that person) consume the tongues of the birds.
4. (He) offers (fire sticks of *audumbara, palāśa,* and *karkandhu* into the fire).
5. He offers (grains of rice, barley, or sesame into the fire).
6. (The person for whom the rite is to be performed) consumes (milk rice, sacrificial bread, or "saps").[14]
7. (The student) offers the teacher the alms (he has collected).

→ with the (recitation of the hymns or verses) for securing long life." Here the *medhājanana* is a part of the *upanayana*. However, Keśava, the author of the Paddhati on the *KauS* (*KP*), understands the expression *medhājanana āyuṣyair* in the sense of instrumental: *medhājananamantrair āyuṣyamantraiś ca* and cites the pratīkas of the hymns and the verses used in the *medhājanana* and the *jātakarman* (*KauS* II.1[10].1-20): *AVŚ* I.1; IV.30; VI.108 and XII.1.53 (*KP*, p. 294: here a reference to *AVŚ* VII.1.53 instead of XII.1.53 as the last pratīka, appears to be a typographical error; cf. *KP* on *KauS* II.1[10].20, p. 39).

[13] According to the Paribhāṣā, *āśyabandhyāplavanayānabhakṣyāṇi sampātavanti* (*KauS* I.7.15), the substance to be consumed or that to be tied as an amulet has to be consecrated with the remnants of the clarified butter that has been offered into the fire (*sampātavanti*). Only then can the relevant act of consuming or tying be performed. Dārila explains that the practice of tying (an amulet) round the neck is well known (*grīvāyāṁ bandhanaṁ prasiddham, DB* on *KauS* I.1.2, p. 46).

[14] According to the Paribhāṣā, *bhakṣayati kṣīraudanapuroḍāśarasān* (*KauS* I.7.6), the verb *bhakṣayati* implies one of the substances — namely, milk rice, sacrificial bread, or a "sap". According to another Paribhāṣā, *dadhi ghṛtaṁ madhūdakam iti rasāḥ* (*KauS* I.8.19), by the word *rasa-* "sap" are meant the substances curd, ghee, or honey mixed in water.

8. (The teacher) consecrates[15] the ear (of the student with the recitation of the hymn) while (the latter) is sleeping.[16]
9. (The student) murmurs (the hymn) while (he) approaches (the teacher).
10. The grains mixed with clarified butter are all offered into the fire.
11. Having offered (the grains mixed with sesame) into the fire, (the student) consumes[17] (what is left over).
12. Having fixed a spotted staff[18] (into the ground) in front of the fire, and having placed the grains on the skin of a black antelope that has been placed to the west of the fire, (the student) consecrates them with the recitation of the hymn.

---

[15] MW translates the root *anu+√mantr-* as "accompany with or consecrate by magic formulas". Gonda translates the verb *anumantrayate* as "accompanies" or "accompanies, consecrates". See his translation of the *Savayajñas*, particularly, *KauS* VIII.1[60]. 19, 22, 23, 24, etc. (Gonda 1965: 77 and 78). He explains that "very often the function of a mantra is 'sacramental' or consecratory (the text using the verb *anumantrayate* 'to accompany with or consecrate by mantras' . . .)" (Gonda 1980: 215).

[16] Keśava explains that the student performs this act while the teacher is sleeping. Sāyaṇa follows his interpretation (see his introduction to *AV* I.1). Keśava offers an alternative explanation, saying that the father performs this act with respect to the student or the child (*KP*, p. 37).

[17] Since the verbal form *prāśnāti* has the root *√aś-* with the prefix *pra-*, the Paribhāṣā *KauS* I.7.15, mentioned in note 10 above, is not to be applied here. It is applied when the act is mentioned with the verbal form *aśnāti* or *āśayati* without any prefix. This particular act, therefore, does not involve the act of consecrating the substance with the remnants of clarified butter (*sampātakaraṇa*). Therefore Dārila says elsewhere: *na sampātāḥ propasr̥ṣṭatvāt* (*DB* on *KauS* II.1[10].16, p. 47). Rotaru (2010: 71, fn. 165; 80) argues that the device prescribed by the Paribhāṣā (*KauS* I.7.15) is not constantly carried out at the places where the causative form *prāśayati* is used.

[18] Gonda (1975: 165) points out the significance of fixing the staff into the ground. According to him, this ritual act is reflected by the words of the mantras: "The object is fixed and the god is besought to make fast what is heard by the pupil." He further suggests that the staff, which is "speckled with black" (*kalmāṣa*), reveals its vajra-like character. Cf. Gonda 1980: 159.

13. Having gone to the end[19] of (the recitation of) the hymn, (the teacher) gives (the grains placed on the black antelope skin to the student).
14. (The student) offers (the grains) at once (by means of the black antelope skin).
15. (The student) gives the staff, (the leftover) grains, and the black antelope skin (to the teacher).[20]

The most peculiar among the acts here is that of tying an amulet made of bird tongues and feeding it to the child or student. There is no indication for that act in the hymn (*mantraliṅga*); however, we may guess that the word *tri-*, occurring in the compound *triṣaptā́ḥ* in the first verse, forms a magical connection (*bandhutā*) with the act, on the basis of which the author of the *KauS* prescribes the three birds. The verse speaks of "the thrice seven" (*triṣaptā́ḥ*), that "go about, bearing all forms" (Whitney 1905: 1). These mystic entities have been interpreted by Sāyaṇa and modern scholars including Weber, Whitney, Vishva Bandhu, Thieme, and others, in various ways.[21] In the present

[19] The text in the *DB* has *antam* in the place of *pāram* (*DB*, p. 47). This appears to be a scribal error. The reading is not supported by MSS. Dārila cites the sūtra elsewhere with the reading *pāram* (*DB* on *KauS* 8.10, p. 41).

[20] This is according to the commentators, Dārila and Keśava. Other Gṛhya-Sūtras, however, prescribe a staff made of a branch of the palāśa tree that is to be given to the student by the teacher. Cf. Gonda 1975: 167.

[21] Sāyaṇa offers a number of explanations for the word *triṣaptāḥ*. First, he explains the word as "three or seven"; secondly, "three sevens"; and thirdly, "thrice seven or twenty-one". Having summarized Sāyaṇa's explanation, Whitney (1893: 94) remarks: "It does not once enter his mind to look at the rest of the hymn and see what its general sense suggests or requires; his discussion is carried on throughout as if the word had been taken out of the pages of a dictionary." Weber (1958: 393) refers to one of Sāyaṇa's interpretations in the sense of the word *trisatyāḥ* and says that the word *triṣaptāḥ* might refer to the gods of the three spheres — namely, the heaven, the firmament, and the earth. According to Whitney (1971: 1-2), "*triṣaptā́s* is plainly used as the designation of an indefinite number, = "dozens" or "scores". Supposing *śruta* to signify one's acquired sacred knowledge, portion of *śruti*, it perhaps refers to the sounds or syllables of which this is made up. If, on the other hand, *śruta* (as in vi.41.1) means "sense of hearing," the *triṣaptās* may be the healthy hearers, old and young (so R.)". In the General Introduction, Part I, Lanman (1905: cv) gives "R." as an abbreviation of "Roth" and then, under "Roth", mentions four of →

context, the word may be understood as *tri-saptā́ḥ*, where the second member may be taken as a past passive participle of the root √*sap-*, a secondary form of √*sac-*, "to cleave to, to follow or seek after", and is indicative of the birds.[22]

The names of the three birds given by Kauśika are *śuka*, *sāri*, and *kr̥śa*. Since the birds have not been mentioned in the verse itself, Sāyaṇa does not identify the names given by Kauśika and simply says "parrot and so on" (*śukādijihvānām . . . bandhanam* I Vishva Bandhu 1960: 29). In his Bhāṣya on *KauS* II.1[10].2, Dārila identifies them as such: *śukaḥ. prasiddhaḥ* I *sārir iti prasiddhā* I *kr̥śaḥ gomeṇaka iti prasiddhābhidhānaḥ kr̥ṣṇavarṇo dīrghapucchavāṁś ca* I (*DB*, p. 46). That is, "The parrot is well known; the *sāri* is well known; and the *kr̥śa* is well known by the name *gomeṇaka*, a bird of black colour, with a long tail".[23] The bird

→ his works. It is yet to be traced which of those works includes Roth's interpretation of the word *triṣaptā́ḥ*. According to Whitney (1905: 2), the thrice seven "are gods, who are to render aid". Griffith refers to the mantra *trisaptā́so marutaḥ* (*AV* 13.1.3) and identifies the word as one denoting the Maruts. Vishva Bandhu (1967: 14) refers to Whitney and thinks that the "three-time sevens" are all other "hearers" in general. Thieme (1985: 563-64) finds it hard to subscribe to Whitney's comment for, according to him, the context does not speak of aid; it speaks of powers. He thinks that the word denotes 21 items of the old varṇopadeśa — namely, 8 vowels (*svara-*, i.e. *a, i, u, r̥, e, o, ai, au*), 4 half-vowels (*antastha-*, i.e. *y, r, l, v*), 5 occlusives (*sparśa-*, i.e. *k, c, ṭ, t, p*), 3 sibilants and 1 *h* (*ūṣman-*, i.e., *ś, ṣ, s*, and *h*). Cf. Bronkhorst (2001: 161-62). Deshpande (1997: 33ff.) thinks that "such a listing . . . is a reflection of this early pre-scientific phase, rather than an explicit representation of the 'types' of Sanskrit sounds". While teaching this hymn to his M.A. class at the University of Pune, R.N. Dandekar used to explain the word *triṣaptāḥ* as one denoting the vowels with their varieties: short vowels *a, i, u*, and *r̥* with their varieties: the short (*hrasva*), the long (*dīrgha*), and the prolonged (*pluta*), thus making the number 12; *ḷ*, only one short vowel; and the diphthongs — *e, ai, o*, and *au*, with their varieties, the long and the prolonged, making the number 8. We thus have a total of 21 varieties of vowels. I have not been able to find this explanation in any of his works. These interpretations of the word, signifying Speech, indicate that the hymn is appropriate for the *medhājanana*.

22 Weber (1858: 393) understands the grammatical form in this way and translates it as "triply combined".

23 Dave (1985: 99) thinks that the reference to a black and a long-tailed bird is to the "wire-tailed swallow" which, according to him, is erroneous.

called *sāri* is most probably *sārikā*, the Indian mynah. The birds *śuka* and *sārikā* are known for their ability, respectively, to imitate the human voice and to chirp sweetly. A child first learns language by imitating his parents, and the student learns the Veda by imitating the recitation of the teacher. Therefore, the tongue of a parrot is used in the rite. *Sārikā* or the Indian mynah is likewise endowed with the same quality. The third bird *kr̥śa* — or, according to Dārila, *gomeṇaka* — is perhaps *gomeda*, the black Drongo, called Kotvāl in Marathi.[24] Keśava has the following gloss: *śukaḥ prasiddhaḥ* ı *sāri saraṇṭikā prasiddhā* ı *kr̥śo bhāradvājaḥ* (*KP*, p. 36). That is, "*Śuka* is well known; *sāri* is well known as *saraṇṭikā*; *kr̥śa* is *bhāradvāja*". The name *saraṇṭikā* appears to be a *deśī* word used by Keśava in its Sanskritized form. He paraphrases *kr̥śa* as *bhāradvāja* — "a skylark" (Dave 1985: 99ff.).

The transfer of the qualities in relation to birds can also be found elsewhere in the *AV*. In *AV*. I.22.4, for example, three birds — a parrot, a *ropaṇākā*, and a *hāridrava* — are mentioned in the context of the yellowness caused by jaundice. Here, however, the transfer of the qualities is reversed. The yellowness of the patient is to be deposited in these birds having yellow colour. This is a case of homeopathic magic[25] based on attractio similium (Bloomfield 1897: 241ff.): *śúkeṣu te harimā́ṇaṁ ropaṇā́kāsu dadhmasi* ı *átho hā́ridraveṣu te harimā́ṇaṁ ní dadhmasi* (*AVŚ* I.22.4). That is, "In the parrots, in the *ropaṇā́kās*, we put your yellowness; likewise, in the *hā́ridravas*, we deposit your yellowness".[26]

The three birds mentioned by the *KauS* are the birds that make sweet sounds and are endowed with the power of speech. Their tongues can magically transfer that power to the child or student. The amulet of tongues prescribed in the *KauS* is to be consecrated with the recitation of the hymn in question and is to be hung around the neck of the child or student.[27] According to the Paribhāṣā, *KauS* I.7.15, when

---

[24] I am thankful to my friends and ornithologists Dr. Suruchi and Dr. Satish Pande for this valuable information.

[25] For detailed discussion, see Marett 1915: 245-52.

[26] Translation by Whitney (1905: 23), slightly modified here. The verse is also found at *R̥V* I.50.12, where the word *me* occurs in the place of *te* in pādas *a* and *c*.

[27] Caland (1967: 18) understands that by the use of the word *badhnāti* in this sūtra, it is intended that Paribhāṣā, *KauS* 7.19 is to be applied here and that the procedure of preparing an amulet prescribed therein is to be →

the tying of the amulet is mentioned by using the verbal form of √*badh-*, it is necessary to consecrate the amulet by pouring "the remnants of clarified butter after it is offered into the fire" (*sampāta*).[28]

The next act with the tongues of the three birds is to feed them to the child or student. Similar acts occur elsewhere. The *Sāmavidhāna Brāhmaṇa* (*SVBr*) II.7.8 prescribes the consumption of a skylark's tongue for being able to reproduce what has been learned:

> He must take the tongue of a skylark. It must be pulverized on the same day and mixed with honey and butter. He must allow his son . . . to eat . . . the son must repeat what he is capable of hearing.[29]

Caland (1967: 19, n. 3) mentions a similar practice in Bohemia:

> . . . In Bohemia, if a child has difficulty in learning to speak, he is made to eat tongues of a skylark (Wuttke §606).[30]

It is quite "magical", if not logical, to consume the tongues of sweet-chirping birds in order to gain a sweet voice. This crude magical practice is extended to this rite for the purpose of increasing intelligence. Dārila and Keśava, as well as modern scholars such as Caland (1967: 19) and Gonda (1980: 85),[31] understand the *KauS* 10.3 in

---

→ followed. He therefore provides the necessary explanation in a bracket. See also Gonda (1980: 85) quoted below. This is, however, not correct. The Paribhāṣā is applicable only in the case of the expression *vāsitaṁ* (or *vāsitān*) *badhnāti* and not merely in the case of *badhnāti*. For explanation, see Bahulkar 1994: 76, n. 2.

[28] See note 10 above.

[29] *bhāradvājikāyā jihvām utthāpya tadahaś cūrṇaṁ kārayitvā madhusarpibhyāṁ saṁyūya prāg annaprāśanāt kumāraṁ prāśayed indram id gāthino bṛhad* (grām. 5.5.198.1) *ity etena śrutanigādī bhavati* (*SVBr* II.7.8, p. 142). Sāyaṇa merely says that Bhāradvāja is a particular bird (*pakṣiviśeṣa*). Bharatasvāmin, in his commentary *Padārthamātravivṛti*, identifies it as a particular bird having red wings (*bhāradvājikā nāma raktapakṣaḥ pakṣiviśeṣaḥ*).

[30] I am thankful to Ms. Anita Shroff for correcting the English translation of the original German passage.

[31] "Parrots and other birds that possess the faculty of imitating human voice or speech or are believed to speak or to sing beautifully are made to transmit this ability and their wisdom to a student when in a special ceremony (*Kauś.* 10,1ff. with *AVŚ* 1,1 'for the retention of sacred learning') their tongues after being put in coagulated milk and honey, and being →

the same way. According to them, the tongues are to be consumed by the child or the student.

However, there is one technical point that may be taken into consideration in trying to understand the practice of consuming the tongues of the birds. The point concerns the two sūtras that can be understood in a different way: *śukasārikṛśānāṁ jihvā badhnāti* । *āśayati* ।। The second sūtra does not have the particle *ca,* showing the continuity of the act. The absence of the particle may be justified. Perhaps it is not used because the two acts are optional and are not performed together. Still, the methodology of the *KauS*, based on its Paribhāṣās, may point to a different understanding of the sūtra. The Paribhāṣā, *aśnāty anādeśe sthālīpākaḥ* (*KauS* I.7.1), posits that when the act of eating is mentioned by the verb *aśnāti* — present, 3rd person singular of the root √*aś*- "to eat" — and when there is no mention of the substance to be consumed, one should understand that cooked rice (*sthālīpāka*) is implied. Dārila explains that when the act is mentioned by using the verb form *aśnāti* or its causative *āśayati,* the same Paribhāṣā is to be applied (*DB*, p. 33). If we apply that Paribhāṣā in the present case, the substance to be consumed would be the cooked rice and not the tongues of the birds. This interpretation, however, is not tenable. In this context, another Paribhāṣā is to be taken into consideration. The Paribhāṣā *viśaye yathāntaram* (*KauS* I.8.10) explains that whenever there is a doubt regarding the mantra, the act, or the substance in a particular rite, one should take the imminent one. Accordingly, in the present context, the substance, i.e., the tongues of the birds, mentioned in the immediately preceding sūtra, are to be understood.[32]

Although the acts to be performed in the rite of *medhājanana* include the eating of birds' tongues, which were part of an amulet, the practice must have become obsolete after Keśava composed his commentary. The Prayogas have more simple and common acts. An example from the *Atharvaveda-Prayogabhānu* by Raviśaṅkara Nāgara or Divedī, a late

→ besmeared with the residue of the ghee that has been sacrificed, are hung round the neck of that youth who should also eat them." (Gonda 1980: 85)

32 Dārila, commenting on this Paribhāṣā, refers to *KauS* II.1[10].13, where the substances to be offered, namely, the staff and the grains, are to be taken from the preceding sūtra (*DB*, p. 47).

Prayoga text, may be cited in this context. He describes the rite in the *medhājananaprayogaraśmi*, section 16 of the second book (*prakāśa*) (*MS* fol. 353A-357B).[33] He explains the *medhājanana* in the context of a student and not a child. Curiously, he omits the first six sūtras (*KauS* II.1[10].1-6), which discuss the tying of the amulet of birds' tongues, the eating of the tongues, offerings of various fire sticks, etc. He simply begins the explanation with *KauS* II.1[10].7, prescribing the act of giving alms to the teacher. This shows that the typically Atharvanic practices became obsolete over time and that more simple practices, common to other Gr̥hya-Sūtras, continued until the composition of the late Prayoga texts. It is doubtful whether the Atharvavedins of recent centuries have ever performed the rite of the *medhājanana* for a newborn child.

References

PRIMARY SOURCES

ĀGS — *Āśvalāyana-Gr̥hya-Sūtra*, cited from Oldenberg 1892.

ĀpDhS — *Āpastamba-Dharmasūtra* with Haradatta's Ujjvalā, ed. A. Mahádeva Śástri, Government Oriental Library Series, Mysore: Government Oriental Library, 1898.

ĀpGS — *Āpastamba-Gr̥hya-Sūtra* with two commentaries, the Anākulā of Haradatta Misra and the Tātparyadarśana of Sudarśanācārya, Kashi Sanskrit Series No. 59, ed. A. Chinnaswami Saastri, Benares: Chowkhamba Sanskrit Series Office, 1928.

AV — *Atharvaveda* (Śaunaka) with the pada-pāṭha and Sāyaṇācārya's commentary edited and annotated with text-comparative data from original manuscripts and other Vedic works. Part I (Kāṇḍas I-V), ed. Vishva Bandhu et al., Hoshiarpur: Vishveshvaranand Vedic Research Institute, 1960.

AVP — *The Paippalāda Saṁhitā of the Atharvaveda*, vol. I, ed. Dipak Bhattacharya, Calcutta: The Asiatic Society, 1997.

AVŚ — *Śaunakīya Saṁhitā of the Atharvaveda*. See *AV* above.

DB — *Kauśikasūtra-Dārilabhāṣya*, ed. H.R. Diwekar et al., Poona: Tilak Maharashtra Vidyapith, 1972.

GDhS — *Gautama-Dharmasūtra with Maskaribhāṣya*, ed. L. Srinivasacharya, Government Oriental Library Series, Mysore: Government Oriental Library, 1917.

[33] For a detailed description of the work, see Bahulkar 2002: 148-53.

GGS — *Gobhila-Gṛhya-Sūtra*, cited from Oldenberg 1892.

HGS — *Hiraṇyakeśi-Gṛhya-Sūtra*, cited from Oldenberg 1892.

KauS — *Kauśika-Sūtra of the Atharvaveda*, cited from Bloomfield 1890.

KhGS — *Khādira-Gṛhya-Sūtra*, cited from Oldenberg 1892.

KP — *Keśava's Kauśikapaddhati on the Kauśika-Sūtra of the Atharvaveda*, ed. V.P. Limaye et al., Shri Balmukund Sanskrit Mahavidyalaya Research Series No. 1, Pune: Tilak Maharashtra Vidyapith, 1982.

ManuSm — *Manusmṛti with Manvarthamuktāvalī* of Śrīkullūkabhaṭṭa, Mumbai: Lakṣmī Veṅkaṭeśvara Press, 3rd edn., 1867.

PGS — *Pāraskara-Gṛhya-Sūtra*, cited from Oldenberg 1892.

SVBr — *Sāmavidhāna Brāhmaṇa with Vedārthaprakaśa of Sāyaṇa and Padārthamātravivṛti of Bharatasvāmin*, ed. B.R. Sharma, Kendriya Sanskrit Vidyapeeth Series No. 1, Tirupati: Kendriya Sanskrit Vidyapeeth, 1964.

ŚGS — *Śāṅkhāyana-Gṛhya-Sūtra*, cited from Oldenberg 1892.

VasiṣṭhaSm — *Vasiṣṭhasmṛtiḥ. The Sacred Law of the Āryas, as taught in the school of Vasiṣṭha and Tattvaprakāśikā commentary of Kulamani Mishra*, ed. Biswanath Swain, Puri: Sri Jagannath Veda Karmakanda Mahavidyalaya, 2005.

ViṣṇuSm — *Viṣṇusmṛti with the commentary Keśavavaijayantī of Nandapaṇḍita*, ed. V. Krishnamacharya, Adyar: Adyar Library and Research Centre, 1964.

MODERN WORKS

Bahulkar, S.S., 1994, *Medical Ritual in the Atharvaveda Tradition* (Shri Balmukund Sanskrit Mahavidyalaya Research Series, 8), Pune: Tilak Maharashtra Vidyapeeth.

———, 2002, "Atharva-Veda-Prayogabhānu (Dharmaśāstra of the Atharvavedins)", in *Ātharvaṇa (A Collection of Essays on the Atharvaveda with Special Reference to its Paippalāda Tradition)*, ed. Abhijit Ghosh, pp. 146-54, Kolkata: Sanskrit Book Depot.

Bloomfield, Maurice, 1890, *The Kauśika Sutra of the Atharvaveda with Extracts from the Commentaries of Darila and Keśava* (*Journal of the American Oriental Society* XIV.), repr. 1972, Delhi: Motilal Banarsidass.

———, 1897 (tr.), *Hymns of the Atharvaveda, together with Extracts from the Ritual Books and the Commentaries* (Sacred Books of the East, XLII), Oxford: Oxford University Press, repr. 1973, New Delhi: Motilal Banarsidass.

Bronkhorst, Johannes, 2001, "Etymology and Magic: Yāska's Nirukta, Plato's Cratylus, and the Riddle of Semantic Etymologies", *Numen* **48**(2), 147-203.

Caland, Willem, 1900, *Altindisches Zauberritual: Probe einer Übersetzung der wichtigsten Theile des Kauśika Sūtra*, Amsterdam: Verhandelingen der Koninklijke Akademie van Wetenschappen, repr. 1967, Wiesbaden: Dr. Martin Sändig.

Dave, K.N., 1985, *Birds in Sanskrit Literature*, Delhi: Motilal Banarsidass.

Deshpande, Madhav M., 1997 (ed. and tr.), *Śaunakīya Caturādhyāyikā: A Prātiśākhya of the Śaunakīya Atharvaveda, with the Commentaries Caturādhyāyībhāṣya, Bhārgavabhāskaravr̥tti and Pañcasandhi* (Harvard Oriental Series, 52), Cambridge, MA/London: Harvard University Press.

Griffiths, Arlo, 2009, *Kauśikasūtra*, the 5th electronic edn., Göttingen Register of Electronic Texts in Indian Languages (GRETIL).

Gonda, Jan, 1965 (tr.), *The Savayajñas (Kauśikasūtra 60-68, Translation, Introduction, Commentary)*, Amsterdam: N.V. Noord-Hollandsche Uitgevers Maatschappij.

———, 1975, "A Note on the Vedic Student's Staff", in *Selected Studies, Part IV: History of Ancient Indian Religion*, pp. 160-70 (repr. from *Journal of the Oriental Institute of Baroda,* **14:** 262-72, 1964-65) Leiden: E.J. Brill.

———, 1980, *Vedic Ritual: The Non-Solemn Rites*, Leiden: E.J. Brill.

Marett, R.R., 1915, "Magic (Introductory)", in *Encyclopaedia of Religion and Ethics*, ed. James Hastings, vol. VIII, pp. 245-52 (4th Impression 1958).

Müller, Max, 1859, *A History of Ancient Sanskrit Literature so far as it Illustrates the Primitive Religion of the Brahmanas*, London: Williams and Norgate, repr. 1926, Allahabad: B.D. Basu.

Oldenberg, Hermann, 1892 (tr.), *The Gr̥hya-Sūtras: Rules of Domestic Ceremonies*, Part II, Oxford: The Clarendon Press.

Pandey, Rajabali, 1949, *Hindu Saṁskāras: Socio-religious Study of the Hindu Sacraments*, Banaras: Vikram Publications, 2nd rev. edn., 1969, Delhi: Motilal Banarsidass.

Rotaru, Julieta, 2010, "Towards a Methodology of Applying the Paribhāṣās in the Kauśikasūtra (I) (with special reference to 7.1)", *Acta Orientalia Vilnensia,* **9**(2): 57-82 (2008).

Thieme, P., 1985, "The First Verse of the *triṣaptīyam* (AVŚ 1.1 ~ AVP 1.6) and the beginnings of Sanskrit Linguistics", *Journal of the American Oriental Society,* **105**(3): 559-65.

Vishva Bandhu, 1967, "Vedic Textuo-linguistic Studies, 4: Atharvaveda I.1", *Vishveshvaranand Indological Journal* **5**(1): 13-24.

———, et al. 1960 (eds.), *Atharvaveda (Śaunaka) with the pada-pāṭha and Sāyaṇācārya's Commentary edited and annotated with Text-Comparative data from Original Manuscripts and other Vedic Works,* part I (Kāṇḍas I-V), Hoshiarpur: Vishveshvaranand Vedic Research Institute.

Weber, Albrecht, 1858 (tr.), "Das erste Buch des Atharvaveda", *Indische Studien* **4:** 393-430.

Whitney, William Dwight, 1905 (tr.), *Atharvavedasaṁhitā*, tr. into English with critical and Exegetical Commentary by W.D. Whitney, rev. and ed. Charles Rockwell Lanman, 2 vols. (Harvard Oriental Series, VII and VIII), Cambridge (Mass.): Harvard University Press, 2nd repr., 1971, New Delhi: Motilal Banarsidass.

———, 1893, "The Native Commentary to the Atharvaveda", in *Festgruss an Rudolf von Roth zum Doktor-Jubiläum, 24 August 1893, von seinen freunden und schülern*, pp. 89-96, Stuttgart: Kohlhammer.

7

Aitareya Āraṇyaka and the Origin and Development of the Mahānāmnī Verses

Ambarish Khare

1. Introduction

THE verses called Mahānāmnīs along with the mantras called Purīṣapadas occur in the khila portion of the *Ṛgveda* (5.4.1-11) for the first time. They also form the basis of the Mahānāmnyarcika in the *Sāmaveda Saṁhitā*. They appear in the *Aitareya Āraṇyaka* (*AiĀ*) and are usually considered the fourth book (āraṇyaka) of this text. We find references to these verses in other Vedic texts such as the *Ṣaḍviṁśa Brāhmaṇa* (*ṢBr*),[1] *Bṛhaddevatā* (*BD*),[2] and *Śāṅkhāyana-Gṛhya-Sūtra* (*ŚGS*).[3]

The Mahānāmnīs are nine in number and basically eulogize the deity Indra. The *Aitareya Brāhmaṇa* informs us that Indra created a "great self" with these verses and hence they are named Mahānāmnīs.[4] Although they appear as one of the khila hymns, it is interesting to note that Gārgya Nārāyaṇa, the commentator of the *Āśvalāyana Śrautasūtra*, mentions the Mahānāmnīs separately, together with some

---

[1] See for example, *ṢBr* 4.5.6-7.

[2] Macdonell translates, "Mahānāmnī stanzas are mystical (*guhya*) and they are addressed to Indra: whosoever repeats (them) obtains a day of Brahmā which lasts for a thousand years." (*BD* 8.98)

[3] See *ŚGS* 2.12.13.

[4] *Indro va etābhir mahān ātmānam niramimīta tasmān mahānāmnyo . . .* (*AB* 5.7.2). This is followed by another story telling why they are also called śakvarī (in spite of the fact that they do not have seven pādas and are in anuṣṭubh meter).

other verses.[5] Kashikar too, opines (1946: 902) that the khilas in general belong to some lost śākhā, other than the one redacted by Śākalya, and were collected later. The reason for the appearance of the verses in the *AiĀ* is disputable due to the problem of authorship of that text, which will be dealt with in brief at the outset.

2. Mahānāmnīs in the *AiĀ*

The fourth āraṇyaka is merely a collection of the verses called Mahānāmnīs and Purīṣapadas. The fifth, that is, the last āraṇyaka is in sūtra-style, and explains the Mahāvrata, which has already been dealt with in the first āraṇyaka. The difference in nature between the first three and the last two āraṇyakas gives rise to the question of their authorship. The repeated subject matter in the first and last āraṇyaka (i.e. the description of the Mahāvrata) shall also be considered while dealing with this question. The problem about the authorship of the *AiĀ* was put forth by Oldenberg (1886) and was argued by Keith (1909).

In his commentary on *AiĀ*, Sāyaṇa says[6] that it is not at all erroneous to discuss the same topic of Mahāvrata twice (i.e. in the first and the fifth āraṇyaka) because the two āraṇyakas differ from one another in the same way as a brāhmaṇa and a sūtra differ. The first āraṇyaka is a brāhmaṇa and the fifth is a sūtra. Therefore the first āraṇyaka explains the rites along with the arthavāda and this arthavāda is absent in the fifth āraṇyaka. We also find ample mantras from other Vedic schools in the fifth āraṇyaka. Thus the fifth āraṇyaka is a sūtra and not a brāhmaṇa.

---

[5] *etasya iti śabdo nivit-praiṣa-puroruk-kuntāpa-vālakhilya-mahānāmnī-aitareyabrāhmaṇasahitasya śākalasya bāṣkalasya cāmnāyadvayasya etad āśvalāyanasūtraṁ nāma* . . . (from the commentary of Gārgya Nārāyaṇa on *Āśvalāyana Śrauta-Sūtra* I.1.1).

[6] *nāyaṁ doṣaḥ* । *sūtrabrāhmaṇarūpeṇa tayor vibhedāt* । *pañcamāraṇyakam ṛṣiproktaṁ sūtram* । *prathamāraṇyakaṁ tv apauruṣeyaṁ brāhmaṇam* । *ata eva tatrārthavādaprapañcena sahitā vidhayaḥ śrūyante* । *pañcame tu na ko 'py arthavādo 'sti* । *śākhāntaragatamantrāś ca bahava upalabhyante* । *tasmād athaitasya samāmnāyasya ityādidvādaśādhyāyīvat mahāvratasya pañcaviṁśatim ityādi pañcamāraṇyakaṁ sūtram eva* ।

Ṣaḍguruśiṣya — a commentator of the *Sarvānukramaṇī* — on the other hand, informs us in his *Vedārthadīpikā*[7] that the fourth āraṇyaka belongs to Āśvalāyana.[8]

3. Oldenberg and Keith on the AiĀ

In his Introduction to the *Āśvalāyana-Gṛhya-Sūtra*,[9] Oldenberg refers to the above-mentioned passage of Ṣaḍguruśiṣya, which states that the fourth āraṇyaka belongs to Āśvalāyana. He further quotes Sāyaṇa's commentary on the *Ṛgveda*, which mentions Śaunaka as the author of the fifth āraṇyaka.[10] Thus it seems that the tradition ascribes the fourth āraṇyaka to Āśvalāyana, and the fifth one to Śaunaka.

Oldenberg states that it is impossible to assume with Ṣaḍguruśiṣya that the Mahānāmnī verses were composed by Āśvalāyana. The term *āśvalāyanasūtrakam* used by Ṣaḍguruśiṣya is more appropriate for the fifth āraṇyaka written in sūtra style; the Mahānāmnī verses can never be called "sutra". He says,[11]

> There seems to me, therefore, to be little doubt as to the fifth āraṇyaka really being the text referred to by Ṣaḍguruśiṣya, though I do not know how to explain his setting down this book as the fourth.

He further quotes another reference from Sāyaṇa's commentary on the *Sāmaveda*, which ascribes the fifth āraṇyaka to Āśvalāyana, and not to Śaunaka. By taking these facts into consideration, he concludes,

> Instead of asserting, therefore, that of the two last āraṇyakas of the Aitareyinas the one is ascribed to Śaunaka, the other to Āśvalāyana, we must state the case otherwise: not two āraṇyakas were, according to Sāyaṇa and Ṣaḍguruśiṣya, composed by those sūtrakāras, but one, viz. the fifth, which forms a sort of supplement to the great body of sūtras of that caraṇa, and which is ascribed either to Śaunaka or to Āśvalāyana.

---

[7] This passage from the *Vedārthadīpikā* was first published by Max Müller. However, the second revised edition (1860: 235-39) has been referred to for the present paper.

[8] *dvādaśādhyāyakaṁ sūtraṁ catuṣkagṛhyameva ca* ।
caturthāraṇyakaṁ ceti hyāśvalāyanasūtrakam ॥

[9] See Oldenberg 1886: 153ff.

[10] *pañcamāraṇyaka auṣṇihatrikasitir iti khaṇḍe śaunakena sūtritam . . .*

[11] For details, see Oldenberg 1886: 156-58.

Keith in his edition of *AiĀ*[12] deals with the statements made by Oldenberg about the authorship of the fourth and the fifth āraṇyaka. He argues that Oldenberg's view that the Mahānāmnī verses cannot be called sūtra is not correct. Instead, he argues that the Mahānāmnī verses may not have been composed by Āśvalāyana, but merely collected by him, and the fourth āraṇyaka "is sort of *Āśvalāyana Saṁhitā* like the Śākala Saṁhitā".[13] He says,

> With reference to Oldenberg's remark (p. 157) that *Āśvalāyanasūtrakam* cannot refer to the Mahānāmnīs, I would observe that the expression refers to the Śrauta and Gr̥hya-Sūtras with the āraṇyaka IV thrown in.[14]

He concludes,

> It is impossible to argue that in Ṣaḍguruśiṣya's eyes the term *caturthāraṇyakam* covered the fifth book also, for the two are quite distinct and cannot ever have been combined into one book.
>
> — 1909: 21

As evinced elsewhere, some citations from the *Vedārthadīpikā* of Ṣaḍguruśiṣya, however, make it amply clear that the existing fifth āraṇyaka was in fact the fourth āraṇyaka in Ṣaḍguruśiṣya's eyes.[15] By the term *caturthāraṇyaka* Ṣaḍguruśiṣya meant the fifth āraṇyaka, and not the Mahānāmnī verses. This evidence shows that Oldenberg was correct in his conjecture regarding the authorship of the present fifth āraṇyaka.

Another first-hand source is the *Mokṣapadāvr̥tti*, the commentary of Ṣaḍguruśiṣya on the *AiĀ* itself. This commentary was not available to both Oldenberg and Keith.[16] Ṣaḍguruśiṣya incorporates the Mahānāmnīs and Purīṣapadas as a *sakr̥dukti-adhyāya*, an additional chapter at the end of the third āraṇyaka. He further counts the fifth (sūtra-style) āraṇyaka as the fourth. This commentary, thus, presents

---

[12] See Keith's Introduction (1909: 18ff.).

[13] Keith 1909: 18.

[14] Keith 1909: 20 fn.

[15] See Khare 2009 and 2010 for details.

[16] Even the present author was unable to refer to this commentary in his earlier articles.

a tradition in which the Mahānāmnīs and Purīṣapadas were not counted as a separate book, although they were part of the *AiĀ*.

Though this evidence strongly establishes the present fifth āraṇyaka as the fourth in the eyes of Ṣaḍguruśiṣya, the origin of the Mahānāmnī verses remains unclear. There is no confusion in the tradition regarding the authorship of the first three āraṇyakas: Mahidāsa Aitareya had composed them. The question remains only about āraṇyakas IV and V: Who was the author and why were the Mahānāmnī verses added in the *AiĀ*.

According to Keith, for understanding some details in the fifth āraṇyaka, a knowledge of the *Āśvalāyana Śrauta-Sūtra* is necessary. This indicates that the fifth āraṇyaka presupposes the *Āśvalāyana Śrauta-Sūtra*. Thus, it can be said that the present fifth āraṇyaka — which was known as the fourth āraṇyaka in the tradition of Ṣaḍguruśiṣya — would have been authored by Āśvalāyana.

The problem that still remains unsolved is why Sāyaṇa ascribed the fifth āraṇyaka to Śaunaka if it was composed by Āśvalāyana. A simple answer (that was in the mind of Keith) can be given to this question. Macdonell has explained that the *Bṛhaddevatā* was the work of some pupil of Śaunaka, but it was credited to Śaunaka. Similarly, it can be said that some part (i.e. the fifth Āraṇyaka) of the *Āśvalāyana Śrauta-Sutra* was credited to his teacher Śaunaka. This again matches with the story recorded by Ṣaḍguruśiṣya,[17] that the sūtra of Āśvalāyana was better than that of Śaunaka. Therefore Śaunaka, out of affection for Āśvalāyana, removed his own sūtra and made his followers accept the sūtra of Āśvalāyana. Thus the statement of Sāyaṇa mentioning the fifth āraṇyaka as of Śaunaka instead of Āśvalāyana is not a major problem.

4. Employment of the Mahānāmnīs in the Vedic Ritual

A plausible explanation for the inclusion of the Mahānāmnīs in the *AiĀ* can be given on the basis of the employment of the verses in the

[17] *śaunakasya tu śiṣyo 'bhūd bhagavān āśvalāyanaḥ* ।
. . . sahasrakhaṇḍaṁ svakṛtaṁ sūtraṁ brāhmaṇasannibham ।।
śiṣyāśvalāyanaprītyai śaunakena vipāṭitam ।
uktaṁ tat tatkṛtaṁ sūtram asya vedasya cāstv iti ।।

Vedic sacrifices. It is interesting to see whether there is any relation between the Mahānāmnīs and the fifth āraṇyaka.

It can be clearly seen that both the Mahānāmnīs and Mahāvrata are related with the sattra, i.e. the Gavāmayana sacrifice. Kashikar (1977: 126 fn.) states that the Pr̥ṣṭhastotra in which six sāmans (*gāyatra, br̥hat, rathantara, bhadra,* and *rājana*) are combined is called Mahāvrata. The sacrifice, in which this Mahāvrata Pr̥ṣṭhastotra is used, gets the same name, i.e. Mahāvrata. The Mahānāmnī verses are also related with the Ṣoḍaśin sāman.[18]

The Pr̥ṣṭhya-ṣaḍaha is a six-day sacrifice coming before the Mahāvrata sacrifice. If the Śakvara-pr̥ṣṭha is used on the fifth day of this sacrifice, then the stotrīya-tr̥ca of the Mahānāmnīs becomes necessary. The three verses are grouped together and are recited with a pause (*avasāna*) in between (i.e. by reciting one-and-a-half verses together, then taking a pause followed by the recitation of the remaining one-and-a-half verses). After the implementation of nine Mahānāmnīs in this way, the Purīṣapadāni verses are recited.

This makes clear that the Mahānāmnī verses are necessary for the hotr̥ in the Pr̥ṣṭa-ṣaḍaha only when the Udgātr̥ uses the Śākvara Pr̥ṣṭha. These verses may not have been part of the proper *Śākala Saṁhitā* earlier as they are required optionally.

Thus a suggestion may be given that at an earlier time the Mahānāmnīs were not part of any Saṁhitā or khilas. They were considered a separate group of verses. Further, the verses regarding the Mahāvrata were to be recited in the *araṇya* (wilderness).[19] Therefore, the part of the Āśvalāyana Sūtra related to the Mahāvrata came to be included in the *AiĀ*. Later on, the Mahānāmnī verses were added to the *AiĀ* by observing their use in the Śrauta sacrifice. As they are used in the Pr̥ṣṭhya-ṣaḍaha, before the Mahāvrata sacifice, they were treated as the fourth āraṇyaka. Thus the former fourth āraṇyaka (i.e. sūtra part) became today's fifth āraṇyaka.

---

[18] *tasya mahānāmnyaḥ ṣoḍaśisāma bhavanti* || *vajro vai mahānāmnyaḥ* | *vajraḥ ṣoḍaśiḥ* | *vajreṇaivasmai vajraṁ praharati str̥tyai* (*ṢBr* 4.5.6-7).

[19] *araṇya eva etad adhyeyam ity abhipretyādhyetāro 'raṇyakāṇḍe 'ntarbhāvyādhiyate* (Sāyaṇa's commentary on *AiĀ* 5.1.1).

5. Mahānāmnīs in the Later Vedic Texts

The *Ṛgvidhāna* mentions what may be considered secondary employment of the verses. It states that these verses in combination with some other mantras should be recited by a person to cause rain.[20] They are also said to have some beneficial powers and powers to destroy the enemies.[21]

We find references to several *vrata*s (vows) to be followed by a brahmacārin. The four vratas mentioned in the *Gautama Dharmaśāstra* are Mahānāmnī, Mahāvrata, Upaniṣad, and Godāna. A brief outline of the Mahānāmnī vrata is as follows:

This shall be performed in the 13th year of age from birth. After setting the sacred fire and performing ājyahoma, he should change the sacred thread. Then the teacher says: *mahānāmnīvrataṁ saṁvatsaraṁ cara. Cariṣyāmi,* replies the disciple. He should then live for one year by observing the regular rules set down for a brahmacārin, and without shaving his hair. After that he again follows the ritual of setting fire and offering a few oblations to various deities. The teacher shall then tie the cloth on the face of the disciple thrice and keep him in the same position for a night. Next day he shall teach the verses to the disciple. After reciting the verses, the teacher shall remove the cloth and the disciple shall see the risen sun. This ritual is further followed by some more acts and ends in the evening.

6. Conclusion

As noted in the beginning of the paper, the verses under discussion are found in the khila portion of the *Ṛgveda*. Taking into consideration the opinion of Gārgya Nārāyaṇa, it may be concluded that these verses, although included in the khila portion, formed a separate category. The ritual of the Mahānāmnī-vrata, which was especially crafted for learning the verses, supports this opinion in a way. As the verses are absent in the tradition of the *Yajurveda*, the sūtras of this Veda do not tell us anything about the Mahānāmnī-vrata. In connection with the

---

[20] *vṛṣṭikamo japec caitā āpo hi ṣṭha sanātanāḥ* । *oṁkārapūrvā vyāhṛtayo madhucchandasa āditaḥ* ।। *sūktāny ante mahānāmnyaḥ saṁhitā sāmṛtā smṛtā* (*Ṛgvidhāna* 4.127-28).

[21] *mahānāmnyaḥ paraṁ brahma śukraṁ jyotiḥ sanātanam* । *sapatnaghnyaś ca puṇyaś ca pāvamānyaḥ parāḥ smṛtāḥ* (*Ṛgvidhāna* 4.126).

ritualistic employment of the Mahānāmnī verses, it may be concluded that these verses were recited as an option, to be selected by the Hotr̥ according to the sāman sung by the Udgātr̥. This practice connects the verses with the Mahāvrata sacrifice.

The above-mentioned ritualistic practice as well as the tradition of learning these verses outside the village would have promoted the incorporation of the Mahānāmnīs and the sūtra portion related to the Mahāvrata (probably composed by Āśvalāyana) in the *AiĀ*. From the commentary of Ṣaḍguruśiṣya, we have at least one tradition before us that presents a different understanding of this text which supports the view that the authorship of the complete āraṇyaka cannot be credited to Aitareya Mahidāsa: The fourth and fifth books are later additions.

The Mahānāmnīs were also used by later Vedic texts such as the *R̥gvidhāna* for some secondary purposes. Their employment in a rain charm would have been based on the fact that the verses praise Indra.

Several vratas and practices have vanished in the course of time. Similar is the case of the Vedavratas. Disciples learning the *R̥gveda* by the traditional method learn the Mahānāmnī verses even today, but now usually they do not observe any vrata before beginning the process of learning.

7. Colophon

I am thankful to Prof. Timothy Lubin (Washington and Lee University) for his suggestions after the presentation at the 15th World Sanskrit Conference, New Delhi.

Abbreviations and Primary References

AB	*Aitareya Brāhmaṇa*, ed. K. Agashe, 1896.
AiĀ	*Aitareya Āraṇyaka*, ed. A.B. Keith, 1909.
BD	*Br̥haddevatā*, ed. A.A. Macdonell, 1904.
R̥gvidhāna	*R̥gvidhāna*, ed. M.S. Bhat, 1987.
ṢBr	*Ṣaḍviṁśa Brāhmaṇa*, ed. B.R. Sharma, 1967.
ŚGS	*Śāṅkhāyana-Gr̥hya-Sūtra*, ed. S.R. Sehgal, 1960.

General References

Agashe, Kashinathshastri (ed.), 1896, *Aitareyabrāhmaṇam*, 2 vols., Pune: Anandashram.

Bhat, M.S. (ed & tr.), 1987, *Vedic Tantrism: A Study of the Ṛgvidhāna of Śaunaka with Text and Translation*, Delhi: Motilal Banarsidass.

K. Raghavan Pillai (ed.), 1968, *Aitareyāraṇyaka with Mokṣapadāvṛtti of Ṣaḍguruśiṣya*, Trivandrum: Oriental Research Institute and Manuscripts Library, University of Kerala.

Kashikar, C.G., (ed.), 1946, *Khilāni or the Supplementary Hymns of the Ṛgveda*, chiefly based on the text in Kashmir MS (Reprinted from the *Ṛgveda Saṁhitā*, vol IV), Poona: Vaidika Saṁśodhana Maṇḍala.

———, 1977, *Śrauta dharmācī svarūpacikitsā* (Marathi), Pune: Pune Vidyapeeth.

Keith, A.B., (ed. & tr.), 1909, *The Aitareya Āraṇyaka*, ed. from the manuscripts in the India Office and the Library of the Royal Asiatic Society with Introduction, Translation, Notes, Indexes, and an Appendix containing the portion hitherto unpublished of the *Śāṅkhāyana Āraṇyaka*, Oxford: Clarendon Press, repr. 1969, London: Oxford University Press.

Khare, Ambarish Vasant, 2009, "The Aitareya Āraṇyaka and Āśvalāyana", *Annals of the Bhandarkar Oriental Research Institute* XC: 1-10.

———, 2010, "The Composition and Authorship of the *Aitareya Āraṇyaka*", in *The Studies in the Āraṇyaka-s*, ed. Bhagyalata Pataskar, pp. 297-322, Pune: Adarsha Sanskrit Shodha Samstha.

Macdonell, A.A., (ed.), 1886, *Kātyāyana's Sarvānukramaṇī of the Rigveda with extracts from Ṣaḍguruśiṣya's commentary entitled Vedārthadīpikā*, ed. with critical notes and appendices, London: Oxford University Press.

———, (ed. & tr.), 1904, *The Bṛhad-devatā attributed to Śaunaka: A Summary of the Deities and Myths of the Ṛgveda*, critically edited in the original Sanskrit with an introduction and seven appendices, and translated into English with critical and illustrative Notes. Parts I & II (Harvard Oriental Series 5 & 6), repr. 1965, Delhi: Motilal Banarsidass.

Müller, F. Max. 1850, *A History of Ancient Sanskrit Literature*, so far as it illustrates the primitive religion of the Brāhmaṇas, rev. 2nd edn., London: Williams and Norgate.

Oldenberg, Hermann, (tr.), 1886, *The Grihya-Sūtras*, Part I (Sacred Books of the East, 29) repr., 1997, Delhi: Motilal Banarsidass.

Rajwade, V.K. et al., (eds.), 1933, *Ṛgveda Saṁhitā with the Commentary of Sāyaṇacārya* (vol. I), Poona: Vaidika Samshodhan Mandal.

Sehgal, S.R., (ed.), 1960, *Śāṅkhāyana Gṛhyasūtra*, Delhi: Munshiram Manoharlal.

Sharma, Bellikoth Ramachandra, (ed.), 1967, *Ṣaḍviṁśa Brāhmaṇa with Vedārthaprakāśa of Sāyaṇa*, Tirupati: Kendriya Sanskrit Vidyapeetha.

8

Some Thoughts on *padavī́* and *padám̐ véḥ*

Frank Köhler

1. Introduction

ONE of the distinctive features of poetic language is the use of ambiguities on all linguistic levels, and the *R̥gveda* (= R̥V) has more than enough examples to offer. Far from being l'art pour l'art, these devices are often used to encode the central element of a hymn, its ENIGMA. And it is partly due to these ambiguities that even in cases where there appears to be no serious disagreement about the basic semantics of a given word, new perspectives may be opened up by analysing the pragmatics of these words in their precise use. In this article it will be argued that the syntagm *padám̐ véḥ,* which is attested six times in the *R̥V* (I.164.7; III.5.5/6; III.7.7; IV.5.8; X.5.1), can/could be seen as such an example: This syntagm is usually translated as "track" or "place of the bird" (*véḥ* being the gen. sg. of *vi-* m. "bird"). However, if *véḥ* is understood as an inflected form of *vī-* "to trace", the phrase can also mean "you or he/she/it traces the track/word". All occurrences of *padám̐ véḥ* except one come from hymns to Agni. It will thus be tested in the following discussion whether it is possible to understand *padám̐ véḥ* in the latter sense and to integrate it into the context of the respective hymns. Since *padá-* contains a semantic ambiguity ("track/abode" vs. "word") it is suitable for the generation of multiple semantic layers. Furthermore, words for speech and its parts are often used by the poets when referring to their own activities. It may therefore be conjectured that *padám̐ véḥ* in its double meaning proposed here functions as a poetic self-reference by which the poets of the *R̥V* were able to comment on the different criteria involved in the process of creating, reciting, and receiving poems. Before I will argue for this interpretation a short summary of the prevailing views on *padá-* (n.) and *vī-* is given below.

2. The Semantics of *padá-*

This word has been subjected to an analysis by Renou and Thompson with the following results. According to Renou the original meaning of *padá-* was "foot, track". From the latter meaning it evolved into "abode" in analogy to other words denoting paths. *Padá-* is also used figuratively in connection with the sacrifice and with esoteric doctrines.[1] Furthermore, the semantics of *padá-* came to include the meaning "word" and the compound *padavī́-* in combination with *kavīnā́m* could be understood as "path-finder" as well as "someone who reveals words" to the poets.[2] Renou also ascribes this double meaning of *padá-* to the syntagm *padáṁ véḥ*, which is supposed to refer to the orbit of the sun and to poetic speech; the latter meaning is comparable to *padáṁ góḥ* "track of the cow".[3]

Thompson, while subscribing to most of the results of Renou in his thorough study,[4] searches for an explanation for the development from "track" to "word". The reason for this he finds in the fact that *padá-* in most of its attestations is used figuratively. He also identifies in these passages the topos of either "hidden" or "revealed" tracks.[5] Comparable to *nā́man-* Thompson considers *padá-* as a term for an indexical sign employed by the poets of the *R̥gveda* to communicate with their audience. In its use he sees one of the means by which these poets were able to hint at, rather than elucidate, their poetic enigmas.[6] With reference to *padáṁ véḥ* he agrees with Renou in ascribing to it the double meaning "orbit of the sun" and "poetic speech" (which is supposed to be of an esoteric character).[7]

---

1 Renou 1958: 21.

2 Renou 1958: 22, fn. 1.

3 Renou 1958.

4 Thompson 1995.

5 Thompson 1995: 11.

6 Thompson 1995: 19, 27.

7 Thompson 1995: 13.

The reasoning and the results of Renou and Thompson are sound[8] and there are no real objections to them.[9] Some minor points of divergence will be discussed in the context of the analysis of *padáṁ véḥ*. Previous to this, some peculiar features of *vī-* deserve consideration.

3. *vī-*

This root displays some peculiarities which have been analysed by Malzahn, who deals with the finite form *veḥ* which allows for several interpretations:[10] It occurs as a 2nd person present injunctive but has been reinterpreted as a 2nd person aorist injunctive and further as a 3rd person aorist injunctive as well (in both cases with irregular guṇa-strengthening).[11] Three attestations of *véḥ* which indubitably are to be considered as 3rd person aorist injunctive (*R̥V* I.77.2; II.5.3; IV.7.7) have Agni as their subject and are found in verses which deal with his function in the ritual.[12] As a result of Malzahn's study it should be borne in mind, that if *véḥ* in the syntagm *padáṁ véḥ* is interpreted as a form of *ví-*, there are at least in theory three options for determining the verbal form: *véḥ* can be understood as the 2nd person present injunctive, as the 2nd person aorist injunctive, or as the 3rd person aorist injunctive.

4. Attestations of *padá-* and *vī-*

The proposal of an alternative rendering of *padáṁ véḥ* as "you trace" or "he/she/it traces the track/abode" or "word" needs further

---

[8] Thompson has some difficulties in reconciling *padá-* as a term for a metrical unit, i.e. a line of a verse in *R̥V* I.164.23-24 with the meaning "word" (Thompson 1995: 7[-10]). But if *padá-* is taken rather loosely as a designation for a semantic unit (of vague boundaries), its meaning can include the metrical sense as well. For the sake of convenience, *padá-* has been rendered as "word" throughout in this paper whenever its linguistic meaning is at issue.

[9] In his dictionary Mayrhofer doesn't accept the meaning "abode" for *padá-*, apparently for etymological reasons (Mayrhofer 1996, s.v. *padá-*). But the examples given by Renou and Thompson as well as by the dictionaries (cf. for example the respective entries in Grassmann 1996 and Böhtlink 1865) strongly suggest this meaning.

[10] Malzahn 2002.

[11] Malzahn 2002: 200.

[12] Malzahn 2002: 197.

support than a mere analysis of the isolated parts of the syntagm. The corpus of the R̥V has to be checked for combinations of *padá-* and inflected forms of *vī-*. The result seems to be somewhat sobering: There are only three instances of a combination of *padá-* with a form of *vī-* in free syntax. The first one of these, R̥V I.48.6, deals with Uṣas in a rather enigmatic way and does not address the issue of poetry. The remaining two attestations are more relevant, both of them occurring in hymns addressed to Agni. The first one is concerned with the search for the hidden Agni:[13]

VI.1.4 *padáṁ devásya námasā vyántaḥ śravasyávaḥ śráva āpann ámr̥ktam* ।
nā́māni cid dadhire yajñíyāni bhadrā́yāṁ te raṇayanta sáṁdr̥ṣṭau ॥

> Tracing the track of the god with reverence the seekers of fame have obtained unscathed fame. They have established even sacrificial names for themselves, they rejoice about your auspicious sight.

It is tempting to assume a double meaning for *padá-* in this verse: On the one hand, those searching for Agni, presumably the Aṅgiras, succeeded in finding the hiding-place of the god himself. On the other hand, they are at the same time looking for the correct poetic expression to address Agni. But the evidence in this hymn is not sufficient enough to allow for such conclusions.

This changes with the third attestation. It comes from the hymn R̥V IV.5, which is described as highly mysterious by Geldner and which also contains one of the attestations of *padáṁ véḥ*.[14] The entire hymn abounds in incomprehensible passages. Among other things it features the opposition between an anonymous group of poets with dubious reputation on the one hand and the speaker of this hymn on the other. *Padá-* is attested six times in this hymn and has been understood here as having the double meaning of "track" and "word".[15] In verse 3 it is Agni who has found the deliberation (*manīṣā́*) reflected in the poem and he communicates his accomplishment to the speaker:

---

13 Geldner 1951, vol. 2: 92.

14 Geldner 1951, vol. 1: 423.

15 E.g. Geldner 1951, vol. 1: 424; Renou 1964b: 96.

IV.5.3 *sā́ma dvibárhā máhi tigmábhr̥ṣṭiḥ sahásraretā vr̥ṣabhás túviṣmān* ।
padáṁ ná gór ápagūḷhaṁ vividvā́n agnír máhyam préd u vocan manīṣā́m ॥

And since Agni, who is of doubled strength and has sharp spikes, the powerful bull of a thousand seeds has found the great melody which was hidden like the track of the cow, he proclaims the poetic deliberation to me.

The fifth verse of the hymn features the evil-minded rivals of the poet:

IV.5.5 *abhrātáro ná yóṣaṇo vyántaḥ patirípo ná jánayo durévāḥ* ।
pāpā́saḥ sánto anr̥tā́ asatyā́ idám padám ajanatā gabhīrám ॥

Tracing like brotherless young women, like wives of evil intent deceiving their husbands, you created this deep trace/word, though being sinful, unrighteous, and insincere.

ajanata: "you created"; this form has been understood to be either 3rd pers. sg. (with passive meaning) or 3rd pers. pl. ātmanepada,[16] but according to Gotō these proposals are untenable due to the lack of parallels.[17]

With regard to the analysis of this verse Oldenberg seems to be right: The rivals of the poet have themselves given the impetus for creating the poem which by its magical force will lead to their destruction, and *padám gabhīrám* corresponds to *manīṣā́m* in the previous verse.[18]

5. *padavī́-* and *padavī́ya-*

Despite the rare use in free syntax, a compound *padavī́-* has been coined,[19] which is attested seven times in the *R̥V* (I.72.2; III.5.1; III.31.8; III.56.4; VII.36.2; IX.96.6/18). In four places the compound has an effect on the interpretation of *padáṁ véḥ*. The first of these, like *R̥V* VI.1.4, deals with the search for Agni, but the poet has modified the topic: there are two searching parties, the unsuccessful gods (a-b) and the first poets (c-d), who have succeeded in finding him:

---

[16] E.g. Geldner 1951, vol. 1: 424; Renou 1964b: 9 (3rd pers. pl. ātmanepada) or Oldenberg 1909: 270 (3rd pers. sg. ātmanepada with passive meaning); but Oldenberg is skeptical about his own proposal.

[17] Gotō 1987: 145(-147), with reference to Narten 1964.

[18] Oldenberg 1909: 270.

[19] For the morphosyntactical analysis of *padavī́-* cf. Scarlata 1999: 499.

I.72.2 *asmé vatsám pári ṣántaṁ ná vindann ichánto víśve amṛ́tā ámūrāḥ* ।
śramayúvaḥ padavyò dhiyaṁdhā́s tasthúḥ padé paramé cā́rv agnéḥ ॥

All the immortal knowing ones, searching, do not find with/for us him who surrounds the calf. The toiling track-finders, the makers of visionary poems stand favourably at the farthest trace of Agni.

dhiyaṁdhā́-: "maker of visionary poems" according to Gonda.[20]

cā́ru: Following Mādhava[21] most translators consider *cā́ru* to be an abridgement of the locative *cā́ruṇi*.[22] But as Debrunner and Wackernagel emphasize, there are no clear attestations of locatives ending in *-u*, *-ū* in the *Ṛgveda*.[23]

In this verse a double meaning for *padá-* can certainly be assumed, at least for the first member of *padavī́-* since it is related to the following *dhiyaṁdhā́-*: The making of poems implies that the poets have been searching for and found the correct poetic expressions.

The syntagm *padavī́ḥ kavīnā́m* can be found thrice in the *Ṛgveda*. One of the involved passages is the first verse from *ṚV* III.5, a hymn addressed to Agni, which also contains two quotations of *padáṁ véḥ*.

III.5.1 *práty agnír uṣásaś cékitānó 'bodhi vípraḥ padavī́ḥ kavīnā́m* ।
pṛthupā́jā devayádbhiḥ sámiddhó 'pa dvā́rā támaso váhnir āvaḥ ॥

Towards the dawns Agni just awoke being recognized time and again, the inspired word/track-finder of the *kavís*. Of broad surface, kindled by those craving for the gods, the charioteer has just opened the doors of darkness.

It is possible here to interpret *padavī́-* literally as "track-finder", which implies that Agni is the one who finds the right path for the delivery of the oblations to the gods. And since oblations include poetry, Agni also traces the poetic words attached to the sacrificial gifts. Seen this way the use of *padavī́ḥ kavīnā́m* points to Agni's ability to comprehend the build-up of the poem recited. Yet there is another possibility to be

---

20 Gonda 1963: 87.

21 A.k.a. Sāyaṇa; in a recent article Slaje has convincingly demonstrated that Mādhava is the real name of the famous commentator of the Rig Veda (Slaje 2010).

22 Mādhava ad loc.; Geldner 1951, vol. 1: 94; Renou 1964a: 18, 90; Witzel et al. 2007: 131.

23 Debrunner/Wackernagel 1930: 154.

taken into consideration: Agni is not only the priest among the gods but also the source of inspiration for the Vedic poets. In this sense, *padavī́ḥ kavīnā́m* may be understood as "word-finder of the *kavís*", and this view finds support in pāda d, which can be understood literally as well as figuratively: Agni has been kindled before the break of dawn, but as an inspirational force he stimulates the poets as well.

The remaining two quotations of *padavī́ḥ kavīnā́m* occur in *R̥V* IX.96, a hymn dedicated to Soma Pavamāna. Without wanting to exclude the literal meaning, both passages taken together again suggest the meaning "word-finder of the *kavís*":

IX.96.6 *brahmā́ devā́nām padavī́ḥ kavīnā́m ŕ̥ṣir víprāṇām mahiṣó mr̥gā́ṇām* ।
śyenó gŕ̥dhrāṇāṁ svádhitir vánānāṁ sómaḥ pavítram áty eti rébhan ।।

As *brahmán* among the gods, word/track-finder of the *kavís*, *ŕ̥ṣi* among the inspired, buffalo among wild animals, falcon among the greedy (vultures?), axe among the lumbers, Soma passes through the sieve while singing.

It is far from obvious whether the combinations of nominatives and genitives all exhibit the same structure: whereas *ŕ̥ṣir víprāṇām* and *mahiṣó mr̥gā́ṇām* point to a superlative this is dubious for the remaining syntagms in this verse.

IX.96.18 *ŕ̥ṣimanā yá r̥ṣikŕ̥t svarṣā́ḥ sahásraṇīthaḥ padavī́ḥ kavīnā́m* ।
tr̥tī́yaṁ dhā́ma mahiṣáḥ síṣāsan sómo virā́jam ánu rājati ṣṭúp ।।

Who with the mind of a *ŕ̥ṣi-* is a maker of a *ŕ̥ṣi-*, a sun-winner, a word/track-finder of the *kavís* having a thousand ways, Soma, desiring to win the third form, rules as a praiser according to the Virāj.

sahásraṇītha-: "having a thousand ways"; the second member of this compound is either *ṇīthá-* "manner of singing" or *ṇī́thā-* "way, manner"; in accordance with the double meaning of *padaví-* it seems legitimate to assume a similar ambiguity for *sahásraṇītha-*.

virā́j-: not clear, due to the disputed meaning of *rāj-* ("to rule" and presumably also "to beam") and the problematic allocation of the respective forms.[24] In this pāda, Geldner sees an allusion to the metres *virāj* and *anuṣṭubh*.[25]

---

24 Mayrhofer 1996: 444 and Roesler 1997: 173(-185).

25 Geldner 1951, vol. 3: 94.

The first of these two verses consists of nothing more than a list of titles, in which Soma is singled out as the best of a specific group. Because of this, the verse seems to be less informative for our purpose. This changes, when we take a look at the second verse; here, Soma is furnished with attributes which refer to poetry, and it is therefore clear that *padavī́ḥ kavīnā́m* belongs to this domain as well. In the immediate context of verse 6 Soma is eulogized as the inspiring force for the poet,[26] and for that reason *padavī́ḥ kavīnā́m* apparently points to the process of creating poems rather than to the god's comprehension of an already existing poem.

Apart from the presented forms of *padavī́-* we can also trace an abstract noun *padavī́ya-*, which is derived from *padavī́-*. It occurs once in the *R̥gveda*. The relevant verse *R̥V* X.71.3 raises the issue of the discovery and distribution of the sacrificial poetry.

X.71.3 *yajñéna vācáḥ padavī́yam āyan tā́m ánv avindann ŕ̥ṣiṣu práviṣṭām* ।
tā́m ābhŕ̥tyā vy àdadhuḥ purutrā́ tā́ṁ saptá rebhā́ abhí sáṁ navante ॥

They went by means of the sacrifice/during the sacrifice in order to trace the speech, they found her entered into the *ŕ̥ṣis*; after fetching her they distributed her in many ways, the seven *rebhás* bellow towards her together.

ŕ̥ṣi-, rebhá-: The semantics of and the relationship between the different terms for "poet" in the *R̥gveda* are still far from settled;[27] in this particular verse one encounters the additional problem of the unexpressed subject of *āyan*, *avindann*, and *vy àdadhuḥ*.

This verse again is about the search for *padás*, and the genitive *vācáḥ* makes it sufficiently clear that *padá-* figures as a term for word. However, the context of this verse is somewhat broadened in relation to the verses discussed so far. It cannot be reduced to the finding of the tracks of a specific god or his proper designations. Rather, the establishment of sacrifice per se comes to the fore in this verse.

---

[26] Verse 5a-b *sómaḥ pavate janitā́ matīnā́ṁ janitā́ divó janitā́ pr̥thivyā́ḥ* "Soma purifies himself as the creator of thoughts, creator of heaven, creator of earth" and verse 7a-b *prā́vīvipad vācá ūrmíṁ ná síndhur gíraḥ sómaḥ pávamāno manīṣā́ḥ* "As the stream [whirls up] a wave, Soma Pavamāna has whirled up the speeches, the eulogies, the poetic considerations".

[27] For an attempt to this effect cf. Köhler 2011, esp. chapter 3.

Nevertheless it is obvious that the combination of *padá-* and *ví-* was thought suited to characterize the process of making poetry.

Thus, the use of the syntagm *padavī́ḥ kavīnā́m* for expressing the creative activity of the poets has been demonstrated, and this holds also for *padavī́ya-* in R̥V X.71.3.

6. An Additional Interpretation of *padáṁ véḥ*

One may go a step further and make *padáṁ véḥ* the subject of a similar analysis. This syntagm is in all attested quotations more or less unanimously rendered as the "track/abode of the bird" and these translations appear to be correct.[28] With regard to its interpretation, however, there do exist diverging opinions. The majority of Vedists consider it to be a reference to the sun or Agni, and sometimes also to esoteric doctrines of the poets. A much more elaborated interpretation, which is mainly based on the analysis of R̥V III.5.5-6, has been proposed by Lüders:[29] He interprets *rípo ágram* in III.5.5 as a place in the highest heaven. Because of its juxtaposition with *padáṁ véḥ*, the latter is placed there as well by Lüders. It is an abode guarded by Agni, identical to the celestial ocean *samudrá-*, from which the sun starts its daily course. Although Lüders' interpretation is largely based on his understanding of *r̥tá* as "truth" he is certainly right in arguing against a simple perception of *padáṁ véḥ* as the orbit of the sun, as will be seen below. But even regardless of Lüders' work there are reasons to reconsider *padáṁ véḥ*: 1. If *padáṁ véḥ* referred to the orbit of the sun, a significant number of attestations of *ví-* should refer to the sun as well. 2. Furthermore, *padá-* should not only occur in connection with *véḥ*, but also with other words denoting "bird" or "sun". These occurrences are missing. In spite of the explanations given by Renou and others it seems therefore legitimate to look for further reasons which motivated the coining of this syntagm. One of these reasons might be the morphological ambiguity of *padáṁ véḥ* mentioned above. It is possible to understand this syntagm not only as a juxtaposition of nominative and genitive, but also as a short phrase in which *véḥ* is used as a finite form of the root *vī-* "to trace". The result then means:

28 Geldner 1951, vol. 1: 228, 341, 345, 425; vol 3: 126; Renou 1964a: 54, 56; 1964b: 9, 96; 1965: 4; Elizarenkova 1989: 201, 295, 298, 366, 646, 692, 693, 728; Elizarenkova 1999: 120, 415.

29 Lüders 1951: 303.

"you/he trace(s) the track/the word". This alternative meaning is supported by the proposals of the native commentators already: Mādhava as well as Veṅkaṭamādhava unanimously equate *véḥ* with *gaccha* in their commentary on *R̥V* X.5.1.

Even according to the standards of the *R̥gveda*, the verses in which *padáṁ véḥ* is attested are highly incomprehensible and they will not become more intelligible once the possibility of an additional interpretation is admitted. In order to avoid further confusion, the individual verses will not be dealt with in isolation but in the context of their respective hymns. However, the analysis should not be understood as an attempt to clear up all occurring mysteries. A glance at the translations of Geldner, Renou, Elizarenkova, and Witzel et al. (to which, for the 3rd Maṇḍala, the works of Velankar and Shukla may be added)[30] is enough to make any such attempt a futile enterprise. Rather, the intentional use of a morphosyntactic ambiguity shall be analysed here, which (to some degree at least) supports the understanding of these hymns on a pragmatic level.

The hymn, which proves to be central to this argument, is *R̥V* III.5, in the first verse of which *padavī́ḥ kavīnā́m* is used. Here we also have two quotations of *padáṁ véḥ*, as has been noticed before:

III.5.5 *pā́ti priyáṁ ripó ágram padáṁ véḥ pā́ti yahváś cáraṇaṁ sū́ryasya* ।
pā́ti nā́bhā saptáśīrṣāṇam agníḥ pā́ti devā́nām upamā́dam r̥ṣváḥ ॥

He protects the dear peak of the *rip*, the trace of the bird, the youngest one protects the course of the sun. At the navel, Agni protects him of seven heads, he protects the stimulator of the gods, the lofty one.

ríp-: Word of unknown meaning; whilst the resembling *rúp-* from IV.5.7/8 may allow for an explanation this cannot be said for *ríp-*.[31] For this reason Bloomfield and Shukla suggested to emend it to *rúp-*.[32] But *ríp-* is attested in *R̥V* X.79.3 and since there is no convincing explanation for the change from *rúp-* to *ríp-* it seems more appropriate to refrain from this emendation.

III.5.6 *r̥bhúś cakra ī́ḍyaṁ cā́ru nā́ma víśvāni devó vayúnāni vidvā́n* ।
sasásya cárma ghr̥távat padáṁ vés tád íd agnī́ rakṣaty áprayuchan ॥

---

30 Velankar 1968; Shukla 2001.

31 Cf. Schindler 1972: 42.

32 Bloomfield 1906: 74; Shukla 2001: 148.

> He has made himself a lovely praisable name as skilful, knowing all covers. The ghee-possessing skin of seed, the track of the bird, just this does Agni protect untiringly.

These verses are composed in the esoteric style common to many hymns addressed to Agni. The focus of this hymn is the kindling of Agni in the morning, but by using *padám̐ véḥ* the interpretive perspective becomes more complex. If *padám̐ véḥ* is simply understood as "the course of the bird", thus designating the track of the sun, *cáraṇam̐ sū́ryasya* appears like an explication of it in plain language. This is of course possible but unlikely, given the sophisticated idiom of the *R̥gveda*. Furthermore, *padám̐ véḥ* in both verses occupies a prominent place at the end of the pāda and both verses in turn occupy a prominent position within the hymn: Since *R̥V* III.5 contains eleven verses and the two verses are placed in the middle, they are likely to contain the central meaning.[33] And finally, *padám̐ véḥ* responds to *padavī́ḥ* in the opening verse. Thus, on the one hand the poet illustrates the kindling of the fire in the morning with attributes pointing to its cosmic significance, while he simultaneously refers to the importance of his poetic language by characterizing Agni as *padavī́ḥ kavīnā́m* in verse 1 (to be understood as "track-finder of words") and returning to it in the middle of the hymn by the use of *padám̐ véḥ* (to be understood as "he traces the word"). This interpretation is also in line with Thieme's interpretation of *vayúna-* as "cover" in the sense of covered, i.e. enigmatic poetical language.[34] Since all other verbal forms in *R̥V* III.5.5 and 6 belong to the 3rd person it seems plausible to interpret *véḥ* correspondingly, and Agni seems to be the most likely subject, as he is explicitly praised as "knowing" *vidvánt-* in verse 6. As he is also the subject of those three attestations of *véḥ* which are to be considered as 3rd person aorist injunctive, a similar classification for *véḥ* suggests itself here.[35]

Two verses of the next hymn in which *padám̐ véḥ* occurs, *R̥V* IV.5, have already been discussed. For a better understanding of *padám̐ véḥ*

33 As Jamison has demonstrated for some hymns, aptly terming this feature as an "omphalos-structure" (Jamison 2004).

34 Thieme 1949: 22.

35 Since according to Hoffmann aorist and present injunctive show overlapping functions (Hoffmann 1967: 119[-130], 135[-140]), one may be allowed to desist from a definite classification.

the verses 6 to 9 will be analysed in the following. Verse 6 contains a complaint of the poet who — unsure about his own nature — compares the poem (*mánman-*) with a heavy burden.

IV.5.6 *idám me agne kíyate pāvakā́minate gurúm bhārám̐ ná mánma* ।
br̥hád dadhātha dhr̥ṣatā́ gabhīrám̐ yahvám pr̥ṣṭhám práyasā saptádhātu ॥

O Agni, of what nature am I, pure one, that you have boldly out of favour provided me, who is not harming, this thought like a heavy burden, lofty, deep, youngest riddle, consisting of seven layers?

pr̥ṣṭhá-: "riddle" after Mayrhofer, following Thieme.[36]

In verse 7 the climax of the mystical message of this hymn is reached: It is marked by the use of the hapax *jábāru-*, which appears to have been coined exclusively for this hymn.

IV.5.7 *tám ín nv èvá samanā́ samānám abhí krátvā punatī́ dhītír aśyāḥ* ।
sasásya cármann ádhi cā́ru pŕ̥śner ágre rupá ā́rupitam̐ jábāru ॥

May this visionary poem, purifying by efficaciousness, only reach him, the same one now, in the same way. The dear [udder/name?] of the speckled one [is] on the hide of the grain, the *jábāru-* has [been?] mounted on the tip of the *rúp-*.

rúp-: Like *ríp-* in R̥V III.5.5 of unknown meaning; a prima-facie convincing explanation was given by Bloomfield: He interprets *rúp-* as "a back-formation from the causative stem *ropaya*" with the meaning "height, ascent".[37] Shukla gives a similar etymology but considers *rupáḥ* to be the nominative singular of a verbal noun *rupá-* "emplanted, established".[38] Oldenberg rejects this derivation, arguing that *ropaya-* serves as the causative stem for *ruh-* only from the Brāhmaṇas onwards; he proposes instead a derivation from *rup-/lup-* "to suffer pain/to break".[39] But *āropayaḥ*, which is attested in *Paippalāda Saṁhitā* IX.10.11,[40] seems to allow for a different derivation (either along the lines proposed by Bloomfield or, with Werba, from a root *rup-* "to ascend").[41]

36 Mayrhofer 1996: 166; Thieme 1938: 65.

37 Bloomfield 1906: 75f., cf. Schindler 1972: 42.

38 Shukla 2001: 149.

39 Oldenberg 1913: 135f.

40 Bhattacharya 1997: 569.

41 Werba 1997: 373, with some hesitation.

cā́ru pŕ̥śneḥ: "the dear of the speckled": since *pŕ̥śni-* can be used as a term for "cow", "udder" or "name" is presumably to be added.[42]

The interpretation of this verse follows that of Jamison, who has pointed out that *jábāru-* admits of no translation since it was meant to embody the very enigma inherent in this hymn.[43] According to Gonda the visionary poem (*dhītí-*) discerns the character of Agni as being the same in all his manifestations.[44] In verse 8 *padáṁ véḥ* is apparently used to confront the poet with another group, perhaps the same which is mentioned in verse 5.

IV.5.8 *pravā́cyaṁ vácasaḥ kím me asyá gúhā hitám úpa niṇíg vadanti* |
yád usríyāṇām ápa vā́r iva vrán pā́ti priyáṁ rupó ágram padáṁ véḥ ||

What of this speech is to be proclaimed by me? Secretly they speak to the concealed, which they open like water of the reddish ones; he protects the dear peak of the *rúp-*, the track of the bird.

In the following verse the poet states that either he or Agni now has found the "shining" one (*dī́dyānam*) at the "track of order":

IV.5.9 *idám u tyán máhi mahā́m ánīkaṁ yád usríyā sácata pūrvyáṁ gaúḥ* |
r̥tásya padé ádhi dī́dyānaṁ gúhā raghuṣyád raghuyád viveda ||

This is the previous great face of the great ones, which the reddish cow follows. At the track of order I have found the shining, the secretly fast-running and hurrying one.

r̥tásya padé: "track of order": according to Lüders this is the abode of *r̥tá-* and the sun.[45] Perhaps it is more appropriate to assume a meaning "track of *r̥tá-*" which is to be understood as a term for expressing the effectiveness of poetical speech: It is effective since it consists of "tracks of order" and thereby participates in it and its power.

It is far from obvious who has found what, but one may at least take into consideration a reference to the speaker who has found a poem. This would also establish a connection with the previous verse 8. It becomes obvious that here again the stanzas are composed in a self-

[42] So Geldner (Geldner 1951, vol. 1: 425).

[43] Jamison 2004: 245.

[44] Gonda 1963: 183.

[45] Lüders 1959: 612.

referring manner: *R̥V* IV.5 is exactly the poem which is shining at the track of order. In this hymn the juxtaposition of *padá* with a form of *vī-* occurs in verse 5, where the rivals of the poet figure as the subject. *Padáṁ véḥ* in verse 8 might therefore be considered as a means to connect the activities of the speaker with those of his rivals and simultaneously with his ponderings on the mystery of creativity, which is referred to in the verses 3, 6, and 9. The poet uses *padáṁ véḥ* in a way to emphasize his superiority: Though he is involved in the same activities as his rivals, only he succeeds because he receives the inspiration by Agni. Once again *véḥ* can be translated as a 3rd person singular aorist injunctive, which is used for a general statement: A true poem relies on inspiration given by Agni. He therefore is again to be considered the subject for *padáṁ véḥ*.

In contrast to the verses discussed so far an interpretation of *padáṁ véḥ* in the following verse according to the schema proposed above proves to be more complicated. The verse again occurs in a hymn addressed to Agni, from the 3rd Maṇḍala:

III.7.5 *jānánti vŕ̥ṣṇo aruṣásya śévam utá bradhnásya śā́sane raṇanti* ।
divorúcaḥ surúco rócamānā íḷā yéṣāṁ gáṇyā mā́hinā gī́ḥ ॥

They know the precious of the red bull and they rejoice in the rule of the reddish one, those who shine from heaven, of good splendour, shining, whose host includes Iḍā and the great song.

śéva-: "precious"; Geldner adds "name", which would suit the context.[46]

III.7.6 *utó pitŕ̥bhyām pravídā́nu ghóṣam mahó mahádbhyām anayanta śūṣám* ।
ukṣā́ ha yátra pári dhā́nam aktór ánu sváṁ dhā́ma jaritúr vavákṣa ॥

And they led the snorting of the great with foresight after the noise for/towards the great parents, where the bull has grown up around the cover of the night according to the singers' own foundation.

Pādas a-b are interpreted by Renou as hinting at the combination of *r̥c* and *sāman*, since the medial forms of *nī-* are sometimes used in the sense of "musically conducting". This is possible but does not really fit in with the singular of *jaritŕ̥-* in pāda d.[47]

---

46 Geldner 1951, vol. 1: 344.

47 Renou 1964a: 56, 117.

> *pravíd-*: "foresight", according to Scarlata ("Vorausschauen").[48]
>
> *dhā́na-*: Renou: for **apidhā́na-* "cloture"; Geldner, Velankar: haplology for *paridhā́na-* or *paridhí-* "cloak, cover"; according to Kim something like "the time for discarding the night" ("Absetzungszeit der Nacht") is meant, which is determined by the poets.[49]

Kiehnle assumes that this verse is about how the poets lead their songs to the nightly abode of the sun-god in order to raise him in the morning.[50] This possibility cannot be ruled out, but since the verse is attested in a hymn to Agni, it is he who is most likely addressed here as a "bull" (*ukṣán-*), despite the difficulties to get a grip on the bull's "growing"; but *ánu sváṁ dhā́ma jaritúr* in pāda d points to the performance of the singer: It is by his poems that the god arises to his true greatness.

The next verse introduces several groups of priests in a rather puzzling way:

III.7.7 *adhvaryúbhiḥ pañcábhiḥ saptá víprāḥ priyáṁ rakṣante níhitam padáṁ véḥ* ।
prā́ñco madanty ukṣáṇo ajuryā́ devā́ devā́nām ánu hí vratā́ gúḥ ।।

> The seven inspired ones together with the Adhvaryus protect the dear track of the bird, which has been laid down. Forward-facing/facing eastward the young unaging bulls rejoice, the gods follow the commandments of the gods.

The content of this stanza is fairly obscure, since the identity of the *ukṣans* cannot be determined. It seems to be certain, however, that beyond this verse there is a ritualistic setting, since terms belonging to the domain of ritual, such as *adhvaryú-* and *vípra-*, are explicitly mentioned,[51] and so are the *vratás* "commandments", i.e. the acts of the gods which are meant to be re-enacted by their followers in ritual.[52] The *vratás* also occur in the next verse:

---

48 Scarlata 1999: 486.

49 Renou 1964a: 117; Geldner 1951, vol. 1: 344; Velankar 1968: 24; Kim 2010: 293.

50 Kiehnle 1979: 76.

51 An interpretation in terms of ritual priests was already proposed by Mādhava (Mādhava ad loc.).

52 For this meaning cf. esp. Hacker 1973.

III.7.8 *daívyā hótārā prathamā́ ny ṛ̥ñje saptá pṛ̥kṣā́saḥ svadháyā madanti* ।
ṛ̥táṁ śáṁsanta ṛ̥tám ít tá āhur ánu vratáṁ vratapā́ dī́dhyānāḥ ॥

The two divine hotṛ̥s I win over as the first ones; the seven powerful ones rejoice with autonomy. Reciting order they speak exactly of order, as protectors of the commandments reflecting according to the commandment.

saptá pṛ̥kṣás: seven priests (Mādhava) or the seven primordial seers with whom the ritualists of the Ṛ̥gvedic sacrifice identify themselves (Geldner).[53]

This verse also appears as *ṚV* III.4.7 in one of the so-called Āprī hymns, where the evocation of the two divine hotṛ̥s has its fixed place.[54] Irrespective of its exact meaning, it refers to a ritualistic setting.

Verses 5, 6, and 8 of this hymn seem to allude to poetry or poets, and this shall provide a subtle hint. In verse 6 it is said, that the young one has grown according to the establishment of the singer. In verse 8 the seven strong ones rejoice according to "own autonomy". The first and perhaps natural association would be with the subject of this pāda: The seven powerful ones rejoice according to their own autonomy. But when read, or more exactly heard, in connection with verse 7 it is also possible to relate *svadháyā* to the poet! In a way this fits well into the suggested meaning of *padáṁ véḥ*: The god Agni understands what has been laid down by the poet, although he is not directly mentioned as the subject of *véḥ*. The form itself is again to be interpreted as 3rd person singular aorist injunctive.

The preceding verses all contain a reference to the ongoing ritual activities which constitute the background of their recitation. This changes with the remaining two attestations of *padáṁ véḥ*; the hymns which provide their framework display a more speculative character. The first verse is part of *ṚV* X.5, a hymn of seven verses which deals with the nature of Agni, poetry, and ritual.

X.5.1 *ékaḥ samudró dharúṇo rayīṇā́m asmád dhṛ̥dó bhū́rijanmā ví caṣṭe* ।
síṣakty ū́dhar niṇyór upástha útsasya mádhye níhitam padáṁ véḥ ॥

---

[53] Mādhava ad loc.; Geldner 1951, vol 1: 339.

[54] Cf. Bosch 1985.

> The one sea, the keeper of riches of many births looks out from us, from the heart. He follows the udder in the lap of the two concealed ones; the track of the bird is laid down in the well.

Although it is perhaps impossible to understand every detail of this verse it seems at least plausible to assume Agni to be the subject of the pādas a to c and to consider the topic of the verse to be inspiration: A hidden Agni resides in the heart of the poet. Simultaneously, *útsa-* and *ū́dhar-* probably refer to the cosmic abode of Agni in form of the sun, as has been argued for by Lüders who pointed to *R̥V* X.177.2[55] and X.45.2.[56] Interestingly, both Indian commentators, Mādhava and Veṅkaṭamādhava, gloss *véḥ* with *gaccha* and consider Agni to be the subject.[57]

The second verse of the hymn goes deeper into the aspects of poetry:

X.5.2 *samānám̐ nīḷám̐ vŕ̥ṣaṇo vásānāḥ sám̐ jagmire mahiṣā́ árvatībhiḥ* ।
r̥tásya padám̐ kaváyo ní pānti gúhā nā́māni dadhire párāṇi ॥

> The male buffalos, dressed, have come together with the mares to the same nest. The *kavís* protect the abode/word of order, they have hidden for themselves the highest names.

Whereas the first part of this verse may have the flames of Agni as a subject,[58] the second part refers to the activities of the poets in expressions which have already been encountered: They protect the *padá-* of order, i.e. the poetic creation which carries magical power due to its formulation of a cosmic truth. The last pāda reveals the way of protecting it: by keeping the poetic vocabulary secret. Since these terms are part of the poetry which is openly recited, this can only mean that the poets (including the author of this very poem) shall give no information on the objects of reference for them, since

---

[55] See above, notes to *R̥V* IV.5.9.

[56] *vidmā́ te agne tredhā́ trayā́ṇi vidmā́ te dhā́ma víbhr̥tā purutrā́ vidmā́ te nā́ma paramám̐ gúhā yád vidmā́ tám útsam̐ yáta ājagántha* "We know your three times three, Agni, we know your forms, multifariously distributed, we know your highest name which is hidden, we know the spring, from where you have come". Cf. Lüders 1959: 614.

[57] Mādhava, Veṅkaṭamādhava ad loc.

[58] Geldner 1951, vol. 3: 126.

the terms themselves are heard by the audience and cannot be said to be secret.

In this spirit the next verse of the same hymn continues:

X.5.3 *ṛtāyínī māyínī sáṁ dadhāte mitvā́ śíśuṁ jajñatur vardháyantī* ।
víśvasya nā́bhiṁ cárato dhruvásya kavéś cit tántum mánasā viyántaḥ ।।

The two who act according to order, possessing the power to create forms, have united; after having formed a baby they gave birth to it, making it grow. [The *kavís* weave] the thread by separately going with their mind to the navel of all that moves or is fixed, [to the navel] even of the *kaví-*.

māyín-: "possessing the power to create forms"; according to Gonda *māyā́-* is the "power of creating or constructing objects characterized by forms and dimensions".[59]

The translation given above follows Velankar who assumes an ellipsis of *kaváyaḥ* and (*ā́*) *tanvate*, referring to *ṚV* I.159.4c-d *návyaṁ-navyaṁ tántum ā́ tanvate diví samudré antáḥ kaváyaḥ sudītáyaḥ* "The *kavís* of good splendour spread out always new threads inside the sky, [inside] the ocean."[60]

All three verses seem to raise the subject of the interplay of poetic creativity and the essence of Agni, culminating in the rather cryptic statement of verse 3 with its ellipsis and the lack of numerical agreement. The root *vī-*, even if not considered as the base for the derivation of *viyántaḥ*,[61] resonates phonetically and is thereby connected to *véḥ* from the first verse. In addition to that, the mentioning of *kaví-* connects this verse with the previous one, even if the bearer of this designation cannot be determined with certitude. An interpretation "he tracks the place/the poetic word" for *padáṁ véḥ* would nicely go with the hymn: Agni resides in the poet's heart and looks out; he traces the word which in turn is guarded by the *kavís*, i.e. it is added to their poetic vocabulary. Correspondingly, *véḥ* can be seen here again as a 3rd person singular aorist injunctive. Thus, *padáṁ véḥ* in this hymn may form part of an explanation for the creativity of the poet. A complexity is added to the hymn by the

[59] Gonda 1959: 129.

[60] Velankar 1958: 6.

[61] Oldenberg 1912: 201.

referential indeterminacy which occurs in verses 1 and 3: The object of reference of "the one ocean" is as unclear as that of *kaví*. This points to the conclusion that for a poem to be formulated it takes the poet and Agni, both of them involved in a reflective interplay of composing and perceiving.

The final attestation of *padáṁ véḥ* can be found in *R̥V* I.164, the famous "riddle-hymn".[62] Here, the syntagm is embedded in a verse which marks the end of a series of questions concerning the nature of Agni, sacrifice, the One and the origin of the sun:[63]

I.164.4 *kó dadarśa prathamáṁ jā́yamānam asthanvántaṁ yád anasthā́ bíbharti* ।
bhū́myā ásur ásr̥g ātmā́ kvà svit kó vidvā́ṁsam úpa gāt prá́ṣṭum etát ॥

Who has seen the first one being born, when the boneless one carries him who has bones? Where, then, has been the vital power, the blood, the self of the earth? Who will approach a knowing person to ask this?

Apart from a probable but disguised reference to Agni this verse displays an interesting shift of perspective in pāda d: The focus of the interrogation is shifted from inquiring about some entities to the very process of asking. It becomes clear in the next verse that the speaker only talks about himself:

I.164.5 *pā́kaḥ pr̥chāmi mánasā́vijānan devā́nām enā́ níhitā padā́ni* ।
vatsé baṣkáyé 'dhi saptá tántūn ví tatnire kaváya ótavā́ u ॥

Immature I hereby ask, unknowing in my mind about the laid-down tracks of the gods. Over the grown-up calf (?) the *kavís* have stretched seven threads in order to weave.

In this stanza the poet asks about the *níhitā padā́ni* of the gods which could not only mean "the traces" but also "the words of the gods", i.e. their poetic designations, since the *kavís* are mentioned here as well. Furthermore, by contrasting the knowing *kavís* with himself — pretending to be nescient — and by repeatedly referring to the "One" the poet transcends the ritual activities and searches for the entity which enables the interplay between cosmos, poetry, and ritual.

---

[62] Cf. Houben 2000 and the literature cited there.

[63] Brown 1978: 61.

In the next verse the attention is turned towards a cosmogonical question:

I.164.6 *ácikitvāñ cikitúṣaś cid átra kavī́n pr̥chāmi vidmáne ná vidvā́n* ।
ví yás tastámbha ṣáḷ imā́ rájāṁsy ajásya rūpé kím ápi svid ékam ॥

Unperceiving I ask just the perceiving *kavís* here, not knowing, in order to know: Just what is the One in form of the Unborn, who propped apart these six regions?

This is one of the verses where the "One" is mentioned.[64] It is particularly interesting here that the poets are being addressed for giving an answer. Whatever the right answer may be, it has to be in the right, i.e. metrical form.

In the next verse, which again contains *padáṁ véḥ*, the mode of speech changes from interrogative to imperative:

I.164.7 *ihá bravītu yá īm aṅgá védāsyá vāmásya níhitam padáṁ véḥ* ।
śīrṣṇáḥ kṣīráṁ duhrate gā́vo asya vavríṁ vásānā udakám padā́puḥ ॥

Let him who knows for sure proclaim here the laid-down track of this dear bird; from his head the cows give milk, dressed in his cover they drank water with the foot.

Beginning with Mādhava most of the commentators interpret this verse as a poetic allusion to the Vedic theory of rain, and in this interpretation the "placed-down track of the dear bird" is seen as the track of the sun, accordingly.[65] It has furthermore been argued that at least large parts of this hymn refer to the Pravargya ritual. Both points of view do not necessarily contradict each other.[66] While acknowledging the soundness of these interpretations it is nevertheless possible to adduce additional arguments for a more detailed interpretation: This verse is the end of a series of questions beginning with verse 4 about cosmos, ritual, and knowledge. *Níhitam padám* in verse 7 ties in with *níhitā padā́ni* in verse 5 where the *kavís* are described as "stretching threads", presumably performing their poetical and ritual activities. From mentioning the *kavís* in verse 5 the poet proceeds

---

[64] Forms of *éka-* are also used in vv. 2, 10, 44, 46, 48.

[65] Mādhava ad loc.; Geldner 1951, vol 1: 228f.; Witzel et al. 2007: 736.

[66] Houben 2000.

to address them directly in verse 6. Verse 7 marks the end of this sequence and is a turning point, since a new topic is introduced here. The shift of mode from indicative to imperative may be taken as a token of self-assertion, if it is considered to be rhetorical in character: The poet has laid down the track of the bird, and no one apart from him is able to proclaim it, not even the *kavís*. In this context *padáṁ véḥ* gets its importance: It could be understood as referring to the subject of *bravītu* (the contemporary audience would also have noticed the assonance of *vī* and *véḥ*): The one possessing knowledge is requested to speak out since he has traced the right poetic designation for the dear one, which is presumably the sun or Agni. By implication it is only the poet himself who understands the enigmatic expressions and proclaims them. But though there is a change in the subject for *véḥ*, the morphological analysis remains the same; here again it could be assumed to be a 3rd person singular aorist injunctive.

7. A Problematic Udātta

Before coming to a conclusion, a formal objection with regard to the view of *véḥ* as a verb may come up: *véḥ* carries the udātta whereas verbs in main clauses do not. This objection may turn out to be not as serious as it looks: It may be argued that the perception of *padáṁ véḥ* as containing additional semantic content could be purely based on phonetic similarity.[67] However, there is a difference between the mere assonance of sounds and the complete reinterpretation of a syntagm. There may be two options for tackling this problem: 1. Grammaticalization or 2. Translation of *padáṁ véḥ* as a subordinate clause. Regarding 1: In his revision of the material collected by Oldenberg with regard to the accentuation of verbs in the *R̥gveda*, Klein has dealt with the irregular accent of *mr̥ḷátā* followed by *naḥ* in *R̥V* VII.60.10.[68] He explained its accent by drawing attention to the fact that eight out of ten attestations of *mr̥ḷatā* in the *R̥V* carry the udātta, including all six attestations of *mr̥ḷatā naḥ*. Klein considers this last syntagm as a clause with initial position of a verb which keeps its accent even when embedded in larger units.[69] It seems tempting to explain the udātta of

---

[67] Comparable to what Elizarenkova has called "grammar of expression"; see Elizarenkova 1995a: 107(-152).

[68] Klein 1992: 78, working on the material collected in Oldenberg 1906.

[69] Klein 1992: 78.

véḥ along similar lines: Six out of its seven attestations as an inflected verb in the *R̥V* carry the udātta. However, this explanation would not work for *padáṁ véḥ*, since the first place of this syntagm is not occupied by a verb. Thus, the udātta of *véḥ* cannot be said to have been taken over from its occurrence in isolation and this explanation is therefore ruled out. Regarding 2: It would also be possible to consider *padáṁ véḥ* as a subordinate clause. It is well known and undisputed that verbs in subordinate clauses carry the udātta, even if there is no segmental subordinator. Hence, it may be promising to interpret *padáṁ véḥ* in this way, although this is not a flawless explanation at first sight. To what syntactical unit should *padáṁ véḥ* be subordinated? It was argued above that the additional interpretation of this syntagm is related at least to the complete content of the verse where it is attested, if not to larger units of the respective hymn. Subordination to smaller units within a verse would render this approach unconvincing. Perhaps a solution for the problem of the udātta of *véḥ* can be found in another direction:[70] If understood as "track or place of the bird" *padáṁ véḥ* can be seen as an element of the esoteric lexicon of the Vedic poets to be used in verses of mysterious content. However, if this syntagm is supposed to carry an additional semantic content which is hidden from common understanding, the occurrence of the udātta could fulfil another purpose. By furnishing *véḥ* with an udātta, the esoteric meaning of "you" or "he/she/it traces the word" is concealed by the (relatively speaking) more comprehensible meaning "track or place of the bird", and only those who really know would perceive the more esoteric meaning. To this effect it would contribute to the enigma of the R̥gvedic hymns where *padáṁ véḥ* was used. This leads to the final question of the nature and of the aim of this enigma.

8. Self-reference, Enigma, and Epiphany in Vedic Poetry

I hope it has become clear from the considerations presented above that it is possible to understand *padáṁ véḥ* in all its R̥gvedic attestations not only as nom./acc. sg. + gen. but simultaneously as acc. sg. + verbal form of *vī-* and that its double meaning suits the respective contents of the hymns in which the syntagm occurs. Nevertheless, a more pragmatic question arises even if the proposed interpretation be

[70] I owe this idea to Hans Henrich Hock.

accepted: Is it necessary to understand the syntagm this way? As has been seen, the traditional view of *padáṁ véḥ* as referring in one way or another to Agni goes well with the context of the respective verses even if there may be some disagreement about the exact object of reference. Given the nature of the Ṛgvedic hymns this is but to be expected and, furthermore, a diverging translation of *padáṁ véḥ* does not solve existing problems but instead raises new ones. Exactly that is the point: All attestations of *padáṁ véḥ* are situated in verses which despite their syntactical lucidity are completely enigmatic with regard to their content. It is therefore possible to consider the use of *padáṁ véḥ* as a means used by the poets to add to the complexity of their poems by benefitting from semantic and morphological ambiguities of the language they used and invented. And lest we forget, there existed an objective for this complex poetical language: The Vedic cult was, as far as we know, aniconic, so the only means to show the presence of the divinity was the poetical language of the poet. But there are two exceptions: Agni as well as Soma are perceivable by everyone being present at the sacrificial ground. To render these two phenomena into two lofty divinities was perhaps the most challenging task for the Vedic poets. And every kind of enigma in use contributed to the revelation of the mysteriousness and majesty of the praised divinities. Furthermore, the poets seem to have felt the necessity to reflect on their own activity within their poems. Especially in hymns addressed to Agni, both aspects — enigma and auto-commentary — sometimes have been linked.

One may even go a step further and ponder the subject of *véḥ* in the attestations of this syntagm. Except for *ṚV* I.164.7 Agni seems to be the most likely candidate, given his designation as *padavī́-* in *ṚV* III.5.1, his agency in passages where *véḥ* is used as a 3rd person singular aorist, and the contexts of the verses in which *padáṁ véḥ* occurs. However, since the poets, or more specifically the Aṅgiras, are said to trace the *padá-* in *ṚV* VI.1.4, the possibility of ascribing the action of "tracing" with regard to *padáṁ véḥ* to the poet himself opens up as well. It seems likely that the respective verses have been deliberately furnished with this indeterminacy. Thus the poets enabled themselves to link the enigma of the god, whose presence is perceived by everyone, but whose true majesty lies in secret and is approachable only for the gifted poet, to the mystery of poetic creativity. *Padáṁ véḥ* may therefore be understood as one example of this entanglement.[71]

References

PRIMARY

R̥V: *R̥gveda Saṁhitā*, cited from Müller 1890-92 and Vishva Bandhu 1963-66.

SECONDARY

Bhattacharya, Dipak, 1997, *The Paippalāda-Saṁhitā of the Atharvaveda*, Critically ed. from palm-leaf manuscripts in the Oriya script discovered by Durgamohan Bhattacharyya and one Śāradā manuscript, Volume One: Consisting of the First Fifteen Kāṇḍas (Bibliotheca Indica Series; 318), Calcutta: The Asiatic Society.

Bloomfield, Maurice, 1906, "Seven Emendations of the Text of the Rig Veda", *Journal of the American Oriental Society*, **27:** 72-78.

Böhtlingk, Otto v., et al. 1855-75, *Sanskrit-Wörterbuch*, Bearbeitet von Otto v. Böhtlingk und Rudolf Roth, 7 vols. St. Petersburg: Kaiserliche Akademie der Wissenschaften.

Bosch, Lourens V.D., 1985, "The Āprī hymns of the R̥gveda and their Interpretation", *Indo-Iranian Journal*, **28:** 95-122, 169-89.

Brown, W. Norman, 1968, "Agni, Sun, Sacrifice and *vāc*: A Sacerdotal Ode by Dīrghatamas (Rig Veda 1.164)", *Journal of the American Oriental Society*, **88:** 199-218 (= Brown 1978: 53-74, with the new title "Dīrghatamas's Vision of Creation").

———, 1978, *India and Indology: Selected articles by W. Norman Brown*, ed. Rosane Rocher, Delhi: Motilal Banarsidass.

Debrunner, Albert, and Jacob Wackernagel, 1930, *Altindische Grammatik, Bd. 3: Nominalflexion, Zahlwort, Pronomen*, Göttingen: Vandenhoeck & Ruprecht.

Elizarenkova, Tatyana, 1989, 1995, 1999, *Rigveda*, Mandaly I-IV, Mandaly V-VIII, Mandaly IX-X, Moskva: Nauka.

———, 1995a, *Language and Style of the Vedic R̥ṣis*, Albany/New York: State University of New York.

———, 2001, "Contribution to the Status of Name in the R̥gveda", *Indologica Taurinensia*, **27:** 35-54.

Geldner, Karl F., 1951, 1957, *Der Rig-Veda: Aus dem Sanskrit ins Deutsche übersetzt und mit einem laufenden Kommentar versehen*, 4 vols. (Harvard Oriental Series 33-36), Cambridge/Mass.: Harvard University Press.

[71] For criticism and advice I would like to thank Hans Henrich Hock, Mareike Heinritz, Marc Lücke, and the audience at the 15th World Sanskrit Conference in New Delhi.

Gonda, Jan., 1959, *Four Studies in the Language of the Veda* (Disputationes Rheno-Trajectinae; 3.) 's-Gravenhage: Mouton.

———, 1963, *The Vision of the Vedic Poets*, The Hague: Mouton.

Gotō, Toshifumi, 1987, *Die "1. Präsensklasse" im Vedischen: Untersuchung der vollstufigen thematischen Wurzelpräsentia*. (Veröffentlichungen der Kommission für Linguistik und Kommunikationsforschung; 18), Wien: Verlag der Österreichischen Akademie der Wissenschaften.

Grassmann, Hermann, 1996, *Wörterbuch zum Rig-Veda: 6., überarbeitete und ergänzte Auflage* von Maria Kozianka, Wiesbaden: Harrassowitz.

Hacker, Paul, 1973, *"Vrata"*, in *Nachrichten der Akademie der Wissenschaften in Göttingen. I. Philologisch-historische Klasse*, 1973: 5.109-142.

Hoffmann, Karl, 1967, *Der Injunktiv im Veda: Eine synchronische Funktionsuntersuchung*, Heidelberg: Winter.

Houben, Jan E.M., 2000, "The Ritual Pragmatics of a Vedic Hymn: The 'Riddle Hymn' and the Pravargya Ritual", *Journal of the American Oriental Society* **120:** 499-536.

Jamison, Stephanie, 2004, "Poetry and Purpose in the R̥gveda: Structuring Enigmas", in *The Vedas: Texts, Language and Ritual: Proceedings of the Third International Vedic Workshop, Leiden 2002*, ed. Arlo Griffiths and Jan Houben, pp. 237-49 (Groningen Oriental Studies, 20), Groningen: Egbert Forsten.

Kiehnle, Catharina, 1979, *Vedisch* ukṣ *und* ukṣ/vakṣ: *Wortgeschichtliche und exegetische Untersuchungen* (Alt-und Neu-Indische Studien, 21), Wiesbaden: Steiner.

Kim, Jeong-Soo, 2010, *Untersuchungen zu altindischen Abstrakta und Adjektiven im Rigveda und Atharvaveda: Die primären* a-*Stämme und die* ana-*Bildungen* (Münchener Forschungen zur historischen Sprachwissenschaft 10), Bremen: Hempen.

Köhler, Frank, 2011, *Kaví im R̥gveda: Dichtung, Ritual und Schöpfung im frühvedischen Denken*, Aachen: Shaker.

Lüders, Heinrich, 1951, 1959, *Varuṇa: Varuṇa und die Wasser, Varuṇa und das R̥ta*, aus dem Nachlaß herausgegeben von Ludwig Alsdorf, Göttingen: Vandenhoeck & Ruprecht.

Mādhava = "Sāyaṇa"; included in Müller 1890-92 and Vishva Bandhu 1963-66.

Malzahn, Melanie, 2002, "Auf der Spur von Ai. *véḥ*", *Indo-Iranian Journal* **45:** 197-204.

Mayrhofer, Manfred, 1992, 1996, 2001, *Etymologisches Wörterbuch des Altindoarischen*, 3 vols. (Indogermanische Bibliothek: Reihe 2, Wörterbücher), Heidelberg: Winter.

Müller, F. Max, 1890-92, *Rig-Veda-Saṁhitā: The Sacred Hymns of the Brāhmans together with the Commentary of Sāyanākārya*, ed. F. Max Müller, 2nd edn., London: Frowde.

Narten, Johanna, 1964, *Die sigmatischen Aoriste im Veda*, Wiesbaden: Harrassowitz.

Oldenberg, Hermann, 1906, "Vedische Untersuchungen 16: Die Verbalenklisis im Ṛgveda", *Zeitschrift der Deutschen Morgenländischen Gesellschaft* **60:** 707-40 (= Oldenberg 1967: 182-216).

———, 1909, 1912, *Ṛgveda: Textkritische und exegetische Noten. Erstes bis sechstes Buch; Siebtes bis zehntes Buch*, Berlin: Weidmannsche Buchhandlung.

———, 1913, "Ṛgveda 10.13", *Indogermanische Forschungen* **31:** 126-42. (Delbrück-Festschrift.) (= Oldenberg 1967: 813-29).

———, 1967, *Hermann Oldenberg: Kleine Schriften*, ed. Klaus Janert, 2 vols. (Glasenapp-Stiftung, 1), Wiesbaden: Franz Steiner-Verlag.

Renou, Louis, 1958, *Études sur le vocabulaire du Rgveda: Première série* (Publications de l'Institut Français d'Indologie, 5), Pondichéry.

———, 1964a, 1964b, 1965, *Études védiques et pāṇinéennes*, tome 12-14, Paris: Boccard.

Roesler, Ulrike, 1997, *Licht und Leuchten im Rgveda: Untersuchungen zum Wortfeld des Leuchtens und zur Bedeutung des Lichts* (Indica et Tibetica, 32), Swisttal-Odendorf: Indica et Tibetica.

Scarlata, Salvatore, 1999, *Die Wurzelkomposita im Ṛg-Veda*, Wiesbaden: Reichert.

Schindler, Hans Jochem, 1972, *Das Wurzelnomen im Arischen und Griechischen*, Dissertation, Universität Würzburg.

Shukla, Siddh Nath, 2001, *The Ṛgveda, Maṇḍala III: A Critical Study of the Sāyaṇa Bhāṣya and other Interpretations of the Ṛgveda (3.1.1 to 3.7.3)*, New Delhi: Sharada.

Slaje, Walter, 2010, "Sāyaṇa oder Mādhava? Verfasserschaft und Reihenfolge der *Saṁhitā*-Kommentare aus Vijayanagara", *Zeitschrift der Deutschen Morgenländischen Gesellschaft* **160:** 383-414.

Thieme, Paul, 1938, *Der Fremdling im Ṛgveda: Eine Studie über die Bedeutung der Worte* ari, arya, aryaman *und* ārya (Abhandlungen für die Kunde des Morgenlandes 23), Leipzig: Brockhaus.

———, 1949, *Untersuchungen zur Wortkunde und Auslegung des Rigveda* (Hallische Monographien, 7), Halle: Max Niemeyer.

Thompson, George, 1995, "The Pursuit of Hidden Tracks in Vedic", *Indo-Iranian Journal* **38**: 1-30.

Velankar, H.D., 1958, "Hymns to Agni in Maṇḍala X (1-80)", *Journal of the University of Bombay* 27 (New Series), Part 2, Arts Number **33:** 1-28.

———, 1968, *Ṛgveda Maṇḍala III: Translation and Critical Notes by H.D. Velankar; Introduction and Indices by S.A. Upadhyaya*, Bombay: University of Bombay.

Veṅkaṭamādhava; included in Vishva Bandhu 1963-66.

Vishva Bandhu, 1963-66, *R̥gveda: The Padapāṭha and the available portions of the Bhāṣyas by Skandasvāmin and Udgītha, the Vyākhyā by Veṅkaṭa-Mādhava and Mudgala's Vr̥tti based on Sāyaṇabhāṣya*, ed. and annotated with text-comparative data from original manuscripts and other Vedic works, 8 vols. (Vishveshvaranand Indological Series, 19-26), Hoshiarpur: Vishveshvaranand Vedic Research Institute.

Werba, Chlodwig, 1997, *Verba Indoarica: Die primären und sekundären Wurzeln der Sanskrit-Sprache*. Pars 1: *Radices Primariae*, Wien: Verlag der Österreichischen Akademie der Wissenschaften.

Witzel, Michael, et al. 2007, *Rig-Veda: Das heilige Wissen: Erster und zweiter Liederkreis, aus dem vedischen Sanskrit übersetzt und herausgegeben* von Michael Witzel und Toshifumi Gotō unter Mitarbeit von Eijirō Dōyama und Mislav Ježic, Frankfurt a. M.: Verlag der Weltreligionen im Inselverlag.

9

Text-critical Study of the *Pativedanāni* Section of the Kauśika-Sūtra

Nirmala R. Kulkarni

1. Introduction

THE pativedana ritual, alternatively referred to as *patividyam*[1] or *patilābhakarman*,[2] is commonly recorded in the Vedic tradition. It is found in the *Śaunaka* (*AVŚ*) and *Paippalāda* (*AVP*) *Saṁhitā* of the *Atharvaveda* (*AV*), the *Kṛṣṇa Yajurveda* (*Maitrāyaṇī* and *Kāṭhaka*), and the *Śukla Yajurveda*. The Śrautasūtras (ŚS) have incorporated the ritual in the *tryambakahoma*,[3] based on the description in the Saṁhitās, the only exception being the *Vaitāna Śrautasūtra*.

The *Kauśika-Sūtra* (*KS*) records certain rituals under the title *pativedanāni*, based on the *Atharvaveda*, and the hymns employed in the ritual are also referred to as *pativedanāni*.

The *pativedana* ritual, in general, has two objectives: In the case of a spinster it helps in finding a husband; in the case of a woman already married it helps in bestowing marital pleasures (*bhaga*).[4] The *KS* also has extended the oracles for obtaining a husband as a part of marriage

---

[1] *Ṛgveda* X.102.11; *Paippalāda Saṁhitā* XIX.34.8, XX.35.5; *Maitrāyaṇī Saṁhitā* III.8.4; *Kāṭhaka Saṁhitā* 8.17; and *Taittirīya Brāhmaṇa* 2.4.2.7.

[2] Kauśikapaddhati on the *KS* 34.12.

[3] In the following texts the verse *tryambakam yajāmahe sugandhiṁ puṣṭivardhanam* is recited with a change to *pativedanam* if the sacrificer has an unmarried daughter. The daughter circumambulates the fire. *Āpastamba ŚS* 8.18.3; *Baudhāyana ŚS* 5.16-24; *Bhāradvāja ŚS* 8.21.10; *Vādhūla ŚS* 1.7.4.72; *Hiraṇyakeśi ŚS* 5.5.18; *Drāhyāyaṇa ŚS* 13.3.3.

[4] See *KŚS* 5.10.15: *kumāryaś cottareṇobhayatra patikāmā bhagakāmā vā*.

rites.[5] The twofold meaning of the root *vid*[6] as well as the content of the *AV* hymns has given rise to variety of rituals aiming at either *jñāna* (getting information about a husband) or *lābha* (finding a husband for an unmarried girl).

Other hymns and rituals can also be considered *pativedanas*. For instance, the Apālā hymn (*Ṛgveda* VIII.91) expresses a spinster's plight (Jamison 2000: 240).[7] The *Sāmavidhāna Brāhmaṇa* (2.6.14)[8] records a ritual for a similar purpose to be performed by the girl's father. Certain rituals are performed even in modern India for an unmarried daughter who has crossed marriageable age. These rituals include recitation of passages from Purāṇa texts, fasting, etc.

KS 34.12 to 34.24 describes a variety of *pativedana* rituals which confirm the importance given to marriage in case of a girl in the society of that time.[9] Moreover, it employs two complete hymns (II.36, VI.60) and two verses from the fifth kāṇḍa (V.1.4, V.2.8) of the *AVŚ* for these rituals.

In terms of the hymns or verses employed therein, the rituals form four groups displaying a variety of independent rituals.

A. RITUALS TO BE PERFORMED WITH AVŚ II.36

1. In accordance with *KS* 34.13 and 34.14, the performer makes the girl eat rice cooked with sesame seeds and offers ornaments and certain fragrant substances to the girl while reciting the hymn *AVŚ* 2.36.[10] He offers her these substances on an altar

---

5 The hymn *AVŚ* II.36 forms a part of the marriage ritual in the Ātharvaṇic tradition. Compare *KS* 75.1 *pativedanam ca.*

6 *Vid*[2] (parasmaipada) *jñāne* and *vid*[6] (parasmaipada) *lābhe.*

7 Schmidt (1987) instead interprets the hymn as related to a puberty ritual. One might argue, however, that one cannot draw any line of demarcation between puberty rite and *pativedana* ritual. Puberty rites, husband-finding rituals, *caturthīkarma* or *garbhādhāna* are broadly included in the same category as these rites, being aimed at preparing a girl for the next stage, i.e. ceremonial coitus with her husband.

8 *kanyāpravahaṇa ekarātropoṣito 'māvāsyāyāṁ niśi catuspatha 'ehy u ṣu bravāṇi ta'* (Grāmageya 1.1.7.1-2) *ityetena abhiṣiñcet* । *trir abhiṣiktā pradāyate.*

9 See also *Śatapatha Brāhmaṇa* 2.6.4.14: *patayo hy eva striyai pratiṣṭhā.*

10 The second ritual is very interesting. The priest offers the girl auspicious objects that are mainly associated with the marital status of a woman. →

made of clay from an animal lair.[11] The ritual substances probably are intended to confer an economically happy and stable married life.[12]

2. Another ritual, described in *KS* 34.15, is to be performed by the brother of the girl. He places rice and barley in a bronze vessel full of water and makes the girl walk around it from the left. Then he offers libations of rice and barley in the fire for Aryaman, the presiding deity of marriage.
3. According to *KS* 34.16, the performer makes the girl climb a boat (metaphorically the boat of Bhaga, the presiding deity of marital pleasures) and while reciting *AVŚ* II.36.5 he makes her climb down the boat.
4. The girl releases seven calves tied to a rope in the ritual described in *KS* 34.17. If she unties the calves from left to right, she may get married.
5. The last variety of ritual to be performed with the hymn *AVŚ* II.36 is described in the *KS* 34.18-19. In this rite, a bull is covered with a new garment. The place where it rushes implies the direction of the place of the husband.

→ These are gold (representing semen) along with the fragrant substances bdellium and *aukṣa*. Especially in the *Atharvaveda*, fragrance is associated with happy married life for a woman.

[11] According to Jamison (2000: 244), however, ". . . the association of these two fairly rare words, *ākhara* and *ākhu* (which are probably etymologically connected) with two forms of husband finding seems unlikely to be coincidental, especially since burrowing animals and a burrow may not be the first semantic association one makes with marriage. The burrow and its maker may symbolize the cozy home to be made by the newly-married couple, but perhaps more likely given the rampant sexual symbolism elsewhere in the ritual, the burrow may obliquely refer to the woman's sexual organs."

[12] Gonda 1980: 103. According to him "the animals know the essence of the earth and cast the essence up so as to form mole-hills which, therefore, represent this essence and bring about welfare (prosperity, wealth, *śrī* *Śatapatha Brāhmaṇa* 2.1.1.7)". This interpretation seems to be more convincing than Jamison's.

B. THE RITUAL TO BE PERFORMED WITH AVŚ V.1.4

KS 34.20 states that the brother offers rice cooked with sesame seeds to his unmarried sister while reciting the verse *pra yad ete.*

C. THE RITUAL TO BE PERFORMED WITH AVŚ V.2.8

According to *KS* 34.21, the brother makes his sister eat rice cooked with sesame seeds with the verse *imā brahma.*

D. THE RITUALS TO BE PERFORMED WITH AVŚ VI.60

In accordance with *KS* 34.22-24, the performer offers libations to Aryaman early in the morning before crows fly to their nests. The direction of the crows indicates the direction of the husband's place.

2. The Problem

Gonda (1977: 615) states that "the present form of the *KS* is a composite whole made up of parts of different origin and authorship". This argument is yet to be established by a thorough analytical study of the text. The text quotes *sakalapāṭha* mantras, especially from the *Paippalāda Saṁhitā*. This has been supposed to be the main reason for inferring the presence of many redactors (Bahulkar 2009: 13). The *strīkarmāṇi* section does not quote many mantras in extenso and thereby gives the impression of a somewhat more congruent form. Still, it is to be understood that some changes might have crept in during the written transmission of the text. Some of these modifications can be inferred with the help of the *KS* text that appears in the commentaries of Dārila (*DB*, Diwekar et al. 1972), and Keśava (*KP*, Limaye et al. 1982), as well as in the *KS* text quoted by Sāyaṇa (Viśva Bandhu 1960-64) while commenting on the *AVŚ*. These three sources function as testimonia in the textual study of the *KS* (Kulkarni 2010: 220-32).

Sūtras 34.12 to 34.24 describing *pativedana* rituals involve certain textual problems. Out of these, sūtras 34.20 and 34.21 have not been recorded uniformly by the commentators Dārila, Keśava, and Sāyaṇa. The present paper makes an attempt to discuss this problem as well as searching for the reason behind the non-unanimity among the commentators.

3. Discrepancies in the Text of the KS

3.1. SŪTRA 34.20

This sūtra reads *jāmyai pra yad eta* (*AVŚ* V.1.4) *ity āgamakr̥śaram* "while reciting the verse *pra yad ete* the performer makes his sister eat rice cooked with sesame seeds". In the context of this sūtra, the text recorded by Bloomfield (1890) does not vary from the *KS* text of Dārila as well as from that of Keśava edited by Limaye et al. and published by the Tilak Maharashtra Vidyapeeth. In the introduction to each hymn Sāyaṇa generally quotes the appropriate *KS* to explain the viniyoga of the hymn. Even if any verse of a particular hymn shows additional rubrication, he explains the viniyoga and quotes the appropriate sūtra. While explaining the viniyoga of *AVŚ* V.1.4, however, Sāyaṇa does not cite *pativedana* as the employment of the verse.[13] Furthermore, the sūtra does not have any other ritual to prescribe. It simply repeats the instruction of making the girl eat *kr̥śara*.

Though Sāyaṇa has not treated the verse as to be employed in the *pativedana*, the wording of the verse (mantraliṅga) signifies its association with the said rite. The last quarter of the verse reads *jāmyai dhuryaṁ patim airayethām*.[14] However, mantraliṅga is not the only factor accepted to choose a verse. Sometimes the wording of the verse is set aside and another verse, not even referring to the ritual, is employed.[15] Even according to Dārila, the Kauśika has not described rites in accordance with the mantras, in order to avoid a lengthy text.[16]

Against this background, the non-mention of this particular *pativedana* verse by Sāyaṇa suggests two possibilities:

---

[13] Sāyaṇa prescribes employment of this hymn mainly for winning victory in battle. *AVŚ* V.1 together with V.2 is employed in *puṣṭikarman*, *saptagrāmalābhakarman*, and *samr̥ddhikarman*.

[14] ". . . do you send for the sister a capable spouse" (Whitney 1905).

[15] See Sāyaṇa on *AVŚ* I.1 . . . *'aindryā gārhapatyam upatiṣṭhate' itivad balīyasā śrutyā liṅgaṁ bādhitvā guṇakalpanāyāpi viniyogasaṁbhavāt* (Vishva Bandhu 1960: 33).

[16] *mantrādhikareṇāśeṣeṣu vidhivacanaṁ nyāyyaṁ granthagauravān nāha* (Diwekar et al. 1971: 1).

1. Sāyaṇa's text might have undergone some changes and the viniyoga of this verse might have been omitted.
2. It is possible that the text of the *KS* known to Sāyaṇa is the oldest, in comparison to present-day manuscripts. The readings accepted by Dārila and Keśava, then, might have been introduced in the course of transmission.

At least apparently, the second possibility prevails.

3.2. SŪTRA 34.21

The immediately following sūtra 34.21 reads *imā brahma* (*AVŚ* V.2.8) *iti svasre*. It is recorded in the footnotes of Bloomfield's edition (1890: 93). Footnote 16 cites the occurrence of the verse in the *Atharvaveda* as V.2.8 and XX.107.11. The next note reads "This sūtra is wanting in D (i.e. in Dārila)".[17]

The commentary of Sāyaṇa presents interesting evidence. The said verse forms a part of *AVŚ* V.2.8 as well as *AVŚ* XX.107.11. At both places Sāyaṇa does not cite its viniyoga in the *pativedana*.

Thus, it is possible that Sāyaṇa did not know the text version of *KS* that notes the employment of this verse in the *pativedana* ritual.

The absence of this sūtra in the Berlin codex of the *DB* as well as the silence of Sāyaṇa regarding the viniyoga of the *AVŚ* hymns in the *pativedana* indicates the possibility of its later addition in the *KS*. The text of the verse might have favoured its inclusion in the *pativedanāni*. The verse *AVŚ* V.2.8[18] (as well as *AVŚ* XX.107.11) runs as follows:

---

[17] The *Dārilabhāṣya* (*DB*) edited by Diwekar et al. cites the sūtrapāṭha of the *KS* based on Bloomfield's edition. The editors have modified the readings with the help of the *DB*. The readings of Bloomfield are recorded in the footnotes (Diwekar et al. 1971: 1). In the case of the sūtra in question, no change is recorded either in the main body of the text or in the footnotes (Diwekar et al. 1971: 25). Thus, it seems that the *KS* text quoted in the *DB* and the *KS* (edition of Bloomfield) does not show any variance. Diwekar et al.'s edition of the *DB* has reproduced the Berlin codex of the *DB* on which the edition is based. The Berlin codex as seen in the offset copy does not record the sūtra 34.21 *imā brahma iti svasre*. However, the edited text of *DB* reads the sūtra, without showing any variation from Bloomfield (Diwekar et al. 1971: 104). The editors record the sūtra as part and parcel of the text.

[18] The verse also occurs in the *R̥V* X.120.8; *AVP* VI.1.8 (Raghu Vira 1936; Bhattacharya 1997) with variations.

imā brahma bṛhaddivaḥ kṛṇavad indrāya śūṣam agriyaḥ svarṣāḥ ।
maho gotrasya kṣayati svarājā turaścid viśvam arṇavat tapasvān ।।[19]

The padapāṭha glosses *svarṣāḥ* "the heaven-winner" as *svasaḥ*. The similarity between *svasṛ* and *svarṣāḥ*, especially reinforced by the form in the padapāṭha, might have inspired some scribe to identify this passage as a *pativedanāni* verse for *svasṛ*, i.e. for a sister. Sāyaṇa, by contrast, notes that the entire hymn *AVŚ* V.2 should be employed to fulfil any desire. However, he does not specify the viniyoga of V.2.8.[20]

Thus, it seems that sūtra 34.21 finds no space in the *KS* text as it may have been known to Dārila and Sāyaṇa. It could have been added at a later period, in the transmission of the *KP* manuscripts.

4. Conclusions

As mentioned earlier, the present form of the *KS* indicates the presence of many redactors and has been subject to many influences. Not only the text of the *KS*, but even the text of the *DB*[21] as well as that of the *KP* might have undergone some changes in the course of time. All these texts might have been transmitted through either oral (?), i.e. practical ritual tradition, or written tradition for at least six or seven centuries with many interventions. It is natural for these texts to exhibit the influence of the scribes who might have intentionally or unintentionally modified the text.

In the present paper a case of two sūtras from the *Pativedanāni* section is discussed where the text shows variation due to such modification by later scribes. I have tried to show that *KS* 34.20 and 34.21 were

---

19 "These incantations (*brahman*) may Bṛhaddiva, the foremost heaven winner, make a strain (śūṣa) for Indra; he rules an autocrat, over the great stall (*gotra*); may he quick (? Tura), rich in fervor, send (?) all." (Whitney 1905: 224)

20 The performer offers libation to Indrāgnī or he simply meditates upon them with this hymn: *tathā sarvaphalakāmo 'nena sūktena indrāgnī yajate upatiṣṭhate vā*. It is possible that *pativedana* is also included in the sarvakāmanās.

21 Rotaru (2010: 454-67) deals with the manuscript details of the *DB* in detail. Some of the details supplied by her also establish a corrupt condition of the available manuscripts of *DB* for at least two or three centuries. She supports her argument on the basis of a comment of Devabhadra.

probably not included in the earliest layer of the *KS* text. On the basis of the readings presented by three commentators it could be argued that the text recorded by Sāyaṇa may be comparatively the oldest. The text recorded in the known manuscript of the *DB* shows the next stage, and the text known to Keśava shows a comparatively later stage.

Abbreviations

AVP	*Paippalāda Saṁhitā of the Atharvaveda*, ed. Raghu Vira (1966), Lahore, and Dipak Bhattacharya (1997), Calcutta
AVŚ	*Śaunaka Saṁhitā of the Atharvaveda*, ed. Vishva Bandhu (1960), Hoshiarpur
DB	*Dārila-Bhāṣya on Kauśika Sūtra*, ed. H.R. Diwekar et al. (1972), Pune
KS	*Kauśika Sūtra*, ed. M. Bloomfield (1889), Delhi (repr.)
KP	*Kauśikapaddhati*, ed. V.P. Limaye et al. (1889), Pune

Primary Sources

Agashe, Kashinath Sastri et al. (eds.), 1907-32, *Satyāṣāḍha-Hiraṇyakeśi Śrautasūtra,* (Anandasram Sanskrit Granthavali 53), Poona: Anandasram.

Bhattacharya, Dipak (ed.), 1997, *The Paippalāda Saṁhitā of the Atharvaveda,* vol. I (Kāṇḍas 1-15), Calcutta: The Asiatic Society.

Bloomfield, M. (ed.), 1889, *The Kauśikasūtra of the Atharvaveda,* with extracts from the commentaries of Dārila and Keśava, repr. 1972, Delhi: Motilal Banarsidass.

Caland, W. (ed.), 1904-13, *The Baudhāyana Śrautasūtra belonging to the Taittirīya Saṁhitā* (Bibliotheca Indica 163), Calcutta: Asiatic Society of Bengal.

———, 1925, *The Kāṭhakagṛhyasūtra,* with extracts from three commentaries, Lahore: Dayananda Mahavidyalaya Sanskrit Granthamala 7.

Chaubey B.B. (ed.), 1993, *Vādhūla-Śrauta-Sūtra,* Hoshiarpur: Kātyāyana Sahitya Prakashan.

Diwekar, H.R. et al. (eds.), 1972, *Kauśikasūtra Dārilabhāṣya,* Poona: Tilak Maharashtra Vidyapeeth.

Kashikar, C.G. (ed. & tr.), 1964, *The Śrauta, Pitṛmedhika & Pariśeṣasūtras of Bhāradvāja,* Poona: Vaidik Samshodhan Mandal.

Limaye, V.P. et al. (eds.), 1982, *Keśava's Kauśikapaddhati on the Kauśikasūtra of the Atharvaveda* (Shri Balmukunda Sanskrit Mahavidyalaya Research Series No. 1), Pune: Tilak Maharashtra Vidyapeeth.

R. Shamasatri (ed.), *The Taittirīya Brāhmaṇa,* with the commentary of Bhaṭṭabhāskara Miśra, vols. I-III, repr. 1985, Delhi: Motilal Banarsidass.

Raghu Vira (ed.), 1936, *Atharvavedīya Paippalāda Saṁhitā*, vol I, Lahore: The International Academy of Indian Culture.

Satavalekar, S.D. (ed.), 1942, *Maitrāyaṇī Saṁhitā*, Aundh: Swadhyay Mandal.

———, 1943, *Kṛṣṇayajurvedīya Kāṭhaka Saṁhitā*, Aundh: Swadhyay Mandal.

———, 1946, *Vājasaneyi Mādhyandina Śukla Yajurveda Saṁhitā*, Aundh: Swadhyay Mandal.

Sharma, B.R. (ed.), 1964, *Sāmavidhāna Brāhmaṇa with Vedārthaprakāśa of Sāyaṇa and Padārthamātrāvivṛti of Bharatasvamin*, Tirupati: Kendriya Sanskrit Vidyapeeth.

——— (ed.), 1983, *Drāhyāyaṇa-Śrauta-Sūtra*, with the commentary of Dhanvin, Allahabad: Rashtriya Sanskrit Sansthan.

Sontakke, N.S., and C.G. Kashikar (eds.), 1933-41, *Ṛgveda Saṁhitā with Sāyaṇa's commentary*, vols. I-V, Pune: Vaidik Samshodhan Mandal.

Thite, G.U., 2005, *Āpastamba-Śrauta-Sūtra: Sanskrit text with English translation and notes*, Delhi: New Bharatiya Book Corporation.

Viśva Bandhu (ed.), 1960-64, *The Atharvaveda Saṁhitā with padapāṭha and Sāyaṇa's commentary*, Part I-IV, 2nd edn. (Series 13-17), Hoshiarpur: Viśhveśvarananda Vedic Research Institute.

——— (ed.), 1967, *Vaitāna-Śrauta-Sūtra*, with the commentary called Ākṣepānuvidhi by Somāditya, Hoshiarpur: Vishvesvarananda Vedic Research Institute.

Weber, A. (ed.), 1992, *The Śrautasūtra of Kātyāyana*, repr., Varanasi: The Chaukhamba Sanskrit Series.

———, 1964, *The Śatapatha Brāhmaṇa* (The Choukhamba Sanskrit Series 96), repr., Varanasi: The Chaukhamba Sanskrit Series Office.

Whitney, William Dwight (tr.), 1905, *The Atharvaveda Saṁhitā: Translated with a critical and exegetical commentary, revised and brought nearer to completion and edited by Charles Rockwell Lanman*, vol. 1 & 2, repr., 1984, Delhi: Motilal Banarsidass.

General References

Bahulkar, Shrikant S., 2009, "Paippalāda in the Śaunakīya Literature of the Atharvaveda", paper presented at the 14th World Sanskrit Conference, Kyoto.

Gonda, Jan, 1977, "The Ritual Sūtras", in *A History of Indian Literature*, ed. J. Gonda, vol. I, fasc. 2, Wiesbaden: Otto Harrassowitz.

———, 1980, *Vedic Rituals: The Non-solemn Rites*, Leiden: Brill.

Jamison, Stephanie, 2000, *Sacrificer's Wife: Sacrificed Wife*, New York/Oxford: Oxford University Press.

Kulkarni, Nirmala, 2010, "Manuscript Translation and Discrepancies in Interpretation", in *Proceedings of the Third International Symposium "The*

Book, Romania, Europe", Section "Veda, Vedāṅga and Avesta: Between Orality and Writing, ed. Jan Houben and Julieta Rotaru, pp. 220-32, Bucharest: Bibliotheca Bucarestilor.

Rotaru, Julieta, 2010, "Habent sua fata libelli: The Dārilabhāṣya and its Manuscripts", in *Proceedings of the Third International Symposium "The Book. Romania. Europe", Section "Veda, Vedāṅga and Avesta: Between Orality and Writing,* ed. Jan Houben and Julieta Rotaru, pp. 454-67, Bucharest: Bibliotheca Bucarestilor.

Schmidt, Hans-Peter, 1987, *Some Women's Rites and Rights in the Veda* (Post-Graduate and Research Department Series No. 29), Pune: Bhandarkar Oriental Research Institute.

10

A New Edition and an Annotated Translation of the Kauśika-Sūtra*

Julieta Rotaru and *Shilpa Sumant*

1. Introduction

THE *Kauśika-Sūtra* (*KauśS*) is a Sūtra-text of the *Atharvaveda* that secures a very prominent position in this tradition. Although the *KauśS* is utilized as a Gr̥hya-Sūtra in the *Atharvaveda* tradition, its scope is much wider in subject matter as compared to other manuals of domestic rites. Typical Ātharvaṇic rites such as sorcery, medical ritual for curing diseases, Savas, pacification of omens and portents, are prescribed in this Sūtra, and have no parallels, with a few exceptions,[1] in the ritualism of the other three Vedas. We may describe the *KauśS* as a text focused to rubricate the hymns and verses from the *Atharvaveda* into various rites that include the peculiarly Ātharvaṇic practices in the first place, and also the Gr̥hya and some of the Śrauta rites in that tradition. It is worth mentioning that the *KauśS* serving as a Gr̥hya-Sūtra precedes the *VaiŚS* that deals with the Ātharvaṇic Śrauta ritual. The two available commentaries to the *KauśS*, Dārila's *Bhāṣya* and Keśava's *Paddhati*, as well as the entire Atharvavedic exegetical literature, refer to the *KauśS* as saṁhitāvidhi, "a ritualistic manual explaining [the employment] of the [Śaunaka] Saṁhitā [mantras]", thus rendering it an important tool for the interpretation of the hymns of the *Śaunaka Saṁhitā* (*ŚS*).

* We are grateful to Shrikant Bahulkar for his valuable comments on an earlier draft of this paper. We also express our gratitude towards Alaister Gornall, University of Cambridge for his suggestions to improve our English.

1 The *Sāmavidhāna Brāhmaṇa*, for example, discusses the rites connected with omens and portents and bears similarity with the 13th chapter of the *KauśS*.

2. Earlier Editions of the Kauśika-Sūtra

In 1889, in the *Journal of the American Oriental Society* volume 14, Maurice Bloomfield published his complete edition of the *KauśS* for the first time, based on eight manuscripts.

Before that, in 1859, Weber published the 13th chapter of the *KauśS* on omens and portents in the transactions of the Royal Academy of Berlin. In 1862, E. Haas brought out the nuptial ritual of the *KauśS* (chapter 10) along with the passages of the nuptials described in other Gr̥hya-Sūtras. His main aim was a comparative study of the rites in these texts and to present a working translation of these passages. Both scholars did a praiseworthy job since they based their editions on a single Chambers manuscript without the help of ancillary texts. Haas broadly followed traditional kaṇḍikā divisions of the Sūtra but did not follow the breaking of the sūtras in a traditional manner. Undoubtedly, Haas's edition has scope for improvement on the basis of new material coming into light during the last century and a half.[2]

Bloomfield's complete edition of the *KauśS* was a milestone in the Atharvavedic studies. The editor also translated some passages from that Sūtra showing the ritual aspect of the ŚS hymns in the 42nd volume of Sacred Books of the East Series in 1897. C.R. Lanman, while working on the Introduction to Whitney's translation of the *ŚS* regretted the fact that Bloomfield, who edited this arcane text, did not provide a translation of the entire text, in the following manner:

> As I have more than once said, no one ought to be so well able to give a trustworthy translation of a difficult text as the man who has made a good edition of it; and for this reason one must regret that Bloomfield did not give us — in the natural sequences of the sūtras — as good a version as he was at the time able to make, instead of the detached bits of interpretation which are scattered through the notes of SBE, xlii.[3]

Bloomfield's edition is an excellent effort and brought us one step ahead in Atharvavedic studies, but it is also not free from lacunae.

[2] To give one instance, in her 2010 article, Sumant has shown how Haas's interpretation of sūtra 76.12 is not in accordance with the traditional interpretation envisaged in the *Kauśikapaddhati*, *ĀtharP*, and other Śaunaka prayogas such as Daśakarma.

[3] Lanman's introduction (p. lxxvi) to Whitney 1905 (1971).

Bloomfield has also published papers offering his interpretations on the parts of the *KauśS* in the *American Journal of Philology* (vols. 7, 11, 12, and 17), *Journal of the American Oriental Society* (vols. 13, 15, 16) and *Zeitschrift der Deutschen Morgenländischen Gesellschaft* (vol. 48).

Bloomfield has supplied extracts from *Dārila's Bhāṣya* (*DB*), the two paddhatis — *Kauśikapaddhati* (*KauśP*), *Ātharvaṇapaddhati* (*ĀtharP*) — beside some ancillary material such as the *Daśakarmāṇi* and *Antyeṣṭipaddhati*, to support his choice of readings and for understanding the sūtras. But those passages are not sufficient and in this connection Bahulkar (1990: 116) observes that:

> Although Bloomfield has furnished valuable information in the form of the cross-references to the identical verses in other Saṁhitās and excerpts from the exegetical literature on the *KauśS*, the source-material given in his edition was too little to understand the most obscure ritual as well as the special characteristics of the domestic rites in the *Atharvaveda* tradition.

In 1967, the Tilak Maharashtra Vidyapeeth, Pune, envisaged a project of editing the *KauśS* and entrusted the work to the editorial committee of H.R. Diwekar, V.P. Limaye, R.N. Dandekar, C.G. Kashikar, and V.V. Bhide. The committee came up with the idea of first bringing out the critical editions of the *DB* and *KauśP*, which were absolutely necessary for the editorial work of the Sūtra itself. Accordingly, the editions of the *DB* and *KauśP* came to light in 1972 and 1982 respectively. Later on, in 1990, S.S. Bahulkar published as a specimen a critical edition of the first chapter of the *KauśS*, in *Vedic Texts: A Revision: Felicitation Volume in Honour of Prof. C.G. Kashikar*. His edition was based on nine manuscripts, seven of which were not used by Bloomfield. Bahulkar also consulted other source-material, namely *DB*, Keśava's *KauśP*, Sāyaṇa's commentary on the *ŚS* in which the Sūtras are cited, and also other ancillary texts such as *ĀtharP* and *Daśakarmāṇi* which were used by Bloomfield. He also referred to three prayogas, Devabhadra's *Prayogadīpa*, Raviśaṅkara Dvivedī's *Prayogabhānu* and a *Sthālīpākaprayoga* by some unknown authority, which had not been available to Bloomfield. This source-material is extremely important for throwing light on the actual performance of the ritual and for a better understanding of the Sūtra. Bahulkar offers some emendations to the text edited by Bloomfield. Bloomfield's edition divides the text into kaṇḍikās and sūtras, while the specimen edition follows the traditional threefold division of the text, namely, adhyāya, kaṇḍikā, and sūtra. This edition takes into account the evidence of variants of the sūtras found in the manuscripts of the *KauśS* and the sūtras quoted and explained in the commentaries. The methodology of the text and the ritual aspect have also been taken into consideration while breaking the sūtras.

3. Earlier Efforts in Translating the Kauśika-Sūtra

During the past 120 years some chapters of this Sūtra have been translated by various scholars. As mentioned above, Weber and Haas have translated the 13th chapter of the *KauśS* on omens and portents and the 10th chapter on nuptials respectively, along with their editions. In the series Sacred Books of the East, Bloomfield translated some passages from that Sūtra showing the ritual aspect of the *ŚS* hymns. Caland in his *Altindisches Zauberritual* translated the core part of peculiar Ātharvaṇa rites of Abhicāra, and Gonda translated the portions related to Sava rites. Bahulkar has translated the Bhaiṣajya section of the Sūtra in his 1976 Ph.D. thesis, published later on as *Medical Ritual in the Atharvaveda.* Sumant has presented a revised translation of nuptials in her 2007 doctoral dissertation. For this, she consulted ancillary source material such as *KauśP*, *ĀtharP,* and Daśakarmāṇi, which was not available to Haas. Rotaru has translated for her doctoral thesis (submitted in 2008, University of Bucharest; unpublished) the sūtras for the śāntyudakavidhi and other, prenatal, birth, and infancy rites, along with an edition and translation of the respective passages from the ancillary Atharvavedic texts, among which is the unedited prayoga, *Saṁskāraratnamālā*.[4] In her studies on paribhāṣā applications in the *KauśS*, Rotaru (2009 and 2010) has focused on several single particular sūtras that are difficult to understand and has come up with a new interpretation with the help of the ancillary materials. There has been a long-felt need for a complete translation of this important text.

4. The New Project of Edition and Translation

The current project of preparing a new edition and translation, supported by the Centre for Euroasiatic and Afroasiatic Studies (Bucharest) is undertaken under the guidance of S.S. Bahulkar on

[4] MS accession number 4290, hand-written catalogue, Pune: Vaidika Samshodhana Mandala.

editorial principles similar to those laid out by him in his specimen edition of 1990. We aim at critically editing the *KauśS* on the basis of the manuscripts used by Bloomfield and some newly available manuscripts. To date, in addition to the manuscripts used by Bloomfield and Bahulkar, we have collected four more manuscripts, two from the Oriental Institute, Baroda, namely 889 and 6854, and two from the Staatsbibliothek, München with the accession numbers 177 and 178. We are in the process of acquiring the rest of the manuscripts known from the *New Catalogus Catalogorum* and from private collections in Gujarat.

5. Methodology to be Adopted for the New Edition

The collation of the new manuscripts has given us an opportunity to reconsider and emend Bloomfield's readings wherever necessary. The most reliable ones out of all the available manuscripts will be selected and grouped. A positive apparatus will appear in the critical notes. A list of manuscripts where the adopted reading appears will be noted in the beginning, followed by variants in other manuscripts. The variant readings from Bloomfield's edition will be noted in the critical apparatus. Variant readings of *DB*'s printed text will be noted, and when the *DB*'s manuscript reading differs from its printed text then that will be noted separately.

6. Some Important Features of the New Edition

1. This edition will follow the traditional threefold division of the text, namely, adhyāya, kaṇḍikā, and sūtra. A concordance of Bloomfield's division and our division will be provided in appendices, and additional numbering of consecutive kaṇḍikās by giving continuous numbering in square brackets will be adopted in the main body of the text. E.g. the first kaṇḍikā of the second chapter will appear as 2.1[10].

2. The edition will also reconsider the division of sūtras made by Bloomfield. For this edition, the division of kaṇḍikās into sūtras will be done mostly on the basis of *DB*, where Dārila quotes the sūtra and comments upon it. We have therefore decided to treat each quoted portion as one sūtra. The editors of *DB*, by contrast, do not change Bloomfield's numbering of sūtras. They probably assume that Dārila had divided one sūtra into two, i.e. yogavibhāga. They therefore give a

punctuation mark (*daṇḍa*) after the first part of the sūtra and show the end of the sūtra after the second part with the appropriate number of the sūtra.

3. While giving references to the pratīkas of hymns, verses, and verse-portions a hymn will be indicated by kāṇḍa and hymn, such as 1.1. A verse will be indicated by kāṇḍa, hymn and verse number, such as 1.1.1. A portion of a verse (pāda), less than a pāda or more than a pāda will be indicated by kāṇḍa, hymn, verse, and pāda, e.g. 12.3.31a (see *KauśS* 1.1.27). Cross-references to the mantras found in Vedic texts other than the *ŚS* will be given following a tentative chronology. However, in the case of mantras found in the *PS*, the reference to the *PS* will be given first, following the references to other texts.
4. The edition will also present an English translation of the sūtras. We will consult published and unpublished ancillary texts, namely, *DB*, *KauśP*, *ĀtharP*, and prayogas in the tradition of the Śaunaka *AV* such as *Prayogadīpa*, *Prayogabhānu*, *Daśakarmāṇi*, and *Saṁskāraratnamālā*, as well as other prayogas for which manuscript material has been reported (Bahulkar 1978: 31, 2002: 149) and, if necessary, the priestly manuals of the Paippalādins, namely *Karmapañjikā* and *Karmasamuccaya*. The exegetical notes including relevant passages with their translation will be supplied along with the English translation of the sūtras.

7. A Case Study: The Editing and Translation of KauśS 43.3

1. Sūtra 43.3, prescribing a rite for building a house, is among the most difficult passages in the whole *KauśS*, wherein all available MSS concord in presenting a corrupt reading, which has been emended differently by the two scholars who have critically dealt with this passage, M. Bloomfield and W. Caland.

   KauśS 43.3: **ati dhanvanīty** (7.41) avasānaniveśanānu-caraṇāni[5] nayanejyā[6] |

[5] Thus Bh1 Bh2 Bh3 Bh6 V1 M2; *avasānāniveśanānucaraṇāni* Bh4; *avaśānaniveśanānucaraṇāni* Bh5 sec. man.=K Bloomfield Dārila (text and school.); *avasānābhiniveśanānucaraṇāni* M1. For the sigla and information of the *KauśS* MSS, cf. Bloomfield 1889 and Bahulkar 1990.

[6] Thus Bh2 Bh3 Bh4 Bh5 Bh6 M1 M2; *nayenejyā* Bh1; *rayenejyā* V1.

2.1. Bloomfield emends: **ati dhanvanīty** (7.41) avasānaniveśanānucaraṇāni ninayanejyā. Thus, he views the awkward lectio *nayanejyā* as a haplology. He translates this emended passage elsewhere (1896: 12): "while reciting *AV* VII.41.1, alighting (upon the spot where a house is to be built), sitting down upon it, and walking along it, one performs the sacrifice of pouring water upon the place". Bloomfield (1893) thinks that a better emendation suiting the meaning of the translation would be *avasānaniveśanānucaraṇānāṁ.*

2.2. Turning to Bloomfield's understanding of the passage, we quote his remark:

> It is striking that the text of the Kauçika does not present the word *çyena* at all. If we regard the last syllables of the undoubtedly corrupt sūtra, namely *nyejā*, the suspicion that the syllable *çye* has fallen out is hardly to be suppressed. Possibly then, once more, the sūtra was . . . *avasāna-niveçana-anucaraṇa-ninayanānāṁ çyenejyā*, or something similar.
>
> — 1896: 13

2.3. In fact the reading *śyenejyā* is recorded in the MS of Sāyaṇa's commentary (MS S′ in S.P. Pandit's edition): *ityāvasanāniveśānucaraṇāniḥ śyenejyeti.* This reading was rejected by the editor probably because the first compound is corrupt.

2.4. An hypothesis, then, is that the sūtra should be emended in contrast to all MSS readings as:

ati dhanvanīty (7.41) avasānaniveśanānucaraṇāni śyenejyā.

Professor Bahulkar (1999) has shown a similar instance, wherein the lectio *śayanavidham* (having the shape of a couch), in *KauśS* 16.30,[7] has to be emended, against all the manuscript evidence, as *śyenavidham* (having the shape of a hawk). His assumption is also supported by a gloss in Keśava's commentary, *śyenākāram.* The hymn employed in that rite suits well the new meaning of the sūtra. The hymn *ŚS* 3.3.3-4, mentions that a falcon is employed in a rite for a dethroned king, wherein a sacrificial cake has to be offered for a dethroned king. As per the emendation of the sūtra, the cake should be hawk-shaped rather than couch-shaped.

---

[7] *acikradat* (3.3) *ā tvā gan* (3.4) *iti yasmād rāṣṭrād avaruddhas tasyāśāyāṁ śayanavidhaṁ puroḍāṣaṁ darbheṣūdake ninayati* |

In the present instance, it is possible that *śyenejyā* belonged to the original text of the *KauśS* 43.3, and that later diaskeuasis, or later ritual tradition, has removed it or rather made it obscure, as in all other occurrences of the term *śyena*, probably due to the connotation of the dreadful rite (v. Medhatithi on Manu V.157, Śabara on Jaimini I.1.2, Mitākṣara on Yājña. I.86, terming the Śyenayāga as adharma). However, the Śyenayāga seems to evoke the Agnicayana's hawk-shaped altar (Śyenaciti) (Parpola 1983: 47-48; 1988: 252), wherein the hawk is the symbolic means by which one attains victory over an enemy on earth.[8]

In the following discussion we shall demonstrate why this emendation is not tenable.

3. Caland emends the sūtra as follows:

ati dhanvanīty (7.41) avasānaniveśanānucaraṇātinayanejyā

and translates according to his understanding of the difficult commentary of Dārila:

> Mit dem Liede VII.41 findet statt das Haltmachen (in der Nähe der Stätte, wo man sich die Wohnung machen will), das Betreten (derselben), das Sich-auf-derselbenbewegen, das Herüber-führen auf derselben (des Viehs und der zukünftigen Bewohner) und das Opfer) (an die im Liede genannte Gottheit: den männerschauenden Falken d.h. die Sonne).[9]

Caland explains his emendation *avasānaniveśanānucaraṇātinayanejyā* in a note:

> We have here a compound the last member of which has preserved its own gender and number. Dārila explains the passages as follows (we agree with his observations with some minor modifications which we find necessary): *avasānaṁ nidhānadeśaḥ; niveśanaṁ* <u>*gṛhaḥ;*</u> *avasāne anucaraṇam;* <u>*niveśane ninayanam;*</u> *anucaraṇaṁ śāntyudakena*

[8] However, it appears that this Śyenejyā is different from the Śyenayāga. This so-called Śyenejyā of the *KauśS* might be a domestic rite and not the solemn one. At this moment, we do not know much about this sacrifice.

[9] With the hymn VII.41 the halt [near the place where a house is to be built] takes place, the entering [into the same], the going around at the same, the leading towards the same [of the kine and the future inhabitants], and the offering [to which reference is made by the deity named in the hymn: a falcon looking at men, i.e. the Sun]. — tr. J.R.

saṁprokṣaṇam; ninayanam udakāvasarjanam; ijyāyāḥ śyeno devatā[10] [. . .]. According to Dārila, sūtra 3 would mean: "with the hymn VII.41 water is poured on the spot where one intends to stop, the house is sprinkled with pacifying water, and the offering takes place". The explanation given by Dārila to the words and the compounds seems to me to be forced. The fact that he mentions here the action sought by him in the sūtra 3 seems to be forced, because the preparation of the pacifying water takes place later on, merely in the sūtra 5.

— tr. by Julieta Rotaru

Caland's emendation of sūtra 43.3 is not supported by Dārila's commentary, since *atinayana* is nowhere hinted at. We differ from Caland's emendation of the sūtra and also from some of his emendations to Dārila's text, as we will show below.

4. Dārila ad *KauśS* 43.3 quotes the mūla with the same lectiones as our available manuscripts. His commentary on this sūtra is likewise extremely corrupt. We have followed some of the emendations proposed by the editors and tried to emend it in some places and translate. The passage as recorded by the codex displays a series of uncalled-for glosses, resembling rather Sāyaṇa's style, as if Dārila tried to convince himself that the glossed terms do not bear special meanings. Sometimes Dārila's discussion appears to be an abridged speech and expedited explanations by reference to other contexts. We have taken recourse to Professor Bahulkar for the translation of the whole passage.

ati dhanvanīty[11] (7.41.1-2) avasānaniveśanānucaraṇa-ninayanejyāḥ[12] [।] **ati dhanvānī**ti dvyṛcam [।][13] **ihaiva dhruvām** (3.12) ity aṣṭabhir[14] dhārayati । **ati dhanvānī**ti kasmāt । ucyate[15]

---

10 We have underlined Caland's emendations to Dārila's text.

11 Thus our emendation, ***ati dhanvānī****ti dvyarcā* ***dhanvānīty*** codex.

12 Thus emended by Caland and editors, *avaśānaniveśanānucaraṇāni nayanejyā* codex.

13 Thus emended, *dvyarcaṁ* codex, v. editors.

14 Thus emended, *aṣṭabhi* codex, v. Bloomfield and editors.

15 Thus emended, *kasmād ucyate* codex, v. editors, cf. *kasmād ucyate* । Bloomfield.

ijyāyāḥ[16] vighnaśāśamanārthatvāt[17] । evaṁ[18] sthite ninayanānucaraṇāyārtha[ṁ][19] [ya]thā saṁkhyatvāt[20] । avasānaṁ[21] nidhānadeśaḥ [।] niveśanaṁ[22] gr̥ham[23] । avasāne[24] anucaraṇaṁ [।][25]niveśane ni[na]yanam[26] anucaraṇaṁ śāntyudakena saṁprokṣaṇam [।] ni[na]yanam[27] udakā['']va[sa]rjanam[28] [।] ijyāyāḥ śyenadevatā[29] mantraliṅgāt (i.e. *ŚS* 7.41) । evam asya sūktasya prayogā[t] tu[30] gr̥hasthāne śyenejyā**ti dhanvānī**ti dvābhyāṁ homaḥ । pākayajñatantram[31] ।।

[With the hymn] "**ati dhanvāni** (7.41) [are performed the acts, namely,] the sprinkling of the pacifying water at the spot for placing [the pitcher], the pouring of water in the house and the sacrifice [for the falcon]. [The hymn] "Beyond dry sandbanks" [is] of two verses. With eight [verses] [of the hymn beginning with] "Right here firm", he holds [the pitcher full of water for the rite that follows]. For what purpose [are] the verses beginning with "Beyond dry sandbanks" [employed]? The answer is: because the sacrifice has the purpose of the pacification of evil. This being

[16] Thus emended, *ijdāyāḥ* codex.

[17] Thus emended, *vaśāśamanārthatvāt* codex, cf. *vaśāśamanārthatvam.*

[18] Thus emended, *eva* codex, v. Bloomfield and editors.

[19] Thus our emendation, *ninayanānucaraṇāyārtha-*, cf. *ninayanān ucaraṇayor* editors.

[20] Thus emended, *-thāsaṁkhyatvāt* codex, v. editors.

[21] Thus emended, *avaśānaṁ* codex, v. Caland and editors.

[22] Thus emended, *nidhānadeśaniveśanaṁ* codex, v. Caland and editors.

[23] Cf. *gr̥haḥ* Caland.

[24] Thus emended, *avaśāne* codex, v. editors and Caland.

[25] Thus emended, v. Caland and editors.

[26] Thus emended, *niveśananiyanaṁ* codex, v. editors and Caland, cf. *niveśananinayanam* Bloomfield.

[27] Thus emended by Caland and editors, *saṁprokṣaṇaniyanam* codex, cf. -*ninayanam* Bloomfield.

[28] Thus emended by Caland, *udakāvarjanam* codex, cf. *udakā''varjanam* editors.

[29] Although Caland's emendation as *śyeno devatā* might do justice to the meaning, "the deity is the hawk", it would be different from what the passage is, namely, as said above, a series of glosses and abridged speech.

[30] Thus emended, *prayogātu* codex, cf. *prayogo gr̥hasthāne* editors.

[31] Thus emended, *pākayajñatatre* codex, v. editors.

the case, "pouring of water" (*ninayana*) and "sprinkling with the pacifying water" (*anucaraṇa*) have the characteristic of relative enumeration (*yathāsaṅkhyatva*).[32] *Avasāna* [means] the spot for placing the pitcher,[33] *niveśana* [means] a house. The sprinkling with the pacifying water [is done] at the spot for placing the pitcher. The pouring of water [is done] in the house. *Anucaraṇa* [means] "sprinkling with pacifying water". *Ninayana* [means] "the pouring of water". The hawk [as] the deity of the sacrifice [is known] from [its] indication in the mantras. Thus being the performance of this hymn, the sacrifice [is to be performed] with [the invocation to] the hawk. The oblation [is to be made] with [the recitation of] the two [verses] [of the hymn, beginning with] "Beyond dry sandbanks". The basic ritual (*tantra*) [is that of] the pākayajña.

5. Keśava ad *KauśS* 43.3 takes cognisance and understands sui generis Dārila's commentary to the difficult sūtra, which prescribes a rite for the purification of the ground (*bhūmiśuddhi*) on which a house is to be built.

ati dhanvāni iti dvābhyām udapātram abhimantrya tatra ninayati bhūmau yatra gr̥haṁ kariṣyati । tatra vighnaśamanaṁ bhavati । śyenadevatāyai[34] pākayajñavidhānenājyabhāgāntaṁ kr̥tvā **ati dhanvāni** iti dvābhyām r̥gbhyāṁ caruṁ juhoti । pārvaṇādyuttara-tantram । bhūmisthāne yatra gr̥haṁ kariṣyati tatra[35] śyenayāgaṁ kr̥tvā gr̥haṁ kuryāt । athavā nave gr̥he śyenayāgaḥ kartavyaḥ । vikalpa iti bhāṣyakāraḥ । prathamato vā śyenayāgo nave gr̥he ।।

---

32 Dārila points out that the compound *avasānaniveśanānucaraṇaninayanejyāḥ* has to be explained using the device of "the relative enumeration" or "one-to-one correspondence" (*yathāsaṁkhya*), a device adopted by the Grammarians (P. 1.3.10) and followed by the authors of Sanskrit Poetics in respect to the figure of speech called *yathāsaṁkhya*. Here, the first member of the compound is connected with the third and the second, with the fourth. Thus *avasāna* is connected with the act called *anucaraṇa*, and *niveśana* with *ninayana*. See a similar compound at *KauśS* 30.16 and Dārila's gloss thereon (*DB*, p. 97). This explanation has been communicated by S.S. Bahulkar, January 2012, Delhi.

33 V. also Renou (1939: 482) "lieu ou l'on dételle (après la course)", "emplacement de la maison" (apud Gobh IV 7.15).

34 *-devatā* Ga, Vā, Sā, Bhā1.

35 *tatredaṁ* Bhā2.

Having consecrated the water jar with two [stanzas of the hymn] 7.41, [the priest] pours [the water] on the earth where [the sacrificer] shall build the house. On that spot the pacification of obstacles takes place. Having performed the ājyabhāga up to the end on the pattern of the pākayajña, he should offer a rice oblation to the deity Śyena with two stanzas of the hymn 7.41. Next he continues with the second part of the rite, beginning with the pārvaṇa offerings. On that place where [the sacrificer] shall build the house, there (itself, cf. Bhā2), after having performed the hawk sacrifice (*śyenayāga),* he should build the house. Or he should perform the *śyenayāga* in the new house. [There is] an option, thus [says] the commentator. Or, with priority, the *śyenayāga* [should be done] in the new house.

6. *ĀtharP* (in the text available in the three manuscripts in our possession) divides Keśava's commentary a bit differently, resulting in a different translation. While its discussion does not alter the general sense of the passage, it does provide an alternative reading of *senedevatā* instead of *śyenadevatā.*

atha bṛha[c]chālākarma ucyate । **ati dhanvānī**ti (7.41) *dvābhyām ṛgbhyāṁ*[36] *udapātram abhimaṁtrya bhūmau*[37] *ninayati* । *yatra gṛhaṁ kariṣyati tatra vighnaṁ śamayati*[38] । *senedevatā*[39] *pākayajña-vidhānenājyabhāgāṁtaṁ kṛtvā*[40] । **ati dhanvānī**ti (7.41) *dvābhyām ṛgbhyāṁ caruṁ juhoti* । *pārvaṇādyuttarataṁtraṁ* ।। ornamentation ।। *bhūmisthāne yatra gṛhaṁ kariṣyati* । *tatra śyenayāgaṁ kariṣyati*[41] । *kuryāt* ।।[42] *athavā nave gṛhe śyenayāgaḥ karttavyaḥ* । (Keśava on 43.3) iti dārilabhāṣyakāraḥ ।।[43]

---

36 *AthPaddh* gloss.

37 Cf. *tatra ninayati bhūmau* Keśava.

38 Cf. *vighnaśamanaṁ bhavati* Keśava.

39 Sic! *śyenadevatā-*. Thus Keśava MSS Ga Vā Sā Bhā1, cf. *śyenadevatāyai* Keśava MSS Ba Bhā2.

40 Thus Keśava MSS Ba Bhā2, cf. *bhavati* Keśava MSS Ga Vā Sā Bhā1.

41 Cf. *kṛtvā gṛhaṁ kuryāt* Keśava.

42 *AthPaddh* Berlin uses distinctly the single and the double daṇḍa whereas *AthPaddh* BORI uses the single daṇḍa throughout.

43 V. Keśava: *vikalpa iti bhāṣyakāraḥ* ।. Thus *AthPaddh* glosses Dārila for the commentator.

> Now the rite of building a big house is described. Having consecrated the water jar with two stanzas of the hymn 7.41, [the priest] pours [the water] on the earth. On that spot where one builds a house he should pacify the obstacle. Having performed the ājyabhāga up to the end on the pattern of the pākayajña, with two stanzas of the hymn 7.41 he should offer a rice oblation to the deity Śyena. Next he continues with the second part of the rite, beginning with the pārvaṇa offerings. On the place where one will build a house he shall perform a *śyenayāga*. He does that. Or he should perform the *śyenayāga* in the new house, thus says the commentator Dārila.

In conclusion, we have thus seen that out of the three proposed emendations, two by Bloomfield, and one by Caland, the gist of the sūtra as understood by the traditional exegesis, starting with Dārila, would support the emendation accepted by Bloomfield in his edition, which we retain for the moment, until further investigations can be carried out concerning the subject and purpose of domestic Śyenayāga.

Our reading, therefore, is as follows:

> *KauśS* 43.3: **ati dhanvanīty** (7.41) avasānaniveśanānucaraṇā-ninayanejyā ।
>
> [With the hymn] "**ati dhanvāni**"(7.41) [are performed the acts, namely,] the sprinkling of the pacifying water at the spot for placing [the pitcher], the pouring of water in the house and the sacrifice [for the falcon].

References

MANUSCRIPTS

Ātharvaṇapaddhati, Berlin, Mss. Accession no. 1495 and 1496 in Verzeichnisse der Kgl. Bibliothek zu Berlin, vol. V: Verzeichniss der Sanskrit-Prakr̥t-Handschriften, vol. II, ed. Albrecht Weber, pp. 86-87, Berlin.

Ātharvaṇapaddhati, BORI, MS accession no. 1870-71, Pune: Bhandarkar Oriental Research Institute.

PRIMARY SOURCES

Bahulkar, S.S. (ed.), 1990, "Kauśikasūtra", in *Vedic Texts: A Revision: Professor C.G. Kashikar Felicitation Volume*, ed. T.N. Dharmadhikari et al., pp. 115-34, Delhi: Motilal Banarsidass.

Bloomfield, Maurice, 1889, "The Kauçika Sūtra of Atharvaveda with extracts from the commentaries of Darila and Keçava", *Journal of the American Oriental Society*, **14:** v-422.

Diwekar, H.R. et al. (eds.), 1972, *Kauśikasūtra: Dārilabhāṣya: Critically edited for the first time on the basis of a single codex which is reproduced by offset process*, Poona: Tilak Maharashtra Vidyapitha.

Limaye, V.P., et al. (eds.), 1982, *Keśava's Kauśikapaddhati on the Kauśikasūtra of the Atharvaveda* (Shri Balmukund Sanskrit Mahavidyalaya Research Series 1), Pune: Tilak Maharashtra Vidyapeeth.

SECONDARY SOURCES

Bahulkar, S.S., 1978, "The Prayoga-Dīpa of Devabhadra: A Brief Survey", *Journal of the University of Pune, Humanities*, **43:** 31-35.

———, 1994, *Medical Ritual in the Atharvaveda Tradition* (Shri Balmukund Sanskrit Mahavidyalaya Research Series, No. 8), Pune: Tilak Maharashtra Vidyapeeth.

———, 1999, "A Note on Kauśika Sūtra 16.30", in *Wisdom in Indian Tradition: Prof. K.P. Jog Felicitation Volume*, ed. Shoun Hino and Lalita Deodhar, pp. 1-7, Delhi: Pratibha Prakashan.

———, 2002, "Atharvaveda-Prayoga Bhānu (Dharma Śāstra of the Atharvavedins)", in *Ātharvaṇa (a collection of essays on the AtharvaVeda with special reference to its Paippalāda tradition)*, ed. Abhijit Gosh, pp. 146-54, Kolkata: Sanskrit Book Depot.

Bloomfield, Maurice, 1896, "Contributions to the Interpretation of the Veda", *Journal of the American Oriental Society*, **16:** 1-42.

———, 1897, *Hymns of the Atharva-Veda Together with Extracts from the Ritual Books and the Commentaries*, tr. Maurice Bloomfield, Oxford: Sacred Books of the East, XLII, repr., 1992, Delhi: Motilal Banarsidass.

Caland, Willem, 1900, *Altindisches Zauberritual, Probe einer Uebersetzung der wichtigsten Theile des Kauśika Sūtra* (Verhandelingen der Koninklijke Nederlandse Akademie van Wetenschappen, Nieuwe Reeks, Deel III. No. 2), Amsterdam: Johannes Müller.

Gonda, Jan, 1965, *The Savayajñas (Kauśikasūtra 60-68: Translation, introduction, commentary)*, Amsterdam: N.V. Noord-Hollandsche Uitgevers Maatschappij.

Haas, E., 1862, "Die Heiratsgebräuche der alten Inder, nach den Gṛhyasūtra", *Indische Studien*, **5:** 267-412.

Parpola, Asko, 1983, "The Pre-Vedic Indian Background of the Srauta Rituals", in *Agni: The Vedic Ritual of the Fire Altar*, ed. Frits Staal, vol. 2, pp. 41-75 and plates 7-8, Berkeley: Asian Humanities Press.

———, 1988, "The Coming of the Aryans to Iran and India and the Cultural and Ethnic Identity of the Dasas", *Studia Orientalia*, **64:** 195-302, Helsinki: Societas Orientalis Fennica.

Renou, Louis, 1939, "La maison védique", *Journal Asiatique* **231:** 481-504, Paris: Société Asiatique et Centre National de la Recherche Scientifique.

Rotaru, Julieta, 2009a, "Towards a Methodology of Employing the Paribhāṣās (II)", Paper read at the 14th World Sanskrit Conference, Kyoto University, Japan, 1-5 September 2009.

———, 2009b, "Śāntyudakavidhi in the Atharvavedic Tradition", in *Śrīnīdhī: Prof. Shrikant Shankar Bahulkar's Gratitude Volume*, ed. Shripad G. Bhat (Chief Editor), Shilpa Sumant, and Ambarish Vasant Khare, pp. 317-54, Pune: Saṁvidyā Institute of Cultural Studies.

———, 2010, "Towards a Methodology of Employing the Paribhāṣās in the KauśikaSūtra (I), with special reference to 7.10", *Acta Orientalia Vilnensia* **9**(2): 57-82 (2008), Vilnius: Vilnius University Publishing House.

Sumant, Shilpa, 2007, *Vivāha: The Development of the Ritual from Saṁhitā to Prayoga in the Atharvaveda Tradition,* Thesis submitted to Tilak Maharashtra Vidyapeeth, Pune [Unpublished].

———, 2010, "The Bride with the Yoke: Interpretation of Kauśikasutra 76.11-13", in *The Proceedings of the International Symposium "The Book: Romania.Europe" 20-24 September 2009*, ed. Julieta Rotaru, pp. 720-30, Bucharest: The Metropolitan Library of Bucharest.

Weber, Albrecht, 1859, *Zwei vedische Texte über Omina und Portenta*, Berlin: Druckerei der Königl, Akademie der Wissenschaften.

Whitney, William Dwight, 1905, *The Atharva-Veda Saṁhitā: Translated with a Critical and Exegetical Commentary, Revised and Brought Nearer to Completion and edited by Charles Rockwell Lanman*, vols. 1 and 2, Cambridge, Mass.: Harvard University Press, repr., 1971, Delhi: Motilal Banarsidass.

Part 3
Culture, Philosophy, Mythology

11

The Objects and Contexts of Vision of the Ṛṣis in the Pañcaviṁśa Brāhmaṇa

Giacomo Benedetti

IN the Vedic literature we can distinguish four aspects of the Ṛṣi: (1) the priestly function in the sacrifice; (2) the creation and recitation of religious poetry and his connection with the sacred Word; (3) the divine inspiration and the faculty of spiritual vision; (4) his ethic and ascetic traits.

In the *Pañcaviṁśa Brāhmaṇa,* as is natural for a Brāhmaṇa of the *Sāmaveda,* the ṛṣi is essentially the person who could see a sāman, a Vedic "melody" or "chant", and who received a specific benefit from that. So, we could say that the main aspect is the second one, the creation of religious poetry, but, as usual in the Brāhmaṇas, through "vision" (the third aspect). However, since the sāman has a *ṛc* or Ṛgvedic "strophe", as a base,[1] we should think that what is "seen" by the ṛṣi are not words in a metrical form, but the way to arrange in a Sāmavedic chant some verses already seen and revealed by a Ṛgvedic ṛṣi. Having seen this chant, the ṛṣi can apply it in the ritual (the first

[1] As observed by Caland 1931: ix, "From a verse (a *ṛk*) a sāman is made by musical notation, by certain changes as stretching of vowels, and repetition of syllables, and by inserting different sounds and syllables, sometimes whole sentences or verses. These insertions are called *stobhas*." In the *ChUp.* I.6.1.1-4 it is said: 1. *iyam evark* । *agniḥ sāma* । *tad etad etasyām ṛcy adhyūḍhaṁ sāma* । *tasmād ṛcy adhyūḍhaṁ sāma gīyate* "This (earth) is the Ṛk. Agni is the sāman. This sāman rests on that Ṛk. Therefore the sāman is sung as resting on the Ṛk.", and the same formula is repeated for the following sentences (I.6.2-6).

aspect). About the fourth aspect, it is sometimes said that before seeing the sāman, the person in question had to practice *tapas*, the ascetic austerities which are able to bring a man (particularly a brāhmin) to the status of a ṛṣi, stimulating, in this context, the vision of the sāman apt to accomplish the wished purpose.

So, the main object of vision of the ṛṣi is the sāman, but there are also other objects, which sometimes can be seen through the sāman previously discovered. In *PB* XII.5.14 we read:

> The Niṣkirīyas[2] performed a Sattra. They did not know (the ritual of the) third day. The Word (*vāc*) inundated them singing this sāman,[3] through it they knew the third day. They said: 'She forsooth, has let us see the third day!' This (chant) is the vision of the third day.[4]

In this case, the object is a part of the ritual, which is usual also in other Brāhmaṇas.[5] The ṛṣis discovered not only the words employed in the ritual, but also the other elements of the sacrifice, thus achieving its completeness. Such episodes, though mythical, seem to preserve a memory of the process which led to the formation of the ritual system,[6]

---

[2] This name can indicate a śākhā or a gotra according to Sāyaṇa. In the corresponding passage of *JB* III.52 the *niṣkaryā devā*s occur, which seems to indicate that they were conceived as a category of gods. In *JB* II.357, on the other hand, we read: *niṣkaraṇīyā iti brāhmaṇāḥ pūrviṇas satraṁ niṣeduḥ* "the ancestral brahmins (called) 'niṣkaraṇīya' performed a sattra".

[3] In *PB* XII.5.12 it is called *vācaḥ sāma* "melody of the Word".

[4] *niṣkirīyāḥ sattram āsata te tṛtīyam ahar na prājānaṁs tān etat sāma gāyamānā vāg upāplavat tena tṛtīyam ahaḥ prājānaṁs te 'bruvann iyaṁ vāva nas tṛtīyam ahar adīdṛśad iti tṛtīyasyaivaiṣāhno dṛṣṭiḥ.*

[5] Cf. e.g. *AB* VI.34; *KB* IV.6.7-11; XXX.2.12. In the version of *JB* III.52, they do not know not only the third day, but also the heavenly world, according to an usual expression (*te svargaṁ lokaṁ na prājānann etat tṛtīyam ahaḥ*). Cf. also *AB* IV.32, where the Aṅgirases become confused (*muhyanti*) on the second day of the twelve-day-rite, and Śāryāta Mānava makes them recite a hymn which stimulates in them the knowledge of the sacrifice and of the heavenly world (*pra yajñam ajānan pra svargaṁ lokaṁ*). In *AB* V.14, the Aṅgirases become confused on the sixth day. In that case Nābhānediṣṭha makes them recite two hymns, causing, again, the knowledge of the sacrifice and of the heavenly world.

[6] Cf. the preceding note and *ŚB* XI.2.3.7, where the gandharvas correct the ṛṣis after they have performed the sacrifice, explaining what was defective and what exceeding.

which is seen as a result of sudden intuitions rather than as a reasoned elaboration. But the Vedic tradition could not represent the ṛṣis as inventing new rites: the underlying concept is that the third day has an ideal form which should be discovered; since the niṣkirīyas could not yet achieve a "vision" of that form, they had to receive a kind of revelation, conferring authority to the new elements introduced. In this case, the revealer is Vāc, the "Word" itself, not in a female human form, as in other stories,[7] but as an immaterial voice, inundating, that is, pervading the space around the niṣkirīyas with the sounds of the sāman.[8] This chant stimulates in them the vision of the third day's ritual: thus, we find that the sāman can have the function to stimulate knowledge, and not only to produce some external effect. This function remains in this sāman, defined as the "vision" (*dṛṣṭi*) of the third day.

Other visions of rites, but without mention of a previous vision of a sāman, are also in *PB* XIV.11.26, where Kutsa sees "the separate drinking of the (two) juice(s)";[9] XXI.9.2, where Atri sees his four-day rite; XXI.11.2, where Vasiṣṭha sees another rite of four days; XXI.12.2, where Viśvāmitra sees his four-day rite.

We have also objects which are not sacred chants or rituals. In *PB* XV.5.24, we read:

> The ṛṣis did not see Indra face to face. Vasiṣṭha desired: "How could I see Indra face to face?" He saw this nihava (chant) and then, he saw Indra face to face. He (Indra) said to him: "I will reveal to you a Brāhmaṇa, so that the Bharatas, with you as purohita, will be multiplied, but do not tell the other *ṛṣis* of me." He told him these stomabhāgas, then the Bharatas with Vasiṣṭha as purohita were multiplied. This sāman is associated with Indra. That there is this Sāman, (is) for the association with Indra.[10]

---

[7] Cf. *AB* I.27; *ŚB* III.2.4.3-6; *BD* V.97-101. On the other hand, *TB* III.10.9.11 speaks of an invisible voice (*vāg adṛśyamānā*) that reveals to Devabhāga Śrautarṣa the knowledge of Agni Sāvitra.

[8] Cf. *PB* XII.5.10-11, where Paṣṭhavāh Āṅgirasa hears "the voice (or Word) of the fourth day" which speaks through the Pāṣṭhauha sāman (*pāṣṭhauhaṁ bhavati* । *paṣṭhavāḍ vā etenāṅgirasaś caturthasyāhno vācaṁ vadantīm upāśṛṇot*).

[9] See Caland 1931: 384-85.

[10] *ṛṣayo vā indraṁ pratyakṣaṁ nāpaśyan sa vasiṣṭho 'kāmayata katham indraṁ pratyakṣaṁ paśyeyam iti sa etan nihavam apaśyat tato vai sa indraṁ pratyakṣam* →

This privilege of Vasiṣṭha is mentioned also in *TS* III.5.2 and *KS* XXXVII.17,[11] but there, in a Yajurvedic context, it is not said that he saw Indra through the sāman. *BD* V.156cd-7ab, gives us another explanation: There it is said that Vasiṣṭha could see Indra, invisible to other ṛṣis, through ascetic practice (*adṛśyam* ***ṛṣibhir*** *hīndraṁ so 'paśyat tapasā purā*). Anyway, the passage is very significant in our context because it says that the other ṛṣis could not see Indra: they are not depicted as omniscient, and only Vasiṣṭha, because of his special interest in direct knowledge of this god, comes to have this perception, through a sāman which he has seen. It is not the god who reveals himself, but the ṛṣi who has to search for him and to chant a special sāman in order to pierce the veil which hides the god. Indra does not want to be perceived, on the contrary, when he is discovered, he reveals special formulas in exchange for the silence of the ṛṣi.[12]

Another special object of vision is mentioned in *PB* XIV.11.19: "Asita, son of Devala, through this (āsita chant) saw the vision of the three worlds."[13] The three worlds should here be those of gods, men, and Fathers, because in a parallel passage of *JB* III.270-271, we find that Asita, after having seen a sāman, can move in those three worlds.[14] In

→ *apaśyat, sa enam abravīd brāhmaṇaṁ te vakṣyāmi yathā tvatpurohitā bharatāḥ prajaniṣyante 'tha mānyebhya ṛṣibhyo mā pravoca iti tasmā etān stomabhāgān abravīt tato vai vasiṣṭhapurohitā bharatāḥ prājāyanta sendraṁ vā etat sāma yad etat sāma bhavati sendratvāya.*

11 Cf. Krick 1975: 62, where the special relationship of the Vasiṣṭhas with Indra (and as a consequence their excellence as purohitas) is already traced in *ṚV* VII.33.

12 As it is observed by Lévi 1898: 148: "Impuissant à lutter contre la force supérieure qui le contraint à paraître, Indra n'a pas d'autre ressource que d'acheter la discrétion du ṛṣi."

Cf. *KS* XXXVII.17: *ṛṣayo vā indraṁ pratyakṣaṁ nāpaśyaṁs taṁ vasiṣṭha eva pratyakṣam apaśyat so 'bibhed itarebhyo marṣibhyaḥ pravakṣyatīti so 'bravīd brāhmaṇaṁ te vakṣyāmi yathā tvatpurohitāḥ prajāḥ prajaniṣyante 'tha metarebhya ṛṣibhyo mā pravoca iti.* "The ṛṣis did not see Indra face to face. Vasiṣṭha saw him face to face. He feared (thinking): 'He will tell of me to the other ṛṣis.' He said: 'I will tell you a formula, so that the people with you as purohita will multiply. But do not tell the other ṛṣis of me.'"

13 *asito vā etena daivalas trayāṇāṁ lokānāṁ dṛṣṭim apaśyat.*

14 *JB* III.271: *taṁ haivāvekṣyaitat sāma dadarśa | tenāstuta | rāye agne mahe tvā dānāya samidhīmahi | iḷiṣvā hi mahe vṛṣaṁ dyāvā hotrāya pṛthivī || iti |* →

a passage of *KS* XXII.11, we read that by means of verses addressed to Yama, the worlds on this and the other side appeared to Asita Devala.[15] This vision is reminiscent of the clairvoyance or "divine eye" (*divyacakṣus*) of the yogic tradition,[16] and it is interesting that it is attributed to a late ṛṣi like Asita Devala.[17] Differently from the yogic system, where the vision is produced by meditative practice, this vision is simply given by the sāman, although we can presuppose that Asita was a *tapasvin*. In *MBh* IX.48.23 we read that Asita Devala, ṛṣi of great

→ *dyāvāpṛthivī sarva ime lokāḥ* ׀ *tato vai sa sarvān imān lokān anusamacarat* ׀ *sa ha pūrvāhṇa eva devānāṁ samityām āsa, madhyandine manuṣyāṇāṁ drupadasya vārddhraviṣṇasya, aparāhṇe pitṝṇām* ׀ Caland 1931 383-84, n.1: "Having looked down on this (soma-cup), he (Asita) saw this sāman and lauded with it: *rāye agne mahe tvā dānāya samidhīmahi iḷiṣvā hi mahe vṛṣaṁ dyāvā hotrāya pṛthivī* (*Jaim. Saṁh.* I.1.10.3=*SV. Kauth.* I.93). Heaven and earth are (equal to) all these worlds. Thereupon, he moved along all these worlds: during the first part of the day he stayed at the meeting of the gods, at midday, of the meeting of men: of Drūpada Vāddhraviṣṇa [sic], at the afternoon at the meeting of the Fathers." Cf. *BĀU* I.5.16 for this division of worlds.

15 *KS* XXII.11.67.9: *atha yāmīr etābhir vā asitāya devalāyeme lokā arvāñcaś ca parāñcaś ca prābhur* "As to the verses addressed to Yama, by means of these the worlds, as well those that are on this (on the nearer) side as those that are on the other side, became visible to Asita, the son of Devala." (tr. Caland 1931: 383, n. 1).

16 Cf. *YS* III.26, where the knowledge of the world(s) comes from concentration on the sun (*bhuvana-jñānaṁ sūrye saṁyamāt*); *MBh* XII.52.20-21 about the divine eye and the eye of knowledge (*jñānacakṣus*) in a Sāṁkhya context; XVIII.5.31-33, about the omniscience and divine eye of Kṛṣṇa Dvaipāyana; *Vism* 427-29, about the divine eye in Buddhist Theravāda tradition; Lamotte 1970: 1557-59, about the divine eye and the knowledge of worlds in Buddhist Mahāyāna tradition. Cf. also the epithet *lokavid* "knower of the world(s)", e.g. in *BĀU* I.7.4.

17 The Ṛgvedic hymns ascribed to Asita Kāśyapa or Devala Kāśyapa belong to the late IXth Maṇḍala. In *MBh* I.48.8 he is mentioned together with Uddālaka, Śvetaketu, Nārada, and Parvata at the sacrifice of Janamejaya Pārikṣita; in *MBh* I.94.73 it is said that the *devarṣi* Asita asked for Satyavatī in marriage; in *MBh* II.4.8 he is together with the Pāṇḍavas, and the ṛṣis Baka Dālbhya and Kṛṣṇa Dvaipāyana. His younger brother Dhaumya is appointed as purohita of the Pāṇḍavas in *MBh* I.174. Pargiter 1922: 192, places him in the generation no. 93, two generations before the Mahābhārata battle, see also ibidem: 233f.

tapas, practising the supreme yoga, obtained yoga in a certain Tīrtha.[18] Then is narrated his encounter with the yogī and muni Jaigīṣavya, how Asita follows him in different heavens and how Jaigīṣavya becomes his teacher of yoga, when Asita has adopted the *mokṣadharma*, that is, an ascetic rule which is different from the traditional Brahmanic way of life. In *MBh* XII.267, Nārada asks Asita Devala[19] about the creation and dissolution of the universe, receiving an explanation about the five elements and in general about Sāṁkhya metaphysics.

Another interesting tradition tells us that Asita Devala was a celebrated ṛṣi astronomer,[20] which is surely something related to the vision of worlds, although in a more ordinary, physical sense, which apparently cannot be stimulated by a sāman like a sudden intuition. However, the fact that astronomy was attributed to ṛṣis like Garga and Asita suggests that such knowledge was also connected with some kind of special "vision".[21]

---

18 *asito devalaś caiva tasminn eva mahātapāḥ* ı *paramaṁ yogam āsthāya ṛṣir yogam avāptavān* ı

19 *MBh* XII.267.1-3: 1. *atraivodāharantīmam itihāsaṁ purātanam* ı *nāradasya ca saṁvādaṁ devalasyāsitasya ca* 2. *āsīnaṁ devalaṁ vṛddhaṁ buddhvā buddhimatāṁ varaḥ* ı *nāradaḥ paripapraccha bhūtānāṁ prabhavābhyayam* 3. *kutaḥ sṛṣṭam idaṁ viśvaṁ brahman sthāvarajaṅgamam* ı *pralaye ca kam abhyeti tad bhavān prabravītu me* "(Bhishma said): 'In this connection is cited the old narrative of the discourse that took place between Nārada and Asita-Devala. Once on a time Nārada, beholding that foremost of intelligent men, viz., Devala of venerable years, seated at his ease, questioned him about the origin and the destruction of all creatures. Nārada said, "Whence, O brāhmaṇa, hath this universe, consisting of mobile and immobile objects, been created? When again doth the allembracing destruction come, into whom doth it merge? Let thy learned self discourse to me on this.'" (tr. Ganguli).

20 See Kern 1865: 41, who defines Asita-Devala as "one of the most celebrated of ṛṣi astronomers", and says: "The work ascribed to Asita-Devala has never come to my notice; from quotations I know that Asita-Devala, or at all events Devala, was acquainted with the signs of the Zodiac, from which it is to be inferred that he (I mean his work) was posterior to Garga." Asita Devala is cited among the authorities about comets in *VarBṛS* XI.1.

21 For a comparison, it is interesting that in *MBh* IX.36.15 it is said that Garga has acquired knowledge of Time and of astral bodies being a practitioner of *tapas* (15. *yatra gargeṇa vṛddhena tapasā bhāvitātmanā* ı *kālajñānagatiś caiva jyotiṣāṁ ca vyatikramaḥ* 16. *utpātā dāruṇāś caiva śubhāś* →

A frequent object of vision of the ṛṣis in the *Pañcaviṁśa Brāhmaṇa* is the heavenly world (*svarga loka*), expressed in a repeated formula. We find the first instance in *PB* XI.8.14:

> Vasiṣṭha, son of Vīḍu, having lauded with this (Vāsiṣṭha sāman), saw directly the heavenly world; (so it serves) for beholding the heavenly world. He who lauds (with this chant) does not fall from the heavenly world.[22]

We find the same phrase for many different ṛṣis (often from the Āṅgirasa gotra[23]), as a stereotyped description of their achievement. The phrase *añjasā paś* appears to be the same as *añjasā vid* of *ŚB* XIII.2.3.1[24] and as *pra-jñā* that we find in the *Pañcaviṁśa*[25] and elsewhere,[26] and also in *svargasya lokasya prajñātyai* of *PB*

→ *ca janamejaya | sarasvatyāḥ śubhe tīrthe vihitā vai mahātmanā | tasya nāmnā ca tat tīrthaṁ garga srota iti smṛtam).*

22 *vasiṣṭho vā etena vaiḍavaḥ stutvāñjasā svargaṁ lokam apaśyat svargasya lokasyānukhyātyai svargāl lokān na cyavate tuṣṭuvānaḥ stomaḥ.*

23 XII.5.16 (Śukti Āṅgirasa); XIII.9.18 (Ukṣṇorandhra Kāvya); XIII.11.22 (Śnuṣṭi Āṅgirasa); XIV.5.25 (Suhavis Āṅgirasa); XIV.9.15 (Iṭan Kāvya); XIV.9.29 (Puruhanman Vaikhānasa); XIV.10.9 (Vyaśva Āṅgirasa); XV.3.13 (Babhru Kaumbhya); XV.5.11 (Śammad Āṅgirasa). So, on ten cases, we have five Āṅgirasas, two Kāvyas (Bhārgavas), one Vaikhānasa (an ascetic), one Vasiṣṭha, and one Kaumbhya, which is apparently not known elsewhere, even if in the *Ṛgveda* there is a ṛṣi named Babhru (cf. Keith-Macdonell 1912, II: 60).

24 "The man does not know directly the heavenly world, the horse does directly know it" (*na vaí manuṣyāḥ svargáṁ lokam áñjasā vedā́śvo vaí svargáṁ lokam áñjasā veda*).

25 *PB* VIII.5.7: *purojitī vo andhasa iti padyā cākṣaryā ca virājau bhavataḥ padyayā vai devāḥ svargaṁl lokam āyann akṣaryayā ṛṣayo nu prājānan yad ete padyā cākṣaryā ca virājau bhavataḥ svargasya lokasya prajñātyai* "(The three stanzas, beginning): 'By fore-conquest of your juice (of Soma)' are (both) a Padyā Virāj and an Akṣaryā Virāj. By means of the Padyā (Virāj) the gods went to the heavenly world, by means of the Akṣaryā (Virāj) the ṛṣis knew (it). The reason for which there are these Padyā and Akṣaryā Virāj (stanzas), (is) for the knowledge of the heavenly world."

26 Cf. *AB* II.1.1, where the ṛṣis, thanks to the sacrificial post, knew the sacrifice and the heavenly world (*te pra yajñam ajānan pra svargaṁ lokaṁ*); *ŚB* XIII.2.3.1: "the Gods did not know the Pavamāna (Stotra) at the Aśvamedha to be the heavenly world, but the horse knew it" (*devā vā́ aśvamedhe pávamānaṁ svargáṁ lokaṁ na prā́jānaṁs tam áśvaḥ prā́jānād*); *ŚB* →

VIII.5.7,[27] which, in turn, appears as equivalent to *svargasya lokasyānukhyātyai*.[28] What is significant in this formula is that the sāman stimulates knowledge in the ṛṣi, more precisely the direct knowledge of the supreme world of the cosmology of the Brāhmaṇas,[29] as well as the ultimate goal of their eschatology. This knowledge certainly serves for reaching the heavenly world after death, but it arises here and now for the ṛṣi, and, through the sāman by him discovered, it seems that it can be realized again in the present. Actually, the idea of a present experience of heaven is already alluded to in some Vedic hymns: in *ṚV* VIII.48.3, the priests who have drunk the soma have reached the light and found the gods;[30] in *AV* XVIII.3.64, in a funerary hymn, we find this invite, addressed again to the priests during the Soma sacrifice:

> Ascend to highest heaven, O ṛṣis: do not be afraid. Soma-drinkers, for you is performed this soma-drinker's oblation. We have come to the highest light.[31]

In *TS* V.1.8.6, in the context of the Agnicayana, we read:

> "We have come to the highest light", he says; the highest light is that sun; verily he attains unity with the sun. The year does not halt, his luck does not halt, for whom these are performed. The last he recites with the word "light" in it; verily he bestows on him light above, for beholding the world of heaven.[32]

→ XIII.2.8.1: "The gods, going upwards, did not know (the way to) heaven, but the horse knew it" (*devā vā údañcaḥ svargáṁ lokaṁ na prā́jānaṁs tam áśvaḥ prā́jānād*).

27 Cf. *PB* VIII.2.6, cited below.

28 Cf. *TS* V.1.8.6; VI.5.4.1 (*suvargásya lokásyā́nukhyātyai*); VI.3.4.8 (*suvargásya lokásya prájñātyai*); II.5.11.3; VI.3.7.2 (*yajñásyā́nukhyātyai*); *AB* I.8.16; II.1.2; IV.32.7 (*yajñasya prajñātyai svargasya lokasyānukhyātyai*).

29 According to *AB* VI.9.10, the *svarga loka* is the fourth world (after earth, intermediate space, and sky); cf. *ŚB* I.2.1.12; I.2.4.12; I.2.4.21; Gonda 1966: 91; Lévi 1898: 91-93.

30 *ṚV* VIII.43ab: *ápāma sómam amṛ́tā abhūmā́ganma jyótir ávidāma devā́n*.

31 *ā́ rohata dívam uttamā́m ṛṣayo mā́ bibhītana* । *sómapāḥ sómapāyina idáṁ vaḥ kriyate havír áganma jyótir uttamám*

32 *áganma jyótir uttamám íty āha* । *asáu vā́ ādityó jyótir uttamám ādityásyaivá sā́yujyaṁ gachati ná saṁvatsarás tiṣṭhati nā́sya śrī́s tiṣṭhati yásyaitā́ḥ kriyánte jyótiṣmatīm uttamā́m ánv āha jyótir evā́smā upáriṣṭād dadhāti suvargásya lokásyā́nukhyātyai* ।।

Often in the Vedic sacrifices, there is a symbolic ascension to heaven,[33] and from the stanzas related to Soma we find that this ascension was made possible, in the ṛṣis, by the drinking of the sacred beverage, which stimulated an ecstatic journey like that of the shaman.[34] In the *Pañcaviṁśa*, it seems that the chant of the sāman is used to induce the ecstatic knowledge of the heavenly world, or at least an ideal orientation towards heaven. Normally, it is not explicitly said that the ṛṣi previously had the vision of the sāman, but in *PB* VIII.2.6 we read:

> The Atharvans saw together this sāman, (being) desirous of the (immortal) world, through it they saw the immortal world. The reason for which there is this sāman, (is) for the knowledge of the heavenly world.[35]

Here we find mentioned both the vision of the sāman and of the immortal or heavenly world. And we can observe that the primary vision of the sāman is stimulated by desire of the (immortal) world (*lokakāma*), a desire which evidently gives an orientation to the sāman which will be seen. Sometimes we find ṛṣis "desirous of cattle" (*paśukāma*), as in *PB* VIII.5.12:

> Then (there is) this Āndhīgava(-sāman). Andhīgu, desirous of cattle, saw this sāman; by means of it he begot[36] a thousand head of cattle. That there is this sāman, (is) for the flourishing of cattle.[37]

---

[33] Cf. *PB* IV.7.10 (Gavām ayana); XVIII.10.10 (Rājasūya); XXI.8.2-6 (Parāka rite). In *PB* XXI.4.3, the performer of the Aśvamedha joins the celestial world "with his body": *eṣa vāva saśarīraḥ sambhavaty amuṣmai lokāyayo 'śvamedhī*. Cf. Gonda 1966: 89.

[34] Cf. Deeg 1993: 117-37.

[35] *atharvāṇo vā etal lokakāmaḥ sāmāpaśyaṁs tenāmartyaṁl lokam apaśyan yad etat sāma bhavati svargasya lokasya prajñātyai.*

[36] Caland 1931: 175, translates "created", thus giving a more miraculous appearance to the story, but I think that "to beget" or "to generate" would be more suitable to the context, indicating that Andhīgu fostered the birth of many calves, not that he created them ex nihilo. The root meaning of *sṛj-* is "to let go, let flow", so it should refer to an act which goes along with a natural process. Cf. also Varenne 1982: 60-62.

[37] *athaitad āndhīgavam andhīgur vā etat paśukāmaḥ sāmāpaśyat tena sahasraṁ paśūn asṛjata yad etat sāma bhavati paśūnāṁ puṣṭyai* [. . .] Cf. VIII.9.4 (Harivarṇa), XIII.11.15 (Karṇaśravas), XV.5.14 (Dāvasu), all obtaining the result of generating a thousand head of cattle.

In *PB* XXI.9.2, we have a desire for sons:

> Atri desired: "May four heroes be born to me!" He saw this (rite and practised it), to him four heroes were born. Four heroes are born to him who knows this.[38]

Also in *PB* XV.5.24 we have found Vasiṣṭha seeing the sāman after having desired to see Indra. Often, we have the formula *tad vāva sa tarhy akāmayata* "that, forsooth, he had wished at that time", about the desired result of the sāman, which implies that this desire was the origin of the vision of the sāman. In a very particular case (*PB* VIII.2.2), we find the R̥ṣi Kaṇva searching for a "finale" (*nidhana*), which was the concluding passage of a sāman sung in chorus:

> Kaṇva saw this sāman without (any) finale. He did not find stability. He heard (the noise) "*āṣ*" of a cat sneezing, he saw this as finale, then he found stability.[39]

We observe here the process of creation of a sāman, and in this context the problem that the r̥ṣi faces here is purely related to this creation. The solution comes from an unexpected sound, the sneeze of a cat, which suggests to Kaṇva the "vision" of the finale: there is nothing supernatural or revelatory, it seems only the inspiration of a poet, using the sounds of nature for his composition. However, here we do not have to do with a "normal" poet, interested in creating a beautiful verse to express his feelings, but with a composer of sacred poetry (with a musical aspect), a r̥ṣi who has to find a chant fit for the ritual, complete and effective for a practical purpose. What is also noteworthy about the concept of the r̥ṣi's vision is that we find here not an eternal Veda, already complete from the beginning, but the inspiration of the moment and the search for completeness.

In some cases, the vision seems to be provoked by urgency or necessity, as for the royal R̥ṣi Dīrghaśravas, who, being exiled and wandering hungry, sees a chant procuring food (XV.3.25). Analogous is the case of Śyāvāśva, who, brought to the desert in order to be killed, sees a sāman which creates rain (VIII.5.9). Or of Śarkara, the

[38] *atrir akāmayata catvāro me vīrā ājāyerann iti sa etam apaśyat tasya catvāro vīrā ājāyantāsya catvāro vīrā jāyante ya evaṁ veda.*

[39] *kaṇvo vā etat sāma rte nidhanam apaśyat sa na pratyatiṣṭhat sa vr̥ṣadaṁśasyāṣiti kṣuvata upāśr̥ṇot sa tad eva nidhanam apaśyat tato vai sa pratyatiṣṭhad.*

dolphin-ṛṣi, that, abandoned on dry land by Indra for his disrespect, through the chant reaches the water again (XIV.5.15). Another instance is that of Vasiṣṭha after the killing of his sons, who in IV.7.3 and VIII.2.4 sees a chant which makes him have progeny and cattle again, whereas in XXI.11.2 he sees a particular rite which permits him to "reach the summit".[40] Agastya, in XXI.14.5, is assailed by the Maruts, but seeing a hymn he is able to appease them.

A different kind of urgency is the condition of impurity or sin of gauṣūkti and āśvasūkti, who having accepted many forbidden gifts, thought to have swallowed poison,[41] which is eliminated through the chant seen by them (XIX.4.10). Similar is the case of XIV.3.22, where Ayāsya Āṅgirasa had eaten food of the Ādityas, who had undergone the consecration: through the chant seen by him on that occasion, he "redressed himself" (*ātmānaṁ samaśrīṇād*). But in a parallel passage, XI.8.10, we find that Ayāsya is taken by grief after this mistake and practices *tapas*, then he sees the two sāmans able to free him from grief. So, we can also suppose that *tapas*, the ascetic "heat", is always implied before the vision of a ṛṣi. The fact that the vision of the sāman is the final effect of an ascetic effort, is often repeated in the course of the Brāhmaṇa.[42] As usual, we find only the formula *tapo 'tapyata* (which can be translated "he heated the heat"), without explanation of the actual practices implied. According to Oldenberg,[43] in the oldest times the most important aspect was heat as vehicle of penance, connected with fire and sun, like in the late yogic practice of staying among four fires and under the sun; he mentions also fasting, staying awake, and holding the breath. *BauDhS* III.10.13 gives us a list of the different practices of *tapas*:

> Practising non-injury; speaking the truth; refraining from theft; bathing at dawn, noon, and dusk; obedience to elders; chastity; sleeping on the floor; wearing a single garment; and fasting — these

[40] *PB* XXI.11.2: *vasiṣṭhaḥ putrahato hīna ivāmanyata sa etam apaśyat so 'graṁ paryaid yo hīna iva manyeta sa etena yajeta.*

[41] Interpreted as moral or ritual impurity by Caland 1931: 506, based on *JB* III.250, which also describes the desire of the two ṛṣis to expel the "poison", preceding the vision of the sāmans.

[42] Cf. *PB* XII.11.25; XIII.6.10; XIII.11.10; XIV.12.5; XX.11.3.

[43] See Oldenberg 1917: 402-03. Cf. Oldenberg 1919: 146-49.

> are the austerities.[44]

These practices had the purpose of developing an internal energy which would have given magical power and spiritual "vision". They were also often intended to expiate sins: the previous citation of the *Baudhāyana Dharmasūtra* is in the context of expiation, and in *BauDhS* III.10.9 *tapas* is explicitly cited as one of the means of redemption (*niṣkrayaṇāni*).[45] We can cite in this context *PB* XI.8.8:

> Yuktāśva Āṅgirasa exchanged two young ones (just) born, from him the mantra withdrew. He underwent austerities, he saw this Yauktāśva. To him the mantra returned. That, forsooth, he had then desired.[46]

---

[44] The translation is from Olivelle 2000: 325. Here is the original text: *ahiṁsā satyam astainyaṁ savaneṣūdakopasparśanaṁ guruśuśrūṣā brahmacaryam adhaḥśayanam ekavastratānāśaka iti tapāṁsi.* According to Oldenberg 1919: 146, n. 3, this is "eine schon merklich modernisierte, abgeflaute Übersicht über Formen des Tapas".

[45] Olivelle 2000: 325: "The expiations for such a man [who has committed wrong actions] are softly reciting prayers, austerity, ritual offering, fasting, and giving gifts." (*tasya niṣkrayaṇāni japas tapo homa upavāso dānam*) Cf. *V.DhS* XX 47; *Manu* V.105-109; XI 242: "Whatever sin people commit through their mind, word, or body — with ascetic toil as their only wealth, they quickly burn off all that simply by ascetic toil." (*yat kiṁcid enaḥ kurvanti manovāṅmūrtibhir janāḥ । tat sarvaṁ nirdahantyāśu tapasaiva tapodhanāḥ*) (translation and text from Olivelle 2005: 228, 882). Cf. Kaelber 1989: 45-60, who connects the purification with *tapas* as a destructive force (like fire), and with the pain involved in the ascetic "mortifications", since "to suffer or feel pain" is one of the connotations of the root *tap-*.

[46] *yuktāśvo va āṅgirasaḥ śiśū jātau viparyaharat tasmān mantro 'pākrāmat sa tapo 'tapyata sa etad yauktāśvam apaśyat taṁ mantra upāvartata tad vāva sa tarhy akāmayata kāmasani sāma yauktāśvaṁ kāmam evaitenāvarundhe.* This story is more detailed in *JB* III.23, where Yuktāśva is the younger brother of Vasiṣṭha, who is Purohita of Sudās Paijavana. Sudās entrusted his mares to Vasiṣṭha, who gave them to his brother. This one exchanged the young ones born from the king's mares with those that belonged to himself, which were worse. When this deed was discovered, Yuktāśva was driven away as a thief and non-ṛṣi (*anṛṣir*). In order to find again trust and invitations, he saw the sāman and applied it. So, the two stories are very different, but it is probable that young horses are meant also here: actually, it is the name itself, Yuktāśva "having yoked horses", which can be connected with this story.

Sāyaṇa, commenting on this passage, writes that this *tapas* had the character of expiation (*prāyaścittātmakaṁ tapas tepe*), and, purified by this *tapas*, this ṛṣi saw the sāman (*tena ca tapasā viśuddhaḥ sa ṛṣiḥ etad yauktāśvaṁ sāmā 'paśyat*). Evidently, he sees a relation of cause and effect between the purification created by the *tapas* and the vision of the sāman, and it is possible that this relation was conceived of also in the times of the Brāhmaṇas: the spiritual vision as a natural consequence of the purification of body and mind (or of the "subtle body" made of prāṇas or vital airs) realized by ascetic exercises. In *PB* XIII.6.9 we find another similar story:

> Dīrghajihvī, this demon destroyer of sacrifices, wandered licking at the objects of sacrifices. Indra could not tell by which stratagem to kill her. Sumitra Kutsa was a handsome (young man). To him (Indra) said: 'Call her to you.' He called her to himself, she told him: 'I have never heard this indeed, but it is rather pleasant to my heart.' He announced her (the meeting-place), and at the arranged place they killed her. That, forsooth, they had desired at that moment. The Saumitra is a wish-granting chant. Through it (one) fulfils (one's) wish. 'Being Sumitra ("good friend") you have done a bloody deed!' a voice said to him. Grief came upon him, he performed austerities, he saw this Saumitra (chant), through it he drove away the grief. He drives away the grief who lauds with the Saumitra (chant).[47]

So, the context is given in both cases by a bad deed, and here an immaterial voice (that we are tempted to interpret as a manifestation of the subconscious guilt-feeling[48]) accuses Sumitra for a bloody deed (*krūra*), that is, for an act of violence. As a consequence, Sumitra is seized by grief (*śuc*). Analogously, in XIII.11.10 Vidanvat Bhārgava is

---

[47] *dīrghajihvī vā idaṁ rakṣo yajñahā yajñiyān avalihaty acarat tām indraḥ kayācana māyayā hantuṁ nāśaṁsatātha ha sumitraḥ kutsaḥ kalyāṇa āsa tam abravīd imām acchā brūṣveti tām acchābrūta sainam abravīn nāhaitan na śuśruva priyam iva tu me hṛdayasyeti tām ajñapayat tāṁ saṁskṛte 'hatāṁ tad vāva tau tarhy akāmayetāṁ kāmasani sāma saumitraṁ kāmam evaitenāvarundhe* 10. *sumitraḥ san krūram akar ity enaṁ vāg abhyavadat taṁ śug ārcchat sa tapo 'tapyata sa etat saumitram apaśyat tena śucam apāhatāpa śucaṁ hate saumitreṇa tuṣṭuvānaḥ.*

[48] Cf. *PB* XIV.11.28; XIX.4.7, where it is Indra who, having given the yatis (a kind of ascetics) to the hyenas, is reproached by an inauspicious or blaming voice (*aślīlā vāg abhyavadat*).

seized by remorse for having struck at Indra,[49] and we have already seen the case of Ayāsya in XI.8.10. In all these cases, the ṛṣi practises *tapas* to purify himself and overcome the condition of moral anguish into which he has fallen, but it is the Sāman which finally relieves him. But in the *Pañcaviṁśa* the *tapas* is not always subsequent to sin, it can also be a way of overcoming a difficult situation. For instance, in *PB* XII.11.25, we read:

> Vatsaprī, the son of Bhalandana, could not find faith (*śraddhā*); he performed austerities (*tapo 'tapyata*) and saw this Vātsapra(-chant). Thereupon, he found faith.[50]

We also find that the practice of *tapas* follows the desire, as in XIV.12.5, where Uśanas Kāvya desires to obtain as much "world" as the other Kāvyas possess, then he "heats the heat" (*tapo 'tapyata*) and sees the appropriate sāman. The desire to solve a problem or to get a particular result stimulates a search for vision which normally requires the practice of *tapas*, that is also a practice of concentration. Even when the vision is sudden and there is no time to practice austerities, it is obvious that the ṛṣi is able to see because he is a *tapasvin*, a man who has cultivated the inner energy of *tapas*. So, although there is no explicit description of the process of becoming a ṛṣi, we can say that *tapas* is the force which brings a person (generally a brahmin, sometimes a kṣatriya) to the status of ṛṣi, of one who sees the mantras. This relationship between *tapas* and the sacred word is synthetically affirmed in *TĀ* V.6.7, where we find the phrase *tapojāṁ vācam* "word born from ascetic heat". The same adjective *tapojā́* in *ṚV* X.154.5 is

49 *vidanvān vai bhārgava indrasya pratyahaṁs taṁ śug ārcchat sa tapo 'tapyata sa etāni vaidanvatāny apaśyat taiḥ śucam apāhatāpa śucaṁ hate vaidanvatais tuṣṭuvānaḥ* "Vidanvat Bhārgava struck at Indra. Grief came upon him, he performed austerities, he saw these vaidanvata (chants). By means of them he removed his grief. He removes his grief who lauds through the vaidanvata (chants)." Cf. *JB* III.159-160; *JAOS* XXVI: 63ff.

50 *vatsaprīr bhālandanaḥ śraddhāṁ nāvindata sa tapo 'tapyata sa etad vātsapram apaśyat sa śraddhām avindata*. This means that Vatsaprī lost the trust as a valid priest (cf. Lévi 1898: 110); cf. *PB* XX.11.3, where Haviṣmat and Haviṣkṛt are left behind by the other Aṅgirases on the way to the heavenly world. For the general concept of *tapas* as a means by which to overcome difficulties, cf. Manu XI.239: "What is difficult to cross, what is difficult to obtain, what is difficult to enter, what is difficult to do — all that is →

applied to the ṛṣis,[51] and we can say that it is all related: the ṛṣi is one who sees the sacred and effective word of mantras, this vision is produced by *tapas*, then the ṛṣi is born from *tapas*, from the ascetic practice of "heat".[52]

References

Caland, Willem, 1931, *Pañcaviṁśa Brāhmaṇa*, Calcutta: Asiatic Society of Bengal.

Deeg, Max, 1993, "Shamanism in the Veda: The Keśin-Hymn (10.136), the Journey to Heaven of Vasiṣṭha (*ṚV* 7.88) and the Mahāvrata-Ritual", *Nagoya Studies in Indian Culture and Buddhism*, **14:** 95-144.

Geldner, Karl Friedrich, 1951, *Der Rig-Veda aus dem Sanskrit ins Deutsche übersetzt und mit einem laufenden Kommentar versehen*, 3 vols., Cambridge (Mass.): Harvard University Press.

Gonda, Jan, 1966, *Loka: World and Heaven in the Veda*, Amsterdam: Noord-Hollandsche Uitgevers Maatschappij.

→ accomplished by ascetic toil, for it is difficult to prevail over ascetic toil." (*yaddustaraṁ yaddurāpaṁ yaddurgaṁ yacca duṣkaram* | *tat sarvaṁ tapasā sādhyaṁ tapo hi duratikramam*) (translation and text from Olivelle 2005: 228, 882).

51 *ṚV* X.154.5cd: *ṛ́ṣīn tápasvato yama tapojā́ṁ ápi gacchatāt*, tr. Geldner 1951, vol. III: 385 "zu den Kasteiung übenden Ṛṣi's, o Yama, zu den durch Kasteiung (neu)geborenen soll er gelangen!" The subject is the dead, who should reach the ṛṣis of the past in heaven.

52 Cf. Kaelber 1989: 61-71, where the relationship is analysed between *tapas*, knowledge, and spiritual rebirth, also in connection with ṛṣis. At p. 64 we find this interesting interpretation: "The *ṛṣis* are visionaries; they frequently see that which does not yet exist. Their *tapas* is therefore not only a heated effort but also a "meditative-brooding", a cognitive incubation. And from that cognitive, meditative incubation emerges the reality itself, hatching, as it were, from the egg of thought. The *ṛṣis* see or meditate upon components of creation not yet in existence and by doing so they actually bring those components into being. Within the *tapas* of the *ṛṣis* is thus reflected ascetic effort, cognitive brooding, and hatching heat." Surely, *tapas* is a practice involving concentration and striving for the realization of a particular purpose: in the case of ṛṣis, what is distinctive is the search for the knowledge of the means of that realization, because they are not yet known. In the Brāhmaṇas, this knowledge has mantras or rites as object, because those are the means of achievement of the different purposes, and naturally because the ṛṣis were trained to compose sacred hymns and chants.

Kaelber, Walter O., 1989, *Tapta Mārga: Asceticism and Initiation in Vedic India*, Albany: State University of New York Press.

Keith, Arthur Berriedale, and Arthur Anthony Macdonell, 1912, *Vedic Index of Names and Subjects*, 2 vols., London: John Murray.

Kern, Hendrik, 1865, *The Bṛhat Saṅhitā of Varāha-mihira*, Calcutta: Baptist Mission Press.

Krick, Hertha, 1975, "Der Vaniṣṭhusava und Indras Offenbarung", *Wiener Zeitschrift für die Kunde Südasiens*, **19:** 25-74.

Lamotte, Étienne, 1970, *Le traité de la grande vertu de sagesse de Nagarjuna*, vol. III, Louvain: Institut Orientaliste.

Lévi, Sylvain, 1898, *La doctrine du sacrifice dans les Brâhmaṇas*, Paris: Leroux.

Oldenberg, Hermann, 1917, *Die Religion des Veda*, Stuttgart/Berlin: Cotta.

———, 1919, *Vorwissenschaftliche Wissenschaft: Die Weltanschauung der Brāhmana-Texte*, Göttingen: Vandenhoeck und Ruprecht.

Olivelle, Patrick, 2000, *Dharmasūtras: The Law Codes of Āpastamba, Gautama, Baudhāyana, and Vasiṣṭha*, Delhi: Motilal Banarsidass.

———, 2005, *Manu's Code of Law: A Critical Edition and Translation of the Mānava-Dharmaśāstra*, Oxford: Oxford University Press.

Pargiter, Frederick Eden, 1922, *Ancient Indian Historical Tradition*, London: Oxford University Press; Humphrey Milford.

Varenne, Jean, 1982, *Cosmogonies védiques*, Paris: Les Belles Lettres.

Vira, Raghu, and Lokesh Chandra, 1986, *Jaiminīya Brāhmaṇa of the Sāmaveda*, Delhi: Motilal Banarsidass.

12

Feminine Aspect of the Sun
Vedic, Purāṇic, and Popular

Mugdha Gadgil

1. Introduction

It is well known that ancient humankind has always revered nature to show admiration for the smooth running of the world. As a result, various natural phenomena were transformed into different deities. Deification of the natural powers can be easily seen in the ancient cultures like Egyptian or Vedic. The Sun-god is one of the best examples of such deities. Ra from Egyptian mythology and Apollo from Greek mythology are some of the famous solar deities. As a source of light, warmth, and life, humankind has adored sun-gods worldwide.

Ancient Indian culture is no exception to Sun-worship. One finds ample evidence of solar-worship in different time-frames. Solar deities like Sūrya, or Savitṛ, or Pūṣan from the *Ṛgveda,* or Rohita from the *Atharvaveda* are well-known examples of the same. The Vedic rituals have included the Sun-god in different forms. The later Epics and Purāṇas have given equal importance to the Sun-god. We can certainly observe a similar trend in the popular or folk religion too. Thus Indians have consistently worshipped the Sun throughout the ages.

In the course of the deification of natural powers an enriched personification of the deities can be found in Vedic and later Indian mythology. As a consequence, the deities were even augmented by their own families. The divine families included both male and female members. Study of the family of a deity may help in studying the general development of that deity and it may also help in the study of that particular culture to some extent.

With this perspective, I focus on the feminine aspect of the Indian Sun-god with the help of the Vedic, Purāṇic, and folk traditions. An attempt is made to observe how long a particular female deity has endured and if she possesses any individuality of her own or just resembles the Sun-god. The "feminine aspect" here includes those females who are regarded as wives, mothers, and daughters of the Sun-god.

2. Aditi

Aditi is an important female deity in the Ṛgvedic pantheon. She is referred to as the mother-goddess of the Ādityas in Vedic literature. The group of Ādityas includes different solar deities. So gradually she was also considered the mother of the Sun-god. Sūryā is mentioned as Āditeya in the tenth maṇḍala of the *Ṛgveda*.[1] In the *Atharvaveda*, Rohita, the rising sun, is called the son of Aditi twice.[2] In the *Mahābhārata* Aditi is found as the mother of Mārtaṇḍa or Vivasvat; she was cursed by Budha and her foetus was born as *mṛta aṇḍa*, i.e. a dead egg — hence the name Mārtaṇḍa.[3]

This female deity does not seem to find any place in the popular tradition.

3. Uṣas

Uṣas is celebrated as the goddess of Dawn in the Vedas. The dawn is suggestive of the beginning of the day and especially of the arrival of the Sun-god. Thus Uṣas is closely associated with the Sun-god. It is said that she has opened paths for Sūrya to travel.[4] She is said to

---

[1] *ṚV* X.88.11ab — *yadéd enam ádadhúr yajñíyāso diví devā́ḥ sū́ryam āditeyám* ı

[2] *AV* XIII.2.9cd — *divyáḥ suparṇáḥ sá vīró vyakhyad áditeḥ putró bhúvanāni víśvā* ı and *AV* XII.2.37: *divás pṛṣṭhé dhā́vamānaṁ suparṇám ádityāḥ putrám* . . . ı *sá naḥ sūrya prá tira* . . . ıı

[3] *Mahābhārata* XII.329.44.1-5 — *aditir vai devānām annam apacat* ı *etad bhuktvā asurān haniṣyatīti* ı *tatra budhau vratacaryāṁ samāptāv agacchat* ı *aditiṁ cāvocad bhikṣāṁ dehīti* ı . . . *nānyeneti aditir bhikṣāṁ nādāt* ı *atha bhikṣāṁ pratyākhyānaruṣitena budhena brahmabhūtena vivasvato dvitīye janmany aṇḍasañjitasyāṇḍaṁ māritam adityāḥ* ı *sa mārtaṇḍo vivasvān abhavac chrāddhadevaḥ* ı

[4] *ṚV* I.113.16cd — *ā́raik pánthāṁ yā́tave sū́ryāyā́ganma yátra pratiránta ā́yuḥ* ıı

shine with the light of her lover.[5] Sūrya is imagined to follow her like a man who follows his beloved maiden.[6] Twice the Dawn or Dawns are actually named as the wife or wives of the Sun.[7] In the seventh maṇḍala of the *R̥gveda*, she is said to have given birth to Sūrya, Sacrifice, and Agni.[8] Thus she possesses the unique quality of being a wife and a mother of the Sun.

Though she is regarded as an important female deity in the Vedas, she has not survived to the time of the Purāṇas or the popular tradition.

4. Sūryā

Sūryā is the daughter of the Sun-god Savitr̥ whose marriage is described in *R̥gveda* X.85. A similar account of Sūryā's marriage-ceremony is also found in the 14th kāṇḍa of the *Atharvaveda*. The myth includes other Vedic deities such as Soma, the Aśvins, Pūṣaṇ, and Agni. Consequently we find some references to her in the hymns devoted to these deities too. She is sometimes also named *sūryasya duhitā*; e.g. in hymns to the Aśvins.[9]

The above-mentioned marriage-hymns first describe the marriage of Sūryā and then that of a human bride. The description includes details of Sūryā's accessories and her chariot. The above-mentioned deities are referred to in various roles such as bridesmen and groomsmen. Soma and the Aśvins are alternatively mentioned as her suitors. Though the Sun-god Savitr̥ is said to bestow her upon her Lord, her husband's name is not made clear. Evidently, these hymns do not throw any light on any personality trait of Sūryā. She seems to be a representation of any young human bride who is looking forward to meeting her husband and who is engrossed in thinking of him. So Sūryā can neither be seen as an individual nor does she reflect any solar quality.

---

5 R̥V I.92.11cd — *praminatī́ . . . yóṣā jārásya cákṣasā ví bhāti* ।

6 R̥V I.115.2ab — *sūryó devī́m uṣásaṁ rócamānāṁ máryo ná yóṣām abhyéti paścā́t* ।

7 R̥V VII.75.5ab — *vājínīvatī sū́ryasya yóṣā citrā́maghā rāyá īśe vásūnām* । and R̥V IV.5.13cd — *kadā́ no devī́r amŕ̥tasya pátnīḥ sū́ro várṇena tatanann uṣā́saḥ* ।

8 R̥V VII.78.3 — *etā́ u tyā́ḥ práti adr̥śran purástāj jyótir yácchantīr uṣáso vibhātī́ḥ* । *ájījanan sū́ryaṁ yajñám agním apācī́naṁ támo agād ájuṣṭam* ।।

9 E.g. R̥V I.117.13cd — *yuvó ráthaṁ duhitā́ sū́ryasya sahá śriyā́ nāsatyāvr̥ṇīta* । and R̥V I.118.5ab — *ā́ vāṁ ráthaṁ yuvatís tiṣṭhad átra juṣṭvī́ narā duhitā́ sū́ryasya* ।

However, sometimes this myth is related to the world-famous myth of union of the Sun and the Moon. Lal has proposed that in this myth, if Soma is accepted as Sūryā's spouse then she represents the Sun and Soma is the Moon.[10] However, this idea is manifested in reverse form in the folk-tradition.[11]

Later the name Sūryā is found once again in the *Agni Purāṇa* in the sense of a power of the Sun-god and it is said that she shall be worshipped before going to a battle.[12] Here, in the Purāṇas, from being a daughter of the Sun, Sūryā has turned into his energy.

5. Rohiṇī

The thirteenth kāṇḍa of the *Atharvaveda* is devoted to God Rohita who symbolizes the rising sun. Hymn I.22 and 23 of this kāṇḍa give an account of Rohiṇī as a devoted consort of Rohita.[13]

She is depicted as being great and glorious, and possessing beautiful complexion. It is said that she belongs to Rohita and pursues the yonder path. Different divine individuals like the gandharvas and the Kaśyapas lead her ahead and the sages protect her attentively. The singer expresses a desire to win all the battles and obtain manifold booty through her. Here Rohiṇī is clearly described as a companion of the rising sun and to belong to him. She also is called *suvarṇā* as well as *suvarcā,* indicating her association with the Sun.

She has not found any place in the later Purāṇic or popular Sun-cult tradition.

6. Suvarcalā

The *Rāmāyaṇa* mentions Suvarcalā as the female part of Sūryā twice. She is also referred to in the Umā-Maheśvara-Saṁvāda of the Anuśāsana-Parva of the *Mahābhārata*. While commenting upon the duties of ideal wives, the Goddess Pārvatī refers to Suvarcalā as the

---

10 Lal 1980: 234-35.

11 Bhagavat 1956: 156.

12 Dange 1990, vol. IV: 1412.

13 *AV* XIII.1.22ab — *ánuvratā róhiṇī róhitasya sūríḥ suvárṇā bṛhatī́ suvárcāḥ* । . . . and *AV* XIII.1.23ab. *idáṁ sádo róhiṇī róhitasya asaú pánthāḥ pṛ̥́ṣatī yéna yā́ti* । . . .

wife of Sūryā.[14] Hopkins has opined that this name probably indicates not a female but a sunflower, as Suvarcalā is known as a plant.[15]

Also this name is not associated with the Sun-god in later times.

7. Sāvitrī

The term Sāvitrī has manifold interpretations throughout Sanskrit literature. Initially it is understood as the sacred chant given to a disciple by his preceptor. Secondly, it is the name of a famous princess, daughter of King Aśvapati, who regained her husband Satyavat's life, right from the clutches of the death-god Yama. This legend is found under the title Sāvitryupākhyāna in the *Mahābhārata*. The name Sāvitrī occurs in the Tapatyupākhyāna too as Tapatī's elder sister. Whether as a chant or as the elder sister of Tapatī, she is undoubtedly associated with the Sun-god.

Additionally, Dange[16] regarded her as the personification of the solar energy and according to him, it was she who offered a lustrous daughter to King Aśvapati as well as regained Satyavat's life from Yama.

Even today the vow of Satyavat-Sāvitrī is followed by women in Maharashtra and many other places in India, but she is not worshipped as a solar goddess.

---

14 *Rāmāyaṇa* II.30.30 — *dharmas tu gajanāsoru sadbhir ācaritaḥ purā* । *taṁ cāham anuvarte 'dya yathā sūryaṁ suvarcalā* ।। — *Rāmāyaṇa* V.24.9: *dīno vā rājyahīno vā yo me bhartā sa me guruḥ* । *taṁ nityam anuraktāsmi yathā sūryaṁ suvarcalā* ।। — *Mahābhārata* XIII.134.4: . . . *varuṇasya tathā gaurī sūryasya ca suvarcalā* . . . ।

15 ". . . As Suvarcalā is a plant it may be a sun-flower." (Hopkins 1915: 85)

16 ". . . Like Sanjīvanī, who actually is said to bring the dead to life, 'Sāvitrī' also figures in the well-known story of 'Satyavān-Sāvitrī' as one who vanquishes Yama and brings her husband to life. 'Sāvitrī' actually giving new birth to Satyavat, and 'Sanjīvanī' giving new birth to Kaca, are hence definitely identical. The tale of 'Satyavān-Sāvitrī', it could easily be seen, is the colourful explanation of the main idea in initiation. The effect of the learning of the Sāvitrī ṛk is the aim therein. 'Sāvitrī' — the essence of the sun, ultimately saves the life of Satyavat, who is the symbol of the initiate. He is, as a matter of fact, 'swallowed' by Death himself; and disgorged at the intercession of 'Sāvitrī' — the solar power which is nothing but the same energy the initiate has to meditate . . ." (Dange 1969: 226-27)

Dange added in a note: "It is 'Sāvitrī' (the Solar energy) that stands before king Aśvapati and gives him a daughter made of her own brilliance. →

8. Saraṇyū, Saṁjñā, and Their Popular Adaptation

8.1. SARAṆYŪ

Saraṇyū has a unique and vital position in the myths related to the feminine aspect of the Sun because a long-lasting myth begins with her. The first two stanzas of X.17 of the *R̥gveda*[17] tell us that Tvaṣṭr̥ decided to perform his daughter's marriage and the whole world arrived there for the same. However, the mother of Yama and the wife of the great Vivasvat disappeared while being carried around. Further, for the sake of the mortals, the immortal female was concealed. Her duplicate was given to Vivasvat. Afterwards, having produced the Aśvins, Saraṇyū left (*ajahāt*) both pairs of twins.

This myth tells us that Saraṇyū was Tvaṣṭr̥'s daughter and wife of Vivasvat, the Sun-god. She was the mother of Yama as well as of the Aśvins. The second stanza talks about two pairs of twins. So a twin sister or brother of Yama is indicated by that stanza.

Yāska in his *Nirukta*[18] explains the name Saraṇyū from *saraṇa*. He explains the term *dvau mithunau* in the sense of *madhyama agni* and *mādhyamikā vāk*. He has also puts forward that Saraṇyū means the night who disappeared at the arrival of the Sun.

The *Br̥haddevatā*[19] of Śaunaka also deals with this story in nine verses altogether. It introduces the idea that after creating a substitute, Saraṇyū turned herself into a mare and departed. After her substitute gave birth to Manu, Vivasvat realized the truth. Consequently he went after Saraṇyū, also as a horse.

→ Hence it could be seen that 'SĀVITRĪ' — THE WIFE OF SATYAVĀN, AND THE DAUGHTER OF AŚVAPATI, IS ONLY THE PERSONIFICATION OF THE SOLAR ENERGY."

17 R̥V X.17.1-2 — *tváṣṭā duhitré vahatúṁ kr̥ṇotī́ti idáṁ víśvaṁ bhúvanaṁ sám eti । yamásya mātā́ paryuhyámānā mahó jāyā́ vívasvato nanāśa ।। ápāgūhann amŕ̥tāṁ mártyebhyaḥ kr̥tvī́ sávarṇām adadur vívasvate । utā́śvínau abharad yát tád ā́sīd ájahād u dvā́ mithunā́ saraṇyū́ḥ ।।*

18 *Nirukta* XII.10-11, p. 209 — *ajahād dvau mithunau saraṇyūḥ । madhyamaṁ ca mādhyamikā ca vācam iti nairuktāḥ । yamaṁ ca yamīṁ cety aitihāsikāḥ । . . . yamasya mātā paryuhyamānā mahato jāyā vivasvato nanāśa । rātrir ādityasya । ādityodaye 'ntardhīyate ।*

19 *Br̥haddevatā* VI.162-63 and VII.1-3, pp. 78-79 — *sa vai saraṇyūṁ prāyacchat svayam eva vivasvate । tataḥ saraṇyvāṁ jajñāte yamayamyau vivasvataḥ ।। sr̥ṣṭvā bhartuḥ parokṣaṁ tu saraṇyūḥ sadr̥śī striyam । . . . sa vijñāya tv apakrāntāṁ saraṇyūm aśvarūpiṇīm । . . . tvāṣṭrīṁ prati jagāmāśu vājī bhūtvā salakṣaṇaḥ ।*

Sāyaṇa too in his commentary[20] gives details about Saraṇyū. However he justifies the acts of hiding her and offering her duplicate to Vivasvat as done by the gods. According to him she was taken by the gods to the Uttara-Kuru region. Although not mentioned in the stanza, Sāyaṇa explains that she, in the form of a mare, held the Aśvins in her womb. He interprets the verb *ajahāt* in the sense of giving birth to the pair of twins.

Griffith interprets Saraṇyū as a stormy cloud or Uṣas. He considers these stanzas to be obscure. Both he and Geldner translate that she deserted or abandoned the two pairs of the twins, but they do not offer any further explanation.[21] On the contrary, Sāyaṇa's interpretation matches with the Saṁjñā–Chāyā–Vivasvat myth later fully developed in the Purāṇas.

8.2. SAṀJÑĀ

The later form of Saraṇyū is named Saṁjñā in the *Mahābhārata* and the Purāṇas.

The daughter of Tvaṣṭṛ is seen again in the Ādi-Parva, which refers to Tvāṣṭrī as the wife of Savitṛ, who took the form of a mare. She gave birth to the Aśvins in space. Another similar reference to the birth of the Aśvins, the sons of Mārtaṇḍa, from the nose of Saṁjñā is found in the Anuśāsana-Parva. So, at this stage Tvaṣṭrī has become Saṁjñā and the Saraṇyū-myth is continued.[22]

Saraṇyū has carried on her journey even in the Purāṇas.[23] Here, after the 3birth of Yama and Yamī, the Purāṇic wife of the Sun did not

---

[20] Sāyaṇa's commentary on *ṚV* X.17.1-2 — *tvaṣṭā . . . duhituḥ saraṇyūnāmikāyāḥ vivāham* । *. . . paryuhyamānā vivasvato . . . uttarān kurūn prati naṣṭā* । *agacchad ity arthaḥ* । *. . . etāṁ saraṇyūm . . . devā uapanītavantaḥ . . . api ca sā aśvarūpiṇī saraṇyūs tadā aśvinau svodare garbhabhūtau dhāritavatī* । *. . . tathā dvau mithunau yamayamyau tyaktavatā janitavatīty arthaḥ* ।

[21] See Griffith 1976: 541 and Geldner 1951: 149 — ('. . . als dies geschah, und sie liess die Zwei, die ein Paar waren, im Stich, die Saranyu . . .').

[22] *Mahābhārata* I.60.34 — *tvāṣṭrī tu savitur bhāryā vaḍavārūpadhāriṇī* । *asūyata mahābhāgā sāntarikṣe 'śvināv ubhau* ।। and *Mahābhārata* Appendix I, 18.40, p. 1039: *dharo dhruvaśca somaśca . . .* ।। *nāsatyaścāpi dasraśca smṛtau dvāv aśvināv api* । *mārtaṇḍasyātmajāv etau saṁjñānāsāvinirgatau* ।।

[23] *Matsya Purāṇa* Chapter 11, vv. 02-40, pp. 65-70 — *vivasvān kaśyapāt pūrvam adityāṁ abhavat sutaḥ* । *tasya patnītrayaṁ tadvat saṁjñā rājñī prabhā tathā* ।। *raivatasya sutā rājñī . . . . . . tvastrī saṁjñā tathā manum* ।। *yamaśca yamunā* →

disappear suddenly but she decided to leave her husband because she could not bear his scorching lustre. Before leaving, she prepared her substitute with the name Chāyā and deposited her children to Chāyā. In the Purāṇas, we also find that at this juncture she went to Tvaṣṭṛ's house but he sent her back. So she changed herself into a mare and went to the desert. In the meanwhile two or three more children were born to Vivasvat by Chāyā. Sāvarṇī Manu was the most prominent amongst them. This changed Chāyā's behaviour towards Saṁjñā's children. As a consequence, Vivasvat came to know the real situation and went to Tvaṣṭṛ. When he understood the reason of Saṁjñā's decision he got himself chopped from Tvaṣṭṛ and got his brilliance lessoned. Then he also transformed himself into a horse and approached Saṁjñā. However, considering him foreign or strange she got scared and so his seed fell on the ground. Aśvins were born from that seed. At last, Vivasvat brought her back to his kingdom.

This story presents Saṁjñā and Chāyā as the female parts of the Sun-god. One can easily see the modifications in the Purāṇic story from the Vedic one. The brief and obscure Ṛgvedic reference to Saraṇyū has been converted into a fully developed plot here. Saraṇyū, in the guise of Saṁjñā, seems to be independent and strong enough because she can decide to leave her husband and create a duplicate in her

→ *caiva yamalau tu babhūvatuḥ* I *tatas tejomayaṁ rūpam asahantī vivasvataḥ* II *nārīm utpādayām āsa svaśarīrād aninditām* I *tvāṣṭrī svarūpeṇa nāmnā chāyeti bhāminī tadā* . . . II *chāye tvaṁ bhaja bhartāram asmadīyaṁ varānane* II *apatyāni madīyāni mātṛsnehena pālaya* . . . II *kāmayām āsa devo 'pi saṁjñā iyam iti cādarāt* I *janayām āsa tasyāṁ tu putraṁ ca manurūpiṇaṁ* II *savarṇatvāc ca sāvarṇir manor vaivatasya ca* I *tataḥ śaniṁ ca tapatīṁ viṣṭiṁ caiva krameṇa tu* II *chāyāyāṁ janayām āsa saṁjñeyam iti bhāskaraḥ* I *chāyā svaputre abhyadhikaṁ snehaṁ* . . . II . . . *vivasvān atha taj jñātvā saṁjñāyāḥ karmaceṣṭitam* I *tvaṣṭuḥ samīpam agamad ācacakṣe* . . . II *tam uvāca tatas tvaṣṭā* . . . II *vaḍavārūpam āsthāya matsakāśam iha āgataḥ* I *nivāritā mayā sā tu* . . . II . . . *apaneṣyāmi te tejo yantre kṛtvā divākara* I *tataḥ sa bhagavān gatvā* . . . II . . . *kāmayām āsa kāmārto mukha eva divākaraḥ* II *aśvarūpeṇa mahatā tejasā ca samāvṛtaḥ* I *aṁjñā ca manasā kṣobham agamad bhayavihvalā* II *nāsāpuṭābhyām utsṛṣṭaṁ paro 'yam iti śaṁkayā* I *tad retas tato jātau aśvināv iti niścitam* . . . II . . . *vimānenāgamat svargaṁ patyā saha mudānvitā* II . . . *yamunā tapatī caiva punar nadyau babhūvatuḥ* II

See also *Brahma Purāṇa* 4.2-9 and 5.10-16; *Mārkaṇḍeya Purāṇa* 74.1-40 and 75.21-30; *Viṣṇu Purāṇa*, vol. II, 2.2-12.

place to maintain the household arrangement as it is. She even can decide to go to a desert or forest when her father does not give her shelter. Thus the Purāṇas have offered her some individuality compared to Saraṇyū. The Purāṇas have given a name and a personality to Saṁjñā's substitute too. Discrimination towards the children of another woman is generally understood as a typical personality trait of women. This can be observed in Chāyā's behaviour. However, the Purāṇas do not utter a single word about Chāyā after the reunion of Vivasvat and Saṁjñā.

In addition, the *Matsya Purāṇa* mentions Rājñī and Prabhā as two more wives of Vivasvat.[24] However they do not play any role in the Purāṇic version of Saraṇyū–Saṁjñā myth.

8.3. RĀNDALAMĀ OR RANNĀDE

Rāndala, Rannā, Rānabāī, Rāṇūbāī, etc. are the popular forms of Saraṇyū–Saṁjñā. Rāndala or Rannā can be mentioned as the most significant form of them. This goddess is worshipped in the Saurashtra region of Gujarat and Rajasthan. She is mostly worshipped to begin auspicious events like marriage, upanayana, etc. We can see that the legend related to Rāndala[25] is nothing but the repetition of the myth of Saraṇyū or Saṁjñā explained already. Probably due to the time-factor, certain changes can be observed in this story.

The popular story including such changes can be summarized as follows. Rāndala, daughter of Viśvakarmā and wife of Sūryanārāyaṇa closed her eyes once in the summer season because she could not bear Sūryanārāyaṇa's splendour. As a result the Sun-god cursed her and her children. She became forlorn and decided to go to her parental house. Just as in the Purāṇic story, she placed her shadow (*chāyāsvarūpa*) before she left, and because her father did not accept her she went to the forest in the form of a mare. The popular legend brings in Sage Nārada at this juncture who tries to send her back to her husband's house, but she is firm on doing penance — her expiation for the mistake of abandoning her husband's house. After this part, the story runs similar to that of the Purāṇas. In the popular version of this deity, the first notable change is observed in her name. Modern scholars have suggested the origin of this name from (Sa)raṇyū or

[24] See the preceding reference.

[25] Bhaskar 2003: 17-26.

Rājñī.[26] Secondly the story is provided with a curse by the Sun-god, and that distress made his wife to leave his house. Later Rāndala accepts that action as her mistake. In this she differs in personality from the Purāṇic Saṁjñā.

Thus in the case of the popular story of the Sun-god's wife, her departure no more remains her own decision but is labelled a mistake. By calling it a mistake and trying to amend for it by doing penance, she seems to have incorporated the contemporary social rules.

On the ritual side, it is noteworthy that the vow of Rāndala is started on a Sunday, i.e. the day devoted to the Sun-god. A symbolic action called *ghoḍā khūndanā*[27] is performed by the women. It looks like an imitation of Vivasvat approaching his wife in the form of a horse.

8.4. RĀNABĀĪ-KĀNABĀĪ AND RANUBĀĪ

In the Khandesh region of Maharashtra, Rānabāī is worshipped as the wife of the Sun-god.[28] She is also known as Kānābāī or Kānoḍa. Her vow is undertaken on the first Sunday of the month of Śrāvaṇa or on the Sunday after Nāgapañcamī (the fifth day of the first fortnight in the month of Śrāvaṇa). No symbolic action is performed in the ritual of Rānabāī reflecting the horse-myth. However, the same deity is known as Raṇādevī by some communities and they perform her marriage with a statue of the Sun-god sitting on an earthen horse.[29]

---

26 Agarwal (1970: 162-64) touches on this subject while explaining the Sun-cult. He proposes that Ranā or Ranu are distorted forms of Rājñī. He similarly proposes that Rājñī and Nikṣubhā mentioned in the *Bhaviṣya Purāṇa* are the Indian forms of Iranian Rashna and Nurshef.

27 This custom is explained by some elderly Gujarati women.

28 Karankal 1997: 29 — *tāpī thaḍī ni chikanī mātī, māya chikanī mātī । tathe manī kānabāī ramata hotī māya kheyata hotī । kheyatā kheyatā konī dekhī māya konī dekhī । kheyatā kheyatā sūryānī dekhī māya sūryānī dekhī । sūryānī mhane manī jīvanī sakhī māya jīvanī sakhī ।* This stanza from the folk-tradition of the Khandesh region of Maharashtra describes that Kānabāī has been accepted as life-partner by the Sun-god. Pushpalata Karankal deals with the Goddess Rānabāī-Kānabāī in detail in her Marathi book *Khandeshatila Lokdevata Kanbai*. While explaining the importance of the popular goddess Rānabāī-Kānabāī in that region, the author also discusses her background and other popular goddesses such as Rāndala or Ranubāī belonging to other geographical areas.

29 Dhere 2007: 183 — *rāṇubāī hī khānadeśāta raṇādevī hyā nāvāne nāndate āhe* →

A similar ritual is performed in the Nimad region of Madhya Pradesh for the vow of Goddess Ranubāī as the wife of the Sun-god.[30] She is said to come from the region of Saurashtra.[31]

8.5. ĀDITYA–RĀṆUBĀĪ

Some communities in Maharashtra perform this vow to obtain the blessings of the Sun-god and consequently worldly prosperity. The name of the vow, Āditya–Rāṇubāī, consists of two elements. Āditya is none other than the Sun-god, and Rāṇūbāī is his consort. However, we do not find any significance given to Rāṇūbāī either in the ritual or in the legend narrated in connection with it.[32]

In all the above popular goddesses one can find the continued existence of Vedic Saraṇyū and Purāṇic Saṁjñā. Agarwal[33] has strongly propounded the idea that there is certainly a correlation between Saraṇyū or Rājñī and Ranudevī, Rānabāī, Rāndala.

9. Tapatī

While discussing the most dominant female aspect of the Sun we come across the names of Tapatī and Yamunā as his daughters.

Tapatī is once again a daughter of the Sun-god Vivasvat.[34] In the Tapatyupākhyāna in the Ādi-Parva of the *Mahābhārata* we find the

---

→ *āṇi tithe aneka gharāṇyāta lagnamunjīpūrvī tice sūryāśī lagna lāvaṇyācī prathā cālū āhe* I . . . *mātīcyā ghoḍyāvara basalelyā sūryācyā putaḷyāśī raṇādevīce lagna lāgate* I *purohita raṇādevīcā ullekha rannāsannādevī asā karatāta* I — Here Dhere also shows the similarity between the popular goddesses Rāṇūbāī, Ranubāī, and Raṇādevī.

30 See Karankal 1997: Chapter 6.

31 *thāro kāi kāi rūpa bakhāṇa ranubāī* I *soraṭha desa so āī o* I — This verse from the folk-tradition refers to the Soraṭha or Saurashtra region as the native place of the Goddess Ranubāī. Ranubāī is also known as Rāndala, Rānabāī, Rannā, or Raṇādevī.

32 Dhere (2007: 181-82 explains the ritual of the vow of Āditya–Rāṇūbāī along with the *kahāṇī* or story related to it.

33 See note 26.

34 *Mahābhārata* I.160.6-15 — *yaiṣa divi dhiṣṇyena nākaṁ vyāpnoti tejasā* I *etasya tapatī nāma babhūva sadṛśī sutā* II *vivasvato vai kaunteya sāvitry avarajā vibho* I *viśrutā triṣu lokeṣu tapatī tāpasā yutā* II *na devī nāsurī caiva na yakṣī na ca rākṣasī* I *nāpsarā na ca gandharvī tathārūpeṇa kācanā* II *suvibhaktā anavadyāṅgī svasitāyatalocanā* I *svācārā ca sādhvī ca suveṣā caiva bhāminī* II *na tasyāḥ sadṛśaṁ* →

following story: Tapatī likewise was a daughter of the one who encompasses the heaven with his lustre. This Tapatī was the younger sister of Sāvitrī and she was famous in all the three worlds because of her penance. She was incomparable in beauty and nobility. Hence initially, Savitṛ could not see any match for his daughter. However later a Kuru king named Saṁvaraṇa, who worshipped the Sun-god, was considered a perfect match for Tapatī by the Sun-god.

During a hunting mission Saṁvaraṇa came across Tapatī and thought of her as a goddess just like an embodiment of the sun-rays.[35] Having fallen in love with her, Saṁvaraṇa asked her to marry him. However, being a modest girl she declared that she was a maiden ruled by her father. Afterwards revealing her identity she ascended to heaven. The story moves ahead by mentioning the marriage of Tapatī and Saṁvaraṇa and how the lineage of the Kurus was continued, etc.[36]

Similar to Sūryā, Tapatī is not portrayed very prominently by the poet. Nevertheless some of her behavioural and physical features are mentioned. By calling her an embodiment of the sun-rays, her relation with the Sun-god is highlighted. From a naturalistic perspective she is sometimes interpreted as the bright lightning.[37]

Afterwards, the *Matsya Purāṇa* and *Padma Purāṇa* mention her as Vivasvat's second daughter by Chāyā and she later becomes a river

→ *kaṁcit triṣu lokeṣu bhārata* । *bhartāraṁ savitā mene rūpaśīlakulaśrutaiḥ* ।। . . . . . . *tapatyā sadṛśaṁ mene sūryaḥ saṁvaraṇaṁ patim* ।।

[35] *Mahābhārata* I.160.25 — *sa hi tāṁ tarkayām āsa rūpato nṛpatiḥ śriyam* । *punaḥ saṁtarkayām āsa raver bhraṣṭām iva prabhām* ।।

[36] *Mahābhārata* I.160-63.

[37] "Covertly, the story of Tapatī–Saṁvaraṇa also symbolizes the relationship of the earth with the sun and the cloud. If we pursue this naturalistic interpretation, we may suggest the following points —

. . . The king sees Tapatī, the younger daughter of the sun. This is perhaps the bright lightening. . . . The attraction of the lightening and the cloud towards each other is succinctly expressed in the story." (Patil 1983: 64-65)

". . . The word Sāvitrī is known in a number of contexts. It means the chandas Gāyatrī. It also means the solar energy." (ibid.: 81)

". . . the main purpose of the story seems to glorify Sāvitrī. Sāvitrī is solar energy and is the very principle of procreation. The word Sāvitrī is derived from the root *su* – meaning 'to procreate' or 'to give birth to'." (ibid.: 82)

according to them.[38]

Yamunā too is a daughter of Vivasvat by Saraṇyū or Saṁjñā, previously mentioned as Yamī. She too is said to become a legendary river, the Yamunā.[39]

The Tapatī and Yamunā are revered by the Indians as sacred rivers even now.

10. Pṛthvī

The discussion regarding the female aspect of the Sun would be incomplete without referring to *Pṛthvī*, the Earth. Though not related with the Sun in the Vedas and Purāṇas, Pṛthvī or the Earth is considered the wife of the Sun-god in folk tradition.[40] A vow named Rājñīsnāpana performed in Kashmir is the worship of Goddess Earth as the wife of the Sun-god.[41] How and when she acquired this position remains a topic for further research.

11. Conclusions

On the basis of the careful overview of the feminine aspects of different Indian Sun-gods the following observations can be presented:

1. We can find mothers, wives, and daughters of the Sun as his female parts in Indian mythology during different time-periods. Uṣas, Rohiṇī, and Tapatī are party to the actual solar activity. Sāvitrī and Sūryā too represent solar energy. Even Saraṇyū is interpreted to be either a stormy cloud or Uṣas. Though the names of the Sun-god do differ as per stories, all of them surely belong to the solar pantheon. Hence feminine parts of all of them are included here.

---

[38] See note 23 above and also *Padma Purāṇa* 8.37-75.

[39] See note 23 above.

[40] Bhagavat (1956: 141-42) mentions a folk tale occurring in a Gond song from Dug district, telling the background of the marriage of the Earth and the Sun. According to this tale, initially the God decided to marry the Earth with the Sky and he invited all deities as well as other beings. However he forgot to invite the Jackal and the Jackal decided to break this marriage. He told the God that if the Earth and the Sky get married then all the beings will be crushed in their embrace. The God was convinced and he made the Earth to marry the Sun.

[41] Dhere 2007: 185

2. Out of these, the wife of the Sun-god is prominently and frequently depicted in various forms in traditional literature as well as popular religion. However, these female forms possess more or less a dependent personality.
3. Saraṇyū has travelled a long way from the Vedas till now. Her myth has become more developed in the Purāṇas and in the popular customs, compared to the *Ṛgveda*. Thus she can be depicted as the most influential amongst all the female parts of the Sun.
4. Saraṇyū's name is replaced by different titles such as Saṁjñā, Rāndala, or Rānabāī. Nonetheless they all are daughters of Tvaṣṭṛ or Viśvakarmā.
5. The birth of the Aśvins from Vivasvat and his wife in the form of a horse-pair remains consistent. Though the *Ṛgveda* does not specifically mention the story, it does refer to the birth of the Aśvins. Is it possible that the story came into being only to justify the birth and name of the Aśvins?
6. Yāska has derived the word Saraṇyū from the root *sṛ* which suggests a flow or movement. So Saraṇyū symbolizes fast movement. It might be based on her quick disappearance while she was carried to her husband's house and so she got imagined as a mare later.
7. Popular religion has also strongly retained the concept of the wife of the Sun-god. The goddesses characterized as such do not have an independent personality in the popular myths, but they are capable enough to provide well-being for the worshippers. A reflection of the myth is found in the performance of the popular rituals of both Rāndala and Raṇādevi. The popular vows related to the female aspect of the Sun are mostly performed by females.

References

PRIMARY SOURCES

Atharvaveda Saṁhitā (*Śaunakīya*), vols. I and III, 2nd edn., Hoshiarpur: VVRI, 1993.

Bṛhaddevatā, attributed to Śaunaka, cited from Macdonell, 1904.

R̥gveda Saṁhitā, vols. I, III and IV, Pune: Vaidik Samshodhana Mandala, 1995 and 2005.

Śrī Matsya Purāṇa, cited from Shukla, 2004.

Śrīharivaṁśapurāṇam, cited from Menon, 2008.

Śrīmadvālmīki Rāmāyaṇam, revised by K. Chinnaswami and V.H. Subramanya Sastri, 2nd edn., Madras: N. Ramaratnam, 1958.

The Mahābhārata (crit. edn.), vol. I, Fascicules 35 and 36, and vol. XVI, Pune: BORI, 1933, 1943, 1964, 1966.

The Nighaṇṭu and the Nirukta, cited from Sarup 1920-29.

SECONDARY SOURCES

Agarwal, V.S., 1970, *Ancient Indian Folk Cults*, Varanasi: Prithvi Prakashan.

Bhagavat, Durga, 1956, *Lokasahityachi Ruparekha* (Marathi), Mumbai: Mumbai Marathi Grantha Sangrahalaya.

Bhaskar, Jayavant, 2003, *Shri Randala Mataji* (Gujarati), Ahmedabad: Yogesh Publication.

Dange, Sadashiv Ambadas, 1969, *Legends in the Mahābhārata*, Delhi: Motilal Banarsidass.

———, 1990, *Encyclopeadia of Purāṇic Beliefs and Practices*, vol. IV, Delhi: Navarang.

Dhere, R.C., 2007, *Lokadevatanche viśva* (Marathi), 3rd edn., Pune: Padmagandha Prakashan.

Geldner, Karl Friedrich, 1951, *Der Rigveda*, dritter Teil, Cambridge (Mass.): Harvard University Press.

Griffith, Ralph T.H., 1889, *The Hymns of the Rigveda*, Benares: Lazarus, repr., 1976, Delhi: Motilal Banarsidass.

Hopkins, Edward W., 1915, *Epic Mythology*, Straßburg: Trübner, repr., 1968, Delhi/Varanasi: Indological Book House.

Karankal, Pushpalata, 1997, *Khandeshatil Lokdevata Kanbai* (Marathi), Aurangabad: Godavari Prakashan.

Lal, Shyam Kishore, 1980, *Female Divinities in Hindu Mythology and Ritual*, Pune: University of Pune.

Macdonell, Arthur Anthony, 1904 (ed. & tr.), *The Br̥had-Devatā of Śaunaka: A Summary of the Deities and Myths of the Rig-Veda*, Cambridge (Mass.): Harvard University Press, repr., 1976, Delhi: Motilal Banarsidass

Menon, K.P.A. (ed.), 2008, *Śrīharivaṁśapurāṇam*, Delhi: Nag Publishers.

Patil, Narendranath B., 1983, *The Folklore in the Mahābhārata*, Delhi: Ajanta Publications.

Sarup, Lakshman (ed. & tr.), 1920-29, *The Nighaṇṭu and the Nirukta*, London: Milford, repr., 1998, Delhi: Motilal Banarsidass.

Sharma, R.N., 1995, *Śrīśivamahāpurāṇam*, part II, 2nd repr., Delhi: Nag Publishers.

———, 2004, *Śrīviṣṇumahāpurāṇam*, 3rd edn., Delhi: Nag Publishers.

———, 2007, *Śrībrahmamahāpurāṇam*, repr., Delhi: Nag Publishers.

———, 2008, *Śrīmārkaṇḍeyamahāpurāṇam*, 3rd edn., Delhi: Nag Publishers.

———, 2008, *Śrīpadmamahāpurāṇam*, 4th edn., Delhi: Nag Publishers.

Shukla, S. (tr.), 2004, *Śrīmatsyapurāṇa*, vol. I, Delhi: Nag Publishers.

13

Processing of Dairy Products in the Vedic Ritual, Compared with Pāli

Naoko Nishimura

0. Introduction: Enumerations of Dairy Products in the Veda and Pāli Canon

THE ancient Āryas made their living by raising cattle. We can find references to various dairy products in their religious texts. For example,

ŚB I.8.1.7 *só 'rcañ chrā́myaṁś cacāra prajā́kāmaḥ* । *tatrā́pi pākayajñéneje. sá* ***ghr̥táṁ dádhi mástv āmíkṣām*** *íty apsú juhavā́ñ cakāra . . .* ।।

He (Manu after the Deluge), desiring offspring, kept exerting himself, singing [praising hymns]. At that time, he performed a sacrifice even if [only] with a pākayajña (thus in the manner of a domestic sacrifice). He offered [the following] into the waters: *ghr̥ta, dadhi, mastu,* [and] *āmikṣā*. [Darśapūrṇamāsa, Iḍā portion, legend of Manu and Mānavī]

ŚB III.3.3.2 *gór vái* ***pratidhúk*** । *tásyai* ***śr̥táṁ****. tásyai* ***śáras****. tásyai* ***dadhi****. tásyai* ***mástu****. tásyā* ***ātáñcanaṁ****. tásyai* ***návanītaṁ****. tásyai* ***ghr̥táṁ****. tásyā* ***āmíkṣā****. tásyai* ***vā́jinam*** ।।

To the cow belongs the *pratiduh*. To her the *śr̥ta*. To her the *śaras*. To her the *dadhi*. To her the *mastu*. To her the *ātañcana*. To her the *navanīta*. To her the *ghr̥ta*. To her the *āmikṣā*. To her the *vājina*. [Agniṣṭoma, Somakrayaṇa]

Vinaya-Piṭaka I.244[33-37]

anujānāmi bhikkhave ***pañca gorase khīraṁ dadhiṁ takkaṁ navanītaṁ sappiṁ****.*

"I admit, O monks, the five kinds of essence of the cow: *khīra,*

> *dadhi, takka, navanīta,* [and] *sappi,*" [said the Buddha]. [Mahāvagga, Bhesajjakkhandhaka]

Those products were not only everyday foodstuffs but also principal offerings of the Vedic rituals. Their description in the Veda and Pāli canon, if not always clear, provides us with information about the methods used to process them. This presentation will examine some ritual materials and procedures related to processing fresh milk into some kinds of butterfat in the Veda. It focuses, among others, on the comparison of Vedic material with that in Buddhist scriptures: the Black Yajurveda-Saṁhitās (prose, *c.* 800 BCE), Brāhmaṇas (*c.* 700 BCE), Śrautasūtras (*c.* 500 BCE), and Pāli canon (*c.* third century BCE) with other "Pāli texts".

1. Processing of Butterfat in the Rājasūya Ritual Offering of caru to Mitra and Bṛhaspati

Vedic literature describes in some places how to process the dairy products in detail. The *Yajurveda* texts offer significant information from the description of the offerings of *caru* (a kind of porridge made of husked rice or barley, named after its vessel[1]) dedicated to Mitra and Bṛhaspati in the Rājasūya ritual (royal consecration). Whereas the *caru* for Mitra is cooked with milk, that for Bṛhaspati is prepared with *ājya*. For the preparation, four stages are mentioned: [1] Milking, [2] Curdling (*dadhi*), [3] Churning (*navanīta*), and [4] Melting (*ājya*). Among the Brāhmaṇas only the *ŚB* refers to the intermediate products, *dadhi* and *navanīta*. The *Śatapatha Brāhmaṇa* belongs to the White Yajurveda (YV) School and seems to be codified later than the Brāhmaṇas of the Black Yajurveda. The Śrauta-Sūtras of the Black YV have more detailed descriptions than their Brāhmaṇas. The *KātyŚrSū* of the White YV refers to the procedures only in a simple manner.

[1] Milking of a white cow accompanied by a white calf[2] (*duh*)

a. no reference to any vessels into which the milk is poured: *MS, KS, TS, TB, ŚB* (*M, K*), *MānŚrSū*; *VādhŚrSū* (Yajamāna milks by himself)

[1] Cf. Rau 1972: 19. The *ŚB* employs this word *carú-* in both meanings, viz. a porridge and a vessel.

[2] Before milking of a cow, people seem to let it suckle its calf to make the process of milking more smooth. A mother cow's lactation is prompted by a calf's suckling, cf. *ŚB* XIV.2.1.9-10, *ApŚrSū* I.12.8-13.2 and 14.7. On the verb *prá-dā* "to let a cow give her milk to a calf" cf. Caland *PB*, p. 336 (XIII.9.17).

b. into a leather bag[3] (*dr̥ti-/vināṭa-*): *BaudhŚrSū, HirŚrSū*

c. some leather (raw-hide?) bag: *ĀpŚrSū*

d. no reference to either milking or colour of the cow: *KātyŚrSū*

[2] **Curdling** (→ *dadhi*)

a. curdling without any additives (*svayáṁ mūrch* "curdle of itself" i.e. a fermentation caused by lactic acid bacteria). *MS, KS, TS, MānŚrSū, HirŚrSū, ĀpŚrSū, BaudhŚrSū,*

b. self-curdling together with unnatural coagulation (i.e. with some additives, *ā-tañc* "coagulate"): *VādhŚrSū* (*svayaṁmūrta-* "curdled of itself"; *svayaṁ ātanakti* "he makes [it] curdled by himself"?)

c. coagulation with some additives (*ā-tañc*): *ŚB* (*M, K*)

d. no reference to curdling: *KātyŚrSū*

[3] **Churning** (*manth*) (→ *navanīta*)

a. churning of itself: *MS, KS, TS, MānŚrSū, BaudhŚrSū*

b. churning in a bag containing *dadhi* bound on a running chariot: *ŚB* (*M, K*) (an Adhvaryu priest, pouring *dadhi* into the bag, recites *dedīyitavái* "Jump repeatedly!"), *HirŚrSū, ĀpŚrSū, KātyŚrSū*

c. the sacrificer's churning by himself: *VādhŚrSū*

[4] **Melting** (*vi-lī*) (→ *ājya*: melted butter made of fermented milk?)

a. melting of itself: *MS, KS, MānŚrSū*

b. melting of itself in a sunny place: *ĀpŚrSū, HirŚrSū*

c. no reference to melting: *TS, ŚB* (*M, K*), *BaudhŚrSū, VādhŚrSū, KātyŚrSū* (*svayaṁjātam* "born of itself")

---

3. The *ŚB* (M, K) teaches that *dadhi* (fermented milk) is poured into a leather bag, cf. below. According to *ŚrSūs* of the Taittirīyakas, the milker milks a cow directly into the bag.

2. Processing of ājya in the Rājasūya Ritual: Offering of caru to Mitra and Bṛhaspati

2.1. THE BLACK YV TEXTS

The Brāhmaṇa chapters of the Black YV Saṁhitā do not provide much detail about the relevant procedures. We can only trace the four stages mentioned above: [1] milking, [2] curdling, [3] churning, [4] melting, and the change of milk which is characterized by some natural procedure expressed with the word *svayám* "of itself".

MS II.6.6.66.15-67.5P (~ **KS XV.5**.212.6-11P)

> *svayaṁrugṇā́yā aśvatthaśā́khā́yāḥ pā́traṁ bhavati. átha śvetā́ṁ śvetávatsā́ṁ duhanti. tát svayáṁ mūrchati. svayáṁ mathyate. svayaṁvilīnám ā́jyaṁ bhavaty. átha maitrābārhaspatyáṁ havír nírvapanti. yé kṣódiṣṭhās taṇḍulā́s táṁ bārhaspatyáṁ carúṁ śṛtáṁ kurvanti. tátra tát pā́tram apidhā́yā́jyam āsícya yé stháviṣṭhās taṇḍulā́s tā́n ā́vapanty. ubháu sahá śṛtáu kurvanti. maitréṇa pū́rveṇa prácaranti.*
>
> A vessel [made] of an aśvattha branch broken by itself is used. Then, they milk a white cow accompanied by a white calf. [The milk] curdles of itself. [It] is churned of itself. Having been melted, it is used as *ājya*. Then, they throw/serve [a necessary portion of rice or barley into a basket from a cart] for the *caru* dedicated to Mitra and Bṛhaspati. They boil the husked rice/barley [grains] which are the tiniest[4] as the *caru* for Bṛhaspati. On it, having put that [mentioned] vessel as a cover, having poured *ājya* into [it], they throw the husked rice/barley [grains] which are the biggest[4] into [another vessel]. They make both boiled together. They proceed first with [the *caru*] dedicated to Mitra.

The ***MānŚrSū*** belonging to the *MS* (**IX.1.2.1-4**) has almost the same explanation as the *MS*.

TS.I.8.9.2.3P (quoted in **BaudhŚrSū XII.6**.92.12-14. Cf. **TB I.7.3.7-8**P)

> *maitrābārhaspatyáṁ bhavati śvetā́yai śvetávatsāyai dughdhé svayaṁmūrté svayaṁmathitá ā́jya ā́śvatthe* ׀׀ 2 ׀׀ *pā́tre cátuḥsraktau svayamavapannā́yai śā́khāyai karṇā́ṁś cā́karṇāṁś ca taṇḍulā́n ví cinuyād. yé karṇā́ḥ sá páyasi bārhaspatyó. yé 'karṇāḥ sá ā́jye maitrā́ḥ. . . .* ׀׀ 3 ׀׀
>
> [The *caru*] dedicated to Mitra and Bṛhaspati is employed. In [the milk] milked from a white [cow] accompanied by a white calf, [as well as] in the *ājya* [which is] curdled of itself [and] churned of itself, in a square aśvattha vessel made of a branch broken by itself, [the Adhvaryu priest]

4 On the *-iṣṭha-* form of the elative, cf. Delbrück 1888: 192.

should collect separately "eared" (i.e. unhusked) grains and "uneared" (husked) [grains]. The ones which are eared [become the *caru*] dedicated to Bṛhaspati in milk. The ones which are uneared [become the one] dedicated to Mitra in *ājya*.

The Śrauta-Sūtras of the Taittirīya School inform us in detail about the processing of *ājya*.

In **BaudhŚrSū XII.5**.91.6-7, it is remarkable that the verb *ā́-tañc* "coagulate" appears. The verb suggests that some additives are used to start the process of fermentation. (This might have influenced the meaning of *svayam*, as we will see in the case of *VādhŚrSū* below.) The same chapter (p. 92, lines 9-11) explains that the offerings are offered after thirteen days after the first milking:

> [91.6]*athāsyaitad ahaḥ śvetāyai śvetavatsāyai payo dohayitvā samātacya nidadhāti . . .* [91.9]*prasiddham asyaitad ahaḥ śvetāyai śvetavatsāyai payo dohayitvā samātacyaiva nidadhāty. atha trayodaśe 'hni maitrābārhaspatyaṁ bhavati.*
>
> Then, on this day, [the Adhvaryu priest], having made [someone] milk his (i.e. the sacrificer's) white cow accompanied by a white calf, having [made it] coagulated completely, reserves [it somewhere]. . . . It is clear. . . . Then, after the 13th day, [the offering] dedicated to Mitra and Bṛhaspati occurs.

XXII.17.141.13-15 (Dvaidhasūtra for XII.5) explains how the milk is "churned by itself":

> *dṛtiṁ vā vināḍaṁ vā ratha ādhāya parivahed. yat tatra navanītam utsīdet tad ājyaṁ syād iti* ।
>
> Having set a *dṛti* or a *vināḍa* (kinds of leather bag) on a chariot, he should carry [it] around. When a *navanīta* separates out there (in the bag), it should be *ājya* [says Baudhāyana].

XVIII.20.366.10-11 and 367.10-12 (not on the Rājasūya but the Ekāha) clarifies that the leather bag contains *dadhi*:

> *teṣu kāla eva dadhivinālān āsañjayanti . . . . āgateṣu ratheṣu yad vinālеṣu navanītam utsīdati tad vilāpyotpūyājyakumbhe pratyasyati.*
>
> On those [chariots] they hang leather bags of *dadhi* at the proper time. . . . When the chariots have come, the *navanīta* which separates out in the bags, they put it into an *ājya* jar, having made it melted, having selected out (clarified it).

ĀpŚrSū XVIII.11.2-6 and **12-22** describes, furthermore, the specific way to melt *navanīta* of itself, how many times to polish the rice or barley, and how to use an earthen pan:

> *svayamavapannāyā āśvatthaśākhāyai maitraṁ pātraṁ catuḥsraktiṁ karoti* I 2 I *śvetāṁ śveta-vatsām āmastye*[5] *dr̥tau duhanti* I 3 I *tat svayaṁmūrtaṁ saṁyogena parivahanti* I 4 I *tat svayaṁmathitaṁ ātape viṣajanti* I 5 I *tat svayaṁvilīnam ājyaṁ bhavati* I 6 I . . . *pātrasaṁsādanakāle bārhaspatyaṁ caruṁ maitraṁ ca pātraṁ kapālānāṁ sthāne prayunakti* I 12 I *triṣphalīkr̥tāṁs taṇḍulān vibhāgamantreṇa vivinakti karṇāṁś cākarṇāṁś ca* I 13 I *kṣodiṣṭhāṁś ca sthaviṣṭhāṁś cety eke* I 14 I *ye karṇāḥ sa payasi bārhaspatyaḥ* I 15 I *yadā śr̥to bhavaty athainaṁ maitreṇa pātreṇāpidadhāti* I 16 I *tasmin svayaṁvilīnam ānayati* I 17 I *pavitravaty ājye 'karṇān āvapati* I 18 I *tāv uttarādharau karoti* I 19 I *evaṁ saha śr̥tau bhavataḥ* I 20 I *bārhaspatyam āsādya maitram āsādayati* I 21 I *evaṁ pracarati* I 22 I
>
> 2. [The Adhvaryu] makes a square vessel for Mitra out of an aśvattha branch which fell down of itself. 3. [Milkers] milk a white cow accompanied by a white calf into a raw-hide (?) bag. 4. When it has curdled of itself, they carry it around, by tying [it] together [with a chariot]. 5. When it has been churned of itself, they hang [the bag] down at a sunny place. 6. Melted of itself, it becomes *ājya* (or: [it] is used as *ājya*). . . . 12. On the occasion of setting up the utensils, [the Adhvaryu] applies a pot for Br̥haspati and a vessel for Mitra instead of the (ordinary) plates. 13. He divides grains threshed three times, while reciting the mantra separating (them) into the eared and uneared ones. 14. Some [say]: "[into] the tiniest and biggest ones". 15. The ones which are eared, they [become the *caru*] dedicated to Br̥haspati in milk. 16. When [the *caru* for Br̥haspati] becomes cooked, then he covers this one (the pot for

[5] Neither meaning nor form is clear; variant readings are *āmatsye, āmaste, āmātsye*. Sāyaṇa on *TS* I.8.9 quotes this passage with the reading *āmrasya* and interprets it as *āmreṇa puṣparasena lepitāyāṁ dr̥tau duhanti* "They milk into a leather bag daubed with Mango, [that is,] the essence of its flower" (*dr̥ti-* is originally masculine but later also feminine, as here). Bhaṭṭa Bhāskara, dated probably earlier than Sāyaṇa, has the reading *āmastye*. Also Tālavr̥ntanivāsin's *ĀpŚrSū-Prayogavr̥tti* has *āmastye* according to Caland on XVIII.11.3, n. 2. Since there is no variant such as *āmrasya* in the *ĀpŚrSū* itself, we must start from *āmastye*. The word could be explained as the loc. sg. masc. of *āmastya-*, a derivative of **āmasti-*: *āma-* "raw, immature, not ripe" and *sti-*, which could be an abstract noun of *as* "exist, be" (on *sti-*, cf. Liebert 1949: 12 and 33f.).

> Bṛhaspati) with the vessel for Mitra. 17. Into it he pours the [*ājya*] melted of itself. 18. He throws the uneared [grains] into the *ājya* equipped with purifying [grass]. 19. He makes [the two vessels] top and bottom (i.e. superimposes them). 20. Both are cooked together in this manner. 21. Having set [the pot] for Bṛhaspati on the fire, [he] sets [the vessel] for Mitra. 22. He proceeds in this manner.

The parallel **HirŚrSū XIII.4.16-18** is quite similar to the *ĀpŚrSū*. Both prescribe the use of a leather bag for milking, which is not mentioned in the *TS*. Also the *ŚB* of the White YV School describes the employment of a leather bag, which contains *dadhi* derived from fresh milk. Making of *dadhi* in the *ŚB* is expressed not with the verb *mūrch* but with *ā-tañc* as seen below.

The **VādhŚrSū** which also belongs to the Taittirīya School seems to use the word *svayam* in another meaning, viz. "by [the Yajamāna] himself". This has naturally something to do with the actual handling, although the processing order itself is the same as the one mentioned above: [1] milking, [2] curdling, [3] churning, [4] melting. Particularly, *svayam* in the meaning of "by himself" and the use of the verb *ā-tañc* "coagulate" for making *dadhi* depend on each other. The expression *svayaṁmūrta-* in the Saṁhitās indicates that the milk curdles without any additives, whereas *svayam ātanakti* suggests that the sacrificer himself adds something in order to promote the fermentation of milk.

VādhŚrSū X.3.63-69[6]

> 63. *etāny* +*ahā(ni yajamā)na*[+239] *śvetāṁ śvetavatsāṁ svayan dogdhi. svayam ātanakti svayam*[240] *manthanti*[241]. *svayam* +*aśvatthasya śākhām*[+242] *avavṛścya*[243] *catusraktiñ*[+7] *camasaṁ*[244] *karoti*. 64. *etasyai payo nidhātavā āha*. 65. *vasanti*. 66. *prātar maitrābārhaspatyaṁ*[245] *havir nirvapati*[246]. 67.[247] *śvetāyai śvetavatsāyai dugdhe svayammūrte* [*svayam = sa ājye*[8]] *maitro*[248]. 68. *maitreṇa bārhaspatyam apidadhāty*. 69. *etacśrapaṇa*[249] *eva*[250] +*maitriyopācāraṁ*[+251] *bārhaspatyam*[252] *mekṣayati*.

> 63. During these days, the sacrificer milks a white cow accompanied by a white calf by himself. He coagulates [the milk with some additives] by himself. They churn [the curdled milk] by themselves. He (the

---

[6] Edited with notes by Ikari, for the working group "Kingship and Ritual" organized by Fujii, Kyoto University. Cf. Chaubey ed.: X.3.49-55.

[7] Thus construed at a meeting of the work group (see preceding footnote).

[8] The symbol "=" is used by the editor to indicate a textual abridgement.

Yajamāna), having cut off a branch of aśvattha by himself, makes a square cup. 64. He (The Adhvaryu?) tells [someone] to reserve its (i.e. the cow's) milk. 65. They spend the night. 66. Next morning, [he] prepares for an offering dedicated to Mitra and Bṛhaspati. 67. In [the milk] milked from a white cow accompanied by a white calf, [and] curdled of itself . . . in the *ājya* [the *caru*] for Mitra [is prepared]. 68. He covers the [pot] for Bṛhaspati with [the vessel] for Mitra. 69. As soon as this is cooked, he mixes the service for Bṛhaspati with [something (a fem. noun is expected)][9] for Mitra.

[239]K_4: *ahā. jamāna*; M: *ahāni* . . . [10]*natvetāṁ śvetavatsāṁ**. [240]M: *svayaṁ*. [241]K_4: *unthanti*; M: *mathnanti*. [242]K_4: *aśvatthaśākhām*. [243]M: *avapṛścya*. [244]M: *catasrakticamasaṁ*. [245]M: *maitrābarhaspatyaṁ*. [246]M: *nivapati*. [247]The reconstruction of the sūtra presupposes the existence of an abridgement in the lacuna. The sūtra seems to be made up of a quotation corresponding to *TS* I.8.9.2-3: *maitrābārhaspatyáṁ bhavati śvetā́yai śvetávatsāyai dughdhé svayaṁmūrté svayaṁmathitá ā́jya ā́śvatthe* ।। 2 ।। *pā́tre cátuḥsraktau svayamavapannā́yai śā́khāyai. karṇā́ṁś cā́karṇāṁś ca taṇḍulā́n ví cinuyād. yé karṇā́ḥ sá páyasi bārhaspatyó. yé 'karṇāḥ sá ā́jye maitrā́ḥ* [248]K_1: *sva* . . . (18)*m api da. ty*; K_4: *svayammartte* . . . (5) *maitro*; M: *svayam ā* . . . (15) *maitro*. [249]K_4: *etyacśravaṇa eva*; M: *etacchapa eva maitro vo*. [250]Cf. *VādhŚS* VIII 6: *abhīmām mahinā divam* (*TS* 4.1.6g1) *ity etayaiva maitriyopācāram īkṣate*. (Also cf. *VādhŚS* VII.3). Also cf. *ĀpŚS* XV.4.4: *pacyamānān maitryopacaraty abhimāṁ mahinā divam iti*. [251]K: *maitropāvāraṁ*; M: *maitro vo vāraṁ*. [252]M: *ṁ*.

The different interpretation of *svayam* from that in the Saṁhitās might be based on misunderstanding or reinterpretation by people living in a later period.

2.2. THE WHITE YV TEXTS.

Remarkable points in the relevant chapters of the *ŚB* are: (1) the verb *ā-tañc* is used for the making of *dadhi*, (2) a leather bag is used only after the making of *dadhi*, (3) a mantra is prescribed for the instruction by the Adhvaryu to drive a chariot on which the bag is bound, and (4) there is no reference to the melting of *navanīta*, which suggests the use of *navanīta* in place of *ājya*. We might infer especially from (1)-(3), that such a procedure as described in the *ŚB* could lie at the base of

[9] Ed. Chaubey makes the conjecture *maitreṇa naivāraṁ* in his edition, which would mean "he mixes the [*caru*] of wild rice prepared for Bṛhaspati with that for Mitra".

the instructions of the Śrauta-Sūtras of the Taittirīya School to coagulate milk (*ā-tañc*) with the help of some additives (*BaudhŚrSū*, *VādhŚrSū*), and to drive a chariot with a leather bag attached (*Baudh.*, *Hir.*, and *ĀpŚrSū* beside *KātyŚrSū* belonging to the *ŚB*).

ŚB (M) V.3.2.4-8 . . . *tásmān maitrābārhaspatyáṁ carúṁ nírvapati* ॥ 4 ॥ *tásyāvŕ̥t. yā́ svayampraśīrṇā́śvatthī śā́khā prā́cī vódīcī vā bhávati tásyai maitráṁ pā́traṁ karoti. varúṇyā vā́ eṣā́ yā́ paraśúvr̥kṇā́thaiṣā́ maitrī́ yā́ svayampraśīrṇā́. tásmāt svayampraśīrṇā́yai śā́khāyai maitráṁ pā́traṁ karoti* ॥ 5 ॥ *áthātácya dádhi. vínāṭa āsícya ráthaṁ yúktvābádhya dédīyitavá āha. tád yát svayamuditáṁ návanītaṁ. tád ā́jyaṁ bhavati. varuṇyàm vā́ etád yán mathitám. áthaitán maitráṁ yát svayamuditáṁ. tásmāt svayamuditám ā́jyaṁ bhavati* ॥ 6 ॥ *dvedhā́ taṇḍulā́n kurvanti. sá yé 'ṇiyāṁsaḥ paribhinnā́s té bārhaspatyā́. átha yé sthávīyāṁsó 'paribhinnās té maitrā́. ná vái mitráḥ káṁ caná hinasti. ná mitráṁ káś caná hinasti. nàinaṁ kuśó ná káṇṭako víbhinatti. nā́sya vráṇaś canā̀sti. sárvasya hy èvá mitró mitrám* ॥ 7 ॥ *átha bārhaspatyáṁ carúm ádhiśrayati. táṁ maitréṇa pā́treṇā́pidadhāti. tád ā́jyam ā́nayati. tát taṇḍulā́n ā́vapati. sá eṣá ūṣmáṇaivá śrapyate. varúṇyo vā́ eṣá yò 'gnínā śr̥tó. 'thaiṣá maitró yá ūṣmáṇā śr̥tás. tásmād ūṣmáṇā śr̥tó bhavati* . . . ॥ 8 ॥

4. Therefore, [he] prepares the *caru* dedicated to Mitra and Br̥haspati. 5. Its process is: if an aśvattha branch broken off by itself exists, either eastward or northward, he makes a vessel for Mitra out of it (the branch). To Varuṇa, verily, belongs this [branch], if it is cut off with a hatchet; to Mitra, if it has broken off by itself. Therefore, he makes a vessel for Mitra out of a branch broken off by itself. 6. Then, having coagulated *dadhi*, having poured [it] into a leather bag, having yoked a chariot, having bound [the bag], he tells [horses (?)] to jump repeatedly[10] (cf. the *ŚBK* version below). At that time, the *navanīta* which has risen [to the surface] of itself is used as *ājya* (or, it becomes *ājya*). This belongs to Varuṇa, if it is churned. However, it belongs to Mitra, if it has risen of itself. Therefore, what has risen of itself is used as *ājya*. 7. They divide grains into two. (The ones) which are finer [or] broken belong to Br̥haspati. However, (the ones) which are bigger [or] not broken, belong to Mitra. Mitra, indeed, never harms anyone. No one ever harms Mitra. Neither kuśa grass nor a thorn pierces him (the sacrificer). No scar belongs to him. For, verily, Mitra is in alliance with all. 8. Then, he sets the *caru* (pot) for Br̥haspati [on the fire]. He covers it with the vessel for Mitra as a lid.

10 Whereas the *ŚBM* intimates the meaning of the mantra by using an infinitive + *aha*, *ŚBK* VII.2.1.7 apparently quotes the mantra: *eténa dedīyadhvam íti* "Together with this one, jump repeatedly!" Cf. Gippert 1985: 29ff.

> Into it, he pours *ājya*. Into it, he pours the (husked) grains. This is cooked only with steam. That, indeed, belongs to Varuṇa which is cooked with fire. However, this belongs to Mitra which is cooked with steam. Therefore, [the *caru*] cooked with steam is used.

The square vessel made of a branch seems to be a kind of steaming basket, in which the *caru* (porridge) for Mitra can be cooked with steam above the one for Bṛhaspati cooked in a *caru* (pot) with fire. That the *ājya* is put into a vessel like a basket suggests that *ājya* is not to be as liquefied as oil. The *ŚB* employs *navanīta*, a kind of butterfat, for this.

ŚBK VII.2.1.6-9 explains the procedure in a similar manner. The mantra used for using the chariot is literally quoted in this recension: *eténa dedīyadhvam* "with this [bag (?)] jump!" (VII.2.1.7). The imperative in the 2nd person plural suggests the subject of jumping to be horses.

KātyŚrSū XV.3.42 has a quite brief reference. It uniquely describes *ājya* as *svayaṁjātam* "come out of itself".

3. Materials from Pāli

3.1.0 *khīra, dadhi, navanīta, takka, sappi* (*pañcagorasa-*): *Vin* I.244$^{33-37}$ (see §0.)

3.1.1 *khīra* → *dadhi* → *navanīta* → *sappi* → *sappimaṇḍa*: *S* III.265$^{3-5}$, 272$^{13-15}$, 276$^{16-18}$, 278$^{7-9}$; *A* II.95$^{29-31}$; III.219$^{18-20}$, 220$^{22-24}$; V.182$^{6-8}$; D I.201$^{25-36}$; Pp 69$^{17-19}$, 70$^{3-6}$

3.1.2 *khīra* → *dadhi* → *navanīta*: *Jā* VI.206$^{13-16}$

3.1.3 *khīra* → *dadhi* → *navanīta* → *ghata* (*ghṛta-*): *Mil* 40^{30}-41^{5}

3.2.1 *khīra* → *dadhi*: *Mil* 48$^{14-24}$

3.2.2 *dadhi* → *nonīta* (*navanīta*): *M* III.143$^{19-21}$ (cf. 141$^{17-19}$)

3.2.3 *dadhi* → *takka*: *Mil* 173$^{23-29}$

3.1 THE STOCK PHRASE AND THE ORDER OF PROCESSING OF DAIRY PRODUCTS IN PĀLI

3.1.0 The stock phrase in the Buddhist literature tells us the order of producing the five main products: [1] *khīra* (*kṣīra*, fresh milk) → [2] *dadhi* (fermented milk) → [3] *navanīta* (a kind of butterfat) → [4] *sappi* (*sarpiṣ*) → [5] *sappimaṇḍa* (*sarpir-maṇḍa*).

> **Saṁyutta-Nikāya** III.265$^{3-5}$, 272$^{13-15}$, 276$^{16-18}$, 278$^{7-9}$; **Aṅguttara-Nikāya** II.95$^{29-31}$; III.219$^{18-20}$, 220$^{22-24}$; V.182$^{6-8}$; **Dīgha-Nikāya** I.201$^{25-36}$;

Puggalapaññatti 69$^{17-19}$, 70$^{3-6}$:

seyyathāpi bhikkhave gavā ***khīraṁ****, khīramhā* ***dadhi****, dadhimhā* ***navanītaṁ****, navanītamhā* ***sappi****, sappimhā* ***sappimaṇḍo****. tatra aggam akkhāyati* ।

It is like that, O monks, from a cow [comes out] *khīra*; from *khīra, dadhi*; from *dadhi, navanīta*; from *navanīta, sappi*; from *sappi, sappimaṇḍa*. Among these, [*sappimaṇḍa*] is said to be the summit.

3.1.2 The same order of processing from *khīra* to *navanīta* is found also in **Jātaka-Aṭṭhakathā VI.206$^{13-16}$** (*khīra* → *dadhi* → *navanīta*):

yathāpi ***khīraṁ*** *viparināmadhammaṁ* ***dadhi*** *bhavitvā* ***navanītam*** *pi hoti evam pi aggi viparinamadhammo tejo samorohatī yogayutto*

Just like, furthermore, *khīra* of changing nature, having become *dadhi*, becomes also *navanīta*, in such manner also, the fire of changing nature, condenses into *tejas* (the power of light and heat), when it is bound with concentration.

3.1.3 Milindapañha 40^{32}-41^{5} describes that *ghata-* (*ghr̥ta-*) comes from *navanīta*, namely *khīra* → *dadhi* → *navanīta* → *ghata*:

yathā mahārāja ***khīraṁ*** *duhyamānaṁ kālantarena* ***dadhi*** *parivatteyya* ***dadhito navanītam****,* ***navanītato ghataṁ*** *parivatteyya, yo nu kho mahārāja evaṁ vadeyya: yam yeva* ***khīram*** *taṁ yeva* ***dadhi****, tam yeva* ***navanītam****, tam yeva* ***ghatan*** *ti, sammā nu kho so mahārāja vadamāno vadeyya ti.*

[Nāgasena said to the king:] "Since, O great king, *khīra* (*kṣīrá-*) being milked should change into *dadhi* with passing of time, from *dadhi* into *navanīta*, from *navanīta* it should change into *ghata* (Skt. *ghr̥tá-*) — if one, O great king, argues as follows: That which is nothing but *khīra*, it is nothing but *dadhi*, it is nothing but *navanīta*, it is nothing but *ghata* — would he now, O great king, argue rightly as he is arguing?"

3.2. THE METHOD OF PROCESSING DAIRY PRODUCTS IN PĀLI

3.2.1 According to **Milindapañha 48$^{14-24}$**, ***khīra*** becomes ***dadhi*** of itself on the next day. It does not need any additives:

yathā mahārāja kocid-eva puriso gopālakassa hatthato khīraghaṭaṁ kiṇitvā tass' eva hatthe nikkhipitvā pakkameyya: sve gahetvā gamissāmīti, taṁ aparajju dadhi sampajjeyya, so āgantvā evaṁ vadeyya: dehi me khīraghaṭan-ti, so dadhiṁ dasseyya, itaro evaṁ vadeyya: nāhaṁ tava hatthato dadhiṁ kiṇāmi, dehi me khīraghaṭan-ti, so evaṁ vadeyya: ajānato te khīraṁ dadhi bhūtan-ti; te vivadamānā tava santike āgaccheyuṁ, kassa tvaṁ mahārāja atthaṁ dhāreyyāsīti ।

[Nāgasena said to the king:] "If, O great king, someone would buy a pot of fresh milk from the hand of a herdsman, leave [it] in his hand, and go away, [saying] 'Tomorrow I will go (come) to take [it].' It would become *dadhi* on the next day. He would come back and say as follows: "Give me the pot of fresh milk!" He (the herdsman) would show *dadhi*. The other would say as follows: 'I do not buy *dadhi* from your hand. Give me the pot of fresh milk!' He (the herdsman) would say as follows: 'Your fresh milk became *dadhi*, which you did not recognize. They would, arguing with each other, come to the presence of you — (Then) whose matter, O great king, would you support?

3.2.2 Majjhima-Nikāya III.143$^{19\text{-}21}$ states that churning of ***dadhi*** in a wooden bucket (*kalasa-*, Skt. *kalaśa-*) provides ***nonīta*** (***navanīta***) (cf. 141$^{17\text{-}19}$):

seyyathāpi, bhūmijā, puriso ***nonīta****tthiko* ***nonīta-****gavesī* ***nonīta****pariyesanañ caramāno* ***dadhiṁ*** *kalase āsiñcitvā matthena āviñjeyya.*

As it were, O Bhūmija, a man wishing *nonīta*, seeking for *nonīta*, who is undertaking a search for *nonīta*, would pour *dadhi* into a wooden bucket and extract it by churning.

3.2.3 Milindapañha 173$^{23\text{-}29}$, on the other hand, informs us that ***takka-*** (*takra-*) is also produced after churning of ***dadhi*** (*dadhi* → *takka*):

yathā vā pana mahārāja dadhiṁ manthayamāno takkaṁ manthemīti voharati, na taṁ takkaṁ yaṁ so mantheti, dadhiṁ yeva so manthento takkaṁ manthemīti voharati

Or, as it were, O great king, [one] who is churning *dadhi* expresses "I am churning *takka*".[11] It is not *takka* that he churns. Churning nothing but *dadhi*, he says "I am churning *takka*".

These two passages (3.2.2 and 3.2.3) signify that churning of *dadhi* results in a separation into *navanīta* and *takka*. Because *Vinaya* I.244$^{33\text{-}37}$ enumerates *navanīta* and *takka* as different products, we can exclude the possibility that the two are synonymous with each other; furthermore, *Vinaya* III.112$^{22\text{-}23}$ and *Jātaka-Aṭṭhakathā* I.448^{29} describe *takka* as a liquid.[12]

[11] The accusative *takkam* should be understood to be an "Akkusativ des Effektionsobjekts". Cf. Gotō 2002: 36.

[12] *Vinaya* IV.112$^{22\text{-}23}$ [Suttavibhaṅga, Pācittiya 54, Prohibition of playing with water] *bhājanagataṁ udakaṁ vā kañcikaṁ vā khīraṁ vā takkaṁ vā rajanaṁ vā passāvaṁ vā cikkhallaṁ vā kīḷati āpatti dukkaṭassa* "[In the case where] one →

3.3 FROM KHĪRA- TO SAPPIMAṆḌA OR GHATA

The above-mentioned descriptions would allow us to infer a processing as in ***fig.* 1** below. As to the specific processes, we are at present informed only of two points: 1. fresh milk is turned into *dadhi* without any additives; 2. *navanīta* is obtained by churning up (*manth*) *dadhi*. The stock phrase in Pāli literature would refer to the whole processing, in which some kind of butterfat called *sappi* or *sappimaṇḍa* results.

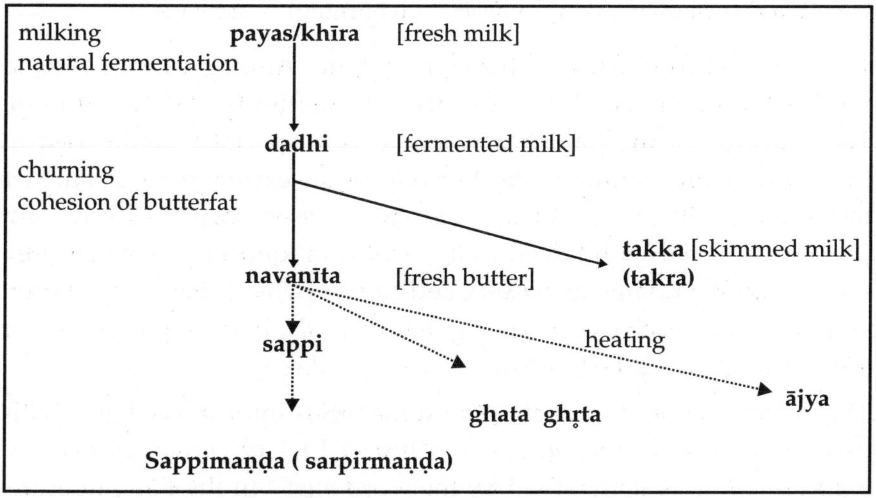

fig. 1: Chart of processing some kinds of butterfat explained in the Veda and Pāli canon

Although both *navanīta/nonīta* and *takka* are produced by churning of *dadhi* (§3.2.2 *Majjhima-Nikaya* III.143[19-21] and §3.2.3 *Milindapañha* 173[23-29]), *takka* is described as a liquid in *Vinaya* III.112[22-23] and *Jātaka-Aṭṭhakathā* I.448[29], as stated above (§3.2). From *navanīta/nonīta*, furthermore, *sappi* or *ghata* are obtained (§3.1.1 *Saṁyutta-Nikāya* III.265[3-5] etc. for *sappi*, and §3.1.3 *Milindapañha* 40[32]-41[5] for *ghata*). Considering the fact that *ghata* (*ghr̥ta*) was used as a kind of butter in Vedic rituals, we might infer that *navanīta/nonīta* is a kind of solid butterfat made from fermented

→ plays with water in a bowl, or rice water, or fresh milk, or buttermilk, or dye, or urine, or mud, [it is] attaining of *dukkaṭa*"; *Jātaka-Aṭṭhakathā* I.448[29] [Naṅgalīsajātaka (123)]: *dadhikhīrāni pana niccaṁ paṇḍarāni pakkhittabhājanasaṇṭhānāni "dadhi* (fermented milk) and *khīra* (fresh milk) are, however, always white [and] have the shape of the bowl [into which they are] thrown".

milk, which is a material for butter, and that *takka* (*takra*) is skimmed milk produced after the separation of solid butterfat. Further research is needed to identify *ājya, ghr̥ta, sappi*, and *sappimaṇḍa*.

4. Conclusion

The processing order of five milk products is given in the Pāli literature. Among them, the first three stages are almost the same as those in the Vedic Rājasūya ceremony:

kṣīrá/khīra — (fermentation) → *dádhi* — (churning) → *návanīta*.

ā́jya is gained from *návanīta* through melting. Among various texts in the Vedas, however, there are different methods of fermentation. The churning of the Rājasūya seems to be a special method used in the ritual, which imitates the lifestyle of an earlier period. Further terms in the milk procession are yet to be precisely identified: *sāṁnayyá* (mixture of *dadhi* with boiled milk), *āmíkṣā* (a kind of cottage cheese), *payasyā̀* (another name of *āmíkṣā*), and *vājina-* (whey), *ātáñcana-* (starter, such as some species of plant, e.g. *pūtī́ka, kvàla*, bark of parṇa tree, or *dádhi* itself as a starter), *mástu-, śáras-, phāṇita-*, etc.[13]

The instruction of the paribhāṣā in some ŚrSūs informs us that *ghr̥ta* is used as a substitute for *ājya*, e.g. *VārŚrSū* I.1.1.19 *ghr̥tam ājyaśabdena pratīyate* "*ghr̥ta* is understood by the word *ājya*". In the Pāli literature, furthermore, occurrences of *sappi-* are much more frequent than those of *ājya* and *ghr̥ta*, whereas *sarpíṣ-* occurs quite rarely in the Veda. *ā́jya-* seems to be an archaic word which was not applied in daily life any more.

Primary Sources

ĀpŚrSū	*Āpastamba-Śrauta-Sūtra*
KS	*Kaṭha Saṁhitā*
KātyŚrSū	*Kātyāyana-Śrauta-Sūtra*
TB	*Taittirīya Brāhmaṇa*
TS	*Taittirīya Saṁhitā*
BaudhŚrSū	*Baudhāyana-Śrauta-Sūtra*

13 On *sāṁnāyyá* (mixture of *dadhi* with boiled milk), *āmíkṣā* (a kind of cottage cheese), *payasyā̀* (another name of *āmíkṣā*), and *vājina-* (whey), cf. Nishimura 2011.

MānŚrSū	*Mānava-Śrauta-Sūtra*
MS	*Maitrāyaṇī Saṁhitā*
VādhŚrSū	*Vādhūla-Śrauta-Sūtra*
ŚB(*M*)	*Śatapatha-Brāhmaṇa* (Mādhyandina)
ŚBK	*Śatapatha-Brāhmaṇa* (Kāṇva)
HirŚrSū	*Hiraṇyakeśi-Śrauta-Sūtra*

All the Pāli texts are cited from the Pali Text Society edition.

References

Caland, Willem, 1924-28, *Das Śrautasūtra des Āpastamba aus dem Sanskrit übersetzt*, 8.-15. Buch, Amsterdam: Koninklijke Akademie van Wetenschappen, repr. 1969, Wiesbaden: M. Sändig.

——— (tr.), 1931, *Pañcaviṁśa-Brāhmaṇa: The Brāhmaṇa of twenty-five chapters*, Calcutta: Asiatic Society, repr. 1982, Delhi: Sri Satguru Publications.

Chaubey, Braj Bihari (ed.), 1993, *Vadhūla-Śrautasūtra*, Hoshiarpur: Katyayan Vaidik Sahitya Prakashan.

Delbrück, Berthold, 1888, *Altindische Syntax*, Halle: Verlag der Buchhandlung des Waisenhauses, repr. 1976, Darmstadt: Wissenschaftliche Buchgesellschaft.

Einoo, Shingo, 1985, "Altindische Getreidespeisen", *Münchener Studien zur Sprachwissenschaft* **44:** 15-27.

Gippert, Jost, 1985, "Verbum dicendi + Infinitiv im Indoiranischen", *Münchener Studien zur Sprachwissenschaft* **44:** 29-57.

Gotō, Toshifumi, 2002, "Funktionen des Akkusativs und Rektionsarten des Verbums anhand des Altindoarischen", in *Indogermanische Syntax: Fragen und Perspektiven*, ed. Heinrich Hettrich and Jeong-Soo Kim, pp. 21-42, Wiesbaden: Reichert.

Liebert, Gösta, 1949, *Das Nominalsuffix* -ti- *im Altindischen*, Lund: Håkan Ohlssons Boktryckeri.

Nishimura, Naoko, 2011, "*Āmíkṣā* and *payasyà*: Processing of Fermented Milk in Ancient India", *Journal of Indian and Buddhist Studies* **59:** 3, 10-16, Tokyo.

Rau, Wilhelm, 1972, *Töpferei und Tongeschirr im vedischen Indien*, Wiesbaden: Verlag der Akademie der Wissenschaften und der Literatur.

14

उपनिषत्सु वैश्वानरसङ्कल्पना

चेतना विभूति वेदी

प्रस्तावना

प्रयोजनदृष्ट्या कस्या अपि सङ्कल्पनाया विकासो वैचारिकपरिवर्तनवशाद् भवति यश्च यथासमयं तत्तद्ग्रन्थेषु सर्वैरवलोक्यते। एवमध्यात्मप्रवणाः पिण्डब्रह्माण्डयोः सूत्रविवेचिका उपनिषदो वेदमूलानां कर्मकाण्डदृष्ट्या विकसितानां सङ्कल्पनानामपि अग्रिमविचारान् वेदाधारेण एव उपबृंहयन्ति। कदाचित् कर्मकाण्डं प्रति भग्नरुचौ समाजे अध्यात्मप्रवणतावशाद् ज्ञानकाण्डस्य उदयोऽभूद् यत्र ब्रह्मवादस्यैव आसीत् प्राधान्यं स एव उपनिषत्कालो विज्ञायते। अत एव वैदिकसङ्कल्पना उपनिषत्सु बहुधा तत्त्वज्ञानबहुला दृश्यन्ते। यथा अग्नितत्त्वस्य विचारो होतृ–हव्यदातृ–दूत–पुरोहित–रत्नधातमादिरूपे नैव कृत्वा एतस्य तेजस्वितायाः सर्वव्यापकतायाः च उपासनादृष्ट्या ब्रह्माण्डान्तर्गतमहत्त्वप्रतिपादनाय उपयोगिनो विचाराः आभिः पुरस्कृताः। तत्समतेजस्विपदार्थानां च स्वरूपेण कर्मव्यापकत्वेन च ब्रह्मबोधनपरत्वं सर्वत्र दरीदृश्यते। अत एव – "एतद् वै तत्", "तदुपासितव्यं", "य एवं वेद" इत्यादीनि वाक्यानि उपलभ्यन्ते। एवं वैश्वानरसङ्कल्पना वेदादारभ्य कीदृशानि वैशिष्ट्यानि उद्वहन्ती उपनिषत्सु विकासं प्राप्ता इति विचारः प्रामुख्येन ऋग्वेदमधिकृत्य अत्र करिष्यते। अस्मिन् निबन्धे अष्टादशोपनिषद[१] एव अनुशीलनाय स्वीकृताः सन्ति।

१. अग्निदेवतायाः स्वरूपम्

वेदेषु नैकाः सङ्कल्पनाः प्राधान्यं भजन्ते। "... एकं सन्तं बहुधा कल्पयन्ति ..." (ऋ. १०.११४.५) इति मन्त्रलिङ्गाद् विविधदेवतानां वर्णनम् अथ च तासां प्रार्थनोपासनोपेता ऋचः अत्र समुपलभ्यन्ते। एवं देवविषयकचिन्तनेऽस्मिन् सर्वातिशायिनी, सन्ततं मानवसहचारिणी किमुत मनुष्याणां देवानामपि या नेदिष्ठा, अहोरात्रं प्रकाशदात्री अग्निदेवता वैदिकदैवतमण्डले राराजते।

---

[१] *अष्टादशोपनिषदः*, वैदिकसंशोधनमण्लेन प्रकाशिता आधारग्रन्थरूपेण अत्र निर्दिश्यन्ते। तासु प्रत्येकमुपनिषदः निर्देशः पृथक् पृथक् कृतोऽस्ति।

एतद्वैशिष्ट्यवशादेव अग्नेर्विविधरूपाणि ऋषिभिर्दृष्टानि अत एव वेदेषु हव्यवाहनः, पुरोहितः, होता, रक्षोहा, रयिपतिः सर्वगर्भस्थोऽयमग्निः कदाचित् पितृरूपे (ऋ. १.१.९; १.३१.१०), सखिरूपे (ऋ. १.२६.३; १.९४.१), मित्ररूपे (ऋ. १.७५.४), रक्षकरूपे (ऋ. ७.१.७; १०.११८.७) वा अवबुध्यते। अस्मिन् बोधावसरे एव अयमग्निर्वैश्वानरेति सङ्कल्पनया अभिहितोऽस्ति।

१.१. *संहितासु वैश्वानराग्निस्वरूपम्*

वेदेषु वैश्वानरशब्दस्य प्रथममभिज्ञानम् अग्निना सहैव वर्तते। वैश्वानराग्निः मुख्यतया पृथ्वीस्थाग्निरूपेण वर्णितोऽस्ति। विश्वानरस्वरूपाभ्यां नाम विद्युदादित्याभ्यां जायमानत्वादयं वैश्वानर इति यास्कमतम्[२]। ऋग्वेदे गौणवृत्या अयमग्निर्विद्युदादित्यरूपेऽपि उपलभ्यते इत्यपि नैरुक्तमतम्[३]।

ऋग्वेदे वैश्वानरस्वरूपम्

ऋग्वेदे प्रामुख्येन अग्नेर्विशेषणरूपेण वैश्वानरशब्दो विद्यते। अयं वैश्वानरो द्वादशसूक्तानां सूक्तभाग् देवता। ऋग्वेदानुसारमयमग्निर्द्यावापृथिव्योः सूनुर्वर्तते। तद्यथा –

स रोचयज्जनुषा रोदसी उभे स मात्रोरभवत् पुत्र ईड्यः... – ऋ. ३.२.२

व्याप्तिश्चास्य भुवनत्रये प्रतिपादिता। तद्यथा –

वैश्वानर तव धामान्या चके येभिः स्वर्विदभवो विचक्षण।
जात आपृणो भुवनानि रोदसी अग्ने ता विश्वा परिभूरसि त्मना॥

– ऋ. ३.३.१०

सकलविश्वो निर्मीयतेऽनेन। तद्यथा –

वि यो रजांस्यमिमीत सुक्रतुर्वैश्वानरो वि दिवो रोचना कविः।
परि यो विश्वा भुवनानि पप्रथेऽदब्धो गोपा अमृतस्य रक्षिता ॥

– ऋ. ६.७.७

अस्य विश्वनिर्माणदृष्ट्या ब्रह्मस्वरूपत्वमपि दयानन्दस्वामिभिः[४] प्रतिपादितम्। विश्वानि भुवनानि वैश्वानराग्नेर्मूर्धनि अधिवसन्ति[५] (ऋ. ६.७.६) इत्यत्रापि सायणाचार्यैः ब्रह्मस्वरूपस्य निर्देशः

---

[२] विश्वानरावेते उत्तरे ज्योतिषी वैश्वानरोऽयं यत्ताभ्यां जायते। – *निरु.* ७.२३

[३] यस्तु सूक्तं भजते यस्मै हविर्निरुप्यतेऽयमेव सोऽग्निर्वैश्वानरो निपातमेवैते उत्तरे ज्योतिषी एतेन नामधेयेन भजेते। – *निरु.* ७.३१

[४] हे मनुष्या येन जगदीश्वरेण सर्वे लोका निर्मिता यः सर्वेषां रक्षिताऽस्ति तं सर्वे उपासीरन्निति। – *ऋग्वेदभाष्यम्* (दयानन्दस्वामिकृतम्) ६.७.७, पृ. ५७

[५] अस्मिन् निबन्धे बहुवारं नैकेषां ग्रन्थांशानां भावानुवादमात्रं कृत्वा तत्तद्ग्रन्थनिर्देशः कृतोऽस्ति, न तु ग्रन्थांशो याथातथ्येन उद्धृतो, यथा अत्र। यत्र यत्र मूलग्रन्थांश उद्धृतः तत्र स्पष्टतया तथा निर्दिश्यते ।

कृतोऽस्ति[६]। लोकत्रयस्य तमांसि अयमाददे (ऋ. ७.६.७)। स्वकीयेन अजस्रेण प्रकाशेन दीप्यमानोऽयं दीप्त्या द्यावापृथिव्यौ विस्तारयति (ऋ. ७.५.४)। बहुविधरूपेण द्यावापृथिव्यौ प्रविशति (ऋ. ३.३.४)। एवं विश्वेषु भुवनेषु स्वरूपेण कर्मणा च व्याप्तस्य वैश्वानराग्नेः कानिचिद् वैशिष्ट्यानि अत्र प्रकटीक्रियन्ते।

• देवसम्बन्धिविविधस्वरूपम्

वैश्वानरोऽमृतेषु देवेषु जागृविर्वर्तते (ऋ. ३.२६.३), विश्वे मरणधर्मरहिताः देवा अस्मिन् मादयन्ते (ऋ. १.५९.१), देवैः सेवितोऽयम् (ऋ. १०.८८.४)। अयममृतोऽग्निर्देवान् हविषां प्रदानेन परिचरति अतः सनातनानि धर्माणि न दूषयति (ऋ. ३.३.१)। वैश्वानराग्निः देवानां यज्ञोऽभवत् (ऋ. १०.८८.८)। देवाः विश्वस्मै भुवनाय वैश्वानरमग्निम् अह्नां केतुम् अकृण्वन् (ऋ. १०.८८.१२)।

• असाधारणबलोपेतः

वैश्वानराग्नेः असाधारणबलस्य वर्णनं नैकेषु मन्त्रेषु वर्तते यत्रायं दिवि, पृथिव्यां, ओषधीषु प्रविष्टो बलेन पृष्टो वर्तते। तद्यथा –

पृष्टो दिवि पृष्टो अग्निः पृथिव्यां पृष्टो विश्वा ओषधीरा विवेश।
वैश्वानरः सहसा पृष्टो अग्निः स नो दिवा स रिषः पातु नक्तम्॥

– ऋ. १.९८.२

अस्य महान्ति कर्माणि कश्चनान्यो न बाधते (ऋ. ६.७.५)। यथा स्थूणा उपस्तभ्नाति तथैव वैश्वानरो जनानामाधारो वर्तते (ऋ. १.५९.१)। एतामेवमृचमुद्धृत्य क्यूपरमहाभागैर्वैश्वानरविषये अभ्युपगमः (Hypothesis) उपस्थापितो यदग्निना सह सम्बद्धो वैश्वानरः अत्यावश्यकशक्तेः सकलपरिमाणो वर्तते अथ च जीवितस्य वृक्षोऽयम्। परं व्रीज़महोदयानामत्र वर्तते मतान्तरम् एतेषां मतेन उपर्युक्तस्वरूपस्य ऋचि नास्ति साक्षान्निर्देशः अत एव विवेचकस्य स्वमतमेतत्। न तु वैदिककवीनाम् (Vries 1979: 8-10)। परमस्मिन् विषये सर्वथा एवं वक्तुं न शक्यते यतो हि ऋगन्तरेषु वैश्वानरस्य विशेषणानि कार्याणि च विवेच्य अर्थापत्त्यापि स्वरूपावाप्तिर्भवितुं शक्यते न केवलमभिधावृत्तिरेव अनुसर्तव्या। यथा अन्यत्रापि अस्य शक्तिमधिकृत्य वैशिष्ट्यानि एवं सन्ति यदयं केनाप्यन्येन हिंसितुं न शक्यते (ऋ. ६.८.७)। अयं द्यावापृथिव्यौ स्तम्भितवान् (ऋ. ६.८.३)। पृथुपाजाः (ऋ. ३.३.१) इति विशेषणोपेतो विश्वं वीर्यं धारयति एषः (ऋ. ६.८.३)। एतैः कार्यैरत्र वैश्वानराग्नेः शक्तेरभिज्ञानं भवति।

---

[६] वैश्वानरात्मकस्य परब्रह्मणो मूर्धन्युपरि प्रदेशे सर्वाणि भूतजातान्यधिवसन्ति। – *ऋग्वेदसंहिता* (सायणभाष्यम्) ६.७.६, पृ. २४

• पराक्रमी रक्षकश्च

अयमग्निः रक्षार्थं प्रार्थ्यते आहूयते च (ऋ. १.९८.२; ३.२६.२)। न केवलं मनुष्याणां परं देवानामपि अयं रक्षकोऽस्ति (ऋ. ६.९.७; ७.१३.२)। असुरघ्नोऽयम् (ऋ. ७.१३.१)। वैश्वानरसकाशात् शत्रूणामभिभवितारो वीरा जायन्ते (ऋ. ६.७.३)। अमृतस्य गोपा अयम् (ऋ. ६.९.३) विश्वे देवा अपि रक्षणाय वैश्वानरं प्रार्थयन्ति (ऋ. ६.९.७)।

• शरीरसम्बन्धिस्वरूपम्

नानाप्रकारेषु जठरेषु सिंह इव नानददयं जिन्वते (ऋ. ३.२.११)। तेजसा वावृधानोऽयमग्निः मनुष्येषु विभाति (ऋ. ७.५.२)। मर्त्येषु इदं वैश्वानराख्यम् अमृतं ज्योतिर्वर्तते (ऋ. ६.९.४)। एष तनूपा अग्निर्वर्तते (ऋ. १०.८८.७, ८)। ध्रुवं जविष्ठं वैश्वानराख्यं ज्योतिः गच्छत्सु प्राणिष्वन्तः स्थापितमस्ति (ऋ. ६.९.५)।

• यज्ञीयस्वरूपम्

अयमग्निः यज्ञानां नाभिरध्वराणां च रथी वर्तते (ऋ. ६.७.२)। यज्ञस्यायं केतुः (ऋ. ६.७.२; ३.३.३) यज्ञानां पिता, ऋत्विजां ज्ञानसाधनम् (ऋ. ३.३.४)। अयं न केवलं मनुष्याणां प्रत्युत देवानामपि पुरोहितोऽस्ति (ऋ. ३.३.२; ३.२.८)। वैश्वानराग्नेः हव्यवाट् (ऋ. ३.२.२), होता, दूतः (ऋ. ३.३.२) इत्येतानि विशेषणान्यपि मन्त्रेषु उपलभ्यन्ते।

• लोकत्रयस्थाग्नीनां विशेषकः

ऋग्वेदे अस्याग्नेः निर्देशः कुत्रचित् पार्थिवाग्निरूपेण (ऋ. ३.३.५; १.९८.१), वैद्युताग्निरूपेण (ऋ. १.५९.६; ६.८.४) सूर्यरूपेण (ऋ. ४.५.९; ६.९.१; ७.१३.३; १०.८८.१२) च उपलभ्यते। यद्यपि लोकत्रये सूर्य एव त्रिधात्मकरूपेण स्थितोऽस्ति इति बृहद्देवताया मतम् (बृहद्दे. १.६३)। अत एव तत्र वैश्वानरः सूर्यो वर्तत इति निर्दिष्टम्। तद्यथा –

> **इहाग्निभूतस्त्वृषिभिर्लोके स्तुतिभिरीळितः।**
> **जातवेदा स्तुतो मध्ये स्तुतो वैश्वानरो दिवि।** – *बृहद्दे.* १.६७

परं पार्थिवाग्निः वैश्वानराग्निरिति शाकपूणेः (*निरु.* ७.२३) मतमनुवर्तते यास्काचार्यः। एवं यास्कमतेन वैश्वानरः पार्थिवाग्निर्वर्तते प्राधान्येन परं बृहद्देवता तु द्युस्थानीयसूर्यरूपेण स्वीकरोति।

बृहद्देवतानुसारं तु अग्निः, जातवेदा, वैश्वानर एते त्रयोऽपि समाना एव, अग्निः वैश्वानरश्च जातवेदस एव रूपे स्तः[७]। यद्यपि पार्थिवाग्नेः प्रतिनिधिभूतेषु देवेषु वैश्वानरस्यापि परिगणनमत्र वर्तते (*बृहद्दे.* १.१०६)। परं याज्ञिकदृष्ट्या वैश्वानरस्तुतौ सूर्य एव सूक्तस्य देवतेति मतान्तरमपि विद्यते (*बृहद्दे.* १.१००, १०१, १०२)।

---

[७] वैश्वानरं श्रितो ह्यग्निरग्निं वैश्वानरः श्रितः। अनयोर्जातवेदास्तु तथैते जातवेदसी। – *बृहद्दे.* १.९७

• धनस्य आकरः

वैश्वानराग्निः सर्वेषां वसूनां ध्रुवमाधारस्थानं विद्यते, यथा ध्रुवा रश्मयः सूर्ये आधीयन्ते तद्वद् वैश्वानराग्नौ वसूनि आहितानि सन्ति (ऋ. १.५९.३)। अयं रमणीयधनानां दाता विद्यते (ऋ. ३.२.११)। अस्य रक्षणेन अन्नस्य प्राप्तिर्भवति (ऋ. ६.८.६)। धनानामयं नेता (ऋ. ७.५.५) रयीणां सदनमस्ति (ऋ. ६.७.२)।

• सुमतिदाता

ऋग्वेदानुसारं वैश्वानरसकाशाद् मेधावी जायते (ऋ. ६.७.३)। प्रार्थ्यते चायं यद् वयं तव सुमतौ स्याम (ऋ. १.९८.१)। अयं मतीनां दाता, धियां धाता च वर्तते (ऋ. ७.१३.१)। तथैव अस्याग्नेर्विचेता (विशिष्टप्रज्ञो), गृत्सो (मेधावी) (ऋ. ४.५.२), चेतिष्ठः (ऋ. ५.२७.१) इत्येतानि विशेषणान्यपि सन्ति।

सातवलेकरमहाभागानां मतेन अग्निशब्दः सर्वत्र भौतिकाग्निरूपेण एव वेदेषु नोपलभ्यते। एवमग्नेः पर्यायवाची वैश्वानरोऽपि भौतिकाग्नौ चरितार्थो न भवति। अत एव एतैः सर्वमानवसङ्घरूपाग्निः, विश्वपुरुषशक्तिः, विश्वस्य चालकः, विश्वेषां नराणां सम्बन्धी इत्येतेऽर्थाः वैश्वानरस्य निर्दिष्टाः (सातवलेकर १९४० : ४, ७)। एवमेतैर्वैश्वानरमधिकृत्य आध्यात्मिकाधिभौतिकव्याख्यापि स्वीकर्तव्येति सूचितम्।

यजुर्वेदे वैश्वानरस्वरूपम्

ऋग्वेदे समागताः काश्चन ऋचः[८] यजुर्वेदेऽपि उपलभ्यन्ते। अस्यां संहितायां वैश्वानरस्य वैशिष्ट्यानि नातिविस्तरेण प्रतिपादितानि। ऋग्वेदे प्रायः अग्नेर्विशेषणत्वेन प्रयुक्तस्य वैश्वानरस्य अस्मिन् वेदे विश्वेदेवदेवतायाः कृते विशेषणत्वेन प्रथमतया निर्देशोऽस्ति। तद्यथा –

...**विश्वे॑ त्वा दे॒वा वै᳚श्वान॒राः कृ॑ण्व॒न्त्वानु॑ष्टुभेन॒ छन्द॑सा**...

– *यजु.* ११.५८, ६०, ६५

वैश्वानरस्य अपरमेकं वैशिष्ट्यमस्यामेव संहितायां दृश्यते यद् अग्निचयनविषये विनियुक्तस्य मन्त्रस्य उवटभाष्ये (*यजु.* १४.७) वैश्वानरपदस्य संवत्सर इत्यर्थः स्वीकृतः, महीधरभाष्ये तु अग्निरूपेणैव निर्दिष्टः। यद्यपि वाजसनेयिसंहितायां वैश्वानराग्नेः सांवत्सरिकरूपस्य साक्षान्निर्देशो नास्ति परं कृष्णयजुर्वेदीयसंहितासु वैश्वानराग्नेः सांवत्सरिकत्वमेव प्रामुख्येन पुरस्कृतं दृश्यते[९]। अस्य राष्ट्ररूपेणापि तैत्तिरीयसंहितायां (*तै.सं.* ५.४.७.७) नूतनं स्वरूपमुपलभ्यते। एवं वक्तुं

---

[८] मू॒र्धानं॑ दि॒वो अ॑र॒तिं पृ॑थि॒व्या... – *यजु.* ७.२४; ३३.८

अस्ता॒व्य॒ग्निर्न॒रां सु॒शेवो॑ वैश्वान॒र... – *यजु.* १२.२९

पृ॒ष्टो दि॒वि पृ॒ष्टो अ॒ग्निः... – *यजु.* १८.७३

[९] *तै.सं.* २.२.५, ६; *मै.सं.* २.१.२, ३; *काठ.सं.* १०.३, ४; *काठ.सं.* १०.४, ५, ६

शक्यते यत् संवत्सरचक्रे सूर्यस्य महतीं भूमिकामनुलक्ष्य सूर्यरूपेण प्रतिपादितस्य वैश्वानराग्नेः सांवत्सरिकस्वरूपे परिणतिः सञ्जाता। अथ च संवत्सरमधिकृत्य यदपि वैशिष्ट्यं वर्तते तस्य सम्बन्धो वैश्वानराग्नौ प्रतिपादितः।

अथर्ववेदे वैश्वानरस्वरूपम्

अथर्ववेदे पूर्वोक्तसंहितासु समागतस्वरूपस्य साम्यमाधिक्येन दृश्यते। ऋग्वेदानुसारं (ऋ. ६.९.७) विश्वैः देवैः रक्षणार्थं प्रार्थितोऽयं यजुर्वेदे (*यजु.* ११.५८) एतेषां विशेषणत्वेन प्रयुक्तः सन् विश्वैर्देवैः सह त्वं मां पाहि (*अथर्व.* २.१६.४) इति प्रार्थनया सह अत्र प्रतिपादितोऽस्ति। पार्थिवाग्निरूपेण पूर्वत्र संहितासु उपवर्णितस्य वैश्वानरस्य एवंविधो निर्देशो वर्तते। तद्यथा –

... **वैश्वानरं बिभ्रती भूमिः** ... – अथर्व. १२.१.६

अत्र वैश्वानराग्निं भूमिः धारयति इत्यभिप्रायः। अयमग्निः ऋग्वेदे सर्वेषां लोकानां निर्माता वर्तते (ऋ. ६.७.७)। सैव सङ्कल्पना अत्र विश्वकृत् (*अथर्व.* ६.४७.१) शब्देन सूच्यते। अस्य ब्रह्मस्वरूपस्यापि प्रतिपादनमनेन भवितुं शक्यते। ऋग्वेदे (ऋ. ७.६.१) इन्द्रवत् स्तुतोऽयमत्र (*अथर्व.* ३.२१.३) इन्द्रेण सह समानरथो विश्वस्य दाहकोऽग्निर्वर्तते।

अथर्ववेदे वैश्वानरस्य पापमोचकस्वरूपम् (*अथर्व.* ४.२३.४), रोगनिवारकत्वम् (*अथर्व.* ६.८५.३), ऋणपाशमोचकस्वरूपं (*अथर्व.* ६.११९.२) नूतनं खलु। ऋग्वेदीयः सर्वेषामाश्रयभूतोऽयमग्निः (ऋ. १.५९.१) अथर्ववेदानुसारं ब्रह्मणि आश्रितोऽस्ति (*अथर्व.* १३.३.५) इति वैशिष्ट्यमत्रैव अवबुध्यते।

एवं संहितासु वैश्वानरस्य निर्देशः प्राधान्येन अग्निना सहैव वर्तते। अन्येऽग्नयः अस्य शाखाः सन्ति (ऋ. १.५९.१)। गौणवृत्त्या अयं विद्युदादित्यब्रह्मसंवत्सरजाठराग्निरूपेणापि अवलोक्यते।

ब्राह्मणग्रन्थेषु वैश्वानरस्य स्थानम्

ब्राह्मणग्रन्थेषु वैश्वानरस्य रूपवैविध्ये सत्यपि अग्निस्वरूपस्य सांवत्सरिकरूपस्य चात्र प्रामुख्येन निर्देशो दृश्यते। तत्र ऐतरेयब्राह्मणानुसारम् –

संवत्सरोऽग्निर्वैश्वानरः। – *ऐ.ब्रा.* १४.३

माध्यन्दिनशतपथब्राह्मणे नैकत्र (*श.ब्रा.* ५.२.५.१४, १७; ६.२.१.३६; ७.३.१.३५) संवत्सररूपेण वैश्वानराग्नेः प्रतिपादनं विद्यते। अत एव "अग्नये वैश्वानराय द्वादशकपालं पुरोडाशं निर्वपति यतो हि संवत्सरे द्वादशमासाः सन्ति" (*श.ब्रा.* ५.२.५.१५)। यद्यपि कृष्णयजुर्वेदीयसंहितासु वैश्वानरस्य संवत्सरेण सह सम्बन्धः प्रतिपादितोऽस्ति परम् ऋग्वेदे एतस्य निर्देश एव नोपलभ्यते। एवं ब्राह्मणग्रन्थेषु वैश्वानरस्य अग्निस्वरूपे ऋग्वेदस्य सांवत्सरिकस्वरूपे च कृष्णयजुर्वेदीयसंहितानां प्रभावः स्पष्ट एव दृश्यते खलु। शतपथब्राह्मणानुसारं पूर्णत्वस्य

द्योतकोऽयं संवत्सरः। तद्यथा –

सर्वं वै संवत्सरः। – *श.ब्रा.* १.६.१.१९

सर्वशब्दश्च पूर्णत्वस्य द्योतकोऽस्ति। तद्यथा –

सर्वं वै पूर्णम्। – *श.ब्रा.* ४.२.२.२

पूर्ण एष यत् संवत्सरः। – *जै.ब्रा.* २.३९३

एवं संवत्सरस्य पूर्णत्वप्रतिपादनाय वैश्वानराग्नेर्नैकत्र संवत्सररूपेण अभिज्ञानमुपलभ्यते। वैश्वानरसङ्कल्पना अध्यात्मदृष्ट्या पूर्णत्वनिर्देशाय पश्चाद् उपनिषत्स्वपि विकसिता।

वासुदेवशरण-अग्रवाल-महाभागैः वैश्वानरस्य स्वरूपविवेचने उक्तं यद् एकतद्वितत्रितनामकस्य अथवा शुचिपावकपवमाननामकस्याग्नेः त्रयाणां बन्धूनां संयुक्तसंज्ञा वैश्वानरेति (अग्रवाल १९६४ : ६)। अग्नितत्त्वमेव विश्वनिर्माणाय त्रेधा विभक्तं, तस्मादेव विश्वत्रयस्य, नरत्रयस्य रूपत्रयस्य च विकासो भवति। एतेषामेव समुदितसंज्ञा वर्तते विश्वरूप्यं वैश्वानरो वा। मतमेतत् ग्रन्थकारेण "*... तमूँअकृण्वन्त्रेधा ...*" (ऋ. १०.८८.१०) "*अस्यवामस्य पलितस्य ..*" (ऋ. १.१६४.१) इति मन्त्रद्वयमाधारीकृत्य स्थापितं (अग्रवाल १९६४:४४), परं मन्त्राधारेण अग्निवाय्वादित्यानां नरेति संज्ञायाः स्पष्टीकरणं न भवति। वस्तुतः शतपथब्राह्मणे एतेषां नराणां निर्देश एवमस्ति –

स यः स वैश्वानरः। इमे स लोका इयमेव पृथिवी विश्वमग्निर्नरोऽन्तरिक्षमेव विश्वं वायुर्नरो द्यौरेव विश्वमादित्यो नरः। – *श.ब्रा.* १.३.१.३

एवम् उपर्युक्तकथनस्य स्पष्टाधारो ब्राह्मणे उपलभ्यते। ब्रह्मचतुष्पदावपि ओझामहाभागैर्वैश्वानरशब्दस्य विवेचनप्रसङ्गे अग्निवाय्वादित्यानां नरसंज्ञा ब्राह्मणग्रन्थाधारेण प्रतिपादिता (ओझा १९५२ : ११२)। एवम् उपनिषत्सु वैश्वानरस्य स्वरूपविकासे वैशिष्ट्यं वर्तते। किमेतद् वैशिष्ट्यं कथमयं वैश्वानरो विकसितोऽत्र इत्येव निबन्धस्यास्य प्रतिपाद्यम्।

१.२. *वैश्वानरपदार्थविचारः*

शब्दनिर्वचनदृष्ट्या विश्वानरः (*अष्टा.सू.* ६.३.१२८) इति शब्देन संज्ञया वा अपत्यार्थे (*अष्टा. सू.* ४.१.९२) सम्बन्धार्थे (*अष्टा.सू.* ४.३.१२०) वा अण्प्रत्यये कृते वैश्वानरेति सिध्यति रूपम्। एवं वैश्वानरो नाम विश्वानरस्य अपत्यं, सकलनरसम्बन्धी वा। निरुक्तदिशा वैश्वानरशब्दस्य निर्वचने वैशिष्ट्यं वर्तते। तद्यथा –

वैश्वानरः कस्मात् ?

१ **विश्वान्नरान्नयति।**

२ **विश्व एनं नरा नयन्तीति वा।**

३ **अपि वा विश्वानर एव स्यात् प्रत्यृतः सर्वाणि भूतानि, तस्य वैश्वानरः।**

– *निरु.* ७.२१

अत्र यास्काचार्यैः "णीञ् प्रापणे" (धातु.भ्वादि. ६४२) इति धातुना आद्यनिर्वचनद्वयं निरूपितम् अन्तिमनिर्वचने च "ऋ गतिप्रापणयोः" (धातु.भ्वादि. ६७०) इति धातुना सिद्धे विश्वानरपदे, ततः तद्धितप्रत्ययेन व्यपदिष्टो वैश्वानरः। एवमत्र विश्वनायकः अथवा सर्वे नरा एनं नयन्ति अथवा विश्वान् (सकलपदार्थान् प्रति) अरः (गतः) विश्वानरः तस्यापत्यं तस्यायं वा इत्येतेषाम् अर्थानामवबोधको वैश्वानरशब्दः सर्वव्यापकत्वं, सर्वपदार्थान्तरवर्तित्वं, विश्वनायकत्वं च सूचयति।

२. उपनिषत्सु वैश्वानरसङ्कल्पनायाः स्वरूपम्

उपनिषत्सु वैश्वानरसङ्कल्पनाया व्यष्टिभूतं समष्टिभूतं च स्वरूपमुपलभ्यते। अत्र प्रथमं तावद् व्यष्टिरूपस्य विवेचनं क्रियते।

२.१. व्यष्टिरूपो अग्निर्वैश्वानरः

वैश्वानराग्नेर्व्यष्टिरूपचिन्तनम् उपनिषत्स्वपि अग्नितत्त्वाधारेणैव विकसितमिति अस्य स्वरूपस्य वैशिष्ट्यं वक्तुं शक्यते। यतो हि वैश्वानरस्य समष्टिरूपचिन्तने उपनिषद इममाधारं परिवर्तयन्तीति विवेचनक्रमे अत्र विज्ञास्यते। वेदेषु वैश्वानराग्नेर्व्यष्टिस्वरूपं सूत्ररूपेण अवबुध्यते परम् उपनिषत्सु एतस्य स्वरूपकर्मणोरुभयोर्वर्णनं समुपलभ्यते।

२.१.१. *देहस्थपाचकाग्निरूपो वैश्वानरः*

अध्यात्मदृष्ट्या व्यष्टिरूपेण वैश्वानराग्नेः स्वरूपं पाचकाग्निरूपेण बृहदारण्यकोपनिषदि उपलभ्यते। तद्यथा –

अयमग्निर्वैश्वानरो योऽयमन्तः पुरुषे येनेदमन्नं पच्यते,
यदिदमद्यते तस्यैष घोषो भवति यमेतत्कर्णावपिधाय
शृणोति स यदोत्क्रमिष्यन्भवति नैनं घोषं शृणोति। – बृ. ५.९.१

जीवितस्य लक्षणभूतोऽपि अयमग्निरत्रावलोक्यते। ननु मैत्रायण्युपनिषद्यपि अल्पेन पाठभेदेन पाचकाग्निरूपे एव वैश्वानरस्य निर्देश उपलभ्यते। तद्यथा –

... **यदौष्ण्यं स पुरुषः। अथ यः पुरुषः सोऽग्निर्वैश्वानरः।** ...

– *मै.* २.६

औष्ण्यभावोपेतशरीरेण पुरुषस्य जीवितलक्षणं ज्ञायते अथ च औष्ण्यस्य निमित्तभूतो वैश्वानरो वर्तते। एवं वैश्वानराग्निद्वारा जीवितलक्षणम् उपनिषदो निर्दिशन्ति।

उपनिषदुक्तस्य वैश्वानराग्नेरेव आयुर्वेदे पश्चाद् जाठराग्निरूपेण विकासोऽवलोक्यते। यद्यपि गर्भोपनिषदि (*गर्भोप.* ५) वैश्वानराग्नेः कोष्ठाग्निरिति अभिधानमुपलभ्यते, न सोपनिषत् प्राचीनासूपनिषत्सु अन्यतमा।

एवमत्र प्रतिशरीरं वर्तमानोऽयमग्निः स्वकर्मणा अन्यान् देहस्थाग्नीननुगृह्य सकलशरीरमेव अनुगृह्णाति तस्माद् वैश्वानरविशेषणेन अभिहितः।

२.१.२. *ब्राह्मणातिथिरूपो वैश्वानरः*

कठोपनिषदि वैश्वानरस्य अभिज्ञानं ब्राह्मणातिथिरूपेण कृतमस्ति। पित्रा मृत्यवे दत्तो नचिकेता यदा यमगृहे तिस्रो रात्रीः अनश्नन् अवसत् तदा उक्तं च तत्र –

> **वैश्वानरः प्रविशत्यतिथिर्ब्राह्मणो गृहान्।**
> **तस्यैतां शान्तिं कुर्वन्ति हर वैवस्वतोदकम्॥** – *क.* १.७

अत्र वैश्वानरस्य अभिज्ञानं ब्राह्मणातिथिरूपेण किमर्थं कृतम् ? अत्र एवं प्रतिभाति यद् एवंभूतस्य असत्कृतातिथेर्गृहवासो वैश्वानराग्नेर्तेजःसदृशो दाहको भवति। अत्र ध्यातव्यमेतत् तथ्यं यद् असत्कृतातिथेर्दाहकत्वस्य साम्यं वैश्वानराग्निसदृशम् उक्तं न तु अन्नपानादिभिः सत्कृतातिथेः। तात्पर्यमेतद् देहस्थजाठराग्निरूपो वैश्वानराग्निर्यदा अन्नपानादिभिरसत्कृतो भवति तदास्य अतृप्तिर्दाहकत्वरूपेण दृश्यते। अत एव एवंभूतस्य अतिथेर्ब्राह्मणस्य दाहकत्वबोधनाय वैश्वानरेति विशेषणं प्रयुक्तमस्ति।

वैश्वानराग्नेर्दाहकत्वं प्राधान्येन निर्दिष्टं ब्राह्मणग्रन्थेष्वपि (*तां.ब्रा.* ५.३.९; *गो.ब्रा.* १.२.२१)। एवमत्र वैश्वानराग्नेः समष्टिगतदाहकत्वस्य व्यष्टिगतपरिवर्तनस्याभिज्ञानं वैश्वानररूपेण प्रतिपादितम्।

२.१.३. *व्यात्तमुखरूपो अग्निर्वैश्वानरः*

बृहदारण्यकोपनिषदि अश्वमेधस्य आधिभौतिकवर्णनप्रसङ्गे अश्वस्य विवृतं मुखं नाम अग्निर्वैश्वानर इति प्रतिपादितम् तद्यथा –

> **उषा वा अश्वस्य मेध्यस्य शिरः सूर्यश्चक्षुर्वातः प्राणो**
> **व्यात्तमग्निर्वैश्वानरः संवत्सर आत्माऽश्वस्य मेध्यस्य।** . . . – *बृ.* १.१.१

अंशतः पाठभेदेन मन्त्रोऽयं तैत्तिरीयसंहितायामपि (*तै.सं.* ७.५.२५) उपलभ्यते। अश्वमेधस्य अभिप्रायोऽत्र कर्मकाण्डपरो नास्ति। अश्वमेध्यस्य अश्वस्य अवयवरूपेण सर्वे स्थूलपदार्थाः सङ्केतिताः। एवमत्र अश्वरूपसृष्टेरङ्गकल्पनायां मुखमिव मुख्यो वैश्वानराग्निर्विवृतं मुखं वर्तते। अत्र प्रतीकरूपेण वैश्वानराग्नेः मुखत्वं सहेतुकं प्रतिभाति, यथा अग्निर्देवानां मुखमिति (*ऐ.ब्रा.* ७.१६; *गो.ब्रा.* १.२३) ब्राह्मणग्रन्थैः याज्ञिकदृष्ट्या निर्दिष्टं तस्यैव देवमुखभूताग्नेर्न केवलं देवमुखत्वं प्रत्युत अश्वरूपसृष्टेर्विश्वमुखत्वज्ञापनपरं लक्ष्यं स्यात्। तस्मादग्नेरभिज्ञानं वैश्वानररूपेण अत्र दृश्यत इति शक्यते वक्तुम्। यथा मुखं प्राप्य सर्वे पदार्थाः सर्वशरीरव्यापिनो भवन्ति तथैव वैश्वानराग्निमुखं प्राप्य सकलपदार्थानां विश्वव्यापकत्वं संभवति नान्यथा। एवमस्या अग्न्याधारितव्यापकक्रियाया बोधाय वैश्वानराग्निरश्वस्य विवृतमुखरूपेण प्रतिपादितः।

२.२. *ब्रह्मरूपोवैश्वानरः*

२.२.१. *वैश्वानरस्य ब्रह्मरूपे अभिज्ञानस्य कारणमीमांसा*

समष्टिचिन्तने उपनिषदो व्यापकतत्त्वानां विचारावसरे यथाप्रसङ्गं वाय्वाकाशादितत्त्वान् निर्दिशन्ति। एतेष्वपि सर्वेषु व्यापकतत्त्वेषु व्यापकतमं यत् तत्त्वं तस्य निर्देशो ब्रह्मशब्देन कुर्वन्ति ताः। एवं प्रयोजनवशाद् ब्रह्मैकलक्ष्यत्वाद् उपनिषत्सु ऋग्वेदीयमग्नितत्त्वं परिवर्तितं परं यतो हि ब्रह्मतत्त्वस्योपलब्धिः सर्वव्यापकतत्त्वान्वेषणसमये उद्भूता तस्माद् वैश्वानराग्नेः सङ्कल्पनातः अग्निमपाकृत्य ब्रह्मणः सर्वव्यापकत्वप्रतिपादनाय ब्रह्मतत्त्वे अनुवर्तिता वैश्वानरसङ्कल्पना दृश्यते खलु। एवं समष्टिगतचिन्तने ब्रह्म एव वैश्वानररूपेण दृष्टत्वादत्र वैश्वानरस्याभिज्ञानं ब्रह्मणा अभवत्। तद्यथा –

> **तान् होवाचाश्वपतिर्वै भगवन्तोऽयं कैकेयः संप्रतीममात्मानं**
> **वैश्वानरमध्येति तं हन्ताभ्यागच्छामेति तं हाभ्याजग्मुः॥** – *छां* ५.११.४

अत्र आत्मशब्देन ब्रह्मण एव ग्रहणं वर्तते इति ब्रह्मसूत्रे (*ब्रसू.* १.२.२४ तः १.२.३१) प्रतिपादितमेव।

२.२.२. *ब्रह्मप्रतीकं वैश्वानरः*

उपनिषद्दृष्ट्या एतद् ब्रह्म विजिज्ञास्यम्, उपास्यम् अन्वेष्टव्यं च वर्तते अत एव उपनिषत्सु ब्रह्मस्वरूपावबोधनार्थं नाना विचारा विविधाश्च प्रतीकोपासनाः आधाररूपेण प्रवर्तिताः याभिर्ब्रह्मस्वरूपं विस्पष्टयेत। आसु वैश्वानरोपासनापि छान्दोग्योपनिषदि प्रतिपादिता। प्रथमतया ब्रह्मणः सर्वव्यापकत्वज्ञापनाय वैश्वानरशब्दो ब्रह्मविशेषणत्वेन प्रयुक्तः तदनन्तरं वैश्वानरब्रह्मणः चिन्तनम् उपासना वा अस्मिन्नेव व्यापकस्वरूपे कथं केन च विधिना भवेदेतदर्थं वैश्वानरब्रह्मणः प्रतीकत्वेन यदा निखिलब्रह्माण्डमेव उपन्यस्तं तदा एतत्प्रतीकमपि वैश्वानरशब्देन अभिज्ञापितम्।

कृष्णानन्दस्वामिभिर्वैश्वानरविद्याविवेचनप्रसङ्गे वैश्वानरस्य विराट्स्वरूपस्य मूलं पुरुषसूक्ते प्रतिपादितम् (Krishnanand, e-book: 72)।

एवममूर्तब्रह्मणो ज्ञापिका वैश्वानरसङ्कल्पना तद्बोधायैव पुनः प्रतीकस्वरूपेणापि स्वीकृता छान्दोग्योपनिषदि दृश्यते । यथा –

> **तस्य ह वा एतस्यात्मनो वैश्वानरस्य मूर्धैव सुतेजाश्चक्षुर्विश्वरूपः**
> **प्राणः पृथग्वर्त्मात्मा संदेहो बहुलो बस्तिरेव रयिः**
> **पृथिव्येव पादावुर एव... आस्यमाहवनीयः॥** – *छां.* ५.१८.२

अत एव एतेषां पृथगुपासना वैश्वानरब्रह्मणः अङ्गोपासना एव अधिगम्यते। तद्यथा -

> **तान् होवाच ते वै खलु यूयं पृथगिवेममात्मानं वैश्वानरं विद्वाँसोऽन्नमत्थ।...**
> – *छां.* ५.१८.१

राजा कैकेयः प्राचीनशालादीन् उवाच यद् युष्माभिर्द्युरूपे, आदित्यरूपे, वायुरूपे वा वैश्वानरब्रह्म उपासितं तदुपासनं पृथगिव नाम अवयवभूतमासीत्।

२.२.३. *वैश्वानराग्निहोत्रम्*

वैश्वानरब्रह्मणो वैश्वानरप्रतीकोपासनया उपासनायाः फलश्रुतिः छान्दोग्ये एवं श्रूयते –

> ... **यस्त्वेतमेवं प्रादेशमात्रमभिविमानमात्मानं वैश्वानरमुपास्ते**
> **स सर्वेषु लोकेषु सर्वेषु भूतेषु सर्वेष्वात्मस्वन्नमत्ति॥** – *छां.* ५.१८.१

यतो हि समष्टिगतब्रह्मणो वैश्वानरस्वरूपं तत्प्रतीकमपि वैश्वानरमाध्यमेन प्रतिपाद्य उपनिषदां कार्यावसानं नैवाभिसम्पद्यते। वैश्वानरप्रतीकस्य सुविस्तृतस्वरूपस्य चिन्तनं ध्यानं वा देहस्थात्मनो विद्यते कर्तव्यकर्म। नरदेहोऽपि वैश्वानरब्रह्मणः प्रतीकभूतेभ्यो ब्रह्माण्डस्थपदार्थेभ्यो विनिर्मितोऽस्ति। तस्माद् वैश्वानरोपासनायाः फलावाप्तये आस्यरूपाहवनीयाग्नौ देहस्थाग्नौ वैश्वानरस्याभिज्ञानं प्रतिपादितं, यत्र पञ्च प्राणान् उद्दिश्य वैश्वानरब्रह्मभावोपेतो याजको भक्ष्यान्नं दैहिकवैश्वानराग्नौ जुहोति चेत् सा हुतान्ननिमित्ता पिण्डस्थतृप्तिर्ब्रह्माण्डतर्पिका अखण्डतृप्तिरूपा सम्पद्यते (*छां.* ५.१९ तः ५.२४)। एवं स सर्वेषु लोकेषु, भूतेषु आत्मसु च अन्नमत्ति। छान्दोग्ये वैश्वानराग्निहोत्रस्य सङ्केतोऽस्य यज्ञस्य फलनिर्देशे सङ्केतितः। तद्यथा –

> **अथ य एतदेवं विद्वानग्निहोत्रं जुहोति तस्य सर्वेषु**
> **लोकेषु सर्वेषु भूतेषु सर्वेष्वात्मसु हुतं भवति॥** – *छां.* ५.२४.२

> **तस्मादु हैवंविद्यद्यपि चाण्डालायोच्छिष्टं प्रयच्छेदात्मनि**
> **हैवास्य तद्वैश्वानरे हुतं स्यादिति।** – *छां.* ५.२४.४

एवं वैश्वानरसङ्कल्पनाया विकासोऽत्र युक्तियुक्तं सूक्ष्मतः स्थूलं प्रति नाम ब्रह्मतः प्रारभ्य ब्रह्माण्डपिण्डान्तर्गतो दृश्यते। एवं ब्रह्माधारं स्वीकृत्य विस्तृता सङ्कल्पनैषा व्यष्टिरूपे पुनः अग्न्याधारेण प्रत्यावर्तिता दृश्यते खलु।

२.२.४. *चतुष्पाद्ब्रह्मणः प्रथमः पादो वैश्वानरः*

उपनिषदि ब्रह्मणः स्वरूपविवेचनं चतुष्पाद्ब्रह्मरूपेण विहितं यत्र पादचतुष्टये प्रथमपादस्य विचारो वैश्वानररूपेण प्रस्तुतः। माण्डूक्योपनिषदि एवमुच्यते यत् –

> **सर्वं ह्येतद् ब्रह्मायमात्मा ब्रह्म सोऽयमात्मा चतुष्पात्॥** – *मां.* २

पादचतुष्टये च प्रथमपादस्य विवरणमेवं प्राप्यते। तद्यथा –

> **जागरितस्थानो बहिःप्रज्ञः सप्ताङ्ग एकोनविंशतिमुखः स्थूलभुग्वैश्वानरः प्रथमः पादः॥** – *मां.* ३

जागरितस्थानो बहिःप्रज्ञः सप्ताङ्ग एकोनविंशतिमुखः स्थूलभुगादिवैशिष्ट्ययुक्तो वैश्वानरो ब्रह्मणः

प्रथमपादरूपेण विज्ञायते। वैश्वानरस्य सप्ताङ्गानाम् एकोनविंशतिमुखानां च स्पष्टीकरणं निर्देशो वा अत्र नैवोपलभ्यते परं भाष्यकारैः सप्ताङ्गानां ब्रह्माण्डस्थैरग्निसूर्यादिभिः सह अन्वयो विहितः, एकोनविंशतिमुखानि च पञ्चज्ञानेन्द्रियैः, पञ्चकर्मेन्द्रियैः, पञ्चप्राणैरन्तःकरणचतुष्टयेन च सहान्वितानि[१०]। एवं भवतु नाम मुखाङ्गानां प्रकारनिर्धारणे मतान्तरं परमेतानि खलु उपभोग-साधनानि इति निश्चितमेव। एवं ब्रह्मणः प्रथमपादस्य जागरितस्थानयुक्तस्य वैश्वानरसङ्कल्पनया अभिज्ञानहेतुरेवं विज्ञायते यद् जागरितस्थाने एव आत्मना समग्रज्ञानकर्मणोः हेतुभूतसाधनैः स्थूलपदार्था उपभुज्यन्ते अतो जागरितस्थानस्यैव वैशिष्ट्यमेतद् यदत्र निखिलसाधनानाम् उपयोगो उपभोगे साकल्येन भवति, नैतत् संभवति स्वप्नस्थाने। अत एव तत्र जागरितस्थानमिव स्वप्नस्थाने समानाङ्गानां मुखानां च निर्देशे सत्यपि तत्स्थानं तैजसाभिधानेन अभिहितम्। तद्यथा –

स्वप्नस्थानोऽन्तःप्रज्ञः सप्ताङ्ग एकोनविंशतिमुखः प्रविविक्तभुक् तैजसो द्वितीयः पादः॥ – *मं.* ४

एवं सुस्पष्टमेतद् यद् जागरितस्थाने सकलज्ञानकर्मरूपिसाधनानां क्रियान्वयित्वम् अशेषतया भवति स्थूलोपभोगाय पालनाय वा तस्माद् जागरितस्थाने एतेषां साधनानां क्रियारूपसर्वव्यापकत्वनिर्देशाय वैश्वानरसङ्कल्पना प्रथमपादत्वेनाभिहिता।

२.२.५. *प्राणाग्निरूपः सूर्यो वैश्वानरः*

कासुचिद् उपनिषत्सु प्राणाग्निरूप उद्यन्नादित्यो वैश्वानराख्यो वर्तते। यथा प्रश्नोपनिषदि –

स एष वैश्वानरो विश्वरूपः प्राणोऽग्निरुदयते। तदेतदृचाभ्युक्तम्॥ – *प्र.* १.७

अस्य प्राणाग्नेः स्वरूपमत्र एवमुक्तम् –

विश्वरूपं हरिणं जातवेदसं परायणं ज्योतिरेकं तपन्तम्।
सहस्ररश्मिः शतधा वर्तमानः प्राणः प्रजानामुदयत्येष सूर्यः॥ – *प्र.* १.८

एवमत्र प्रजानां प्राणभूतः सूर्यो वैश्वानरशब्देन अभिहितोऽस्ति। उद्यन्नादित्यो विश्वस्य बाह्यप्राणरूपो वर्तते इत्यपि उपनिषन्मतम्। तद्यथा –

आदित्यो ह वै बाह्यः प्राण उदयति।... – *प्र.* ३.८

एवमन्तर्वर्तिनः प्राणस्य बाह्यं रूपं सूर्यो वा अग्निर्वा तस्य अभिज्ञापकोऽयं वैश्वानरः। वस्तुतो वैश्वानराग्नेः सर्वव्यापकतेजोऽधिकृत्य यदा चिन्तनमारब्धं तदा सूर्येऽपि तथाभूतं तेजोवृत्तित्वमुप-लब्धम्। अत एव ब्राह्मणग्रन्थेष्वपि सूर्यस्य तेजोनिमित्तकमभिज्ञानं दरीदृश्यते (*श.ब्रा.* १०.५.२.१; *ऐ.ब्रा.* ३०.९)। अग्निना सह सूर्यस्य सम्बन्धस्तु कुत्रचित् स्पष्टतया निर्दिष्टोऽस्ति। तद्यथा –

असौ वा आदित्य एषोऽग्निः। – *श.ब्रा.* ६.३.१.२९

---

[१०] *माण्डूक्योपनिषत्* (शाङ्करभाष्यम्), पृ. १४; *माण्डूक्योपनिषत्*, श्रीपाद दामोदर सातवलेकर, पृ. १६–१७।

"उद्यन्नादित्यः सर्वाणि भूतानि प्रणयति" इति निर्वचनद्वारा प्राणसंज्ञापि ब्राह्मणेन प्रतिपादिता। तद्यथा –

उद्यन्नु खलु वा आदित्यः सर्वाणि भूतानि प्रणयति तस्मादेनं प्राण इत्याचक्षते।

– *ऐ.ब्रा.* २५.६

एवमग्निरूपसूर्यस्य प्राणाग्निरूपे विकसिता ब्राह्मणविहिता सङ्कल्पना उपनिषत्सु स्वीकृता। वैश्वानरमतिरिच्य प्राणसंज्ञा ब्राह्मणैः प्रयुक्ता परम् उपनिषत्सु अग्न्याधारेण विकसितस्य प्राणाग्रेः सूर्यस्य सर्वनायकत्वेन सह सर्वव्यापकत्वनिर्देशाय वैश्वानरसङ्कल्पनापि पुरस्कृता दृश्यते।

२.२.६. *प्राणोऽग्निरूपः परमात्मा वैश्वानरः*

मैत्रायण्युपनिषदि प्राणाग्निरूपसूर्यस्य सङ्कल्पना परमात्मरूपे विकसिता दृश्यते। तद्यथा –

प्राणोऽग्निः परमात्मा वै पञ्चवायुः समाश्रितः।
स प्रीतः प्रीणातु विश्वं विश्वभुक्॥
विश्वोऽसि वैश्वानरोऽसि विश्वं त्वया धार्यते जायमानम्।
विशन्तु त्वामाहुतयश्च सर्वाः प्रजास्तत्र यत्र विश्वामृतोऽसीति॥
एवं न विधिना खल्वनेनात्ताऽन्नत्वं पुनरुपैति॥ – *मै.* ६.९

एवमनेन विधिना यः खलु आत्मेज्यान आत्मानं नाम ब्रह्म अभिध्यायेत तर्हि सोऽयमत्ता पुनरन्नत्वं नाम भोग्यत्वरूपं न उपैतीति प्राणाग्निरूपपरमात्मनः उपासनायाः फलश्रुतिरत्र श्रूयते।

एवमग्नितत्त्वस्य मूलस्वरूपेण सहैव एतस्य विकसितरूपाणामपि सहचारिणी वैश्वानरसङ्कल्पना इदानीम् अग्नितत्त्वस्य स्वरूपविकासस्य परां काष्ठां प्रापयन्ती इह दृश्यते। यतो हि उपनिषदनुसारं यद् भाति विभाति वा तत् सर्वं तमेव भान्तमनुभाति (*क.* ५.१५)।

एवं स्वलक्ष्यम् अनुधावन्त्यः उपनिषदो वैश्वानराग्नेः विकासस्य परां काष्ठां विज्ञापयन्ति यतो हि सर्वेऽपि तपन्तो विभान्तः पदार्था ब्रह्मभासा एव तेजस्विनः सन्ति। अत एव प्राणाग्निरूपसूर्यस्वरूपेण विकसितायाः सङ्कल्पनाया मूलस्रोतः अवबोधनाय, सर्वाग्निरूपेषु ब्रह्मणो व्याप्तिदर्शनाय च प्राणाग्निरूपस्य परमात्मनोऽभिज्ञानमपि वैश्वानररूपेण अत्र दृश्यते।

२.२.७. *ब्रह्मरूपो वैश्वानराग्निः*

उपनिषत्सु प्रायः सर्वत्र ब्रह्मणः सर्वव्यापकत्वनिर्देशाय वैश्वानरसङ्कल्पना ब्रह्माधारेण विकसिता परमार्षेयोपनिषदि अग्न्याधारेण ब्रह्मबोधाय प्रवर्तिता दृश्यते। तद्यथा –

परोवरीयांसमभिप्रणुत्यमन्तर्जुषाणं भुवनानि विश्वा।
यमश्रवन्न कुशिकासो अग्निं वैश्वानरममृतजातं गमध्ययी॥...

– *आर्षेय* ९

३. प्रेतहरणे वैश्वानराग्नेर्भूमिकाया विवेचनम्

निरुक्तशास्त्रे दुर्गाचार्यैः वैश्वानरशब्दस्य निर्वचने स्वीयं मन्तव्यम् एवमुपस्थापितम्। तद्यथा –

विश्वान्नरान् इतो लोकादमुं लोकं नयति यथा पञ्चाग्निविद्यायामुच्यते।

– *निरु.* ७.२१

अत्र छान्दोग्योपनिषदि प्रतिपादितायाः पञ्चाग्निविद्याया (*छां.* ५.४ तः ५.९) निर्देशो दुर्गाचार्यैः कृतो यस्यां पुरुषजन्महेतुभूतपञ्चाग्नीनां वर्णनानन्तरं प्रेतहरणेऽपि अग्नीनां भूमिका प्रतिपादिता। तद्यथा –

स जातो यावदायुषं जीवति तं प्रेतं दिष्टमितोऽग्नय एव हरन्ति
यत एवेतो यतः संभूतो भवति ॥ – *छां.* ५.९.२

एवमत्र सुस्पष्टमेव यत् प्रेतहरणे निर्दिष्टाग्नयः साक्षाद् वैश्वानरशब्देन अनभिहिताः सन्ति। केवलं व्युत्पत्तिसामर्थ्यादाचार्यैरुदाहरणत्वेन छान्दोग्यस्य पञ्चाग्निविद्या पुरस्कृता स्यादिति अनुमातुमेव शक्यते। वेदेष्वपि वैश्वानराग्नेर्वर्णनं प्रेतगतिप्रदाने नोपलभ्यते। केवलम् अथर्ववेदे एतत् सङ्केतितं यथा –

... **वैश्वानरो नो अधिपा वसिष्ठ उदिन्नयाति सुकृतस्य लोकम्॥**

– *अथर्व.* ६.११९.१

अत्र प्रार्थ्यतेऽयं वैश्वानराग्निर्यत् सुकृतस्य लोकम् अस्मान् प्रापयतु। एवं वैश्वानराग्नेः एषा सङ्कल्पना उपनिषत्सु नैव विकसिता परं पुराणकाले अथर्ववेदीया एषा प्रार्थना निवेदनं वा अध्यवसायात्मकतया परिवर्तितं यदयं वैश्वानरः सद्गतिं प्रापयति तस्मादयमग्निर्वैश्वानरनामको वर्तते। तद्यथा –

विश्वान् नरान् हूतो येन नयसे सद्गतिं प्रभो।
अतो वैश्वानरो नाम तव वाक्यं भविष्यति॥ – *वराह पु.* १८.२०

वराहपुराणानुसारम् अग्नेर्मूर्तस्वरूपस्य वैश्वानरेति नाम वर्तते। तद्यथा –

अग्नेर्वैश्वानरो नाम प्राणापानौ तथाश्विनौ।... – *वराह पु.* १७.६६

एवमत्र स्थूलस्वरूपात्मको वैश्वानराग्निः सद्गतिप्रदायको वर्तते। एवं प्रेतहरणे सद्गतिप्रदाने वा वैश्वानरसङ्कल्पना उपनिषदि नैव विकसिता परम् अथर्ववेदीयसाङ्केतिकप्रार्थनाया विकास उपनिषदुत्तरकाले तु दृश्यते।

४. ऋग्वेदीयवैश्वानरसङ्कल्पनाया औपनिषदिकदृष्ट्या परिवर्तनं विकासश्च

ऋग्वेदीयवैश्वानरसङ्कल्पना यज्ञीयाग्निसम्बद्धत्वादेषा प्रायः आधिदैविकवर्णनबहुला दरीदृश्यते। यतो हि वैश्वानराग्निर्मनुष्याणां देवानां च पुरोहितोऽस्ति (*ऋ.* ३.३.२, ३.२.८) अत एव

देवतास्वरूपे विद्यमानम् एतमग्निमुद्दिश्य नैकाः प्रार्थनाः स्तुतयश्च ऐहिकविकासाय आमुष्मिकविकासदृष्ट्या चोपलभ्यन्ते।

ऋग्वेदीयवैश्वानरसङ्कल्पना ऐहिकामुष्मिकसमृद्ध्यर्थम् अग्निशब्दमेव अभिज्ञापयति परम् औपनिषदिकचिन्तनधारा ऐहिकामुष्मिकफलकामनामुल्लंघ्य पारलौकिकविकासाय शश्वत् प्रवहति अत एव उपनिषत्सु वैश्वानरसङ्कल्पना प्रायः ऋग्वेदाधारिता एव विकसिता परमस्या विकासस्य स्वरूपं ब्रह्मस्वरूपबोधाय, तत्साधनीभूततत्त्वानां वैशिष्ट्यबोधाय च दृश्यते, ब्रह्मणो व्यापकस्वरूपस्य प्रतीकत्वेनापि उपलभ्यते। समष्टिगतवैश्वानरसम्बन्धितत्त्वानां दिव्यताया अशेषलाभ उपासकेभ्यो भवेदिति कृत्वा वैश्वानरप्रतीकोपासनाया अनुष्ठानं दैहिकवैश्वानराग्निहोत्ररूपेण प्रतिपादितम्।

व्यष्टौ जाठराग्निरूपे समष्टौ च प्राणाग्निरूपसूर्यस्य स्वरूपे परिवर्तितो वैश्वानरः अग्निरूपस्यैव अभिज्ञापनाय प्रयुक्तो वर्तते। अग्न्याधारेण समुत्पन्नाया वैश्वानरसङ्कल्पनाया विकासस्य औपनिषदिकविवेचनस्य च सा परा गतिर्वर्तते यदा अग्नेरपि अग्नित्वं सूर्यस्य च सूर्यत्वं यस्य कारणवशाद् विद्यते तस्य प्राणाग्निरूपपरमात्मनो व्यापकत्वमभिज्ञापनाय संहितासु दृढमूला वैश्वानरसङ्कल्पना अत्र प्रयुक्ता।

५. उपसंहारः

- वेदेषु सूत्ररूपेण वर्णितस्य वैश्वानराग्नेर्जाठरसम्बन्धस्य ब्रह्मसन्दर्भस्य च स्पष्टतया स्वरूपकर्मणोर्निर्देशे उपनिषदां योगदानं दृश्यते।
- उपनिषत्सु वैश्वानरस्य व्यष्टिरूपं समष्टिरूपं च वर्तते। व्यष्टिरूपस्य विकासः अग्न्या-धारित एव वर्तते परं समष्टिरूपस्य आधारो ब्रह्म वर्तते।
- ऋग्वेदीया सङ्कल्पनैषा या प्रामुख्येन आधिदैविकायतने दृग्गोचरीभवति उपनिषत्सु सा तदायतनमुल्लंघ्य अधिब्रह्मायतने परिणता दृश्यते।
- उपनिषत्सु वैश्वानरसङ्कल्पनाया भौतिकदृष्ट्या विवेचनमपि कुत्रचित् पारलौकिक-दृष्टिम् अधिकृत्य प्रवर्तितमिति विज्ञायते।
- आध्यात्मिक-आधिभौतिक-आधिदैविकस्तरेषु विचाराय स्वीकृतत्वात् चिन्तनस्य समग्रायामे विस्तृता दृश्यते सङ्कल्पनैषा।
- सर्वासु उपनिषत्सु अङ्गोपासनायाः कृते नैकानि तत्त्वानि प्रतीकत्वेन उपात्तानि परं समस्तोपासनायाः कृते प्रतीकत्वेन केवला वैश्वानरप्रतीकोपासना एव यज्ञाङ्गबहिर्भूतासु उपासनासु राराजते।
- एषा अग्नेरथ च तत्तेजःसम्बन्धिपदार्थानां ज्ञापनाय अथवा अग्नेरपि दाहकत्व-प्रदातृशक्तेर्ज्ञापनाय प्रयुक्तत्वादस्या वेदोक्तमूलस्वरूपमेव परिवर्धितमत्र दृश्यते।
- अग्नेरन्यविशेषणानां निर्देशो वैश्वानर इव बाहुल्येन उपनिषत्सु नोपलभ्यते।

आधारग्रन्थाः

ससंक्षेपाः मूलग्रन्थाः

अथर्व. : *अथर्ववेदसंहिता*, सम्पा. श्रीपाद दामोदर सातवलेकर, तृतीय संस्करण, स्वाध्यायमण्डल, पारडी, १९५७।

अष्टादश-उपनिषदः, सम्पा. वि. प्र. लिमये, रं. दं. वाडेकर, प्रथमखण्डः, प्रथमं संस्करणम्, वैदिक-संशोधन-मण्डलम्, पुण्यपत्तनम्, १९५८।

अष्टा. सू. : *अष्टाध्यायीसूत्रपाठः* (पाणिनिमुनिप्रणीतः), सम्पा. ब्रह्मदत्त जिज्ञासु, त्रयोदश संस्करण, रामलाल कपूर ट्रस्ट, अमृतसर, १९८९ (प्रथमप्रकाशनम् १९५५)।

उपनिषत्संग्रहः, सम्पा. जगदीश शास्त्री, प्रथमो भागः, षष्ठं संस्करणम्, मोतीलाल बनारसीदास, दिल्ली, २००६ (प्रथमप्रकाशनम् १९७०)।

ऋ. : *ऋग्वेदसंहिता*, सम्पा. श्रीपाद दामोदर सातवलेकर, तृतीय संस्करण, स्वाध्यायमण्डल, पारडी, १९५७।

ऋग्वेदसंहिता (सायणाचार्यविरचितभाष्यसहिता), तृतीयो भागः (६-८ मण्डलम्), वैदिक-संशोधन-मण्डलम्, पुणे, १९४१।

ऋग्वेदभाष्यम् (दयानन्दसरस्वतीस्वामिनिर्मितम्), अष्टमो भागः, चतुर्थं संस्करणम्, श्रीमती परोपकारिणी सभा, अजमेर, २००१।

ऐ.ब्रा. : *ऐतरेयब्राह्मणम्* (सायणाचार्यविरचितभाष्यसमेतम्), प्रथमो भागः, नूतनेयमङ्कनावृत्तिः, आनन्दाश्रमः, पुण्यपत्तनम्, १९७९।

काठ.सं. : *काठकसंहिता*, सम्पा. श्रीपाद दामोदर सातवलेकर, स्वाध्यायमण्डल, औंध, १९४३।

गो.ब्रा. : *गोपथब्राह्मणम्*, सम्पा. प्रज्ञा देवी, मेधा देवी, द्वितीय संस्करण, इन्द्रदयालसेठ, अथर्ववेदभाष्य कार्यालय, इलाहाबाद, १९७७।

जै.ब्रा. : *जैमिनीयं ब्राह्मणम् (सामवेदीयम्)* सम्पा. रघुवीर, लोकेशचन्द्र, द्वितीय संस्करण, मोतीलाल बनारसीदास, दिल्ली, १९८६।

ता.ब्रा. : *ताण्ड्यमहाब्राह्मणम्* (सायणाचार्यविरचितभाष्यसहितम्), चौखम्बा संस्कृत सीरीज ऑफिस, बनारस, १९३५।

तै.सं. : *तैत्तिरीयसंहिता* (कृष्णयजुर्वेदीया), द्वितीयं संस्करणम्, चौखम्बा संस्कृत प्रतिष्ठान, दिल्ली, २०००।

धातु. : *धातुपाठः* (पाणिनिमुनिप्रणीतः), चतुर्थं संस्करणम्, रामलाल कपूर ट्रस्ट, अमृतसर, १९८९।

निरु. : *निरुक्तम्* (दुर्गाचार्यकृतवृत्तिसमेतम्) संशो. वैजनाथ काशीनाथ राजवाडे, द्वितीयो भागः, आनन्दाश्रमः, पुण्यपत्तनम्, १९२६।

बृहद्दे. : *बृहद्देवता*, सम्पा. एवं अनु. राजकुमार राय, तृतीय संस्करण, चौखम्बा संस्कृत संस्थान, वाराणसी, २००३।

माण्डूक्योपनिषत्, सम्पा. श्रीपाद दामोदर सातवलेकर, प्रथम संस्करण, स्वाध्यायमण्डल, पारडी, १९५२।

माण्डूक्योपनिषत् (गौडपादीयकारिकासहिता), संशो. आबाजी विष्णु शर्मा, षष्ठं संस्करणम्, विनायक गणेश आप्टे, आनन्दाश्रमः, पुण्यपत्तनम्, १९३६।

मै.सं. : *मैत्रायणीसंहिता* (कृष्णयजुर्वेदीया), प्रथम संस्करण, चौखम्बा संस्कृत प्रतिष्ठान, दिल्ली, २००५।

यजु. : *यजुर्वेदसंहिता*, सम्पा. श्रीपाद दामोदर सातवलेकर, प्रथम संस्करण, स्वाध्यायमण्डल, औंध, १९४७।

वराह. पु.: *वराहपुराणम्*, सम्पा. आनन्दस्वरूपगुप्त शास्त्री, पाठसमीक्षात्मकसंस्करणम्, सर्वभारतीय-

काशिराजन्यासः, वाराणसी, १९८१।

श.ब्रा. : *शतपथब्राह्मणम्* (माध्यन्दिनशाखीयम्), संशो. अल्बर्त वेबर, द्वितीयं संस्करणम्, चौखम्बा संस्कृत सीरीज ऑफिस, वाराणसी, १९६४।

शुक्लयजुर्वेदसंहिता (उवटमहीधरकृतभाष्येण संवलिता), हिन्दी व्याख्या रामकृष्ण शास्त्री, द्वितीय संस्करण, चौखम्बा विद्याभवन, वाराणसी, २००५।

शांकरब्रह्मसूत्रभाष्य (मराठी भाषांतर), सम्पा. काशीनाथ वासुदेव अभ्यंकर, द्वितीय संस्करण, सेक्रेटरी, डेक्कन एज्युकेशन सोसायटी, फर्ग्युसन कॉलेज, पुणे, १९५७।

गौणग्रन्थाः

अग्रवाल, वासुदेवशरण, १९६४, *वेदरश्मि*, सम्पा. वसंत श्रीपाद सातवलेकर. पारडी : स्वाध्यायमण्डल।

ओझा, मधुसूदन, १९५२, *ब्रह्मचतुष्पदी*, द्वितीय संस्करण, सम्पा. प्रद्युम्न शर्मा, जयपुर : प्रद्युम्न शर्मा।

सातवलेकर, श्रीपाद दामोदर, १९४०, *ऋग्वेद के अग्निसूक्त*, प्रथम संस्करण. औंध : स्वाध्यायमण्डल।

पाश्चात्यभाषानिबद्धा ग्रन्थाः

Vries, L. de, 1979, "Vaiśvānará", *Zeitschrift für Vergleichende Sprachforschung*, **93**: 8-10.

Electronic Sources

The Chhandoyga Upanishad, e-book by Swami Krishnananda. Rishikesh: The Divine Life Society, Sivananda Ashram. http://www.swamikrishnananda.org/chhand/Chhandogya Upanishad.pdf

Vedic Literature: Agni, Sri Aurobindo, Kapil Sastry Institute of Vedic Culture. http://www.vedah.com/essays-on-veda-upanishad-etc/elementary-topics/59-godsmore-details/464-agni

Agni and the Fire of Self-inquiry, by David Frawley (Pandit Vamadeva), American Institute of Vedic Studies. http:// www.vedanet.com/our-online-articles-topmenu-2/33-the-vedas-and-their-interpretation/4-agni-and-the-fire-of-self-inquiry

Contributors

S.S. Bahulkar, Professor Rtd., Department of Sanskrit and Indological Studies, Tilak Maharashtra Vidyapeeth, Pune (India). Postal address: Plot no. 6, Pushkaraj Society, Dhankawadi, Pune – 411 043. *e-mail*: <shrikant.bahulkar@gmail.com>

Giacomo Benedetti, JSPS Post-Doctoral Fellow, Faculty of Letters, Kyoto University, Yoshida-Honmachi, Sakyo-ku, Kyoto 606-8501 (Japan). Postal address: Yoshidashimoōjichō 65, apartment no. 307, Sakyō-ku, Kyoto (Japan). *e-mail*: <giacomobenedetti@hotmail.com>

Mugdha Gadgil, Assistant Professor, Department of Sanskrit and Prakrit Languages, University of Pune, Pune (India). Postal address: A-54, Rutuparna, S. No. 40/1+2+3, Kothrud, Pune – 411 038 (India).

Hans Henrich Hock, Professor Emeritus, Department of Linguistics, University of Illinois, 707 S. Mathews, Urbana, IL 61801 (USA). *e-mail*: <hhhock@illinois.edu>

Ambarish Khare, Assistant Professor, Shri Balmukund Lohia Centre of Sanskrit and Indological Studies, Tilak Maharashtra Vidyapeeth, 1242 Sadashiv Peth, Pune – 411 030 (India). Postal address: Shree Khunya Muralidhar Mandir, 1236 Sadashiv Peth, Pune – 411 030 (India). *e-mail*: <avkhare@gmail.com>

Jared S. Klein, Professor, Department of Classics, Park Hall, The University of Georgia, Athens, GA 30602 (USA). *e-mail*: <jklein@uga.edu>

Frank Köhler, Lecturer Institute of Asian and Oriental Studies, University of Tübingen, Gartenstraße 19, 72074 Tübingen (Germany). *e-mail*: <frank.koehler@uni-tuebingen.de>

Nirmala Ravindra Kulkarni, Research Scientist, Centre of Advanced Study in Sanskrit, University of Pune, Pune – 411 007 (India). *e-mail*: <nirmala@unipune.ac.in>

Martin Joachim Kümmel, Professor, Friedrich-Schiller-Universität Jena, Philosophische Fakultät, Lehrstuhl für Indogermanistik, Zwätzengasse 12, D-07743 Jena (Germany). *e-mail*: martin-joachim.kuemmel@uni-jena.de>

Naoko Nishimura, Lecturer, Department of Indology and History of Indian Buddhism, Graduate School of Arts and Letters, Tohoku University, Kawauchi 27-1, Aobaku, SENDAI, 980-8576 (Japan). *e-mail*: <gharma@sal.tohoku.ac.jp>

Georges-Jean Pinault, Professor, Ecole Pratique des Hautes Etudes, Paris/ Sorbonne, 23 rue Leon Frot., 75011 Paris (France). *e-mail*: <georges.pinault@wanadoo.fr>

Julieta Rotaru, Researcher, Centre of Eurasiatic and Afroasiatic Studies (CEAS), Tache Ionescu, no. 4, 010352 Bucharest (Romania). *e-mail*: <julieta.rotaru@bibliotecametropolitana.ro>

Shilpa Sumant, Assistant Professor, Deccan Postgraduate Research Institute, Yerwada, Pune – 411 006 (India). *e-mail*: <shilsumant@hotmail.com>

Elizabeth Tucker, Jill Hart Senior Research Fellow, Oriental Institute, Oxford OX1 2LE (UK). *e-mail*: <elizabeth.tucker@orinst.ox.ac.uk>

Chetna Vibhuti Vedi, Ph.D. candidate, University of Pune, Pune – 411 007 (India). Postal address: C/o M.V.M. Avdhut Swami, At-Post: Bhivari, Tal. Purandar (Saswad), Dist. Pune – 412 301 (India). *e-mail*: <chetnavedi@yahoo.com, vedichetna@gmail.com>